T0208744

Lecture Notes in Computer Science

Vol. 1: GI-Gesellschaft für Informatik e.V. 3. Jahrestagung, Hamburg, 8.–10. Oktober 1973. Herausgegeben im Auftrag der Gesellschaft für Informatik von W. Brauer. XI, 508 Seiten. 1973.

Vol. 2: GI-Gesellschaft für Informatik e.V. 1. Fachtagung über Automatentheorie und Formale Sprachen, Bonn, 9.–12. Juli 1973. Herausgegeben im Auftrag der Gesellschaft für Informatik von K.-H. Böhling und K. Indermark. VII, 322 Seiten. 1973.

Vol. 3: 5th Conference on Optimization Techniques, Part I. (Series: I.F.I.P. TC7 Optimization Conferences.) Edited by R. Conti and A. Ruberti. XIII, 565 pages. 1973.

Vol. 4: 5th Conference on Optimization Techniques, Part II. (Series: I.F.I.P. TC7 Optimization Conferences.) Edited by R. Conti and A. Ruberti. XIII, 389 pages. 1973.

Vol. 5: International Symposium on Theoretical Programming. Edited by A. Ershov and V. A. Nepomniaschy. VI, 407 pages. 1974.

Vol. 6: B. T. Smith, J. M. Boyle, J. J. Dongarra, B. S. Garbow, Y. Ikebe, V. C. Klema, and C. B. Moler, Matrix Eigensaystem Routines – EISPACK Guide. XI, 551 pages. 2nd Edition 1974, 1976.

Vol. 7: 3. Fachtagung über Programmiersprachen, Kiel, 5.–7. März 1974. Herausgegeben von B. Schlender und W. Frielinghaus. VI, 225 Seiten. 1974.

Vol. 8: GI-NTG Fachtagung über Struktur und Betrieb von Rechensystemen, Braunschweig, 20.–22. März 1974. Herausgegeben im Auftrag der GI und der NTG von H.-O. Leilich. VI, 340 Seiten. 1974.

Vol. 9: GI-BIFOA Internationale Fachtagung: Informationszentren in Wirtschaft und Verwaltung. Köln, 17./18. Sept. 1973. Herausgegeben im Auftrag der GI und dem BIFOA von P. Schmitz. VI, 259 Seiten. 1974.

Vol. 10: Computing Methods in Applied Sciences and Engineering, Part 1. International Symposium, Versailles, December 17–21, 1973. Edited by R. Glowinski and J. L. Lions. X, 497 pages. 1974.

Vol. 11: Computing Methods in Applied Sciences and Engineering, Part 2. International Symposium, Versailles, December 17–21, 1973. Edited by R. Glowinski and J. L. Lions. X, 434 pages. 1974.

Vol. 12: GFK-GI-GMR Fachtagung Prozessrechner 1974. Karlsruhe, 10.–11. Juni 1974. Herausgegeben von G. Krüger und R. Friehmelt. XI, 620 Seiten. 1974.

Vol. 13: Rechnerstrukturen und Betriebsprogrammierung, Erlangen, 1970. (GI-Gesellschaft für Informatik e.V.) Herausgegeben von W. Händler und P. P. Spies. VII, 333 Seiten. 1974.

Vol. 14: Automata, Languages and Programming – 2nd Colloquium, University of Saarbrücken, July 29–August 2, 1974. Edited by J. Loeckx. VIII, 611 pages. 1974.

Vol. 15: L Systems. Edited by A. Salomaa and G. Rozenberg. VI, 338 pages. 1974.

Vol. 16: Operating Systems, International Symposium, Rocquencourt 1974. Edited by E. Gelenbe and C. Kaiser. VIII, 310 pages. 1974.

Vol. 17: Rechner-Gestützter Unterricht RGU '74, Fachtagung, Hamburg, 12.–14. August 1974, ACU-Arbeitskreis Computer-Unterstützter Unterricht. Herausgegeben im Auftrag der GI von K. Brunnstein, K. Haefner und W. Händler. X, 417 Seiten. 1974.

Vol. 18: K. Jensen and N. E. Wirth, PASCAL – User Manual and Report. VII, 170 pages. Corrected Reprint of the 2nd Edition 1976.

Vol. 19: Programming Symposium. Proceedings 1974. V, 425 pages. 1974.

Vol. 20: J. Engelfriet, Simple Program Schemes and Formal Languages. VII, 254 pages. 1974.

Vol. 21: Compiler Construction, An Advanced Course. Edited by F. L. Bauer and J. Eickel. XIV. 621 pages. 1974.

Vol. 22: Formal Aspects of Cognitive Processes. Proceedings 1972. Edited by T. Storer and D. Winter. V, 214 pages. 1975.

Vol. 23: Programming Methodology. 4th Informatik Symposium, IBM Germany Wildbad, September 25–27, 1974. Edited by C. E. Hackl. VI, 501 pages. 1975.

Vol. 24: Parallel Processing. Proceedings 1974. Edited by T. Feng. VI, 433 pages. 1975.

Vol. 25: Category Theory Applied to Computation and Control. Proceedings 1974. Edited by E. G. Manes. X, 245 pages. 1975.

Vol. 26: GI-4. Jahrestagung, Berlin, 9.–12. Oktober 1974. Herausgegeben im Auftrag der GI von D. Siefkes. IX, 748 Seiten. 1975.

Vol. 27: Optimization Techniques. IFIP Technical Conference. Novosibirsk, July 1–7, 1974. (Series: I.F.I.P. TC7 Optimization Conferences.) Edited by G. I. Marchuk. VIII, 507 pages. 1975.

Vol. 28: Mathematical Foundations of Computer Science. 3rd Symposium at Jadwisin near Warsaw, June 17–22, 1974. Edited by A. Blikle. VII, 484 pages. 1975.

Vol. 29: Interval Mathematics. Procedings 1975. Edited by K. Nickel. VI, 331 pages. 1975.

Vol. 30: Software Engineering. An Advanced Course. Edited by F. L. Bauer. (Formerly published 1973 as Lecture Notes in Economics and Mathematical Systems, Vol. 81) XII, 545 pages. 1975.

Vol. 31: S. H. Fuller, Analysis of Drum and Disk Storage Units. IX, 283 pages. 1975.

Vol. 32: Mathematical Foundations of Computer Science 1975. Proceedings 1975. Edited by J. Bečvář. X, 476 pages. 1975.

Vol. 33: Automata Theory and Formal Languages, Kaiserslautern, May 20–23, 1975. Edited by H. Brakhage on behalf of GI. VIII, 292 Seiten. 1975.

Vol. 34: GI – 5. Jahrestagung, Dortmund 8.–10. Oktober 1975. Herausgegeben im Auftrag der GI von J. Mühlbacher. X, 755 Seiten. 1975.

Vol. 35: W. Everling, Exercises in Computer Systems Analysis. (Formerly published 1972 as Lecture Notes in Economics and Mathematical Systems, Vol. 65) VIII, 184 pages. 1975.

Vol. 36: S. A. Greibach, Theory of Program Structures: Schemes, Semantics, Verification. XV, 364 pages. 1975.

Vol. 37: C. Böhm, λ-Calculus and Computer Science Theory. Proceedings 1975. XII, 370 pages. 1975.

Vol. 38: P. Branquart, J.-P. Cardinael, J. Lewi, J.-P. Delescaille, M. Vanbegin. An Optimized Translation Process and Its Application to ALGOL 68. IX, 334 pages. 1976.

Vol. 39: Data Base Systems. Proceedings 1975. Edited by H. Hasselmeier and W. Spruth. VI, 386 pages. 1976.

Lecture Notes in Computer Science

Edited by G. Goos and J. Hartmanis

39

Data Base Systems

Proceedings, 5th Informatik Symposium,
IBM Germany, Bad Homburg v.d.H.,
September 24–26, 1975

Edited by H. Hasselmeier and W. G. Spruth

Springer-Verlag
Berlin · Heidelberg · New York 1976

Editors
Helmut Hasselmeier
Dr.-Ing. Wilhelm G. Spruth
IBM Deutschland
EF Grundlagenentwicklung
Schönaicher Straße 220
703 Böblingen/BRD

Library of Congress Cataloging in Publication Data

Informatik Symposium, 5th, Homburg vor der Höhe, 1975.
Data base system.

(Lecture notes in computer science ; 39)
English or German.
Sponsored by IBM Germany and the IBM World Trade Corporation.
Bibliography: p.
Includes index.
1. Data base management--Congresses. I. Hasselmeier H. II. Spruth, W. G. III. IBM Deutschland. IV. IBM World Trade Corporation. V. Title. VI. Series.
QA76.9.D3I52 1975 001.6'442 75-46501

AMS Subject Classifications (1970): 00A10, 68-02, 68-03, 68A05, 68A10, 68A20, 68A50
CR Subject Classifications (1974): 4.30, 4.33, 4.34, 4.0, 4.22, 4.6

ISBN 3-540-07612-3 Springer-Verlag Berlin · Heidelberg · New York
ISBN 0-387-07612-3 Springer-Verlag New York · Heidelberg · Berlin

Contents

PREFACE

The papers in these Proceedings were presented at the 5th Informatik-Symposium which was held in Bad Homburg, Germany, from September 24 - 26, 1975. The Symposium was organized by the Scientific Relations Department of IBM Germany and sponsored by IBM Germany and the IBM World Trade Corporation.

The aim of the Informatik-Symposium is to strengthen and improve the communication between universities and industry, by covering a subject in the field of computer science, both from a university and from an industry point of view.

During the last 5-10 years, Data Base Systems have developed from a highly speculative "Management Information System (MIS)" approach to a practical production tool. In the late 50's and early 60's, the application program was viewed as the nucleus of an application, with multiple data sets as accessories to the application program, and multiple, more or less unrelated application programs serving the needs of a larger enterprise or organization. The modern approach views the data base as the nucleus of a data processing operation, surrounded by multiple application programs operating on its data.

This switch has significantly increased the need for features and characteristics, which permit quick adaptions to an ever changing set of external requirements. In the old approach, external changes usually could be contained to one or a few application programs and their associated data sets. Because of the tight coupling between application programs and their data in a Data Base System, external changes are much more pervasive than they used to be. As a consequence, practical Data Base System implementations require a degree of universality and generality unknown in previous data processing installations.

In organizing this Symposium, we structured the subject matter into four topics. The topic of data structures covers the logical view the user has on internally stored data. This topic is closely related to the subject of data base languages. In doing this, we specifically tried to avoid a repetition of the popular argumentation of the pros and cons of the various data representation models, e.g. the hierarchical, network, and relational models.

The second topic deals with components and technology. Today the magnetic disk is the main technology for the storage of large amounts of data. Its peculiarities impact to a large extent the structure of today's data base systems. A major change in data base structures can be expected, if and when we succeed to replace the magnetic disk storage by another, more amenable storage structure.

System aspects is the third topic. It includes problems of data security and data integrity. The evolution of data base systems has generated numerous ethical, social and moral questions. It is the responsibility of the data processing community to assure technically acceptable solutions for those issues.

User aspects is the fourth topic of the Symposium. Data Base Systems require a number of tools for their installation, maintenance, and evaluation. Refinement and enhancement of these tools may be one of the major prerequisites for the further development of Data Base Systems.

The editors would like to express their thanks to everybody who contributed to the Symposium by preparing a talk, providing advice for its content and organization or assisting in its administration.

Boeblingen, October 24, 1975

H. Hasselmeier W.G. Spruth

Überlegungen zur Entwicklung von Datenbanksystemen

Horst Remus, IBM Palo Alto, Californien

Zusammenfassung

Bei der Entwicklung zur integrierten Datenverarbeitung sind zwei Schritte besonders bemerkenswert:

- Die Datenbank als Zentrale, wobei die Anwendungsprogramme im wesentlichen den Verkehr mit der Datenbank regeln (Abfrage oder Aufarbeitung).

- Das Datenfernverarbeitungsnetzwerk, das den gleichzeitigen Zugriff zu einem Programm oder einer Datenbank von mehreren Benutzerstationen aus gestattet.

Die Datenbankzentrale des Datenverarbeitungssystems im Gegensatz zu der Datei als Zugriffsdatei für ein bestimmtes Programm (mit OPEN und CLOSE der Datei von diesem einen Programm) erfordert bestimmte Überlegungen bezüglich ihrer Organisation. Ein weiterer Schritt ist die Einfügung genereller Datenbanksysteme mit der Idee der Datenunabhängigkeit. Andere Überlegungen haben mit der Beantwortungszeit ("performance"), Datenschutz und Datensicherung ("integrity" und "recovery") zu tun. Für den Benutzer stellt sich das System in zwei Teilen dar:

- Das Datenmodell
- Die Sprache mit der diese Daten manipuliert werden ("user interface").

Künftig zu lösende Probleme weisen in die Richtung von Datenbanken mit gleichzeitigem Zugriff von mehreren Systemen und in Netzwerken auf verschiedene Knotenpunkte verteilte Datenbanken.

1. ENTWICKLUNG ZUR DATENBANK

Wir betrachten Mengen, deren Elemente aus alphanumerischen Zeichen zusammengesetzte Daten oder Informationen sind. Für diese Mengen ergeben sich folgende Operationen:

a) Die *Abfrage*, d.h. die Herauskristallisierung gewisser Teilinformation aus der Gesamtmenge.

b) Die *Berichterstellung*, d.h. die (meist summarische) Zusammenfassung der Informationsmenge, oder Teilen daraus, nach gewissen nicht notwendig automatisch in der Mengenstruktur gegebenen Merkmalen.

c) Die *Aufarbeitung* der Informationsmenge, d.h. Hinzufügung, Ausstreichen oder Verändern von Teilen der Informationsmenge. (Eine spezielle Form der Aufarbeitung ist die Formatänderung, d.h. das Hinzufügen oder Fortlassen von Information relativ zu jeder vorhandenen Teilinformation.)

Historisch gesehen ergibt sich bezüglich der Struktur oder Organisationsform von Informationsmengen folgende Entwicklung (Abbildung 1 zeigt einen Versuch zur schematischen Darstellung):

Der erste Schritt zur Zusammenfassung von Information ist die *Liste*, wobei die einfachste Form die *fortlaufende Liste* ist. Als Datenträger in der ursprünglichen Form dienen Medien auf denen lesbar geschrieben werden konnte. Die Abfrage erfolgte manuell, die Liste wird nach dem infrage stehenden Eintrag (normalerweise startend am Anfang der Liste) durchsucht. Eine Berichterstellung ist in den meisten Fällen unmöglich, da Einzelabfragen sehr zeitraubend sind. Die Aufarbeitung erfolgt manuell durch Hinzufügung eines neuen Eintrags am Ende oder durch Streichung überflüssig gewordener Einträge. Eine Änderung im Listenformat (zusätzliche Information per Eintrag) führt normalerweise nicht zu Schwierigkeiten, da die zusätzliche Information ohnehin nur für die neu hinzugefügten Einträge verfügbar ist.

Der nächste Schritt ist die *geordnete Liste* mit den gleichen Medien als Datenträger. Eine geordnete Liste entsteht aus einer fortlaufenden Liste durch Sortierung nach einem Ordnungsbegriff. Es ist auch möglich, daß eine fortlaufende Liste automatisch geordnet ist, z.B. bei chronologischen Listen wie Kirchenbuchregistern.

Die Abfrage ist wesentlich vereinfacht und erleichtert damit die Berichterstellung. Bei der Aufarbeitung treten Probleme mit der Einschiebung von Einträgen auf. Jede Menge dafür vorgesehener Platz erschöpft sich. Das führt entweder zu einer Zerstörung der Ordnung oder es muss eine neue Liste erstellt werden. Ein gewisser Ausweg sind die Ergänzungslisten und Hinweise auf solche in der Basisliste (anstelle des Eintrags der Gesamtinformation). Derartige Verfahren führen jedoch schnell zur Unübersichtlichkeit, z.B. werden eröffnungstheoretische Werke für Schach immer wieder neu aufgelegt.

Der nächste Schritt wäre das Auseinanderbrechen der Liste in Einzeleinträge, die *Kartei*. Sie stellt gewisse spezielle Ansprüche an die Medien. Die Schwierigkeiten in der geordneten Liste bezüglich Hinzufügen von Einträgen sind beseitigt.

Die Erfindung der Lochkarte und die damit verbundene elektromechanische Behandlung von Information bedeutete die Möglichkeit, einzelne manuelle Verarbeitungsschritte zu automatisieren. Die semi-automatische Einzelabfrage ist jedoch im Normalfall zu zeitraubend. Die Berichterstellung kann weitgehend automatisch erfolgen, jedoch muß die *Lochkartenkartei* für das Programm, d.h. die Tabelliermaschinenschaltung, speziell vorbereitet werden (Sortieren, Mischen und andere spezielle Arbeitsgänge). Die Aufarbeitung erfolgt semi-automatisch. Problematisch wird die Formatänderung, die meist zur Erstellung einer neuen Kartei führt.

Benutzung anderer Medien wie Platte oder Band ermöglichen vollautomatische Verarbeitung und führen zur *Datei*. Normalerweise ist diese, ähnlich wie die Lochkartenkartei, relativ zu einer bestimmten Anwendung organisiert. Der Programmierer "öffnet" (OPEN) und "schließt" (CLOSE) die Datei, je nachdem ob die zugehörige Anwendung läuft oder nicht. Läuft die Anwendung nicht, wird die Datei unter Umständen sogar physikalisch vom System entfernt; jedenfalls ist sie normalerweise nicht für andere Anwendungen zugriffsbereit. Abfrage und Berichterstellung sind auch nur für bestimmte Anwendungsprogramme möglich. Die gleichzeitige Bearbeitung mehrerer Anwendungen von ein und derselben Datenstation oder von einer oder mehr Anwendungen von verschiedenen Datenstationen wird problematisch. Aufarbeitung und Formatänderung erfordern die automatische Erstellung einer neuen Datei.

Eine Vielzahl von Anwendungen und Benutzern für ein und dieselbe Datenmenge führt zur Datenbank. Ihre speziellen Erfordernisse werden im folgenden näher erläutert.

2. DATENBANKEN UND DATENBANKSYSTEME

Implizit enthalten in der Definition der Datenbank ist das Konzept der minimalen Redundanz und die Notwendigkeit einer für den Benutzer verständlichen Struktur, dem *Datenmodell*.

Zugriff zu einer Datenbank erfolgt normalerweise von einer Reihe von Benutzern mit verschiedenartigen Anwendungen gleichzeitig. Das erfordert eine fortlaufende Überwachung der Datenbank durch einen *Datenbankverwalter*. Neben der Erhaltung der Integrität der Datenbank streben diese Systemprogrammierer eine optimale Erzielung von Leistungsfaktoren wie Beantwortungszeit und Speicher an. Sie interessieren sich daher für die physikalische Organisation der Datenbank, einschließlich der Wirkungsweise von Indizes und Zeigern.

Die Anwendungsprogrammierer oder "Enduser" interessieren sich für das logische Datenmodell und für Wege zum Wiederauffinden und zur Aufarbeitung von Datenbankelementen.

Um zu verstehen, welche Forderungen beide, der Datenbankverwalter und der Anwendungsprogrammierer, an Datenbanksysteme haben, müssen die Anwendungen von Datenbanken näher untersucht werden.

Zunächst sei an den Unterschied von Stapelverarbeitung (batch processing) und Echtzeitverarbeitung (real time processing) erinnert (Abbildung 2). Bei der Stapelverarbeitung erfolgt die Verarbeitung bezüglich eines Merkmales oder Begriffs gruppenweise an bestimmten festgelegten Terminen oder nachdem eine bestimmte Menge zur Verarbeitung angesammelt ist. Bei der Echtzeitverarbeitung wird jeder Schritt sofort auf der gesamten Datenmenge ausgeführt.

Außerdem sind bei den Anwendungen zwei Parameter von besonderer Bedeutung:

. die Voraussehbarkeit
. die Häufigkeit gleichartiger Zugriffe (Repetivität).

Hierbei gibt es bezüglich beider Merkmale eine Reihe von Mischungen. Man weiß z.B. nicht im voraus, nach welchem Teil eines Lagerbestands ein Magazinverwalter fragt. Was er darüber wissen will, ist jedoch genauestens bekannt. Im allgemeinen kann man Datenbankoperationen in folgende verschiedenartige Operationen einteilen (Abbildung 3):

1. Wirkungsvolle Ausführung sich wiederholender Arbeiten (traditionelle Stapelverarbeitung).

2. Im voraus definierte Abfragen ("Wie groß ist der Lagerbestand an 2 Zoll Nägeln ?").

3. Zufällige, schlecht strukturierte und unvorhergesehene Abfragen ("Wieviele Ingenieure in Hamburg haben ein Monatseinkommen von mehr als DM 6000.-- ?").

Ein System, das Nr. 1 und 2 behandelt, wird *"Operational"* oder *"Supervisory System"* genannt, ein System, das Nr. 3 behandelt, ein *"Informations"* oder *"Executive System"*. Beispiele für beide Gruppen wären:

"Operational" Systeme: Bank mit Datenstationen an jedem Schalter, Flugreservierung, Flugsicherung.

Informationssysteme: Bücherei mit Aufsuchen von Information nach Kennwort, Marktinformation für Management, Datenbank mit Personaldaten.

Ein und dieselbe Datenbank sollte normalerweise die Anwendung beider Systeme erlauben.

3. SPEZIELLE ANFORDERUNGEN AN DATENBANKEN

Es wurde bereits auf die Forderung der *minimalen Redundanz* hingewiesen. Die meisten Band-Bibliotheken enthalten eine Fülle von redundanten Daten. Unkontrollierte Behandlung der Frage der Redundanz kann (wie z.B. bei vielen Büroablagesystemen) zu der Notwendigkeit häufiger Um- oder Neuordnung führen. Eine weitere Frage ist natürlich der Verbrauch an Speicherplatz und die damit verbundene Kostenfrage. Mehrfache Kopien derselben Daten können außerdem wegen eines möglicherweise verschiedenen Aufarbeitungsstandes zu verschiedener Information führen. Ziel einer Datenbankorganisation sollte es also sein, Redundanz zu vermeiden, wo es ökonomisch richtig erscheint. Aus Gründen der Datensicherheit und zur möglichen Wiederherstellung fehlerhafter Daten kann jedoch einige Redundanz erforderlich sein.

Eine weitere Forderung ist die *Vielseitigkeit in der Darstellung* von Datenbeziehungen. Verschiedene Programmierer benutzen unterschiedliche logische Dateien, die jedoch alle auf derselben Datenbank beruhen.

Sehr bedeutend sind die Aspekte der *Leistungsfähigkeit* eines Datenbanksystems. Entscheidende Leistungsfaktoren sind die Antwortzeit für die Benutzer einer Datenstation und die Anzahl der Übertragungen je Zeiteinheit, die ein System bewältigen kann. Es gibt Systeme mit geringerem Verkehrsvolumen, bei denen die Anzahl der Übertragungen je Zeiteinheit (throughput) von geringer Bedeutung ist. Systeme mit hohem Verkehrsvolumen sind z.B. Flugreservierungssysteme und Großbanken. Es gibt heute bereits Anwendungen, die 10 und mehr Übertragungen in der Sekunde erfordern. Bei derartigen Anwendungen ist eine weitere rasche Steigerung zu erwarten (Hinzufügen von weiteren Bank-Zweigstellen etc.). Um die erforderliche Leistungssteigerung besser in den Griff zu bekommen, sind weitere Maßnahmen in Betracht zu ziehen, wie z.B. Aufspaltung der Datenbank in mehrere Einzeldatenbanken (Dezentralisierung) oder Zugriff zu einer Datenbank von mehreren Rechenanlagen aus. Für traditionelle Stapelverarbeitungssysteme ist die Antwortzeit ohne Bedeutung. Ihr Entwurfskriterium ist die Effektivität des "batch processing" (Stapelverarbeitung). Für gewisse Anwendungen ist ein Dialog mit einer Antwortzeit von 2 Sekunden oder weniger erforderlich. Natürlich ist die Leistungsfähigkeit der Recheneinheit von Einfluß auf die Leistungsfähigkeit des Datenbanksystems.

Es ist notwendig, daß Daten und ihre Beziehungen untereinander nicht durch Maschinenfehlverhalten oder andere "Unfälle" zerstört werden (D a t e n s i c h e r h e i t). Jedes System muß daher die Möglichkeit von Datensicherheitstests beinhalten.

In vielen Fällen müssen Daten vor dem Zugriff Unbefugter geschützt werden ("security and privacy" = *Datenschutz*). Diese Forderung kann übertragen werden auf die Forderung, daß das System die Authorisation eines Benutzers und seiner Aktionen überprüft (z.B. durch ein Passwort). Die Kontrollen sollten so gestaltet sein, daß geschickte Programmierer sie nicht ohne weiteres umgehen können. Auch sollten die Aktionen überwacht und notiert werden, sodaß falscher Gebrauch nachträglich herausgefunden werden kann. Ebenso ist es erforderlich, daß die Datenbank selbst laufend überprüft werden kann.

Außerdem tritt die Forderung auf, Anwendungsprogramme unabhängig von der Datenorganisation und Zugriffstechnik zu schreiben (*Datenunabhängigkeit*). Z.B. bietet IMS [3] einen gewissen Grad von Datenunabhängigkeit, indem neue Datensegmente an bestimmten Punkten der Hierarchie ohne Programmänderung hinzugefügt werden können, oder auch die Länge eines Datensatzes oder die Aufteilung der Datenbank in Datengruppen geändert werden kann.

4. DATENBANKSTRUKTUREN

Die Funktion einer Datenbank ist das Abspeichern der Daten und der Beziehungen zwischen den Daten.

Die logische Beschreibung einer Datenbank wird das Datenbankschema genannt. Ein Schema definiert also das Datenmodell für den Anwender. Ein Subschema ist die Aufgliederung der Datenbank für ein spezielles Anwendungsprogramm. Abbildung 4 zeigt das Zusammenwirken der verschiedenen Teile innerhalb eines Datenbanksystems und insbesondere die Bedeutung der Begriffe Schema und Subschema.

Abbildung 5 zeigt die Aufgliederung einer Datenbank zur Arbeitsplatzbeschaffung. Die Beziehungen zwischen den einzelnen Dateien sind klar ersichtlich. Die Arbeitgeberdatei gibt die Einzelheiten zu dem Feld "Arbeitgebernummer", die Talentdatei die Einzelheiten zu dem Feld "Gefordertes Talent" in der Arbeitsplatzliste. Hierbei zeigt sich eine Hauptform für Datenbankstrukturen: die hierarchische Gliederung. Die Dateien "Arbeitgebernummer" und "Talentgruppe" sind Untergliederungen der Datei "Arbeitsplatzliste" (Eltern-Kind-Beziehung).

Die Möglichkeit Beziehungen zwischen den einzelnen Datenfeldern in der Datenbankstruktur zum Ausdruck zu bringen, hat zu drei wesentlichen Datenbankorganisationsformen geführt:

1. Die *hierarchische Datenbankstruktur* (Abbildung 6). Hierbei hat der höchste Level einen und nur einen Knotenpunkt, die "Wurzel des Baumes". Jeder Knotenpunkt eines anderen Levels erhält genau einen Knotenpunkt in dem nächsthöheren Level zugeordnet.

Knuth [4] definiert einen Baum oder eine hierarchische Struktur entsprechend als "eine endliche Menge T von einem oder mehr Knotenpunkten mit

a. einem speziell ausgezeichneten Knotenpunkt, der Wurzel des Baumes und
b. m≥0 verbleibenden disjunkten (unverbundenen) Teilmengen $T_1 \ldots\ldots T_m$, wobei jede dieser Teilmengen ein Baum ist. Diese Teilmengen werden Teilbäume genannt."

IMS [3] verwendet die hierarchische Datenbankstruktur.

2. Falls ein Knotenpunkt auf mehr als einen Knotenpunkt einer höheren Ebene zurückgeführt werden soll, kann die Beschreibung nicht mehr durch einen Baum erfolgen. Die entstehende Struktur wird als "*Netzwerkstruktur*" bezeichnet. Wegen des vielseitigen Gebrauchs des Wortes Netzwerk in der Datenindustrie wird im angloamerikanischen Sprachbereich häufig die Bezeichnung "plex structures" verwendet. Abbildung 7 zeigt einige einfache Beispiele von Netzwerkstrukturen. Natürlich ist eine hierarchische oder Baumstruktur nur ein spezieller Fall derselben. Ein Beispiel einer einfachen Netzwerkstruktur ist ein Stammbaum. Komplexere Strukturen entstehen, wenn mehrfache, nicht algorithmisch bestimmbare Beziehungen zwischen den Elementen verschiedener Level existieren. Unter Einführung von Mehrfachindizes und Redundanz können Netzwerkstrukturen auf Baumstrukturen zurückgeführt werden. Die Ausarbeitungen der Codasylgruppe [1] führen zu einer Netzwerkstruktur.

3. Die Forderung ohne Redundanz auszukommen und die Beziehungen zwischen den Datenbankelementen als algebraischen Kalkül darstellen zu können, führt zu der "relational data base" nach Codd (siehe ausführliche Beschreibung in [2]).

   Die Grundoperationen zur Formung neuer Datensätze sind Vereinigung und Durchschnitt. Die Sprache erscheint vom mathematischen Standpunkt aus sehr elegant, doch haben sich Implementierungen aus Gründen der Leistungsfähigkeit bisher wenig durchgesetzt. Die Vorteile von Datei mit Datensätzen auf dem gleichen Level gliedern sich um Übersichtlichkeit des Datenmodells und Einfachheit der Sprache mit denen Beziehungen manipuliert werden können. Darstellungen in "relational data base"-Form können durch Verwendung von Mehrfachindizes und Redundanz auf obige Formen der hierarchischen oder Netzwerkstrukturen zurückgeführt werden.

Im Zusammenhang mit Datenbankstrukturen wird häufig von Listen und Ringen gesprochen (chains or lists, rings). Diese Strukturen beziehen sich jedoch auf die Art, in der Datensätze innerhalb einer Datei untereinander verbunden sind. Sie beschreiben daher Techniken, wie logische Strukturen aus physikalischen erreicht werden, während die unter 1-3 beschriebenen Strukturen spezielle Formen logischer Strukturen darstellen. Ein entscheidendes Element für beide, die Listen- als auch die Ringstruktur, sind die Zeiger (pointer), die von einem auf den folgenden Datensatz weisen. Bei der Ringstruktur sind dabei normalerweise zweiseitige Zeiger gebräuchlich.

5. DATENBESCHREIBUNGSSPRACHEN

Eine Sprache, die die logische Datenstruktur beschreibt, sollte die folgenden Forderungen erfüllen:

Die Gliederung in Datenmengen wie Dateien, Sätze, Segmente, Datenelemente, sollte klar beschreibbar sein.

Jeder Typ einer solchen Mengeneinheit sollte spezifisch bezeichnet sein (z.B. sollten 2 verschiedene Satztypen verschiedene Bezeichnungen haben).

Die Untergliederung einer bestimmten Datenmenge in bestimmte Untermengen sollte klar erkennbar sein (welche Datenelemente in einer bestimmten Datengruppierung enthalten sind etc.). Die Aufeinanderfolge muß spezifiziert und Wiederholungen sollten aufgezeigt sein.

Die Sprache sollte ausdrücken, welche Datenelemente als Indizes benutzt werden.

Beziehungen zwischen Satztypen, Segmenttypen etc., die die Grundlage der Datenstruktur bilden, müssen spezifiziert und klar bezeichnet werden.

Nach J. Martin [5] ergeben sich je nach dem Gesichtspunkt des Benutzers verschiedene Level der Datenbeschreibungssprachen (Abbildung 8):

1. Die Sprache für den Anwendungsprogrammierer, die das Datenbanksubschema beschreibt (z.B. die Datendivision in COBOL oder die PSBs in DL/1 (PSB = program specification block)).

2. Die generelle Beschreibung des Schemas der Datenbank, die vom Datenbankverwalter angewandt wird (z.B.: DL/1 logical data base description). Die COBOL Datendivision erlaubt z.B. nicht, die Beziehungen in einem Schema zu beschreiben. Sie kann daher hier nicht verwendet werden.

3. Die physikalische Datenbeschreibung (z.B.: DL/1 physical data base description). Im Gegensatz zur logischen Datenbeschreibung, die völlig losgelöst ist von Hardware- und Speicherüberlegungen, sind diese jedoch für Leistungsoptimierung sehr interessant.

Außer DL/1 ist wahrscheinlich CODASYLs data description language DDL die bekannteste Datenbankbeschreibungssprache.

6. ÜBERLEGUNGEN BEI DER HARDWARE

Es sind Datenbanken von der Größenordnung von mehr als 4 Milliarden Bytes bekannt. Das entspricht 40-50 Platteneinheiten IBM 3330. Es ist denkbar, eine Platteneinheit durch eine größere Speichereinheit mit längerer Zugriffszeit zu unterstützen, ähnlich wie beim virtuellen Speicherkonzept zwischen Kernspeicher und Platte. Die vor etwa einem Jahr angekündigte IBM 3850 liefert z.B. 10^3 bis 10^4 mehr Speicherraum mit einer um den Faktor 10^2 verlängerten Zugriffszeit. Der Benutzer sieht das System als ein einziges Plattensystem, für Leistungsfähigkeitsbetrachtungen sind die Hardware-Parameter jedoch von größter Bedeutung. Zum Beispiel bestehen strenge Abhängigkeiten zwischen Antwortzeit, Übertragungsrate und Direktspeichergröße, oder Speicherverfügbarkeit in der niedrigsten Stufe der Speicherhierarchie. Die Antwortzeit wächst mit der Übertragungsrate und fällt mit mehr Direktspeicherverfügbarkeit (weniger paging). Die Übertragungsrate kann mit mehr Direktspeicher gesteigert werden.

Andere Hardware-Parameter sind natürlich die Geschwindigkeit des Computers, der Aufbau und die Komponenten des Nachrichtennetzes.

7. AUSBLICK

Die zusätzlichen Anforderungen für Erweiterungen bestehender oder Entwicklung zukünftiger Datenbanksysteme gliedern sich um die folgenden Aspekte:

a) *Steigerung der Leistungsfähigkeit.* Wachstum der Datenbank und der Anzahl der Datenbankbenutzer erfordern höhere Übertragungsraten und kürzere Antwortzeiten. Die Antwort liegt in geeigneteren Datenbankorganisationen und einer Minimisierung von Verwaltungsfunktionen. Gewisse Hilfsmittel der Hersteller ermöglichen ein "tuning" der Datenbank, dazu ergeben sich Anwender-beeinflußte Verbesserungsmöglichkeiten. Gewisse Verbesserungen sind durch geeignetere Verwendung von Hardware erzielbar (multiprocessing oder ähnliche Verfahren).

b) *Fortlaufende Operation.* Die Forderung einer 24-stündigen Zugriffsmöglichkeit zur Datenbank führt zu gewissen Konsequenzen bei der Implementierung.

   Zunächst wird bei Unterbrechung durch Fehlverhalten eine schnelle Wiederherstellung der Datenbank und kurzfristige Wiederaufnahme der Operationen notwendig. Das erfordert die Führung eines schnell zugriffsbereiten "Journals". Außerdem sollte an den besten Techniken zur Fehlerverhütung, -auffindung und -korrektur gearbeitet werden.

   Eine weitere Forderung ist, die Datenbank - bei gleichzeitiger Fortführung des Routinebetriebs - zu reorganisieren. Ein Dictionary [7] kann dabei als wesentliche Hilfe zum Management der Datenbanken dienen.

c) *Einfachheit der Installierung und Benutzung.* Die Parameter, die zur optimalen Organisation einer Datenbank führen, sind sehr komplex. Systemhersteller helfen allgemein mit automatischen Organisationshilfen oder Hinweisen in der Dokumentation.

   Die Frage der Installierbarkeit ist weitgehend identisch mit der Möglichkeit, die physikalische Repräsentation der Datenbank zu verstehen. Wiederum kann ein Dictionary [7] nützlich sein.

Einfachheit der Benutzung hängt wesentlich mit der Beschaffenheit der Sprachen zur Datenmanipulierung und -beschreibung und dem "interface" zu den Programmierungssprachen ab.

Weitere Funktionen, die zur Vereinfachung der Benutzung führen, haben mit der automatischen Regelung des Informationsflusses zu tun. Wesentlich ist hierbei die Handhabung der Kontrollinformation (Kontrollblöcke), wie sie z.B. bei der standard network architecture erfolgt.

Um die spätere Benutzung zu vereinfachen, müssen Datenbanken und zugehörige Systeme auf die Möglichkeit zur späteren Veränderung bzw. Erweiterung ausgelegt sein.

Literatur

[1] CODASYL, "1974 Status Report on Data Base Activities"

[2] Date, C.J., "An Introduction to Database Systems". Addison-Wesley, Reading, Mass. 1975

[3] Information Management System, "System/Application Design Guide" IBM Form No. SH 20-9025

[4] Knuth, D.E., "The Art of Computer Programming; Vol. 1, Fundamental Algorithms". Addison-Wesley, Reading, Mass., 1968

[5] Martin, J., "Computer Data Base Organization", Prentice-Hall, Englewood Cliffs, N.J., 1975

[6] Senko, M.E., Altman, E.B., Astrahan, M.M and Fehder, P.L., "Data Structures and Accessing in Data-Base Systems". IBM Systems Journal 12, 30-93 (1973)

[7] Uhrowczik, P.P., "Data Dictionary/Directories". IBM Systems Journal 12, 332-350 (1973)

Datendarstellung	Datenträger	Abfrage	Berichterstellung	Aufarbeitung	Formatänderung
Fortlaufende Liste	Medium, das menschliches Schreiben und Lesen erlaubt.	Manuelles Durchsuchen (generell: Start am Anfang)	Manuell, bestimmt durch zeitraubende Einzelabfragen	Manuell, Zufügung neuer Einträge am Ende	Kein Problem, neues Format bleibt auf neue Einträge beschränkt.
Geordnete Liste	– " –	Manuell, unter Benutzung des Ordnungsbegriffs	Manuell	Häufige Neuerstellung wegen Ausschöpfung des Platzes für Zufügungen	– " –
Kartei	Medium, separierbar je Eintrag	– " –	– " –	Manuell, unbegrenztes Hinzufügen möglich	– " –
Lochkartenkartei	Lochkarte	Manuell oder semiautomatisch (sehr zeitraubend)	Semiautomatisch, die Kartei wird für das entsprechende Programm vorbereitet	Semiautomatisch	Erfordert normalerweise Neuerstellung der Kartei
Datei	Band, Platte	Automatisch, beschränkt auf die zu dieser Datei gehörende Anwendung	Automatisch, die Datei wird für das entsprechende Programm vorbereitet	Automatisch, mit häufiger Neuerstellung	Erfordert normalerweise Neuerstellung der Datei
Datenbank	– " –	Automatisch unbegrenzt	Automatisch soweit Information vorhanden unbegrenzt	Automatisch unbegrenzt	Automatisch unbegrenzt

ENTWICKLUNG ZUR DATENBANK

Abbildung 1

STAPELVERARBEITUNG (BATCH PROCESSING)

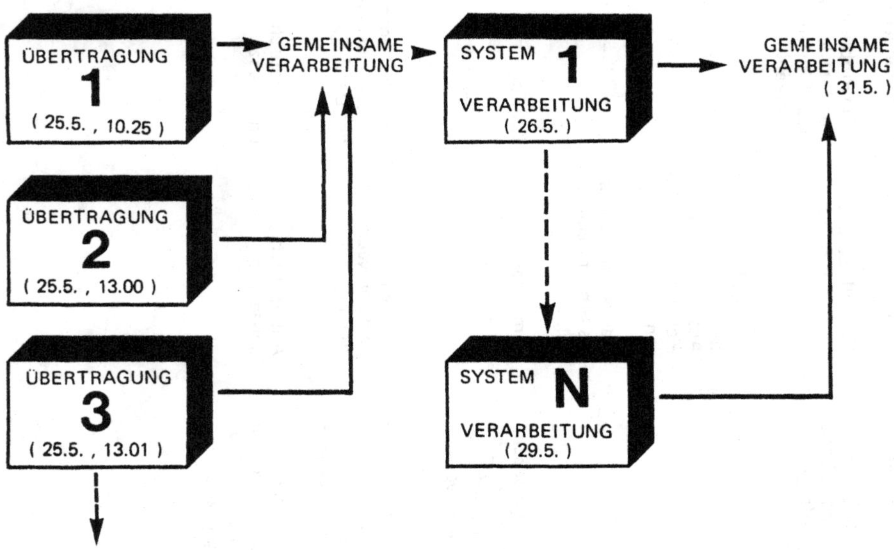

ECHTZEITVERARBEITUNG (REAL TIME PROCESSING)

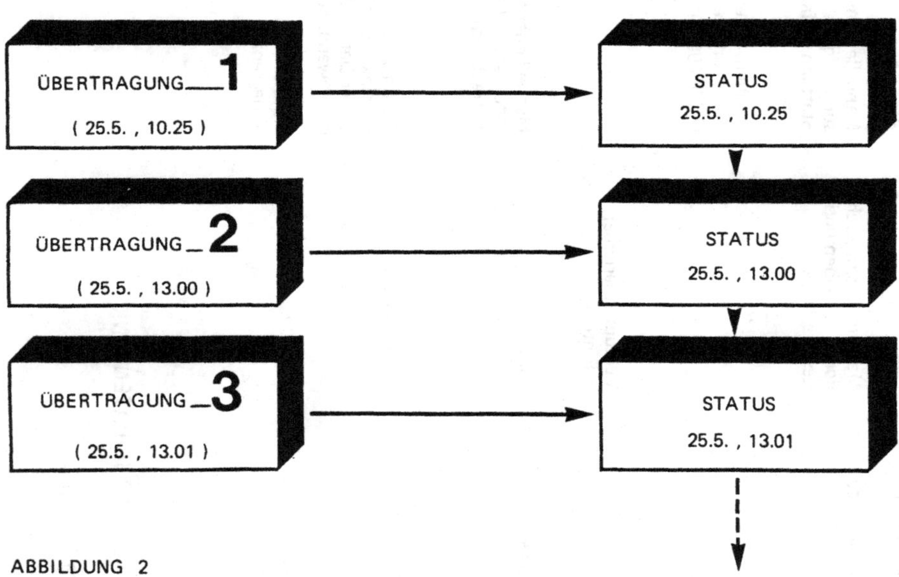

ABBILDUNG 2

	Operational Systeme	Informations-Systeme
Zugriff	geplant oder vorausprogrammiert	spontan, nicht vorausprogrammiert
Typische Beispiele	Bankschalter Flugreservierung	Verkaufsanalyse, Personalinformation
Typische Benutzer	Bankschalterbeamte, Vorarbeiter, Unteres Management	Informationsstab, Mittleres Management, Assistenten des höheren Management
Normalzweck	Unterstützung von Routine Operationen	Unterstützung von Planung und dringenden Informationsbedürfnissen
Antwortzeit	Sekunden	Minuten oder Stunden
Implementierer der Anwendung	Programmierer	Informationsspezialist
Implementierungs-zeit	Wochen oder Monate	Stunden
Typische Sprachen	COBOL, FORTRAN, PL/I	IQF, GIS

MERKMALE FÜR DATENBANKSYSTEME (nach James Martin)

Abbildung 3

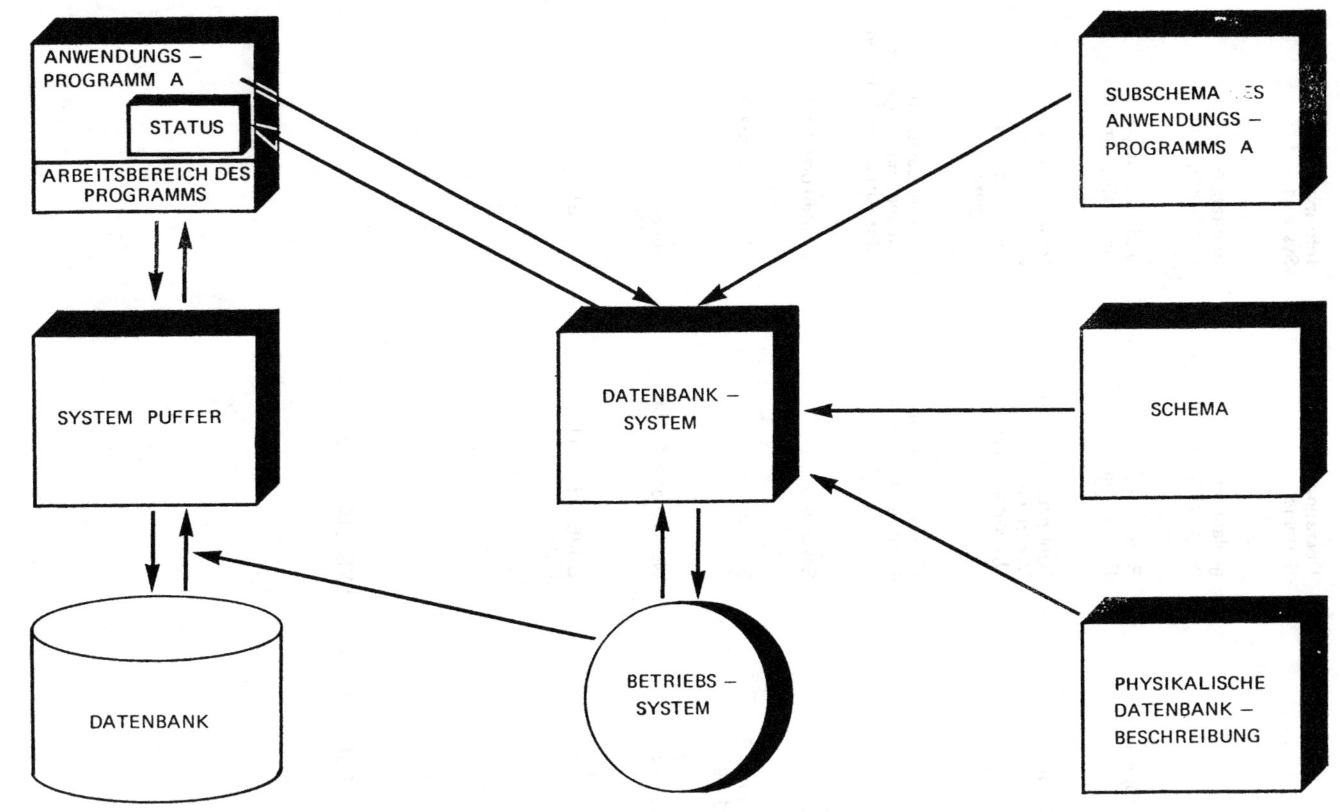

WIRKUNGSWEISE EINES DATENBANKSYSTEMS

ABBILDUNG 4

ARBEITSPLATZLISTE

REFERENZ – NUMMER	ARBEITGEBER – NUMMER	GEFORDERTES TALENT	ANFANG	ENDE	BEZAHLUNG	STATUS

ARBEITGEBERDATEI

ARBEITGEBER – NUMMER	NAME	ADRESSE	ARBEITSKLIMA	SOZIALE LEISTUNGEN

TALENT DATEI

TALENT GRUPPE	NAME	ADRESSE	VERFÜGBARKEIT	AUSBILDUNG	ERFAHRUNG	PERSONAL – DATEN	GEHALT

AUFGLIEDERUNG EINER DATENBANK ARBEITSPLATZBESCHAFFUNG

ABBILDUNG 5

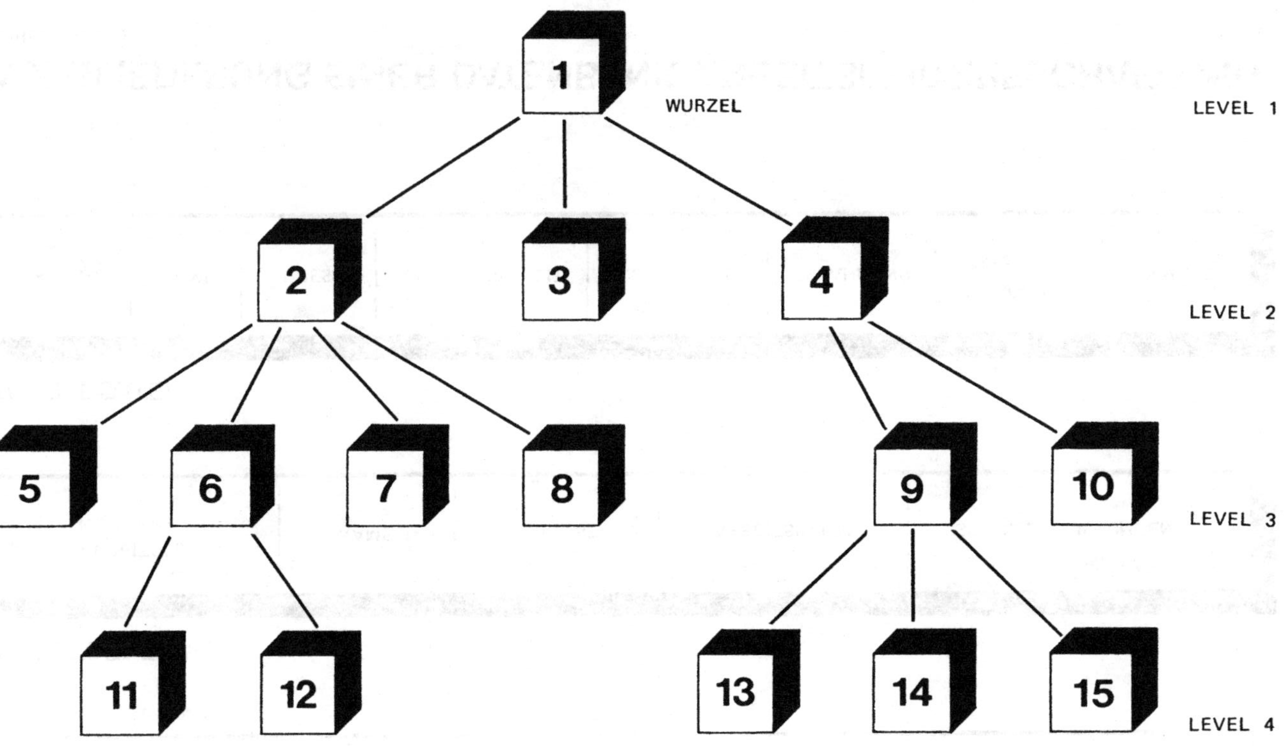

HIERARCHISCHE DATENBANKSTRUKTUR
ABBILDUNG 6

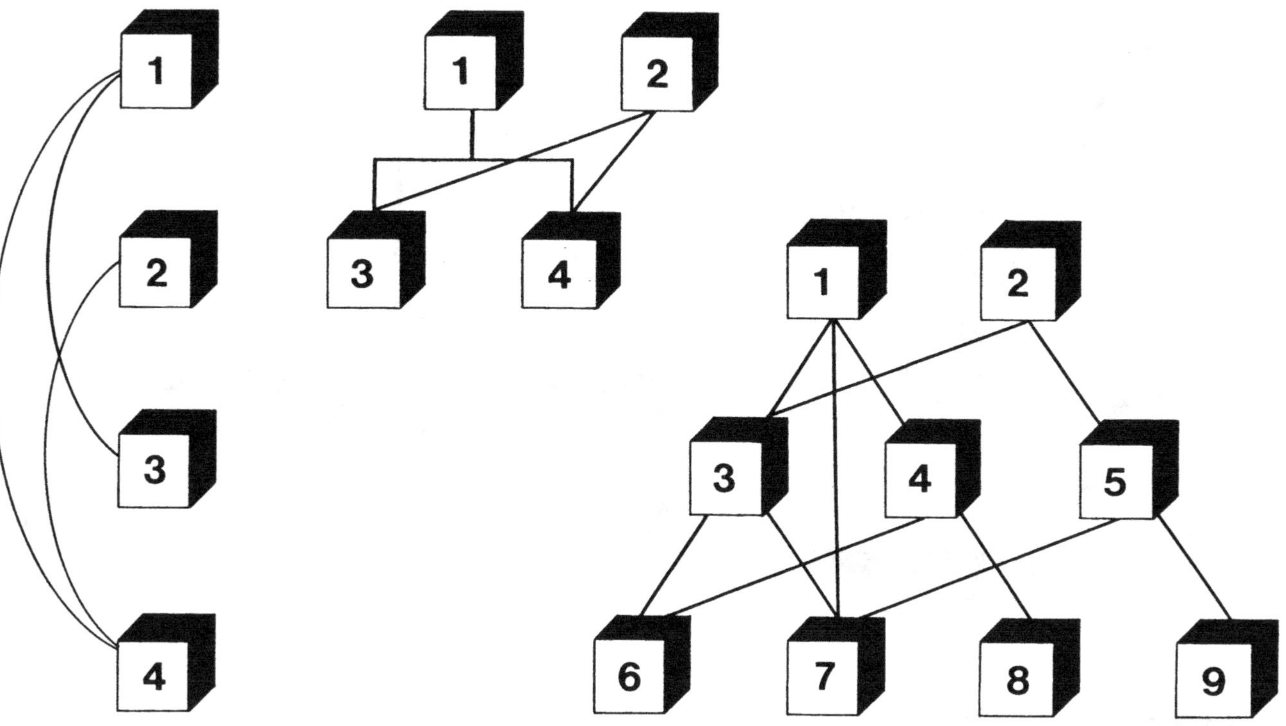

DATENBANKNETZWERKSTRUKTUREN

ABBILDUNG 7

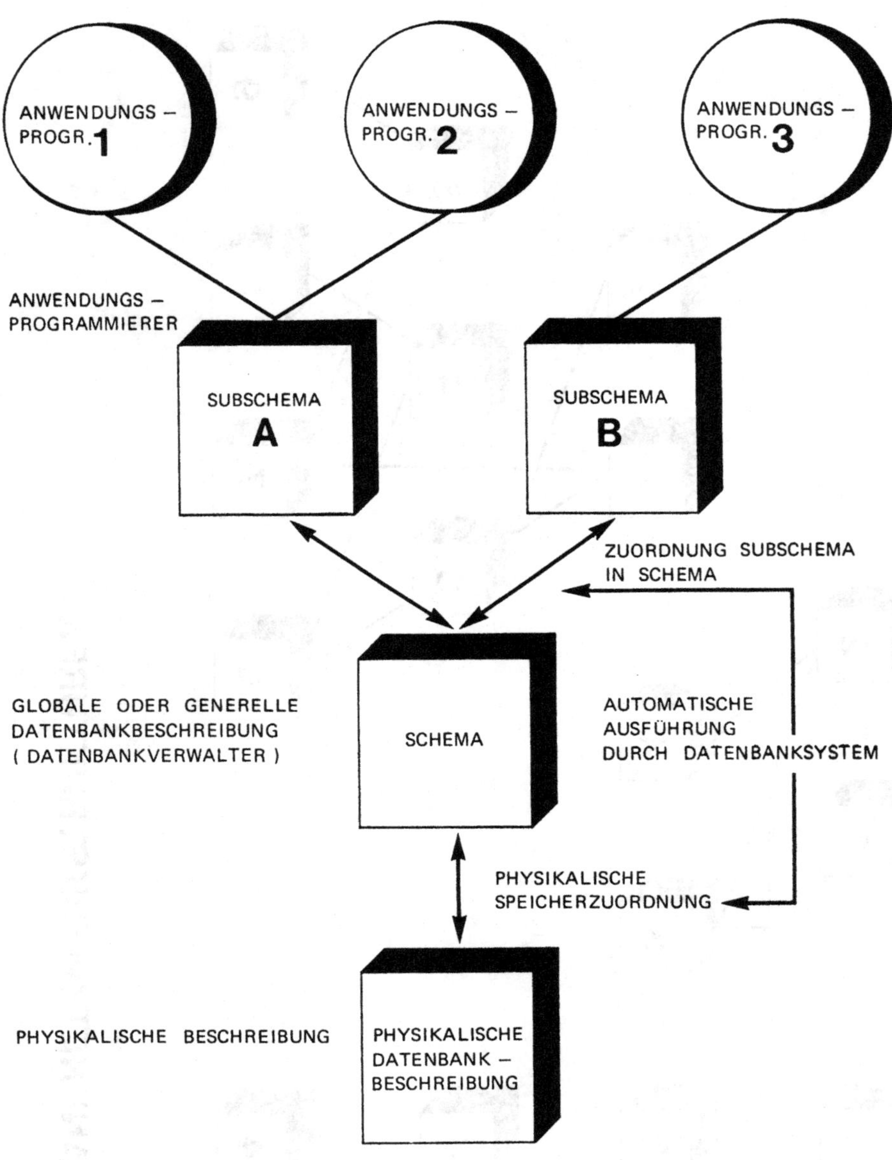

LEVEL DER DATENBESCHREIBUNGEN

ABBILDUNG 8

On the Relationship between Information and Data

Gernot Richter, Gesellschaft fuer Mathematik und Datenverarbeitung (GMD), St. Augustin

Summary

On the background of a general model of information systems a view is analyzed which explicitly distinguishes between information and its representation. Using a conceptual system (IMC) which has been designed to talk about information structures and their manipulation, some ideas on the representation of information are presented. The significant role of type declarations for the information and representation level is shown. For the concepts of format and data a definition is outlined. In the light of these considerations some topics concerning present data base technology are discussed. This gives the motivation to conclude with a plea for conceptual differentiation in the field of data base management systems.

1. A model view of information systems

For information systems a view has been proven to be very useful which considers them consisting of communicating functional units (Funktionseinheiten) in the sense of [DIN]. Recently these functional units have been identified in [ANSI] as roles or work stations characterized only by their function within the system rather than by their technical realization. Years ago this kind of functional units has already been introduced and applied in [ABN] following a suggestion of C. A. Petri. There the term office (Instanz) has been chosen for the functional units under consideration. In information systems the offices influence each other by communicating messages. So the need has been recognized to introduce a complementary functional unit which allows for the exchange of messages between offices. To this kind of functional units the term <u>channel</u> (Kanal) was given in [ABN]. The concept of interface, as used in [ANSI] has a direct relation to the concept of channel: An interface is a system of rules which govern the communication via a considered channel. Also a channel is characterized only by its function within the system serving as a facility where messages can be posted and taken by the communicating offices.

This yields a model view of information systems which provides for the decomposition into two distinct classes of functional units:

- offices   characterized by the processes they can perform
- channels   characterized by the states they can assume.

This model view applied to data base management systems recently has gained some publicity, since the publication of [ANSI] is under discussion both in the world of scientific research (IFIP/TC-2 and IAG) and in the area of standardization (ISO/TC 97/SC 5).

With the above model in mind we want to do a close look to the communication of two offices via one channel. This seems to be an adequate minimum configuration to examine the interrelation between information and data.

To illustrate this configuration we use the graphic notation of [PET], where offices are depicted by boxes and channels by circles (in the cited paper only elementary offices and channels are considered). This yields fig. 1. In the adopted model communication between both offices is done by exchanging messages via the linking channel. The arrows in the above figure only indicate the possibility of access and are n o functional units.

A further aspect is depicted in fig. 1: The exchange of messages makes only sense if both communicating offices have a common background of understanding, which allows them to interpret the messages found in the channel. The assumption of such a "universe of discourse" is a very useful auxiliary model for the understanding of communication also between technical functional units.

2. Model information and abstraction

So far no reference has been made to a distinction between information and data. But words as "represent" and "interpret" indicate a kind of mapping between two things. It is the goal of this section to show that there are two mappings to be considered. Both have the nature of an abstraction, i.e. omission of features not to be considered - but they start at different points.

One kind of abstraction starts with the so-called initial information (Ausgangsinformation), which is to be understood as the whole of knowledge or ideas a person has about something (of the real world or anything else). For a certain pragmatic context, i.e. pursuing an intended purpose it might be that not the whole information is needed but only the "relevant" part of it. The information about a person e.g. is different for administrative purposes and for medical purposes; the information about a technical process for teaching purposes will be different from what is needed for engineering purposes. So it is the intended purpose which controls the abstraction process. In [DURI] the result of the abstraction process has been called the (respective) model information (Modellinformation). In similar considerations of [STEEL] the above abstraction is called the "engineering abstraction" which yields the "engineering model". The term model information indicates, that we are still on the information level. In the present context we do not adopt any definition of information; the concept is used in the sense of knowledge or idea (about something). Thus information is viewed as being of mental nature.

It is obvious, that depending on the respective intended purpose various abstractions can be performed on the same initial information.

It is not of interest in this presentation, whether the model information "exists" or not - whatever that means. However we found the approach very useful which assumes a level of model information (as did also other authors).

Model information cannot be communicated directly because of its mental nature. There must be a representation of it (on a medium) which can be handed out to the addressee (or which can be stored for later use). Such a representation is what usually is called "data". The distinction between information and its representation is the background on which all the following ideas have been developed.

Now it is possible to show the other abstraction mentioned above, which is of a quite different nature. Consider some messages (here in the sense of data) which by agreement between the communicating offices have the same meaning. What is "same meaning" in the present case? Any message is considered to be a representation of model information. As already pointed out, exchange of messages is assumed to have the goal to exchange model information. There are rules for the mapping of messages to model information. Such a mapping usually is called "semantics" and the process of mapping "interpretation". If several messages are mapped onto the same model information, they all have the "same meaning". So we have an abstraction from various representations to the pertinent model information by ignoring the respective representational peculiarities.

There is one problem which might have been apparent already in the above discussion. Considering the communication beween an author and the audience he has the need of representing model information, which he wants to write about. For this purpose a kind of (graphical) reference language is beneficial, in which information can be represented and the interpretation of which is agreed upon. Such a graphical language will be presented in the following and used for canonical representation whenever emphasis is laid on the model information rather than on one of its possible representations.

3. Outlines of a conceptual model of information

Before dealing with any problems of representation the properties of model information itself have to be identified. What is an adequate view of model information with respect to applications? This question brings us into a (at least in the past) very controversal area of argumentation about the advantages and deficiencies of so-called "data models" (hierarchic, network, relational, ...). For general considerations we can avoid this topic by adopting a view which covers the various "data models". This view has been outlined in [DURI] and is reflected in a conceptual system called Information Management Concepts (IMC). These concepts have been developed as a means for talking about model information, in particular in the context of data base management systems. Simultaneously, rules for graphic representation of model information in terms of IMC were developed. Both the basic concepts of IMC and the related canonical representations will be outlined in this section to facilitate the treatment of the topic of "data" (in the sense of representation) and its relationship to information.

In IMC any portion of model information which can be referred to in a communication is called a construct (Gebilde). A construct may be the information about a family, a car in an administration, a book in a library, a process in a factory. A construct is either an atom (Atom) or an aggregate (Aggregat). Whereas an atom is declared to "be", i.e. to be viewed as elementary (in a given situation), an aggregate is a compound construct, the composition of which is relevant in a considered communication. A construct in its capacity as a part of another construct is a component (Komponente). A construct cannot be a component within itself.

Depending on the way of immediate composition (first level) an aggregate is either a collection (Kollektion) or a nomination (Nomination). These two generic types of aggregates differ in that a collection is an unordered finite set of constructs, whereas a nomination is a (mathematical) function from names (Name) to constructs. The domain of a nomination therefore is a set of names. For the property of being a collection or a nomination the nature of the immediate components is of no significance. Names only serve for the selection of immediate components in a nomination (in the same manner as selectors in the Vienna Definition Language, cf. e.g. [ZEM]). Beyond that no meaning of names is involved within the framework of IMC.

To show examples of atoms, collections, and nominations we first have to introduce the above mentioned canonical representation. In IMC a box represents a construct. The composition of a construct is shown either by nested boxes (fig. 2) or by trees (fig. 3). In a tree representation the aggregation of constructs to an aggregate is expressed by the vertex. A combination of both representation techniques is possible. Atoms are always represented by boxes. In the representation of nominations the presence of names is depicted by small circles attached to the component representations. The names are written close to the circles. A detailed example of a "relation" and the corresponding "set network" in IMC representation is given in [DKR].

If we look at the representation of the nomination of fig. 2 or 3 we notice that the same construct may appear in different contexts. In a representation we can point at the various locations where (the representation of) the same construct appears, on the conceptual level of model information we cannot. Therefore a concept is needed which allows to distinguish between different appearances of one construct (within a considered embracing construct). In IMC the concept of spot (Stelle) has been introduced. A spot can be defined as a sequence of pairs (name, construct). In case of a collection the empty name is inserted at the name position in the pair. The first pair of a spot defining sequence always consists of the empty name and the reference construct, in (=relative to) which the spot is considered. So with the symbols of fig. 4 the construct in question appears at the spots

(-,c_1) (home address,c_2) (city,c_3)
(-,c_1) (place of birth,c_3)
(-,c_1) (branches,c_5) (-,c_3)

which are spots in c_1. (The lower case c's stand for the respective construct.) The same construct also appears at the spot

(-,c_2) (city,c_3) in c_2 and
(-,c_5) (-,c_3) in c_5.

Another example is c_7 which appears in c_1 at the following two spots:

(-,c_1) (home address,c_2) (street,c_6) (number,c_7)
(-,c_1) (date of birth,c_4) (year,c_7)

It turns out, that the concept of spot is essential for the discussion and understanding of some sophisticated aspects in data base management systems, not least those concerning the interrelationship between information (constructs) and data (representations).

Fig. 2 and 3 show, by the way, that in canonical graphic representation always constructs a t s p o t s are depicted. As by definition any spot structure is hierarchic, one might be tempted to label IMC a hierarchic system. But it is obvious, that in a l l existing information models (in hierarchic, network, relations, etc.) the spots form hierarchic trees.

So far only individual constructs have been considered. Nothing about types or declarations has been said nor used tacitly. A type in general is a set. But not any set is a type. First of all, it has to be determined what are the elements of such a set. In the present context we focus on types of constructs (Gebildetyp), thus the elements are constructs. In the world of data base management systems instead of "element" the terms "occurrence" or "instance" of a type have been adopted.

But not even any set of constructs is a construct type. A type of constructs has to be declared for a considered communication, saying that only constructs which belong to the specified type(s) are admitted for exchange. More precisely: As only representations of constructs can be exchanged via the channels of an information system, a type declaration specifies what constructs will be represented and can be "understood" by interpretation. A language, in which type declarations are made, should be called a "type definition/declaration language", but unfortunately is often called a "data definition language". This is one example of sloppy terminology which is so characteristic for the field of data processing.

Not even "type declaration language" would be sufficiently precise. As will be shown below, also other types have to be declared (on the representational level). Therefore, strictly speaking such a language is a "construct type declaration language" (CTDL). As far as only the composition of constructs by others is specified in a recursive type declaration, a graphic construct type definition language can be applied in analogy to the canonical construct representation. An example for a graphic type definition is shown in fig. 5, an occurrence of that type is represented in fig. 6, where in both figures the small box in the upper righthand corner provides a place for inserting the name of the type or the _type designation_ (Typenbezeichnung) as we prefer to say. This "type plate" is also used in construct representation, if emphasis is put on the fact that the construct is occurrence of a particular type (cf. fig. 6 and 10).

It would be beyond the scope of this paper to discuss all the aspects involved in the concept of type in general and of construct types in particular. The one or the other will be addressed in the following paragraphs.

After this very short outline, concepts to talk about model information and a canonical representation technique are available. The concept of type has been emphasized because of its great importance for the questions of representation to be discussed in the next section.

4. Data as representations

For convenience the term "data" is used in the following instead of "digital data" indicating that only representations are considered which consist of characters (cf. [DIN]). Other representations (pictures, sounds, etc.) are not investigated with regard to their relationship to information.

Referring to the configuration of two offices with a channel between (fig. 1), let the piece of paper on which fig. 7 appears be a realization of a communication channel. The question is, whether the addressee interprets the five representations there as representations of five, four, three, two or one construct. The example suggests the answer, that the interpretation of the various representations is the subject of agreements between the communicating offices. So according to one agreement all representations might be interpreted as "number seven", according to another agreement the representation 4 + 3 might be taken for an arithmetic expression and not be interpreted as "number seven", or there might be a difference on the construct level even between a "bar seven"(7) and a "plain seven"(7), etc.

A multitude of such agreements are taken for granted in everyday communication. So in usual text the shape of the characters is irrelevant, but in mathematical texts it is not. On the contrary, you have to distinguish carefully between different fonts, because they have a different meaning which usually is agreed upon at the beginning of a paper or is default in mathematical literature. Or: In many programming languages the interspersion of blanks in some places is of no relevance, in other places it is.

These two examples may show that the relationship between information and representation (data) has to be established in advance in order to make possible mutual understanding in communication via a channel. What are the provisions to be made?

For a communication to be possible there must be a prior common background of understanding, i.e. a predefined mapping of representations onto constructs. In the course of communication further agreements may be used to extend this common background: One office passes the declarations to the other, the latter one accepts or rejects them. The declarations comprise

- construct type declaration
- representation type declaration.

Construct type declarations were discussed in the preceding section. The construct type declaration determines the constructs which can be communicated via the considered channel. The construct type declaration language is a part of the above mentioned common background.

The representation type declaration refers to a declared construct type. It determines, what are the admissible representations of constructs of this type which can be exchanged in the regarded channel. Considering the set of all representations of the occurrences of a given type we arrive at the concept of representation type (Darstellungtyp). The representation type declaration language (RTDL) is a further part of the above mentioned common background.

An example may illustrate the relationship between construct type and representation type and their respective occurrences. (The used ad-hoc languages are not to be discussed here and should be understood intuitively.) Although it is a very simple example, many figures have been necessary to depict the ideas presented sc far, which gives an indication about the magnitude of usually implied declarations.

Fig. 8 shows a declaration of the four construct types CALENDAR-DATE, MONTH-NAME, YEAR and DAY-NUMBER. The latter three are types of atoms, the first one is an aggregate type. Additionally the type composition is shown in IMC representation.

Fig. 9 shows a pertaining declaration of four representation types: MONTH REPR, YEAR REPR, and DAY REPR are the representation types for the construct types MONTH-NAME, YEAR, and DAY-NUMBER, respectively. DATE REPR is the representation type for the construct type CALENDAR-DATE.

In spite of the extensive declarations many implicit assumptions still remain: The character sets to be used, the arrangement of characters on the medium (paper e.g.) and other details. They all have to be counted to the pre-existing common background of the communicating offices.

Fig. 10 shows two occurrences of the construct type CALENDAR-DATE (and of course of the component types) and some occurrences of the representation type DATE REPR.

This example suggests that the concept of format belongs to the concept of representation type. Up to here the assumption has been maintained, that only one representation type can be declared for each construct type. This restriction should be dropped now. If multiple declaration of representation types for one construct type is provided, each of the declared representation types could be called a <u>format</u> (Format) in close relation to the common use of this term. Referring to the above example of fig. 9, instead of the one representation type DATE REPR we could declare three representation types (= formats) for the representation of constructs of type CALENDAR-DATE (two "positional" formats, one "key-word" format).

It can be observed that the separation of construct type declaration and representation type declaration (=format declaration) is not explicit in existing systems. The layout of the construct type declaration is often simultaneously the specification of the input and working area format. This might be a reasonable economical approach. But to understand the relationship between information and data one should be aware of the double function of such a "data definition".

Applying the view which has been presented so far of the relationship between information (constructs and construct types) and data (representation and representation types) we outline a flow of information between two offices via one channel: An office B may be requested by an office A to retrieve a construct with given properties (e.g. from a data base). Office B finds the specified construct (i.e. a representation of it), identifies the type of it, chooses one of the pertaining representation type declarations and puts a representation of the construct in question into the channel. As this representation conforms to the representation type declaration established for the regarded channel, office A is able to interpret the data (knowing the representation type and construct type).

Some reader might have noticed, that in the CALENDAR-DATE example an argumentation is missing, why the representations do not show all the details of the represented constructs (cf. fig. 10). Actually, this is not necessarily so, it only corresponds to the practice in data processing, because it is the representation which occupies storage, and not the construct. More extensive representations could be provided in a representation type declaration for various reasons (security, less extensive declarations, etc.). Of course, that would require more capacity of the involved channels (storage). In any case the question arises, whether such a "representation" is really a representation of a construct. Strictly speaking, it is not. Only together with all specifications, which allow the interpretation of the construct, a full representation is there. Therefore a representation in the above sense shows only the individual part (Individualteil) of the represented construct, because the representational part common to all occurrences of that type is in the type declarations. This leads to the idea, that data (e.g. in "input data") usually means individual part of the full representation rather than the full representation itself. With this in mind, the use of the word "data" in the criticized term "data definition" can partly be justified: The "data definition" defines in its representation type declaration the admissible data, i.e. the admissible individual parts of construct representations. However, it should be clear by now, that the omission of the word "type" is entirely misleading.

5. Practice oriented remarks

In this concluding section some applications of the ideas about information and data as discussed above shall be tried.

First a preliminary remark: There might be the impression, that the system of IMC has been offered as a new proposal of a data model to compete with other, well known data models. That would be a misunderstanding. IMC is aiming to be a conceptual tool for speaking about information, on this level comprising the various data models. Nevertheless it is a c o n c e p t u a l model and as such offers a specific view on model information which allows to form a variety of information structures, but has its own limitations, too.

It is not the task of this paper to outline the features of hierarchic, network, relational or other data models. But it might be of interest in this context, to what these attributes refer. They refer to the so-called "data structures" which can be established in a system of the respective model and which are supported by the system's manipulation functions. With the terminology introduced above we would of course say "information structure" instead of "data structure" as meant here. Data structure in our understanding as structure of the information representation normally is left to the implementor, in order to achieve efficiency, security, or any goal else of this nature. For communication purposes the possible structures of constructs and related questions concerning model information are of main interest: On what levels of aggregation are nominations or collections available, what are the restrictions for the nesting of constructs, are there special generic types adjusted to the application in question (e.g. "relations", which in terms of IMC are collections of equally domained nominations, called _collectives_ (Kollektiv)), what is the support for orientation in extensive constructs, what properties can be used to address constructs (independently of their representation), and many other questions. The answers to these questions together with the pertaining operations on the constructs render a data model to be hierarchic, network or relational (or something else).

It is a matter of course, that also efficiency and other aspects influenced by representation techniques are of relevance. The problem of "redundancy" is one of them. It is not intended here to consider the benefits and the disadvantages of redundancy. But it has to be clarified, that redundancy does not refer to the level of constructs, but to the level of their representation. It has been shown, that a construct may appear at several spots as a component of an embracing construct. Spots, at which the same construct appears (necessarily or by chance) are called _parallel spots_ (Parallelstelle). If the appearance of a construct at several spots is r e q u i r e d this has to be specified in the construct type declaration by so-called "consistency constraints" (cf. the SOURCE clause of [DDLC]). Once a consistency specification of this kind has been established, the system (as one of the communicating offices) is free to decide, whether it will store the representation of the construct each time it appears (at a parallel spot) or less often (usually once). The more often the representation is stored, the higher the degree of redundancy is said to be. It is conceivable in principle (and actually is done sometimes) that the same technique could be applied also for other than consistency-conditioned parallel spots. Such a situation is also given with the RESULT feature of [DDLC]). On the model information type level the RESULT clause specifies that the atom at the specified spot is the result of the execution of a specified procedure, which uses constructs at other spots as input. In both the SOURCE and the RESULT clause additionally is specified, whether a representation of the depending atom is maintained permanently (ACTUAL) by the system, or is made up only when required for passing it via the communication channel to the requesting office (VIRTUAL). In the strict sense, the ACTUAL feature causes redundancy. However also another, less restrictive interpretation of the ACTUAL and VIRTUAL feature is conceivable, where the system still remains free to follow the specification verbatim (as assumed above) or to understand it only as an efficiency constraint

Doing a closer look to the discussion of redundancy (in the context of data base management systems) one encounters a system configuration which is a slight modification of that used so far. To show explicitly that one of the offices (the "system") is a computerized functional unit with a storage as a private channel (the "data base"), a diagram like fig. 11 is often preferred rather than fig. 1. With this configuration containing two channels or still better three channels (input channel, data base, output channel) we have also three places to represent constructs. If we consider a representation type declaration, the question has to be answered, what is the object channel which the declaration is applied to? As a matter of fact this is seldom clearly stated. In particular, input format declaration (e.g. sequence of atom representations) and data base format declaration (e.g. SOURCE feature, RESULT feature) are made up to one complex declaration package, the complexity of which is still more increased by packing the construct type declaration into the same package. Such declaration packages are well known under the label "schema". The consequence of such an "optimization" is a minimization of the number of characters to be written by the programmer at the expense of quality of software, in particular of clarity.

Finally some remarks on the relationship between information and data on the one hand and their manipulation on the other hand might be appropriate. It would be an obvious question to ask whether constructs or their representations are manipulated. Strictly speaking, only representations can be handled, as was stated previously. But so-called data manipulation languages do not refer to the representational level only. Primarily they are designed for the manipulation of constructs.

This will be illustrated by an example of the retrieval of a construct: The properties which are specified as parameters of a request refer to a construct rather than to a representation of it. The delivery of the found construct is done by putting it into the respective channel in an agreed representation, i.e. meeting the output format. Another example is "navigation". This term refers to moving from one spot to the other in an extensive construct. Also here no reference to the representation of this construct is involved. Only upon request the navigator gets some representation of the construct (at the spot) where he has arrived at. In case of a data base management system, he does not receive the representation on which the retrieval has been performed, but an output representation. A counter-example, however, is a library, where the representation in the data base (room with book-shelves) is the same as in the output channel (librarian's counter).

Although a "data manipulation" language refers to the level of model information, this does not imply that no actual access to representations takes place in the system. But again, it is up to the implementor, which representations in what way he has provided to be accessed in order to execute manipulation commands. On the other hand the user has several interests to influence also the policies of representation and access. He has time, cost, and security requirements. These requirements which refer to storage and computing time exert some influence to the information level. A good choice of construct types and of manipulation functions as well as a forecast of the user's way of acting in the future (traffic density, update / retrieval ratio, etc.) should yield a balanced compromise between application adequacy and computer efficiency. However, in overall efficiency considerations the influence of storage and computing time resources will decrease. More and more it becomes evident, that we have to move from computer biased concepts, information structures and manipulation facilities to system interfaces, where more preference is given to the involved people and the intended application. This goal includes to support conceptual differentiation wherever useful. The presented view of information and data is intended to be a contribution to this goal.

References

[DIN] DIN/Fachnormenausschuss Informationsverarbeitung (FNI), DIN 44300 "Information processing; vocabulary" (German). German Institute for Standardization, March 1972

[ANSI] ANSI/X3/Sparc/DBMS Study Group, Interim Report. American National Standards Institute, February 1975

[ABN] GMD/Arbeitsgruppe fuer Betriebssystemnormung, "Terminology for the description of models of job processing computer systems" (German). GMD, St. Augustin, 1971

[PET] C. A. Petri, "Grundsaetzliches zur Beschreibung diskreter Prozesse". In: 3. Colloquium ueber Automatentheorie, Haendler, Peschl, Unger, (Hrsg.), Birkhaeuser Verlag, Basel, 1967

[DURI] R. Durchholz and G. Richter, "Concepts for data base management systems". In: Data Base Management, J. W. Klimbie and K. L. Koffeman, (eds.), North-Holland, 1974

[STEEL] T. B. Steel Jr., "Data base standardization - a status report". IFIP-TC-2 Special Working Conference "A technical in-depth evaluation of the DDL", Namur, January 1975

[ZEM] H. Zemanek, "Abstract Objects" (German). Elektronische Rechenanlagen 10/5, 1968

[DKR] R. Durchholz, W. Klutentreter, G. Richter, "Design of a data base management basic system for application programs (DAGS)" (German). In: Datenmodelle und Systementwuerfe fuer Datenbanksysteme, E. Falkenberg und W. Klutentreter, (Hrsg.), GMD, St. Augustin, 1974

[DDLC] CODASYL/Data Description Language Committee (DDLC), "June 73 Report". CODASYL DDL Journal of Development, June 1973

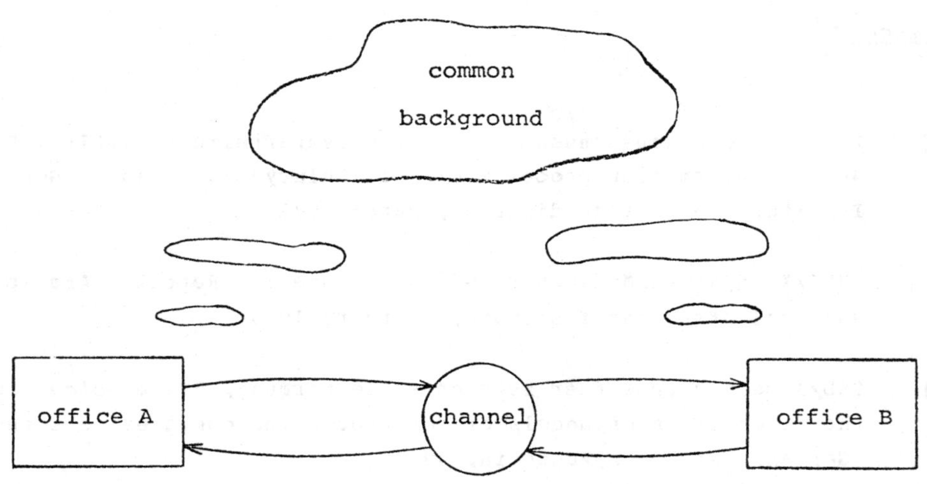

Figure 1 Configuration of communicating functional units

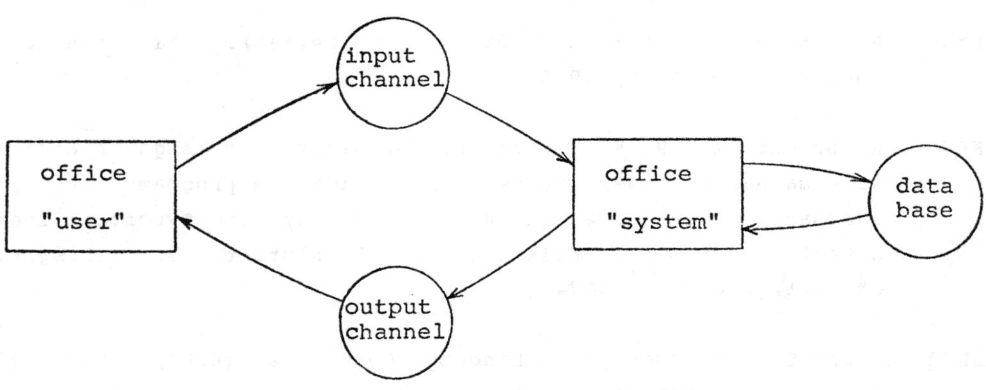

Figure 11 Extended configuration of communicating functional units

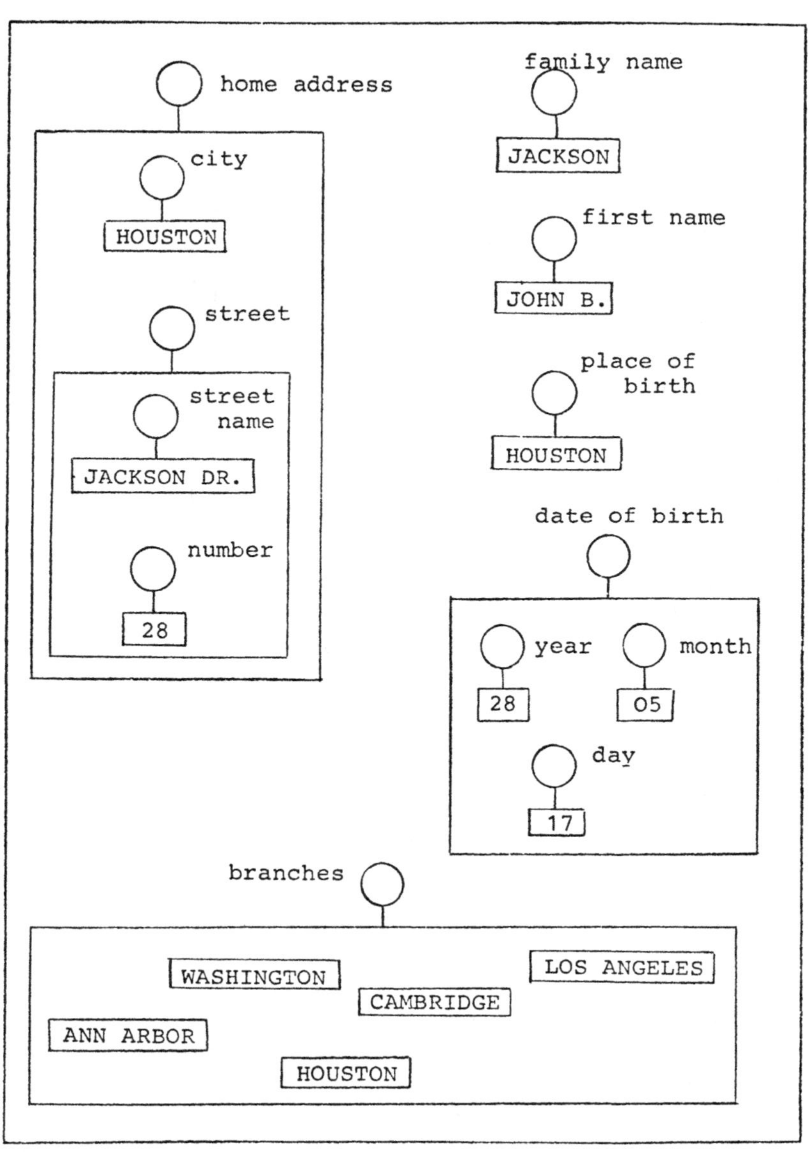

Figure 2 Constructs in IMC box representation

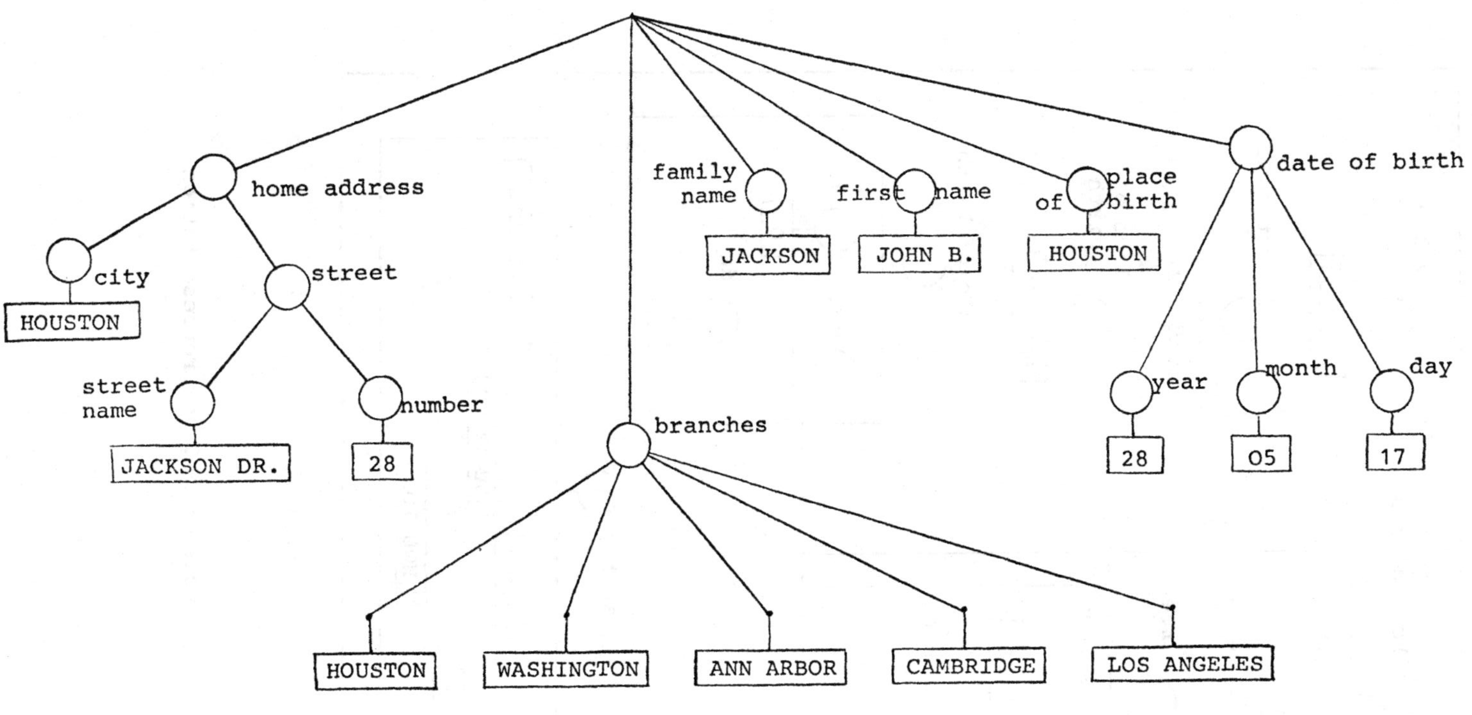

<u>Figure 3</u> Constructs in IMC tree representation

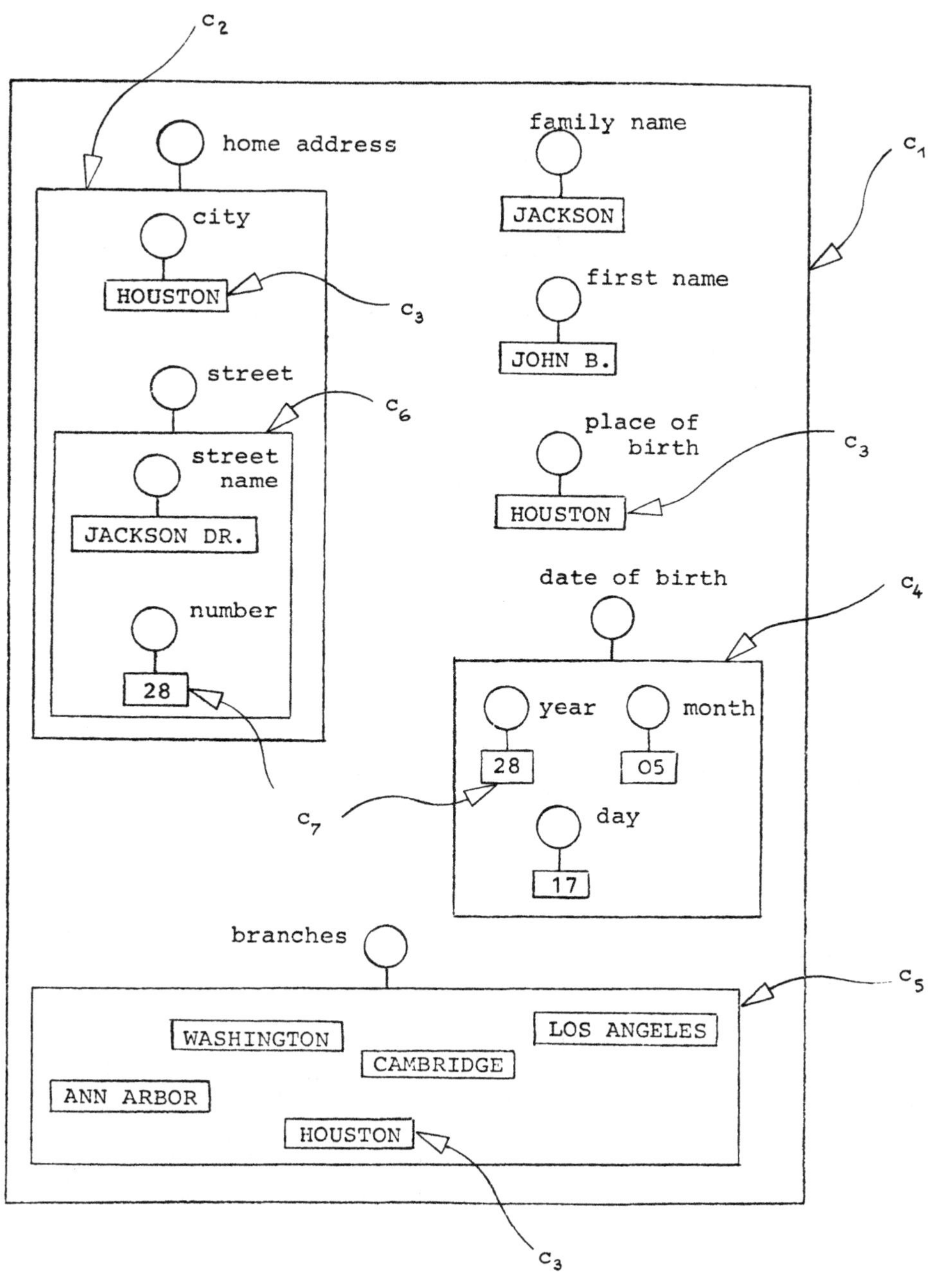

Figure 4 Construct representation of fig. 2 with additional lettering for reference purposes

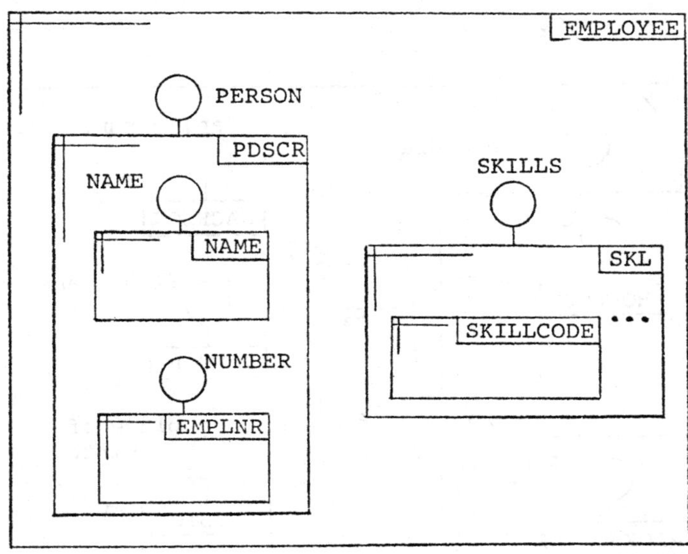

<u>Figure 5</u> Graphic construct type definition

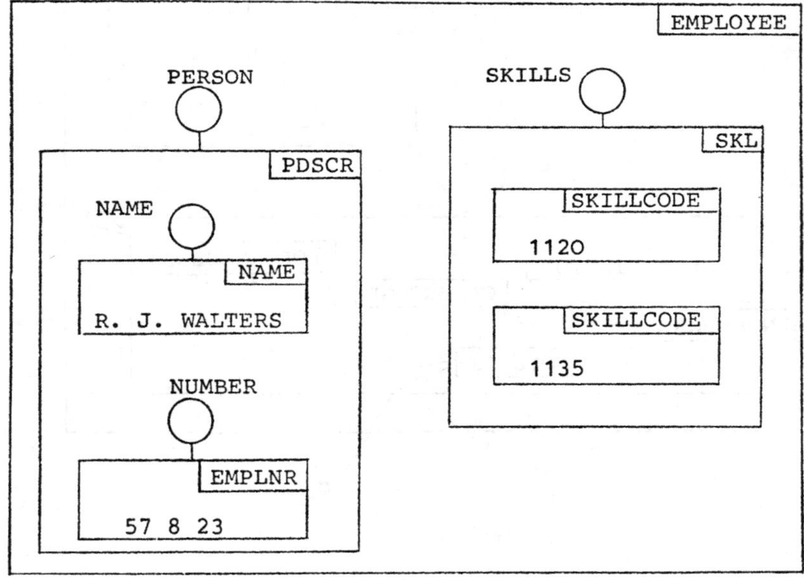

<u>Figure 6</u> Occurrence of construct type defined in fig. 5

Figure 7 see next page

```
construct type MONTH-NAME
atom:   JANUARY, FEBRUARY, ... DECEMBER

construct type YEAR
atom:   1900≤INTEGER≤1999

construct type DAY-NUMBER
atom:   1≤INTEGER≤31

construct type CALENDAR-DATE
nomination:   MONTH -> construct type MONTH-NAME
              YEAR  -> construct type YEAR
              DAY   -> construct type DAY-NUMBER
non-occurrences:  MONTH     | DAY
                  ----------+----
                  FEBRUARY  | 30
                  FEBRUARY  | 31
                  APRIL     | 31
                       etc.
```

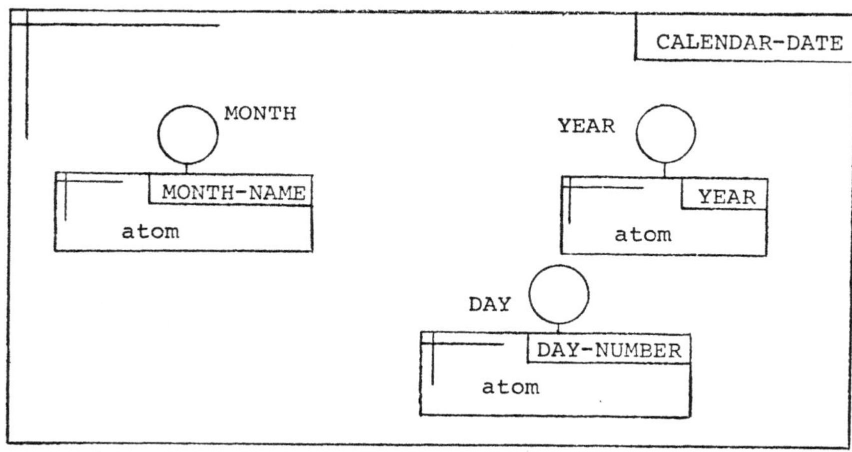

Figure 8 Construct type declarations

```
representation type MONTH REPR
represented construct type MONTH-NAME
string:  1  or  JAN -> atom JANUARY
               ...
        12  or  DEC -> atom DECEMBER

representation type DAY REPR
represented construct type DAY-NUMBER
string: DECIMAL representation

representation type YEAR REPR
represented construct type YEAR
string: DECIMAL representation

representation type DATE REPR
represented construct type CALENDAR-DATE
string: (DAY REPR "-" MONTH REPR "-" YEAR REPR)
      or
        (YEAR REPR "-" MONTH REPR "-" DAY REPR)
      or
        ("D:" DAY REPR /// "M:" MONTH REPR ///
         "Y:" YEAR REPR ; delimiter ",")
```

Figure 9   Representation type declarations

4 + 3

S E V E N

seven

7

7

Figure 7   Five construct representations on paper

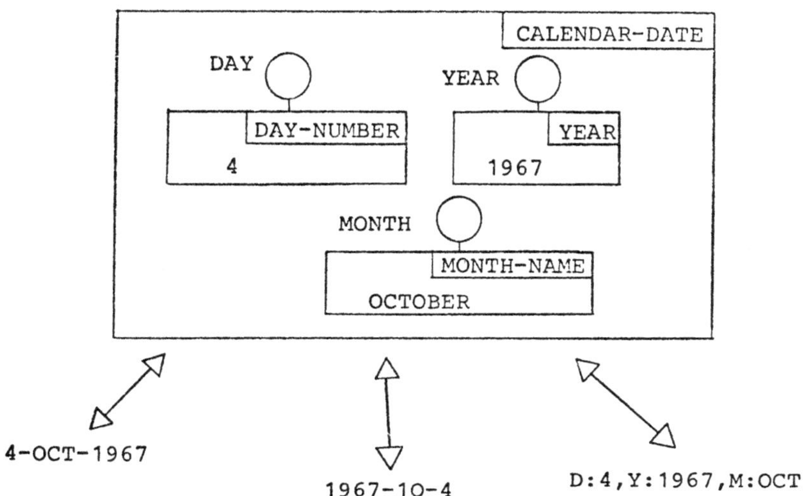

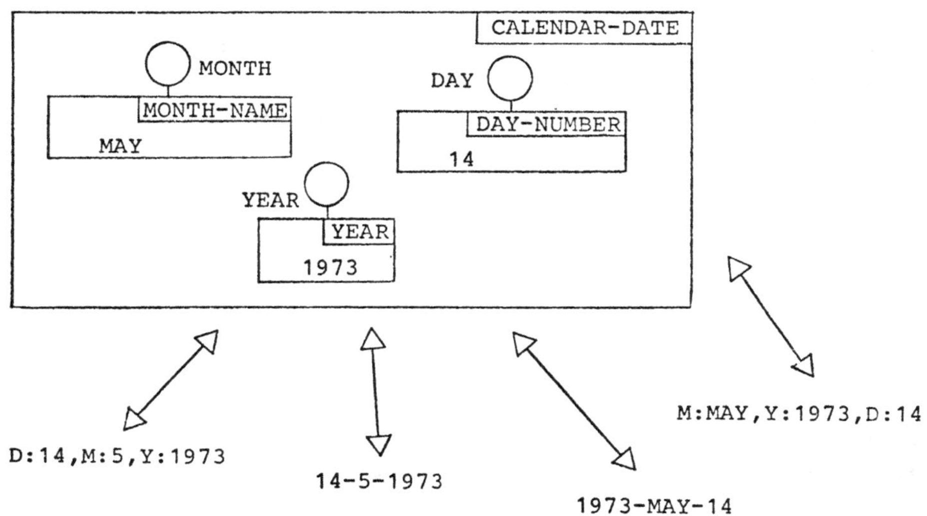

<u>Figure 10</u> Construct type occurrences and representation type occurrences of fig. 8 and 9

<u>Figure 11</u> see first page (fig. 1)

Data Base Research: A Survey

A. Blaser, H. Schmutz, IBM Wissenschaftliches Zentrum, Heidelberg, Tiergartenstr. 15

Abstract

The research activities in the area of data base systems are reviewed. Most of the issues considered by research institutes center around models of information, interactive data manipulation, system aspects, implementation techniques and modelling and analysis. Comparison with industry activities and documented user requirements shows differences of emphasis between research and development. Conclusions are drawn with respect to established and potentially emerging principles in the area of data base design and architecture and with respect to potential future trends in data base research.

TABLE OF CONTENTS

1. INTRODUCTION /49, 192/

The objective of this paper is primarily to provide an overview over past and present research activities in the data base area. This paper does not survey commercially available data base software. Further, information retrieval systems and non-computeroriented aspects of information systems are not addressed. We are well aware of the danger of such limitations and recommend to the reader, who is interested in an introduction to the field, to study in depth some of the commercially available data base systems, such as IMS (A.J. Barnett and J.A. Lightfoot: Information Management System (IMS) - A Users Experience with Evolutionary Development. In Data Base Management Systems (D.A. Jardine editor), North Holland, Amsterdam, 1974) in addition to the literature referenced in this survey.

What is a data base system? This is already a question, which has been and still is subject of debates. We will make our definition with the help of a scheme , which in our experience is widely accepted. It is a simplification of an architecture scheme employed by a major standardization group (ANSI/X3/SPARC) and is very similar to schemes shown in Date's or Wedekind's book. To the authors knowledge, the IMS designer have been the first who implemented, consciously or unconsciously, such a scheme nearly a decade ago.

The scheme is shown in fig. 1 and shows persons, views of information, data mappings, programs and a data flow during retrieval of information. The conceptual view is the central point. It represents the way information is seen by the group responsible for the system aspects of stored, integrated information. This group is usually referred to as the "data base administrator". For a given system installation, a conceptual schema specifies which type of information may exist at the conceptual level. A schema describes, what is legal or "correct" and is therefore similar to a grammar defining the syntax of a language.

The conceptual view is never used directly. It serves as a central reference point for other views of information. For example, the physical or internal view of information reflects the way the information is actually stored in memory. Given the data base in conceptual form, we can construct the corresponding physical form with the help of a mapping, the conceptual to internal mapping (fig. 1 mapping C/I).

The use of conceptual information is through mappings. All of these mappings are in the responsibility of the data base administrator and are specified in a data definition and mapping language. The mappings between conceptual and external views serve a double purpose: (a) to select the subpart of information necessary and sufficient for a spe-

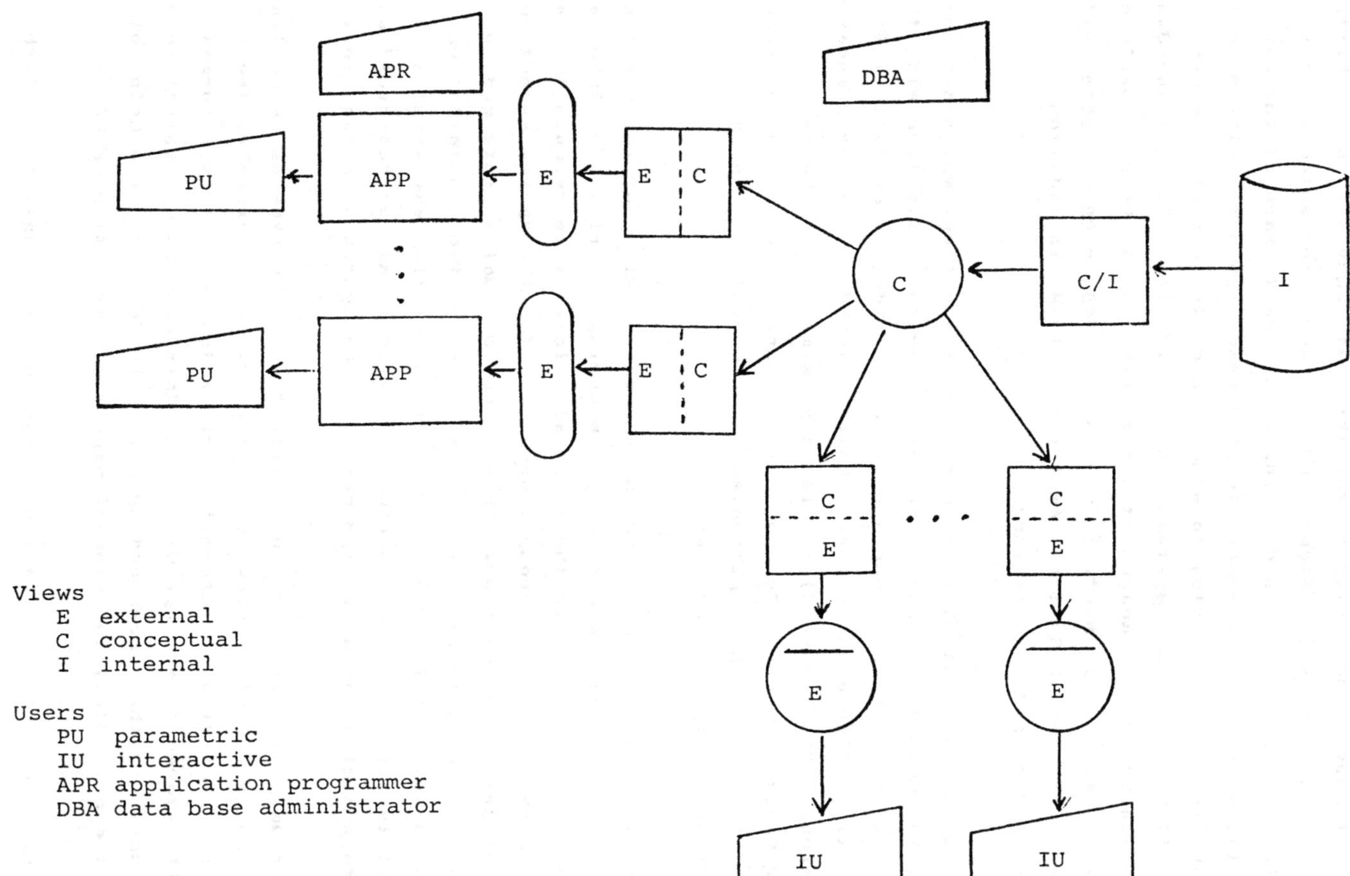

Views
E external
C conceptual
I internal

Users
PU parametric
IU interactive
APR application programmer
DBA data base administrator

Fig. 1:Structure of a data base system

cific use of the data base and (b) possibly, to transform the selected subview to a view, which is "more natural" for the specific use. Point (a) represents the primary purpose and is of importance for reasons of protection, scheduling, user isolation etc., i.e. essentially for systems aspects.

There are two major end-user groups to consider. First we have the query language user, also called the interactive problem solver and typified by the "non-DP-professional". The query language users view of data is very similar to the conceptual view. He performs data manipulation at a fairly high level without needing help by experts. This is different for the "parametric user", who performs well defined actions with parameters of a simple structure. This user interacts with the system via application programs written by application programmers in some programming language into which a data manipulation language is incorporated as a sublanguage. We talk of a host language - sublanguage relationship. In general, the query data manipulation language is at a higher level than the application programmers data manipulation language.

In practice, large amounts of stored information are extremely unlikely to be used by only one person. It is therefore a requirement to a data base management system that it allows sharing of and concurrent access to the stored information. Concurrency creates a number of problems in connection with system integrity, scheduling, deadlock prevention, recovery, protection, and efficiency in solving all these problems.

While commercially employed systems (like IMS) primarily support applications involving parametric users, research concentrates on support of the interactive problem solver. Correspondingly we find a large number of research activities oriented towards the data model used for the conceptual view and to a single user high level query language system. Sections 2 and 3 are devoted to data models and data manipulation languages to describe this research. In section 4 we will discuss research in the area of system aspects. Section 5 describes contributions of research to implementation techniques such as a storage structures and search algorithms. Section 6 will refer to some of the modelling, measurement and analysis efforts and section 7 will contain conclusions with respect to primary results, recognizable trends and some major problems deserving research.

2. DATA MODELS

The conceptual view has been introduced as the central point of reference in a data base management system. Clearly, such a view should be as close as possible to intuitive notions of information. Proposals for a conceptual view are known as data models. A conceptual data model provides a set of possibilities of how to encode conceptually information which exists in the real world. Of course, the mapping between real world information and conceptual information is not formalized.

Closely connected with the notion of a conceptual data model is that of a conceptual schema. For illustration purposes let us consider an extremely simplified real world situation. We have sets P of professors, S of students, and C of courses. Each of the objects in these sets has a number , which is unique within the set, and a name. Further, we know for every professor which students he advises and which courses are tought by him. A student has exactly one professor as advisor and may attend a number of courses and a course is taught by exactly one professor and attended by a number of students. Fig. 2 shows the information in an attempt to be close to reality without biasing towards any data model.

Conceptual data models are all more or less based on the notions of set theory. One of the earlier attempts is the Information Algebra of CODASYL /34/. Other models and stimulating ideas are due to Mealy /124/, Feldman and Rovner /74/, and, Ash and Sibley /3/. The most successful model in terms of acceptance and as a stimulus for data base research has been developed by E.F. Codd in a series of papers to which we will devote the next subsection.

2.1. Codd's Relational Model (CRM) /39-41, 43/

In CRM information is a finite set of named relations of assorted degree. A n-ary relation is a finite subset of a cartesian product

D1 x D2 x ... Dn

where the Di are potentially infinite sets of "scalar" data values such as numerical values or string values. In other words, a n-ary relation is a set of n-tuples. To any relation, the elements of the

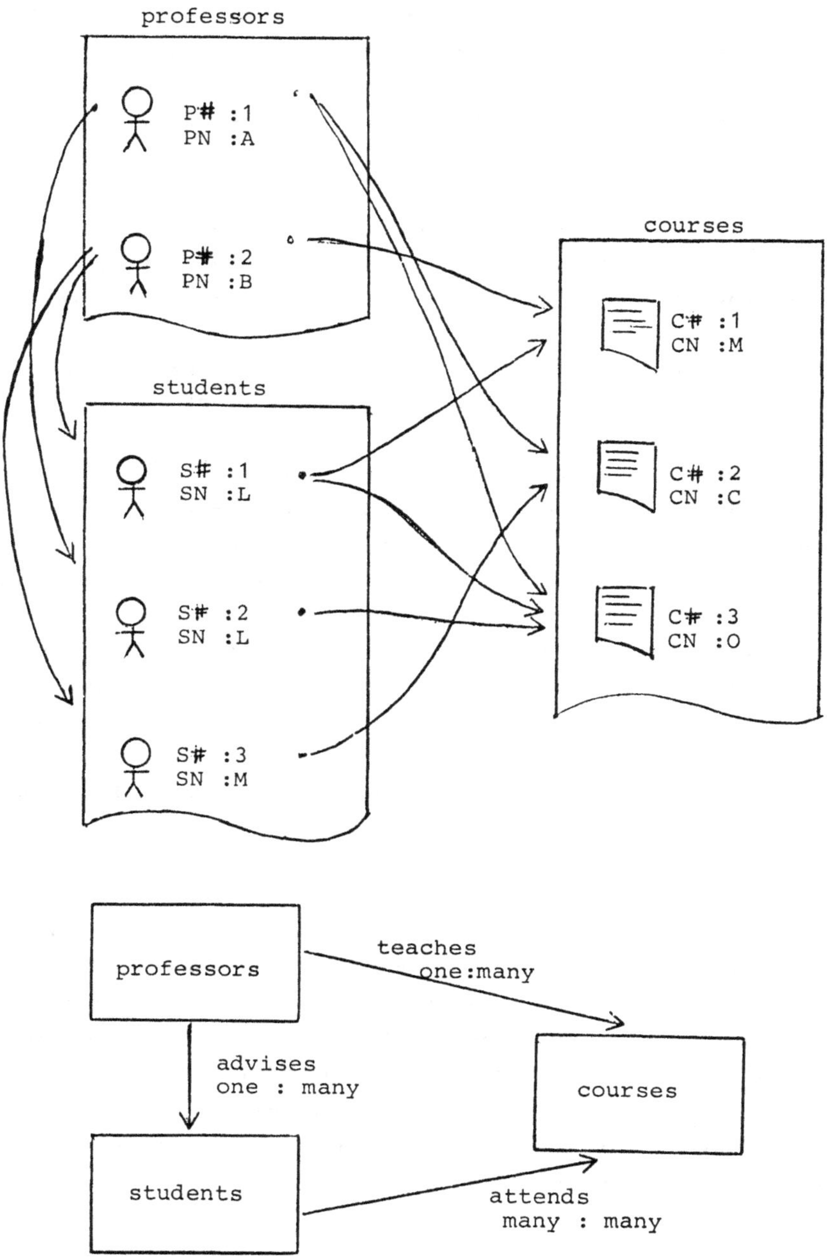

Fig. 2:Example situation and schema

tuples are named with attribute names for ease of reference. A relation is homogeneous, i.e. any two elements of the same relation have the same attribute names associated with them. This allows a tabular listing of a relation as shown in fig. 3, the representation of the example information in CRM.

Some domains within a relation may be keys and/or references. Two distinct tuples in a relation have different values in their key elements. A refernce domain actually is used to refer to some value that is element of another tuple in the same or another relation. For example, P# in P is a key domain, but P# in S is a reference domain which contains only such integer values, which appear as P# in P.

The relations shown in fig. 3 and corresponding to the schema indicated in fig. 4 are all in socalled first normal form. This means, that all elements of a tuple are scalar (and not sets or lists or structural in any other way). This has consequences in the way information can be modeled. Consider the relationship between students and professors. Principally there are at least two ways to store this information:
(a) we can build the set of all students (or their unique numbers) advised by one professor and store this set with the professor tuple or
(b) we store with every student the professor (or his unique number), which advises the student. Case (a) would not be in "first normal form". Fortunately, case (b) is in this form.

The relationships between professors and students or professors and courses are one to many (i.e. <u>one</u> professor advises <u>many</u> students). In these cases we store the converse relation to satisfy normalization. However, the student/course relationship is many to many and therefore requires the introduction of an additional relation, the relation SC. Codd has defined further normalizations, the "second" and "third normal form", which essentially serve to remove some redundancies. The reader is referred to Codd /41/, Date /49/, or Wedekind /192/.

The advantages of CRM are its apparent simplicity and its appeal to those, who are used to "think" in tables, in particular for researchers with a background in the elementary notions of discrete mathematics. Since a relation is a set, set operations like union, intersection, relative complementation etc. can immediately be applied if the relations agree in domain names. More importantly, projection may be

S		
S#	SN	P#
1	L	2
2	L	1
3	M	2

P	
P#	PN
1	A
2	B

C		
C#	CN	P#
1	M	2
2	C	1
3	O	1

SC	
S#	C#
1	1
1	3
2	3
3	2

Fig. 3:Normalized CRM relations

S (S# <u>int</u>, SN <u>char</u>, P# <u>int</u>) <u>key</u> (S#) <u>ref</u> (P# <u>to</u> P.P#)

P (P# <u>int</u>, PN <u>char</u>) <u>key</u> (P#)

C (C# <u>int</u>, CN <u>char</u>, P# <u>int</u>) <u>key</u> (C#) <u>ref</u> (P# <u>to</u> P.P#)

SC (S# <u>int</u>, C# <u>char</u>) <u>key</u> (S# , C#) <u>ref</u> (S# <u>to</u> S.S# , C# <u>to</u> C.C#)

Fig. 4 CRM schema

applied to relations and relations of different structure may be combined using well known methods of composition such as cartesian product or Pierce product, or a generalization called join in Codd's terminology. In a slightly different approach every relation may be viewed as a stored predicate and first order predicate calculus may be applied to define new relations. Codd has investigated both approaches, the "relational algebra" and the "relational calculus" and has shown that they are equivalent /41/.

The relational model has been subject to a number of critical considerations /20, 43/. It is obvious that it does not offer the full range of structures to which we are used within computer science. It has, for example, no equivalent to the hierarchic record organization of COBOL, PL/I, PASCAL or ALGOL68, a structure which is simple, corresponds to intuition and is most frequently used. This is only one important example of a structure violating the "first normal form" condition.

The example of the relationship between students and professors has shown how the schema is affected by constraints. For example, if the one:many constraint of the professor - student relationship is relaxed to a many:many constraint, a completely new relation has to be introduced.

Another consequence of normalization is the fact, that basic information has to be encoded with the help of other information, which is often of no interest to the requestor of the basic information. For example, in order to know the name of the advisor of the student with name "M", the "system" has to learn that this advisor has the professor number 2, since there is no other way to get to his name. This may be considered tolerable, however, more critical situations arise, if we allow a user to see only a subset of domains, which does not contain the key values. For example, a particular user may be allowed to look at every employee's salary and compare it with the employee's manager salary, but for reasons of privacy he is not allowed to look at the man numbers associated with the salaries. There are immediately two problems. First, in order to find a man's manager's salary, the user has to know the man number of this manager, contradicting the privacy constraint. Second, if the man number is projected out it may well happen that two persons with the same salary appear as one tuple in the projection, thus making any statistics on salary distribution in the projection invalid. One can imagine ways around the first prob-

lem though no elegant ways are known to the authors. The second problem is solved in at least some of the experimental systems (like INGRES, SQUARE) by allowing "duplicates in sets". These implementations are actually implementing a homogeneous flat file model as it is described, for example,
by McGee /122/. This model is in turn a special case of the graph model described later in this section. It cannot be claimed that implementations of the homogeneous flat file model find their clean, theoretical foundation in CRM, though some operations, like joins, make sense with both kinds of data structures.

2.2. Graph Oriented Data Models

The common idea behind the data models discussed in this section is the implicit or explicit notion of labeled graphs over entities or named binary relations between entities . The origins of the model in computer science goes back to McCarthy's abstract objects (as models of information) which have to conform to an abstract syntax (as the schema to the model). (McCarthy,J.: Towards a Mathematical Science of Computation. Proc. IFIP Congr. 1962, North Holland, Amsterdam, 1963). McCarthy's work has influenced the activities of a group in the IBM Vienna Laboratories to model the interpreter states during execution of programs (Lucas P. and K. Walk: On the formal description of PL/I. Annual Reviews of Automatic Programming 6, 3 (1969)). The data structures in languages like COBOL, PL/I, PASCAL, and ALGOL68 are adaptations and extensions of this model, in general with restrictions as to what may be specified in a schema. "Schema" appears now as a synonym for "declaration" or "abstract syntax". Some of the data models designers refer explicitely to this origin /1, 56/. Practically all commercially available data base systems are based on the graph model.

Within data base research activities the graph model shows up more or less consciously in a number of papers. McGee discusses a graph model in 1968 /121/. The entity set model of the DIAM system designed by Astrahan, Altman, Fehder and Senko is essentially a binary relational model and therefore a graph model /155/. Other well known graph models are those developed in CODASYL activities and generally known as the DBTG model /35, 37, 38/. We find the graph model also in Abrial's "data semantics" /1/ and many other research papers /20, 56, 63, 158/. Schmid and Swenson employed recently some sort of graph model to establish a connection between relations in CRM and the real world /151/.

Among the earlier data base research activities the DIAM effort deserves special attention /155/. It contributed essentially to the acceptance of a data base system structure as shown in fig. 1. Its data model, the entity set model, had and still has impact on standardization activities. The DIAM data model has not been defined with the same mathematical rigor as CRM. This is related to the fact, that its designers stressed the closeness of the model to the real world more than pure mathematical formalism. We will not discuss the DIAM model in more detail here since it can be mapped in a straightforward way to the subsequently described graph model and as such find a clean mathematical foundation.

The essential notion of the graph model is that of an abstraction of objects as nodes in a graph. To be consistent with the most frequently used terminology we call such a node an entity. An entity may be anything "that has reality and distinction of being in fact or in thought, e.g. objects, associations, concepts, and events" /34, 155/. Some entities have unique denotations like
5, 7 or 'ABC'. Other types of entities can only be uniquely identified with the help of relationships between entities.

Information in the graph model is stored as a finite set of named finite binary relations between entities. Since entities are nodes in a graph, relations can be represented as directed labeled edges in the graph. To represent unary relations (which are sets of entities) we assume a given node as the entry node to the information and interprete the binary relation between entry node and any other node as a unary relation. For simplicity in drawing a graph we represent edges from the entry node to other nodes by labeling these nodes with the relation name. Fig. 5 and fig. 6 show the graph model representation and schema for our example.

A first advantage of the graph model over CRM is the fact that only binary relations are used. This removes the need to distinguish between the domains via symbolic domain names. More importantly, due to its explicit notion of entities, which is not present in CRM, it is clean and clear in the mathematical sense without the need to deviate from it for "practical" reasons of convenience. Like for CRM, it is possible to develop calculus or algebra oriented languages with the

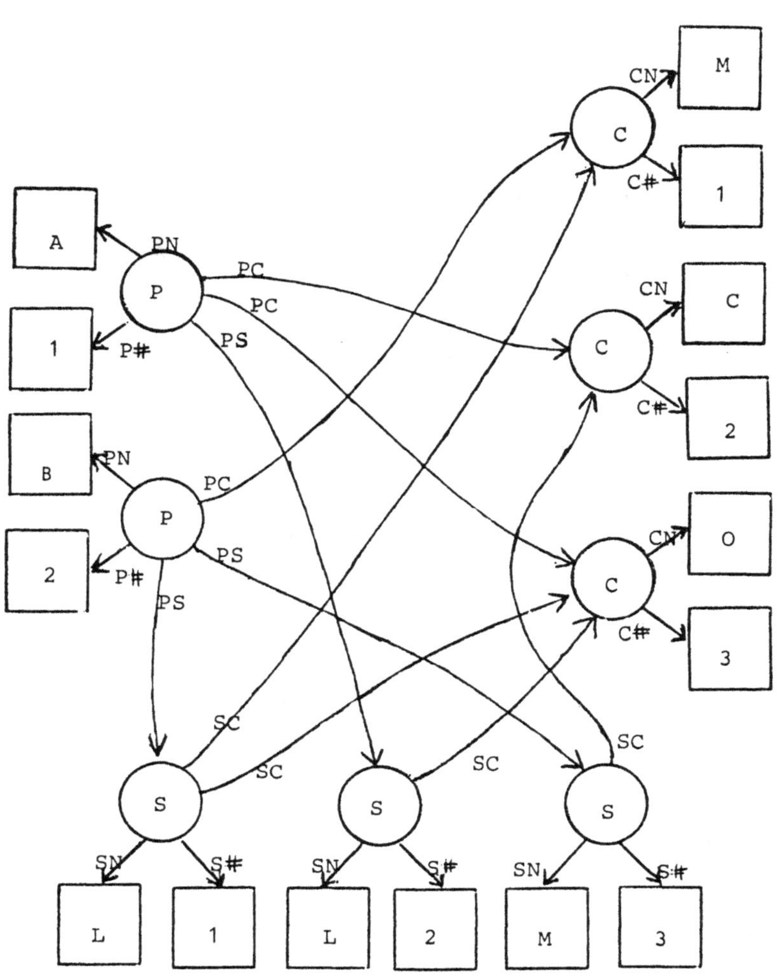

Fig. 5 :Information as a graph

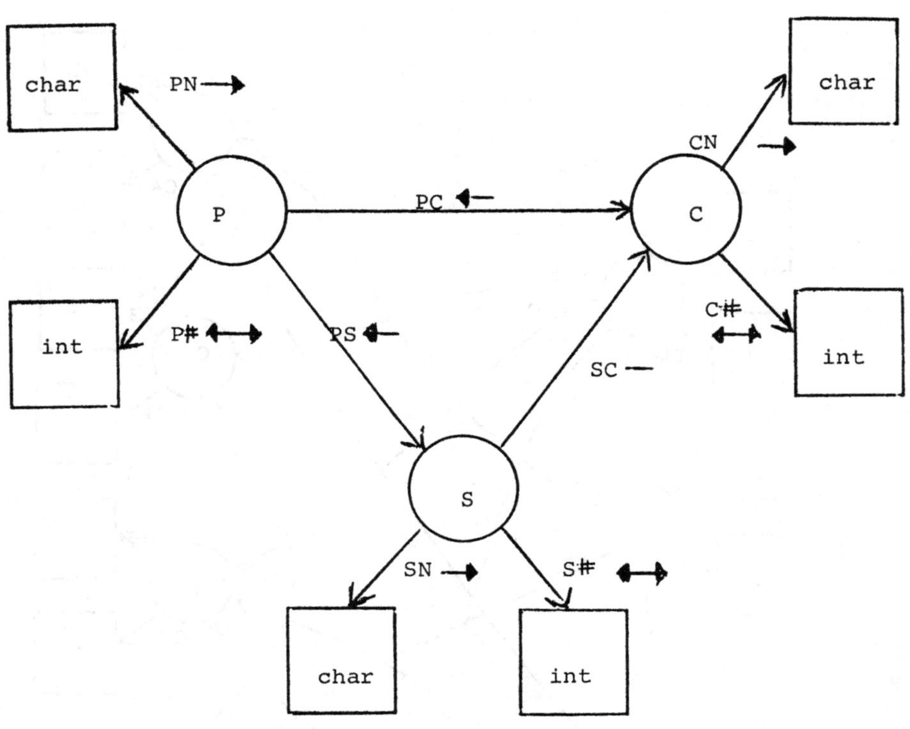

R ↔ one : one

R → many : one

R ← one : many

R — many : many

Fig. 6:Schema to the graph model

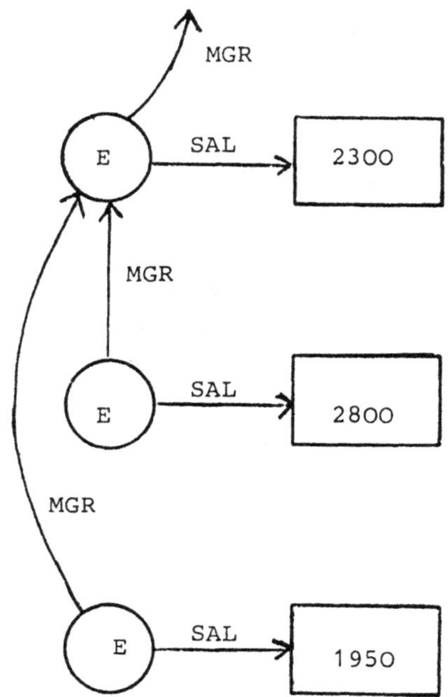

Fig. 7: Subgraph of E, MGR and SAL

same rigor /128/. On the other side it does not provide difficulty to furnish a user with a subview of the data base (i.e. a subgraph) which restricts to the relationships, which may be seen by the user. See fig. 7 for an illustration. Since practically all known structures in computer science can be mapped conveniently to some form of graphs, it does not force us to exclude these structures from our high level data modeling.

2.3. The Equivalence of Data Models

It is not at all surprising that the different models are equivalent in the sense that information encoded in the DBTG or DIAM model can be encoded in CRM and vice versa. Moreover, in most cases there is a simple and straightforward way to convert a schema in one model to a corresponding equivalent schema in the other. The question of choice between two different models must be decided on how "convenient" or "natural" processing becomes in the models. This is, however, not only a question of the data model but also a question of the data manipulation language. In the next section we will therefore come back to the question of equivalence.

The question of equivalence of data models has been investigated by Bobrow /17/, Neuhold /134/, Sibley /167/ and McGee /122/. Different models are likely to coexist for a while (at least in the world of researches), even on the same system. This creates a new mapping problem, namely of how to superimpose a model A on a model B, a problem, which creates the need for a "superimposition theory" as it was stated by E.F. Codd /43/. First results in this direction are reported by Frasson /82/.

3. DATA MANIPULATION LANGUAGES

3.1. Low Level Versus High Level Logic

As we can see in fig. 1, data are accessed in external form either via an application program or interactively at a terminal. In the first case, records are typically retrieved one by one and processed sequentially in a programming language. This type of processing is referred to as "low level" or as "one record at a time logic". Typical for the second case of access is the higher level "multiple records at a time logic". Research activities are primarily oriented towards the higher level logic. It is important to realize that also in the application program case "multiple records at a time logic" is required to specify in advance on which subset of the data the program is going to operate. The system needs this information for scheduling and resource allocation purposes. In effect, the selection of the subspace to a program is a mapping between the conceptual and the external view, which by the nature of its use has to be specified in a high level logic. Even though research projects are primarily oriented towards interactive access to data and even though their implemented systems are modest compared to commercially available systems, their results may very well be of relevance for the type of processing through application programs as it is still more common in todays user installations.

Subsequently some of the data manipulation languages developed by researchers will be referenced. We start with the CRM implementations, then we continue with languages based on other data models. A special subsection is devoted to languages which are characterized by the way in which they are used. Finally we will come back to the equivalence of data models.

3.2. Some CRM Implementations

Table I lists some of the experimental systems, which claim to implement CRM, though for some it would be more correct to claim that they

System	location	remark	reference
IS/I	IBM UK	algebra	Todd
MacAims	MIT	algebra	Goldstein
RDMS	MIT/MULTICS	algebra	Steuert
MORIS	Milano	calculus	Bracchi
SQUARE	IBM Research	mapping	Boyce
SEQUEL	IBM Research	mapping	Chamberlin
INGRES	Berkeley	calculus	Held
ZETA	Toronto	definitional	Mylopoulos
DAMAS	MIT	calculus	Rothnie

Table I. Some relational systems

implement homogeneous flat file. Of the nine systems shown, the first four represent early experiments. SQUARE is a language based on the concept of "mapping", an approach which is somewhere in between relational algebra and relational calculus. It is implemented on top of XRM, a data management supporting n-ary relations or, better, homogeneous flat files /111/. XRM in turn is implemented on top of RAM, a data management, which supports stored binary relations and resembles the graph model /110/. SQUARE has a compact syntax. The query language SEQUEL is derived from it with more English keywords. INGRES stands for a system, which offers QUEL and the graphics oriented CUPID as enduser interfaces /93, 119/. ZETA is a system which is currently being developed at Toronto. It has a data management supporting relations and provides a "syntax directed" definitional tool to let the user implement his high level query language on top of low level primitives. DAMAS is a system specifically used by its implementor to study an optimization aspect of data access.

To give an impression of the different styles of query languages, let us consider the following query:

> What is the name of the advisor of the student, whose name is "M"?

In IS/1, the relational algebra approach, we obtain:

```
( (P * (S; C2 = 'M' )); C1 = C5) % C2
```

This expression is a sequence of a selection (operator = ';'), a cartesian product (operator = '*'), a second selection and a projection (operator = '%'). Ci refers to the value in the i'th domain.

In QUEL, the calculus oriented query language to INGRES, we obtain:

```
RANGE OF PROF IS P
RANGE OF STUD IS S
RETRIEVE INTO R(PROF.PN) WHERE PROF.P# = STUD.P# AND STUD.SN
= 'M'
```

Here the answer is in the result relation R, a unary relation. Clearly PROF and STUD are variables in the predicate calculus sense over which existential quantifications are applied by default.

In SEQUEL, the "mapping" approach, we obtain:

```
SELECT PN FROM P WHERE P.P# IN
SELECT P# FROM S WHERE S.SN = 'M'; ;
```

All of the nine systems represent what might be called first generation research data base systems. This means that their contribution to the solution of data base problems, though already significant as pointed out above, may be increased by follow-on development. At least for the three systems SEQUEL, INGRES, and ZETA we know that such ongoing research is planned. The follow-on system to SEQUEL is called System R.

3.3. Some Non-CRM Systems

As already mentioned, most research activities are using CRM as their data model. In this subsection we will discuss some languages which are using a graph oriented data model.

First there is DIAM with RIL (Representation Independent Language) as its data manipulation language /72/. The DIAM work continues in an effort called DIAM II with FORAL as its query language /157-159/. Senko's FORAL has the interesting property of a graph (or binary relational) model oriented query language for the composition of relations between entities. The example query of the preceding subsection can be formulated in FORAL as follows:

P(PN) <u>where</u> <u>for</u> PS SN = 'M';

FORAL establishes the connection between professors and students with a single identifier where IS/1 or QUEL need at least one comparison. A recently described system, developed in Nice, implements the graph model on top of IMS and offers a query language with similar advantages /82/. McGee describes a data manipulation language to a conceptual graph model, which is very similar to the DBTG model /123/.

A very interesting research developed system is SIMS /194/ which offers a query language and a data definition language. The data definition language allows to map data given in their internal form and possibly generated on another computer, to a hierarchical conceptual form. This hierarchical form can then be accessed by the query language without actually converting the data. SIMS meets with these features objectives, which are missed by most other experimental systems, though SIMS is one of the earlier implementations.

Report generation, i.e. the design of layouts of computer generated reports is a non-trivial problem which to solve with the help of a computer seems natural. Dana and Presser report about an interesting high level language specifically designed for this task /46/.

3.4. User Interface Aspects

In this section we will discuss some data manipulation languages whose designers apply a specific technique with respect to the interface to the user.

A series of research efforts has as its target to embed the query language into a general purpose programming language to combine the data access with powerful computational facilities. Two of these efforts have as their specific research goal to develop and study protection mechanisms /44, 75/. Earley describes a proposal for the inclusion of CRM data structures into an ALGOL like language /59/. Schauer proposes to build an interactive CRM query language in a data base system for the evaluation of measurement data on top of APL /149/.

A question, which is currently still open, is whether the traditional way of defining rigorously a formal language is the best way to attract all end-user groups to the computer. Some researchers believe in the possibility that a freedom in syntax as offered by a natural language, might make the computer more attractive to at least some user groups. Codd proposes such a natural language system, called RENDEZVOUS, which is currently being implemented /42/. TORUS is a natural language system being developed at Toronto. It uses ZETA as its data management /131/. Thompson, Petrick and Kraegeloh report about experimental language systems, which are already implemented /184, 147, 102/. Further references to systems natural language and the linguistic approach can be found in /156/.

The feasibility of the "communication with the computer in natural language" is subject to rather sceptical considerations. In the case of data manipulation languages many of these considerations are not applicable, since the "universe of discourse" is essentially restricted to the objects and verbs stored in the data base and described in a simply structured data dictionary.

A completely different approach is taken by Zloof, McDonald and Schauer /198, 119, 149/. Their method requires a display device, which is used to display the description of the stored CRM relations in some graphical form. In Zloof's Query By Example the user fills "examples" into free spaces of the relation description. Simple queries can be formulated easily and with a low probability of error. In McDonald's CUPID, the user has to draw a flow diagram like picture (with the help of a menue) which expresses the semantics of the query. Schauer's extended query by example is an extension and modification of Zloof's method. It is natural to use a display device if information is associated with geographic locations. GADS /25/ is such a system in which a user can point to locations or subareas within a displayed map to obtain information related to the graphic entities.

The question, wether one user-interface oriented approach is more successful than another cannot be answered by abstract reasoning. Investigations are under way, which employ the methods of experimental psychology to find unbiased answers to the posed question /143, 183/. One of the reported experiments seems to indicate that questions of syntax (or more generally of the form as opposed to the contents) are of a slight significance for the unskilled while questions of semantics are significant independent of the users skill /143/.

3.5. Data Model Equivalence

As pointed out earlier, and illustrated by examples, we know that different data models are (or "can be made") equivalent with respect to corresponding schemata. Subsequently we will briefly indicate that equivalence can easily be extended to the equivalence of the query languages. To this end we introduce informally two query languages, one (CRM) for CRM and the other (GRAPH) for the graph model. Both languages are very similar to SEQUEL. In CRM we deal with relation names, attribute names and variables. A variable is denoted by a relation name followed by a period followed by an attribute name.

Example

S relation name
SN attribute name
S.SN variable

In GRAPH we deal with sets (unary relations) and relations (binary relations). A set denotation is a set name or a set name followed by a period followed by a relation denotation. A relation denotation is a relation name or a relation name followed by a period followed by a relation denotation. A set denotation may also be used as a variable with the obvious meaning that the variable "runs" over all elements of the set.

Example

S, S.SC, S.SC.CN sets (or variables)
PS, PS.SC, PS.SC.CN relations

It should be noted that GRAPH is recursive in the definition of sets while CRM is bound to two levels.

The period is in both languages used as the operator for functional composition from left to right.

A query is of the form:

SELECT list1 FROM list2 WHERE predicate;

In CRM list1 is a list of attribute names, list2 is a list of relation names, and the predicate is over variables which can be built starting with the relations in list2.

In GRAPH list1 is a list of relation denotations, list2 is a list of set denotations and the predicate is over set denotations which can be built with the help of relations starting with the sets in list2.

In both languages the use of subscripts may be necessary to avoid ambiguity. The subsequent examples are such that ambiguity does not arise.

Query 1

Name of the professor, who advises student M.

CRM:

```
SELECT PN FROM P,S WHERE P.P# = S.P# and  S.SN = 'M';
```

GRAPH

```
SELECT PN FROM P WHERE P.PS.SN = 'M'
```

This simple query illustrates already the essential difference between the two data models. CRM normalization requires that some logical relationship between entities are encoded with the help of unique porperties of these entities while in the graph model these relationships may be used directly. Therefore, CRM has to make a comparison where GRAPH simply uses functional composition as we do in natural language. This will become even more apparent in the next query.

Query 2

Names of courses attended by students which are advised by 'B'.

CRM:

```
SELECT CN FROM P, S, C, SC WHERE P.PN = 'B' and  P.P# = S.P#
and  S.S# = SC.S# and SC.C# = C.C#;
```

GRAPH:

```
SELECT PS.SC.CN FROM P WHERE P.PN = 'B';
```

The brevity and elegance of the GRAPH form compared to the CRM form should, however, not be used to conclude an essential superiority of the graph model over CRM. In fact, it is possible to extend the CRM language with a macro processor which accepts as definitions relations between entities in terms of their CRM encodings. This macro processor can then accept GRAPH queries and convert these queries into CRM queries in a simple straight forward algorithm. With other words, we can implement the GRAPH language on top of a CRM implementation such that the user has all the advantages of the graph model. The differences of the languages and their underlying models appear on a level which is primarily of a syntactical nature since they can be transformed away with the help of syntax macros. Issues of one data model versus the other are of little practical relevance given the right sort of implementation. Many other questions like those discussed in subsequent sections deserve and are in the process of receiving more attention.

4. SYSTEM PROBLEMS

4.1. Introduction

The major problems in a data base system like IMS are connected with concurrent access to data shared by many users, with application program management and scheduling, with system enforced data integrity, with locking and recovery or error isolation, with data independence and last, but not least, with high enough transaction rates and short enough response times to make the whole system attractive for the user.

The implementation of such a system, even for experimental purposes, may turn out to be quite costly in time and manpower. It is therefore natural that only few research projects aim at a large portion of the full set of data base management system functions. Among the systems mentioned in section 3, DIAM in its original conception was at least very ambitious with respect to data independence and supported storage structures. System R, the follow-on activity to SEQUEL, though being experimental, plans to provide solutions in nearly all of the problem areas mentioned above.

The fact that researchers so far have not developed full size operational data base systems does not mean that they have ignored problems outside data models and high level query languages. In subsequent sections we will reference a considerable number of relevant papers in the area of data independence and data integrity and recovery in connection with multi-user systems. In addition, the reader will find references to research in the area of security and authorization in the attached bibliography.

4.2. Data Independence /175/

A data base system supports data independence to the extent in which it allows transformations of the internal or conceptual forms of data without affecting (a maximum of) existing programs in the sense that non-affected programs, which run correctly before the transformations, run also correctly after the transformations. Hence, data independence is in effect the independence of programs with respect to data transformations. This makes clear that data independence is not the automatic consequence of the selection of a certain conceptual data model as it is sometimes claimed.

We distinguish between internal and conceptual data independence. The need for internal data independence, i.e. independence of application programs with respect to changes of the internal form of the data, while the conceputal form stays invariant, is a consequence of the widely recognized fact that there is no absolutely best internal data organization /182/. The performance of an application program depends heavily on how many of its access paths are directly implemented (for example via links or inverted files or other storage structures; see section 5). Every such direct implementation means redundancy in storing, i.e. requires additional update activities. The data base administrator will attempt to optimize the internal organization for a given mix of application programs. Since the mix changes with time, there will be a need to adapt the internal data organization.

The need for conceptual data independence arises due to additions of new types of information, or more generally, changes in the conceptual schema. In general, at least some of the existing application programs are affected, while still a large part may remain unaffected. Consider, for example, the addition of a domain to a CRM conceptual data base. There should be no need to alter programs, which only read data, since the old model is a subview (projection) of the new model. This may already be different for programs which update information, since there may be a dependency between the changed domains and the new domain. Certainly, at least some of the programs which insert new elements into relations are affected, since otherwise the new information cannot be entered. Other changes in the conceptual model, for example, relaxing the many to one constraint of a binary relation to a many to many constraint, may even affect read only programs, if these programs are designed such, that they rely on the old many to one constraint.

Support of conceptual data independence requires that the system is capable of determing for each of its application programs, whether it is affected or not. This involves a very complex decision problem, which is not solvable in general. It is therefore necessary to restrict the data mapping languages such that the decision problem remains solvable. This requires a type of theory, which has not been extensively applied /exceptions appear, in other contexts, in 53 and 65/.

Support of internal data independence requires the following:

1. A data definition and mapping language, which specifies the internal form to every conceptual form allowed by the schema. The degree of data independence to a given conceptual schema is the set of different mappings supported for the conceptual schema.

2. To any given application program the system must be capable of recognizing the predefined access paths in the internal schema, which meet "optimally" the program's needs, and exploit these access paths during execution of the program. This process has been called reduction of the external access to the internal access. A system without this optimizing reduction may be "logically" data independent but practically serves no purpose . In other words, what is necessary is a data independence which results in performance gains for the user.

Almost all of the experimental query language implementations described in section 3 support data independence to a limited degree in the following way: When a user (in his "data base administration role") introduces a new relation he may specify which attributes should be inverted. However, a query is formulated independently of whether there exist inversions or not. During execution of a query the system exploits the advantages offered by inversions and maintains the inversions without any burden on the user except unavoidable storage and time overhead /175/.

A more comprehensive approach to data independence starts with the development of a flexible data definition and mapping language. Taylor, and with a slightly modified motivation, Smith have developed such languages for a data model very close to the DBTG model /179,

169/. As pointed out earlier, SIMS has also such a language, which enables it to operate on given data without converting these data as a whole /194/. The importance of the possibility to access data by means of a description and without converting the data as a whole is illustrated by the existence of data collections, which to convert to a standard form is more expensive than rewriting all the application programs operating on these date /166/.

The evaluation of a data definition and mapping language in a full size data base management system is a very complex task. This fact has probably given impetus to experiments with such languages in the area of data translation, which has also a justification in its own right. Data translation is the conversion of data, which have been created and processed in one system, to a data organization which allows processing in another system. The orientation of these projects combines practical orientation with experimental evaluation of the power of mapping languages, while the projects still remain small enough to be conducted in less than a large group.

Ramirez et al. have built a compiler, which generates conversion programs from data descriptions /142/. This work makes use of the mentioned data definition and mapping language developed by D. P. Smith . Similarly, Taylor's language is used in another major activity at the University of Michigan / Merten, Fry, 126/. This work is continuing with increased functions being built into the currently runnning prototypes. The underlying data models in both projects are DBTG oriented. The usefulness of CRM as internal form of data during translation has been investigated by Navathe and Merten /133/ with a negative result. Liu and Heller have used contextfree grammars as data descriptions at the record level /108/. Housel, Lum and Shu have developed a language DEFINE (mapping to a hierarchical structure) for data definition and a language CONVERT (mapping between hierarchical structures) for translation definition and plan to implement these languages in a prototype /95, 165/. Again their model of data is that of a graph, which, for the purpose of translation, is decomposed into hierarchies. In a network of computers, such as the ARPA net, data conversion is of particular importance. Su and Lam, and also Schneider and Desautels describe an approach to data translation specifically oriented towards this use /177, 153/.

4.3. Data Integrity and Recovery in Multi User Systems

Though the problems, which exist with respect to data integrity and recovery are also present in single user systems, they are enormously increased in a system with many concurrent users. In fact, without multi-user support, traditional means under user responsibility may be adequate for dealing with these problems. In a multi-user system the system has by necessity to take over some of the responsibility for the solution.

The notion of data integrity is closely connected with the notion of consistency and the schema. A schema may be viewed as a collection of assertions about the data base contents which stay invariant during processing. These assertions are also called consistency rules. Such rules may state that information is in a certain sense complete (for example, whenever something is known about a person, then its mannumber, name, address and birthdate are known). A more complex rule may require that a person cannot be its own ancestor, or, that the sum of different expenses in a department may not exceed the budget allocated to the department. A data base supports data integrity to the extent in which it allows a user to specify consistency rules, which are subsequently enforced by the system.

A straightforward approach to specifying such rules could consist of the following.

1. Provide the user with a general language like predicate calculus or a query language to specify assertions.

2. Whenever the data base has been modified, the system checks, whether the assertions still hold.

This approach, proposed for example in /1,78/ and recently also in /66/ has to be considered with caution. First, it is for a general language undecidable whether the assertions are in themselves consistent. Second, it has to be carefully defined when the consistency of a data base is checked, since a user must in general perform a number of modifications to a data base before a consistent state is again transformed into a consistent state. Third, checking of a set of complex consistency rules may require access to a large portion of a data base, which can range from hours for small data bases to several weeks for larger data bases in processing time.

The first problem can be solved only, if the language in which the consistency rules are expressed, is simple enough so that the consistency of the rules remains decidable. Practical systems, like IMS, certainly satisfy this criterion.

The second problem has been recognized and has lead to the introduction of the notion of a transaction /65, 66/. A transaction is a sequence of transformations of the data base by one user, which are supposed to transform a consistent state into a consistent state. Beginning and end of a transaction are under user control. Now consistency checking can take place whenever a transaction is complete.

The third problem is in some way connected to the first one. Given a consistency rule, the system must be capable of determing, how costly its checking during data base transformations will be. The variation of costs of checking a consistency rule may be illustrated with an example: Given a father relation, a consistency rule may state that the subgraph containing only edges labeled with father is cycle free. Checking this rule requires an algorithm that is in execution time proportional to n**3, where n is the number of objects participating in the father relation. If the stored information contains in addition for every person the birthdate, the rule that the birthdate of the father precedes the birthdate of the son, serves the same purpose as the previous cycle rule. This rule can, however, easily and efficiently be verfied for every data base change. In most situations "system enforced integrity" makes only sense, if the time needed for the enforcement is bound by a linear function of the time necessary to perform processing without integrity assurance. A compiled approach like the assurance of integrity constraints by query modification, as proposed by Stonebrecker /176/, may help since it allows comparative analysis of the queries with and without constraints. Of course, such an analysis does not have to be at the source level.

The problem of integrity is increased with concurrent access by more than one user. The system has, in addition, to ensure that the users do not interfere with each other during update operations. To this end the system must provide a facility which gives a user exclusive access to a part of the data base for a limited time. Basic mechanisms for granting exclusive access to a user are well known from operating systems under the names of locking or semaphores.

The situation is analyzed in a technical report by Eswaran et al

/65/. A complication of locking in data base systems, also explained in /65/, is the need to lock objects, which may not yet exist, from being created /30/. There are an infinite number of objects which may potentially be created (though the set of created objects is always finite). Such locks may be described by predicates with an infinite extension. Performance requirements dictate that it can be decided for two such predicates whether they overlap. This imposes restrictions on the formulation of predicates to be handled by the system /65/.

Locking has as consequence the danger of deadlocks. As in operating systems there are essentially two ways to deal with deadlocks. The first, proposed for example by Everest /67/ is preclaiming. With preclaiming of resources the system can schedule the user's transactions such that no deadlock appears. The second solution is preemption, i.e. taking away resources from one process to give the resources to the other process. The preempted process has then to be positioned back to a state in which it did not hold the resources. This is possible with the help of journals and checkpoint files, i.e. data sets which record the internal state of a process during its execution /83/. This method is discussed by Chamberlin et al /29/. It should be noted that these files are required in most systems for recovery purpose.

Recovery is necessary whenever it is impossible for a transaction to terminate normally. The cause for this may be a deadlock, a logical error in the user's program (a zerodivide exception or a consistency check failure, for example), a hardware failure, or the failure of a transaction which has directly or indirectly (via the data base) delivered input to the transaction. The first objective of recovery is the isolation of a failure, such that an error does not propagate in the data base. A second objective is to restart all transactions which have been affected by a failure without being the cause such that they continue execution as if no failure had appeared. This is to a large extent possible. Recovery algorithms have been described by Genton /83/, Davies /50/, Bjork /13/, Edelberg /62/ and Sayani /148/. The basis for much of this work has been laid by recovery in operating systems such as MULTICS /81/.

All solutions to the integrity and recovery problems must of course avoid placing an unnecessary burden on the user. The most that should be expected from an application programmer is to inform the system of the beginning and the end of transactions. The interactive problem solver should not be required to know about transactions. He should, as far as the query language is concerned, be able to act as if he were the only user of the system.

As with data independence, the problems discussed in this section are at the beginning to be understood. There is certainly significant room for improvement over proposed and existing solutions, in particular, in providing the functions with improved performance.

5. STORAGE STRUCTURES AND SEARCH ALGORITHMS

Data independence as discussed in the preceding section derives its value (a) from the existence of storage organization techniques which reduce the sometimes enormous search time required otherwise and (b) from the existence of algorithms which allow to utilize the storage structures without binding the programs to these structures. The next two subsections are devoted to these two topics.

5.1. Storage Structures

One of the frequently employed techniques is the acceleration of a search with one parameter with the help of an inverted file. If the inverted file is repeatedly inverted we obtain an hierarchical index organization described by Bayer and McCreight and known as 'B-Tree'. B-Trees allow a logarithmic search time for retrieval, update and insert /9/. Lum introduced multi-attribute indexes which allow quicker answers to queries of higher complexity /112/. Finkel and Bentley describe an extension of binary trees to quad trees supporting logarithmic searches with two parameters /77/. Haerder describes methods of address list compressions ('bit lists') to reduce the storage costs of indices in certain cases /90/.

Another method of reducing search time is hashing. Hashing has been extensively studied in connection with its application to data management /113, 115/. Ghosh and Lum have recently shown that under their assumptions, 'hashing by division' is in general best /85/.

Of course, there are a number of additional, essentially basic techniques applied to data organization such as links between or the splitting of records. These methods may be combined in various modifications. Storage structures have been extensively studied in the past and are well described in textbooks and surveys /54, 99, 100, 118, 120, 135, 160/. The problem remains to offer this richness of structures to programs without binding the programs to specific structures, i.e. to offer the structures with data independence. In the case in which the program does not know the internal organization, it is the system's responsibility to utilize the storage structures optimally. Attempts to solve this problem are discussed in the next subsection.

5.2. The Reduction Problem

Reduction is the problem of reducing external accesses to internal access, where the relationship between internal and external representations are given by mappings of these forms to a conceptual form (fig. 1). Reduction is something like an "optimization" with the primary objective to reduce the number of accesses to secondary storage during execution of a query or an application program. The term "optimization" should not evoke unrealistic expectations; the problem is too complex and is loaded with similar problems as optimization in a compiler.

Variations in the objectives of optimization are connected with the handling of intermediate expressions over data sets. Consider, for example, the expression

(A op1 B) op2 (C op3 D)

where A, B, C, D are large relations and op1 to op3 are operators in the relational algebra. A straightforward evaluation might construct two intermediate relations AB = A op1 B, and CD = C op3 D and then evaluate AB op2 CD. Such an algorithm requires in additon to enormous amounts of secondary storage accesses also an enormous amount of auxiliary storage, which may by far exceed the storage occupied by the underlying relations A, B, C, and D. On the other hand, there are drastic improvements in the evaluation of some queries if during their evaluation at least some temporary inversions can be built. Most of the research in this area is primarily oriented towards the interactive use of a data base of modest size and consequently assumes that auxiliary data sets (i.e. indices) can be built temporarily for one query execution.

One of the earliest comprehensive investigations into this problem is due to Palermo /140/. Palermo claims that for the investigated type of queries no tuple has to be accessed more than once. This is achieved by building indices and restricting the domains of variables in calculus expressions and applying a "least growth principle" for the sequence of operations. A reduction algorithm applicable to the DIAM system is described by Astrahan, Ghosh and Senko /5, 84/ . Greenfeld and Rothnie look at the problem of handling quantification in calculus expressions efficiently /89, 147/. Another implemented version of a reduction algorithm is described by Astrahan and Chamberlin /6/. Their problem consists of primarily taking advantage of inversions, but their algorithm involves also the construction of intermediary lists (indexes) by merging of inversions.

A paper related to the reduction problem is due to Wong/Chiang. They assume that each query is a boolean expression over elementary queries. In this case the data base can be organized according to the elementary queries and reduction becomes essentially the problem of putting a boolian expression into some standard form /195/.

CPU usage has not received much attention, perhaps under the assumption that CPU time is not the bottleneck in the system. This assumption is, however, not always valid. To reduce CPU time, less dynamic and less interpretive search stategies are required, which can be compiled into a CPU efficient search module or access module per application. As mentioned earlier, the compiler approach has been taken or proposed by several researchers primarily, however, for other reasons than efficiency /Mehl, Fernandez, Conway, also Taylor in 125, 75, 44 and 180/.

It should be clear that the reduction problem is very complex. Every algorithm described above has to make a number of assumptions with respect to system structure, which are not generally valid. This has to be so, as long as there is no generally respected data base architecture. Questions, which potentially deserve more attention in future research are the recognition of constraints in storage requirements and CPU time in addition to "minimizing" secondary storage accesses.

6. MODELLING AND ANALYSIS

Research in the area of modeling and analysis has as its objective to learn about existing systems by analyzing their behaviour and to develop simple probabilistic models for the components of a data base management system. Such models may help to predict the influence of changes in a system or system design. Thus the designer of a data base management system and even more, the data base administrator should have primary interest in these research activities.

The need for modeling of data management system and data base systems has been recognized early by Senko and his colleagues and lead to the development of an analysis tool called FOREM and a follow-on tool called PHASE II /154, 138/. Haerder has recently performed a comparative analysis of current indexing techniques using these tools /91/. FOREM and PHASE II are useful to evaluate storage organizations, but limited with respect to overall data base system simulation. Nakamura et al. report about a data base simulation model which they have constructed with the help of a conventional simulation package /132/. Their model is a fairly detailed, event driven simulator of the processes in a data base management system. These processes are so complex that questions of simulation performance may become critical. A possible way out may be the development of comprehensive data base system simulating tools. A step in this direction is proposed by Reiter /144/.

Data base systems have also been objects of analytical modeling activities though they are clearly too complex to be analytically treatable as a whole. Analytical studies restrict themselves therefore to well defined parts of the system. FOREM is an example of a deterministic, analytical tool for the analysis of storage structures. The methods proposed by Cardenas in /22/, Yao in /196/ and Wedekind in /193/ are also essentially deterministic.

To mention is also the analytically tractable queueing model of the DL/I component of IMS developed by Lavenberg and Shedler /103/. Though they allow for "rather general" distributions, their model is at a gross level. For example, it does not explicitly represent the physical storage organization and total I/O is represented by a single server queue. Extensions of the model are, however, likely to make simulation necessary.

Perhaps the most frequently investigated question is the selection of indices to a flat file. Authors, who have contributed to research on this problem under varying assumptions are Lum and Ling /114/, Palermo

/139/, Stonebraker /174/, King /98/, Cardenas /23/, Schkolnick /150/, Yue and Wong /197/ and Farley and Stewart /71/. Shneiderman has investigated the question of index size at different levels /164/.

Data may be allocated to or destributed over a variety of categories: first, data have to be allocated within a storage hierarchy in an attempt to balance between costs and access time, second, data have to be assigned to physical devices to minimize contention given their position in the hierarchy, third, in case of a network (like the ARPA net), data have to be assigned to nodes in the network to improve accessibility and reduce line costs. Lum et al. as well as Buzen and Chen have considered the problem of allocating data within a storage hierarchy, given statistical information on the usage of the data sets /116, 21/. Lum et al. specify a total cost function to an allocation and an algorithm which finds the allocation to a minimal cost. Buzen and Chen's model takes in addition queueing effects at the hierarchy levels into consideration. Their algorithm's target is to minimize response time under given storage constraints.

The second problem, minimizing disk arm contention by suitably distributing data sets over a number of disk drives given their usage statistics, has been considered by Chandra and Wong and recently also by Easton and Wong /31, 60/. There is no best algorithmic solution, but heuristic approaches are given and some bounds for the optimality are derived.

Casey and Chang have considered the third problem of allocating data within a simplified network of computers to reduce line costs /26, 27, 32/. Chang has extended Casey's linear cost functions to a more general function. Both specify algorithms, which attempt to minimize line costs.

With the analysis work reported so far, at least one question remains open: what are the characteristic input data? Or, with other words, how is the workload of a data base system statistically characterized? Nakamura et al. in their simulation raise the further question of the validity of their model. Answers to such questions can only be found by actually observing operational systems and collecting statistics. Rodriguez and Hildebrand describe how relevant data ranging from a log of the user's messages, over a trace of the application program calls (to the data base system) to a trace of physical disk address references can be collected in operational systems /145/. Lewis and Shedler derive from such observations that the interarrival times between transactions can be satisfactorily modeled by a non-stationary Poisson process (i.e. a Poisson process with a time dependent rate) /107/.

In a semi-empirical approach, Ghosh and Tuel, and also Easton, determine the parameters of a theoretically established model to make the model fit to empirical data /86, 61/. Ghosh and Tuel model certain interactions in a data base system by linear relationships and determine the coefficients by comparison with measurements, which are also used to validate the model. Easton has proposed to use an extension of the independent reference model for the sequence of references of application programs to blocks on secondary storage and again has validated this model by comparison with the behaviour of a large data base system.

It is clear that the objective to obtain representative models and validated workload characterizations has not yet been convincingly met. The reasons for this are connected with the current state of the art of data base research in general, which will be summarized in the next section. However, it is also clear that research on modeling and analysis of data base systems as described in this section has made significant progress, and that its continuation is extremely important from a practical point of view.

7. SUMMARY AND CONCLUSIONS

Before we try to summarize the research activities of the past, at least two major factors have to be considered:

Data base systems are in their objectives of a complexity that is in our opinion by far greater than the complexity of programming language implementations or operating systems. Consider alone the goals of data integrity and data independence. In conventional systems, the integrity remains the responsibility of the user, in a data base system the system has to take over a large part of this responsibility. In a conventional system, a user's program may be device independent due to implementation of equivalent storage structures on different devices. The goal in a data base system requires that the user's program is not only independent of different storage on the same (or another) device, but also that the system takes advantage of current structures during access where restructuring is under control of the user in his data base administrator role.

The area of data base systems research is new. Major activities started only a few years ago. Understanding the real problems takes a large amount of time; demonstrating the viability of a solution requires expensive prototype implementation efforts. Before such large implementations are performed, the risk of failure has to be reduced by prior assessment. This justifies that a fair amount of research was spent in clarification. For example, it is sometimes held against the researchers that they are engaged in a "religious war" around data models. The question, which data model is taken, is certainly important and of a similar nature as the question, which programming language should be supported. However, data base researchers are now discussing the problem of different models with a changed attitude: it is not so much the question of selecting between two models but more the question of how one model can be represented on top of the other.

A number of promising activities have been started and will continue, which design and evaluate the man-machine interface for the interactive problem solver. In another branch of research, investigations into the system aspects have reached a level that prototype efforts are justified and now under way.

Data translation, driven by data description and mapping languages, continues to be investigated with increased power of the languages. With respect to storage structures there is already more available than can be intelligently handled by data base management systems. Research probably has to put more emphasis on how these structures can be efficiently utilized.

Modeling systems in a way that significant help results for the data base administrator is in its beginning. It will take some time, before the research which has already been conducted and has to be continued is combined into a useful set of tools for the system designer or administrator.

Comparing the obtained results with industry activities we may see first a difference of emphasis. Systems like IMS are primarily designed for and employed by parametric users while research systems are primarily designed for the interactive problem solver. With the current state of art, it is likely that research changes priority somewhat in favour of the parametric user. The modeling and analysis work described in section 6 is already now primarily oriented towards running, productive systems.

Conclusions

With the wealth of research existing, it becomes meaningful to ask: what are among all these results the major achievements? Are there any trends recognizable with respect to a change of research direction? What are currently the major problems? While we are trying to answer these questions, we are well aware that the reader may wholeheartedly disagree.

Major results

1. Model Development for Data Independence
One of the primary achievements of past research is the agreement on a type of data base system structure, which is shown in fig. 1. In particular, this means that we have to deal with at least three levels of information (conceptual, internal, external) that users assume different roles (parametric, problem solving, application programming, and data base administrating) and finally that the user in his data base administrator function has control over storage structures to tune the performance of his installation.

2. Multiple Records at a Time Logic
Due to the orientation of research to the interactive problem solver, high level multiple record at a time logic has been developed exceeding in power and flexibility the features offered in many commercially available systems. In particular the notions of views and predicate locks are of similar importance to the parametric use of data bases as to the problem solving use.

3. Storage Structures
Storage structures like the B-trees or to say it more generally "what can be found in Knuth vol. 3, chapter 6" or other textbooks represent important results and are basic to future research activities.

Recognizable Trends

1. Data Model Coexistence

After years of controversies, it is increasingly realized that different models have their justification even within the same system. The coexistence of different models in one system is called the superimposition problem and likely to find more attention in the future.

2. Integration of the DBMS into the OS

Past research has made apparent that many of the problems in the area of scheduling, resource management and recovery, i.e. classic operating system functions, cannot be solved outside the data base management system. Increased experience in this area has already lead to systems, which in much respect contain operating system functions. It can be expected that further research makes the need of integrated solutions to operating, time sharing and data base management systems even more apparent.

3. Data Dictionary/Directory

With the current merge of operating system and data base management system arises a large number of places where descriptive information about data and programs is stored in the system. A trend is recognizable to combine these different types of descriptions into a central data dictionary, thereby ensuring more consistency among the descriptive data and generally offering a simpler interface to the user for maintaining the descriptive information.

Major problems

1. Performance

Performance in the sense of throughput and transaction rate constitutes currently the major problem. It is generally felt that current systems do not offer the level of achievable performance, though this can only be proved by better performing alternatives. In particular, that CPU time may constitute a bottleneck has not been recognized in the past and research is necessary in this area.

2. Integrity, Data Independence, Recovery

It is necessary to provide more possiblities of specifying system enforceable integrity rules and data representations, which can be handled by the system with efficiency. The emphasis here is on more <u>functions and efficiency</u> (to provide these functions ignoring efficiency is trivial) so that the users installation as a whole has benefit. Similarly techniques which allow rapid recovery from failures are extremely desirable and lacking.

3. Concurrency

The problems of concurrency (deadlock prevention, scheduling) again in connection with efficiency, have not been solved in a satisfactory way. These problems increase in multiprocessing systems and with data bases, which are distributed on a network of computers.

4. Design Tools

In todays systems, and even more so in future systems, the user has to make a number of decisions like: how to model the conceptual information, or how to select hardware and physical representation. With the current state of the art, he is not given much information, which helps in making these decisions. Some of the research reported in section 6 is certainly relevant for the development of such tools.

5. Data Reorganization

In a dynamic system with addition, deletion and update of stored information it is inevitable to physically reorganize the data from time to time. The reason is a type of physical disorder like storage fragmentation, which does not affect the logical order, but degrades performance and storage utilization. To reestablish physical order, it is, in general, necessary to dump and reload significant parts of the data base as a whole, which is therfore not available during this process for normal use. For large data bases, which are used around the clock, the interruption may become too long to be tolerable. (The time range is from hours to weeks for a reorganization). A solution to the reorganization problem is necessary which avoids interruption.

Acknowledgement

The authors are grateful to their collegues at the IBM Heidelberg Scientific Center, to members of the IBM Research staff at Yorktown Heights and San Jose and to representatives from Universities in Europe and North America for many helpful discussions. Specifically they are grateful to E. F. Codd and M. E. Senko for a critical review of a preversion of this report.

8. BIBLIOGRAPHY

The subsequent list of references contains the basis for this status report. It is hoped that it is also of value as a reference to recent research results. Where present, the annotations are intended to help the reader in selecting literature. They should not be considered as critical reviews, which can be found elsewhere. Subsection I contains alphebetically ordered lists of cross references in numbers referring to entries in subsection II, which is a partially annotated list of references, ordered according to first author.

8.1. Cross References

Data Definition Languages

35 37 82 95 142 152 166
169 179 194

Data Independence

47 48 55 82 125 152 175
180 181 182 194

Data Integrity

1 29 30 45 65 66 78
129 163 176

Data Manipulation Languages

1 3 6 13 16 17 18

8.2. References

1. Abrial, J.R. Data Semantics. Data Base Management, Proc. of IFIP Work. Conf., Cargese, Corsica April 1974. North Holland, Amsterdam 1974.
   The paper is mathematical and philosophical with a scope exceeding the data base management area. It describes and advocates a data model with binary relations between entities.

2. ANSI/X3/SPARC. Interim Report: Study Committee on Data Base Management Systems. ACM SIGMOD Newsletter, 1975.

3. Ash, W. L., and Sibley. TRAMP: An Interpretive Associative Processor with Deductive Capabilities. 1968 ACM Natl. Conference, 144 - 156 (1968).
   TRAMP is the implementation of a binary relational model in a question answering system. It accepts definitions of relations in terms of other relations (e.g. the grandfather as a function of father and mother) which leads to deductive capabilities.

4. Ashany, R. Concepts of Data Manipulation. The Connection Matrix Method. IBM System Development Division, Poughkeepsie, T.R. 00.2200 June 1971
   Information is represented as a binary matrix, where the rows represent entities, the columns represent attributes, and a 1 in a position indicates that the attribute is true with respect to the entity, otherwise false. Sparse matrix techniques have to be applied to reduce storage requirements.

5. Astrahan, M. M., and Gosh, S. P. A Search Path Selection Algorithm for the Data Independent Accessing Model (DIAM). Proc. 1974 ACM SIGFIDET Workshop, ACM, New York, 1974.
   A heuristic algorithm is described which constructs a DIAM access path to a given query in RIL (Fehder).

6. Astrahan, M. M., and Chamberlin, D. D. Implementation of a Structured English Query Language. CACM 18, 580 - 588 (1975).
   Describes essentially the SEQUEL interpreter and the reduction algorithm employed by it to make use of secondary indexes for "minimization" of data accessing operations.

7. Bachmann, C. W. The Programmer as Navigator. CACM 16, 653 - 658

(1973).
C. W. Bachmann's famous 1973 ACM Turing Award Lecture.

8. Bachmann, C. W. Trends in Data Base Management. AFIPS NCC 1975 Proc. vol. 44, 569 - 576 (1975).
Trends are:
1. The evolution of a tripartite data description (conceptual, internal, external) as used by ANSI/X3/SPARC.
2. The current debate data structured model (graph, network) vs relational model contributes to the understanding of the nature of data. 3. The introduction of new hardware to support data base algorithms.

9. Bayer, R., and McCreight, E. Organization and Maintenance of Large Ordered Indexes. Acta Informatica 1, 173 - 189 (1972).
The described hierarchical index organization (B-tree) has become a standard storage structure. Logarithmic search and efficient insert, delete are characteristics of the method.

10. Bayer, R. Symmetric Binary B-trees, Data Structure and Maintenance Algorithms. Acta Informatica 1, 290 - 306 (1972).
Symmetric Binary B-trees are a modification of the storage structure described by Bayer and McCreight.

11. Bayer, R. Storage Characteristics and Methods for Searching and Addressing. Information Processing 74, 440 - 444, North Holland, Amsterdam, 1974.
The paper contains a discussion of hashing and B-trees in random access, pseudo random access (i.e. indexed sequential) and virtual memories.

12. Bennet, B. T., and Kruskal, V. J. Stack Processing for Data Base Systems. To appear in IBM J.of Res. and Dev. (1975).
Traditional stack processing algorithms are inefficient for large average stack distances as they appear in the case of a large number of distinct pages. The authors describe a new algorithm to handle this situation with drastically improved efficiency.

13. Bergen, M., Erbe, R., Pistor, P., Schauer, U., and Walch, G. An Environment for the Interactive Evaluation of Scientific Data and its Application in Computer Aided Design. Proc. Workshop on

data bases for interactive design (W. M. Cleemput and J. G. Linders, editors), Waterloo, Canada, September 15-16, 1975, available from ACM. See also Schauer /149/.

14. Biller, H., and Neuhold, E. J. Formal View on Schema-Subschema Correspondence. Information Processing 74, Proc. of IFIP Congress, North Holland, Amsterdam, 1974.

15. Bjork, L. A. Recovery Scenario for a DB/DC System. 1973 ACM National Conf. Proc., 142-146 (1973).
This paper is the second of two papers describing a recovery concept in a data base system. See C. T. Davies for the first of the two papers.

16. Bjorner, D., Codd, E. F., Decker, K. L., Traiger, I. L. The Gamma-Zero n-ary Relational Data Base Interface: Specifiacations of Objects and Operations. IBM Research Report RJ 1200, 1973.
A detailed description of a low level query language accessing a relational data base.

17. Bobrow, R. J. An Experimental Data Management System. In Data Base Sytems (R. Rustin editor), Prentice-Hall, Englewood Cliffs, 1972.
The paper describes an experimental system implemented in LISP. It contains a brief but excellent discussion of the EDMS (hierarchy or network) approach vs. Codd's relational approach.

18. Boyce, R. F., Chamberlin, D. D., King, W. F., and Hammer, M. M. Specifying Queries as Relational Expressions: SQUARE. Data Base Management, Proc. of IFIP Work. Conf. Cargese, Corsica, April 1974, North Holland, Amsterdam, 1974.
SQUARE is a syntatically terse, set oriented, high level query language based on the so-called "concept of mapping". See also Chamberlin/Boyce for "SEQUEL".

19. Bracchi, G., Fedeli, A., and Paolini, P. A Relational Data Base Management System. Laboratorio di Calcolatori, Instituto di Elettrotecnica, Politechnica di Milano, Internal Report No. 72-5, 1972.
MORIS is a Codd relational system with a calculus oriented manipulation language. The users view (external schema) may include hierarchical structures (i.e. unnormalized data).

20. Bracchi, G., Fedeli, A., and Paolini, P. A Multilevel Relational Model for Data Base Management Systems. In Data Base Management, Proc. of IFIP Work. Conf., Cargese, Corsica, April 1974, North Holland, Amsterdam, 1974.
Advocates the binary relational model (graph model) for the conceptual schema and many models for the external schema (hierarchical, Codd relational, etc.) as well as internal schema.

21. Buzen, J. P., and Chen, P. P.-S. Optimal Load Balancing in Memory Hierarchies. Information Processing 74, 271-275. North Holland, Amsterdam, 1974.
A queuing model for the access to data sets in a memory hierarchy is used to analyze the allocation of data sets. The paper offers a generalization of Chen's results.

22. Cardenas, A. F. Evaluation and Selection of File Organization - a Model and System. CACM 16, 540 -548, 1973.
A program is described, which may be used to estimate total storage costs and average access time given the data organization and device related specifications.

23. Cardenas, A. F. Analysis and Performance of Inverted Data Base Structures. CACM 18, 253 - 263, 1975.
See also King, Farley/Stewart, Schkolnick and Yue/Wong for recent treatments of this subject.

24. Cardenas, A. F., and Sagamang, J. P. Modeling and Analysis of Data Base Organization: The Doubly Chained Tree Structure. Inform. Systems 1, 57 -67, 1975.

25. Carlson, E. P., Bennet, J. L., Giddings, G. M., and Mantey, P. E. The Design and Evaluation of an Interactive Analysis and Display System. Information Processing 74, 1055 - 1061, North Holland, Amsterdam, 1974.
GADS is an interactive graphics system for data related to geographic locations and intended as a tool to be used by non-programmers. It provides a data extraction technique for accessing data stored in a variety of files. The paper discusses experience gained with GADS and the requirements, which must be met by a system of this kind.

26. Casey, R. G. Allocations of Copies of a File in an Information Network. AFIPS SJCC 1972 Proc., vol. 40, 617 - 225, 1972.
The author gives an exact and a heuristic solution to the problem of allocating data sets within a network of computers, given the costs of storing at and transmission between nodes.

27. Casey, R. G. Design of Tree Networks for Distributed Data. AFIPS NCC 1973 Proc. vol. 42, 251 - 257, 1973.

28. Chamberlin, D. D., and Boyce, R. F. SEQUEL - a Structured English Query Language. ACM SIGFIDET Workshop 1974, ACM, New York, 1974.
SEQUEL is a language with semantics very similar to those of SQUARE, however, with a syntax closer to natural English. See Boyce/ Chamberlin for SQUARE.

29. Chamberlin, D. D., Boyce, R. F., and Traiger, I. L. A Deadlock Free Scheme for Resource Locking in a Data Base System. Information Processing 74, 340 - 343. North Holland, Amsterdam, 1974.
The authors propose to use deadlock-detection and backout of processes in case of deadlocks. Their algorithm avoids indefinite delays of a process.

30. Chamberlin, D. D., Gray, J. N., Traiger, I. L. Views, Authorization and Locking in a Relational Data Base System. 1975 AFIPS NCC Proc. vol. 44, 425 - 430, 1975.
A view is a virtual relation derived form other relations via the query language SEQUEL. The problem of updating views is discussed. Views can be used for authorization. Locks temporarily restrict the access to a view for the exclusive use of one user.

31. Chandra, A. K., and Wong, C. K. Worst Case Analysis of a Placement algorithm related to Storage Allocation. To appear in SIAM Journal on Computing.
The authors specify a heuristic algorithm to allocate data sets to disk drives such that the probability of simultaneous access of one disk drive is minimized. The worst case performance of the algorithm is analyzed. See also Easton/Wong.

32. Chang, S.K. Data Base Decomposition in a Hierarchic Computer System. ACM SIGMOD 1975 Int. Conf. on Mgmt. of Data, San Jose,

1975.
The author has extended Casey's results by allowing a non-linear cost function.

33. Chen, P. S. Optimal File Allocation in Multilevel Storage System. 1973 AFIPS NCC Proc. vol. 42, 277 - 282, 1973.
A treatment of the hierarchy allocation problem taking queuing effects into considerations. See also Buzen/Chen.

34. CODASYL Development Committee. Language Structure Group. An Information Algebra. CACM 5, 190 - 204, 1962.
An "oldtimer" and source for many ideas. Contains, for example, the definition of an entity or the idea that files may be interpreted as sets of n-tuples on which then joins, union and intersection can be performed.

35. CODASYL Programming Language Committee. DBTG-Report. 1971. Available from ACM.
The original DBTG proposal.

36. CODASYL Programming Language Committee. DBLTG proposal, February 1973.
Contains the COBOL data manipulation and suvschema data definition language. The languages are essentially those of ref. 35.

37. CODASYL Data description Language Committee. Data Description Language. Journal of Development, June 1973.
Essentially the same data definition language as in 35.

38. CODASYL Systems Committee. Feature Analysis of Generalized Data Base Management Systems. Technical Report, May 1971. Available from ACM.
Primarily compares commercially available systems, contains also a network data model.

39. Codd, E. F. A Relational Model of Data for Large Shared Data Banks. CACM 13, 377 - 387, 1970.
The paper in which Codd introduced the (Codd) relational model of data.

40. Codd, E. F. A Data Base Sublanguage Founded on the Relational

Calculus. 1971. ACM SIGFIDET Workshop, ACM, New York, 1971.

41. Codd, E. F. Further Normalization of the Data Base Relational Model, and Relational Completeness of Data Base Sublanguages. In Data Base Systems (R. Rustin editor). Prentice-Hall, Englewood Cliffs, 1971.

42. Codd, E. F. Seven Steps to Rendezvous with the Casual User. In Data Base Management, Proc. of IFIP Work. Conf. Cargese, Corsica, April 1974, North Holland, Amsterdam, 1974.
The description of seven steps to a proposed natural language question answering system. The steps are: simple data model, high level internal logic, clarification dialogue, query restatement, declarative query, multiple choice interrogation and a definition capability.

43. Codd, E. F. Recent Investigations in Relational Data Base Systems. Information Processing 74, 1017 - 1021, North Holland, Amsterdam, 1974.
A brief survey of Codd's relational model including a discussion of normalization and data sublanguage types. The author lists concurrency, performance, superimposition and storage access theory among the topics needing investigation.

44. Conway, R. W., Maxwell, W. L., and Morgan, H. L. On the Implementation of Security Measures in Information Systems. CACM 15, 211 - 220, 1972.
The main idea in this paper is to perform checking of security only "once at compile time", an approach which is conscious of the CPU as a resource. The paper contains also a discussion of security systems implemented by 1972.

45. Conway, R. W., Maxwell, W. L., and Morgan, H. L. A Technique for File Surveillance. Information Processing 74, 988 - 992. North Holland, Amsterdam, 1974.
A technique implemented by the authors in their system ASAP is described. Each file has associated with it a set of function declarations, which are compiled into a file surveillance program. All accesses to the file have to pass through the surveillance program, which can then be used to perform certain automatic functions.

46. Dana, C., and Presser, L. An Inforamtion Structure for Data Base and Device Independent Report Generation. AFIPS FJCC 1972 Proc. Vol. 41, 1111 - 1116, 1972.
The paper describes high level elements for the generation and manipulation of reports.

47. Date, C. J., and Hopewell, P. Storage Structure and Physical Data Independence. 1971 ACM SIGFIDET Workshop, ACM, New York, 1971.

48. Date, C. J., and Hopewell, P. File Definition and Logical Data Independence. 1971 ACM SIGFIDET Workshop, ACM, New York, 1971.

49. Date, C. J. An Introduction to Data Base Systems. Addison-Wesley, Reading, Massachusetts, 1975.
Similar to Wedekind's book, one of the first attempts of a comprehensive introduction to data base systems. Many annotated references.

50. Davies, C. T. Recovery Semantics for a DB/DC System. 1973 ACM Natl. Conf. Proc., 136 - 141, 1973.
Together with Bjork's paper an easy to understand introduction to a recovery concept.

51. Dearnley, P. A. Operation of a Model Self Organizing Data Management System. Comp. Journal 17, 205 - 210, 1974.
Among others the system observes patterns of usage and restructures the data accordingly. Simulation results are reported.

52. Delobel, C., and Casey, R. G. Decomposition of a Data Base and the Theory of Boolean Switching Functions. IBM J. Res. Develop. 17, 374 - 386, 1973.
Deals with the problem of decomposition of a flat file with (enormous) redundancy into a set of flat files having the minimal cover property, i.e. allowing to derive the same information as the original file without allowing further decomposition.

53. Di Paola, R. A. The Solvability of the Decision Problem for Classes of Proper Formulas and Related Results. Rand Corp., Santa Monica, Calif. Technical Report R-803-PR, August 1971.
The paper deals with the solvability of the decision problem of

a class of questions to be processed by Rands Relational Data File. See Levien/Maron.

54. D'Imperio, M. E. Data Structures and their Representation in Storage. Annual Review in Automatic Programming, vol. 5, Pergamon Press, 1969.

55. Dittmann, E. L. Klassifizierung von Datenunabhaengigkeit fuer den System-Entwurf. Technische Hochschule Darmstadt. Berichte der Informatik- Forschungsgruppen DV75-1

56. Doerrscheidt, A. Das Konzept des Objektbeschreibungsbaumes als Grundstruktur eines graphenorientierten Datenbankmodells. Lecture notes in computer science 26, 532 - 541, Springer Verlag, Berlin, 1975.
Describes a typically graph oriented data model based on LISP ideas.

57. Durchholz, R., and Richter, G. Concepts for Data Base Management Systems. Data Base Management Proc. IFIP Work. Conf. Cargese, Corsica, April 1974. North Holland, Amsterdam, 1974.
Influenced by the data model of the "CODASYL Feature Analysis" the authors discuss a hierarchical data model and schema.

58. Earley, J. Towards an Understanding of Data Structures. CACM 14, 617 - 628, 1971.
Sketches some ideas related to a theory of data structures similar to the available theory of formal string languages.

59. Earley, J. Relational Level Data Structures for Programming Languages. Acta Informatica 2, 293 - 309, 1973.
A proposal for the incorporation of relational level data structures into ALGOL like languages.

60. Easton, M. C., and Wong, C. K. The Effect of Capacity Constraints on the Minimal Cost of a Partition. JACM, 22, 441 - 449, 1975.
A new algorithm to the problem considered by Chandra/Wong is proposed, which accepts capacity constraints.

61. Easton, M. C. Model for Interactive Data Base Reference String. IBM Research Report RC 5050, Sept. 1974.

Describes a modification of the independent references model, which describes measured behaviour well. An advantage of the model is its analytical tractabilitly under working set assumptions.

62. Edelberg, M. Data Base Contamination and Recovery. 1974 ACM SIGFIDET Workshop, ACM, New York, 1974.
The paper describes an algorithm, which for a given error and a given set of data transfers (i.e. log) determines the error propagation into processes and data blocks. A recovery algorithm is also described, which restores blocks and reruns processes.

63. Ehrich, H. D. Grundlagen einer Theorie der Datenstrukturen. Acta Informatica 4, 201 -211, 1975.
A graph oriented data model and graph oriented schemata within the model are investigated from a more mathematical point of view.

64. Engles, R. W. A Tutorial on Data Base Organization. Annual Review in Automatic Programming vol. 7 part 1, Pergamon Press, 1972.

65. Eswaran, K. P., Gray, J. N., Lorie, R. A., and Traiger, I. L. On the Notions of Consistency and Predicate Locks in a Data Base System. IBM Research Report RJ 1487, December 1974.
The paper defines the notion of transaction, consistency within concurrency, and predicate locks and their consequences. A language for predicate specification is proposed, and an algorithm is presented which determines whether two such predicates overlap.

66. Eswaran, K. P., and Chamberlin, D. D. Functional Specifications of a Subsystem for Data Base Integrity. IBM Research Report RJ 1601, 1975.
Contains a classification of consistency rules. Consistency rules are interpreted as routines to be invoked after changes of the data base.

67. Everest, G. C. Concurrent Update Control and Data Base Integrity. Data Base Management, 241 - 270, Proc. IFIP Work. Conf. Cargese, Corsica, April 1974. North Holland, Amsterdam, 1974.
Preclaiming of resources to prevent deadlocks is advocated by

the author.

68. Falkenberg, E., Meyer, B., and Schneider, J. Resultatspezifizierende Handhabung von Datensystemen. Lecture Notes in computer science 1, Springer Verlag, Heidelberg, 1973.
Informal discussion of the "Gegenstandsmodell", a data model, and of a high level manipulation language for it.

69. Falkenberg, E. Time-Handling in Data Base Management Systems. University of Stuttgart, Institut fuer Informatik, Internal CIS-Report 07/74, 1974.
Adds the dimension of time to (for example: A is employee of B from T1 to T2) stored relations and extends a data manipulation language to cope with the time dimension.

70. Falkenberg, E. Strukturierung und Darstellung von Information an der Schnittstelle zwischen Datenbankbenutzer und Datenbank-Management-System. Thesis, University of Stuttgart, 1975.
A detailed description of a data model and a data manipulation language where both are closely related to concepts in natural language. The model is graphoriented though it allows for n-ary relations which can be (and graphically are) interpreted as joins of binary relations.

71. Farley, J. H. G., and Stewart, S. A. Query Execution and Index Selection for Relational Data Bases. Technical Report CSRG-53, University of Toronto, March 1975.
See also Cardenas for recent investigations into this subject.

72. Fehder, P. L. The Representation Independent Language. IBM Research Reports RJ 1121 (1972) and RJ 1251 (1973).
The papers describe RIL, the data manipulation language to the DIAM system.

73. Fehder, P. L. The Hierarchic Query Language (HQL) part 1. IBM Research Report RJ 1307, Nov. 1973.
Describes a query language to operate on IMS like hierarchic data.

74. Feldman, J. A., and Rovner, P. P. An ALGOL based Associative Language. CACM 12, 439 - 449, 1969.
The high level, ALGOL like programming language LEAP is based on

binary associations, which are implemented using a hash coding technique.

75. Fernandez, E. B., Summers, R. C., and Coleman, C. P. An Authorization Model for a Shared Data Base. ACM SIGMOD 1975 Intl. Conf. on Mgmt. of Data, San Jose, 1975.
Authorization is governed by predicates over applications and data base contents and enforced primarily at compile time.

76. Fiedler, H. Datenschutz und Gesellschaft. Lecture Notes in Computer Science, vol. 26, 1975
A survey of the discussions on privacy.

77. Finkel, R. A., and Bentley, J. L. Quad-trees: a Data Structure for Retrieval on Composite Keys. Acta Informatica 4, 1 - 9, 1974.
A generalization of binary trees for the search on composite keys.

78. Florentin, J. J. Consistency Auditing of Data Bases. Comp. Journal 17, 52 - 58, 1974.
Consistency rules are predicate calculus expressions over the data base contents. Problems of their implementation are discussed.

79. Frank, R. L., and Sibley, E. H. The DBTG Report: An Illustrative Example. University of Michigan, ISDOS - working paper - 7.
Shows in detail the steps, which have to be made to get a COBOL application program running in the DBTG approach.

80. Frank, R. L., and Yamaguchi, K. A Method for a Generalized Data Access Method. 1974 AFIPS NCC Proc. vol. 43, 45 - 52, 1974.
Describes ideas and a keyword oriented language to tailor access methods to the users specifications.

81. Fraser, A. G. Integrity of a Mass Storage Filing System. Comp. Journal 12, 1 - 5, 1969.
Describes the recovery in MULTICS.

82. Frasson, C. A System to Increase Data Independence in an Hierarchical Structure. Lecture Notes in Computer Science, vol. 34 (GI 1975), Springer Verlag, Heidelberg, 1975.

Describes how IMS structures can be accessed independent of their position in the hierarchy.

83. Genton, A. Recovery Procedures for direct Access Commercial Systems. Comp. Journ. 13, 123 - 126, 1970.
Describes elementary checkpointing and journaling techniques.

84. Ghosh, S. P., and Senko, M. E. String Path Search Procedures for Data Base Systems. IBM J. Res. Dev. 18, 408 - 422, 1974.
Within DIAM the reduction of queries to access paths in a network is considered. An algorithm is given, which is claimed to yield an access path of minimum "path cardinality".

85. Ghosh, S. P., and Lum, V. Y. Analysis of Collision when Hashing by Division. Inform. System 1, 15 - 22, 1975.
It is analytically shown that "hashing by division" is in general best.

86. Ghosh, S. P., and Tuel, W. G. A Design of an Experiment to Model Data Base System Perfromance. IBM Research Report RJ 1482, Dec. 1974.
The authors construct a linearized performance model and evaluate the model by comparison with measurements in an IMS system.

87. Goldstein, R. C., and Strnad, A. J. The MacAims Data Management System. 1970 ACM SIGFIDET Workshop, ACM, New York, 1970.
MacAims is an early relational system.

88. Gorenstein, S., and Galati, G. Data Base Reorganization for a Storage Hierarchy. IBM Research Report RC 5063, Oct. 1974.
The problem considered is that of clustering records into blocks (i. e. units of transfer) in a way as to minimize the number of transfers necessary.

89. Greenfeld, N. R. Quantification in a Relational Data System. 1974 AFIPS NCC Proc. vol. 43, 71 - 75, 1974.
Discusses optimization techniques for a relational system like LEAP (see Feldman/Rovner).

90. Haerder, T. Die Implementierung von Zugriffspfaden durch Bitlisten. Technische Hochschule Darmstadt, Berichte der Informatik-Forschungsgruppen DV74-2.

The author proposes bit lists as an index organization and investigates when bit lists are superior to conventional methods of indexing.

91. Haerder, T. Zugriffszeitverhalten bei der Auswahl von Saetzen aus einer Datenbank. Technische Hochschule Darmstadt, Berichte der Informatik-Forschungsgruppen DV74-3.
Analysis of access with the help of simulation. Includes a comparison of storage structures for indexes.

92. Hall, P. A. V. Common Subexpression Identification in General Algebraic Systems. IBM UK Report UKSC0060, Nov. 1974.

93. Held, G. D., Stonebraker, M. R., and Wong, E. INGRES - a Relational Data Base System. 1975 AFIPS NCC Proc. vol. 44, 409 - 416, 1975.
INGRES is a relational data management system with calculus based QUEL as its high level query language. An interesting plan of the authors is to incorporate access control and integrity assurance via query modification at preprocessing time.

94. Hoffmann, L. J. (editor). Security and Privacy in Computer Systems. Melville Publishing Company, Los Angeles, 1973.

95. Housel, B. C., Smith, D. P., Shu, N. C., and Lum, V. Y. DEFINE: A Nonprocedural Data Description Language for Defining Information Easily. Proc. of ACM Pacific, San Francisco, April 1975, ACM, New York, 1975.
Describes a language DEFINE to map graph structures to a linear form, which is then referenced by (and processed according to) a translation specification, written in the language CONVERT. See Shu et al.

96. Inglis, J. Iverted Indexes and Multilist Structures. Comp. Journ. 17, 59 - 63, 1974.
Discusses how to use multilist structures in order to maintain inverted files.

97. Karp, R. M., McKellar, A. C., and Wong, C. K. Near-optimal solutions to a 2-dimensional placement problem. IBM Research Report RC 4740, also to appear in SIAM Journal of Computing.
The problem considered is the placement of records in a 2-dimen-

sional storage array, so that the expected distance between two consecutive references is minimized.

98. King, W. F. On the Selection of Indices for a File. IBM Research Report RJ 1341, January 1974.
See also Cardenas for recent research in this area.

99. Knuth, D. E. The Art of Computer Programming, vol. 1: Fundamental Algorithms. Addison-Wesley, Reading, Massachusetts, 1968.

100. Knuth, D. E. The Art of Computer Programming, vol. 3: Sorting and Searching. Addison-Wesley, Reading, Massachusetts, 1973.

101. Kogon, R., Lattermann, D., Lehmann, H., Ott, N., and Zoeppritz, M. User Specialty Languages: General Information. IBM Germany, Scientific Center Heidelberg, Technical Report 75.08.007, 1975.
An interactive system is introduced designed to a data manipulation language,which is very close to natural language.

102. Kraegeloh, K. P., and Lockemann, P. C. Retrieval in a set-theoretically Strucutred Data Base: Concepts and Practical Considerations, Proc. of International Computing Symposium 1973, 531 - 539. North Holland, Amsterdam, 1973.
The described system has a natural language like query language, which is translated into a "set theoretic" intermediate language suitable for interpretation.

103. Lavenberg, S. S., and Shedler, G. S. A Queuing Model of the DL/I Component of IMS. IBM Research Report RJ 1561, 1975.
A simplified, analytically tractable queuing model of the processes during data base access.

104. Lefkovitz, D. File Structures for On-Line Systems. Spartan Books, 1969.

105. Levien, R. E., and Maron, M. E. A Computer System for Inference Execution and Data Retrieval. CACM 10, 715 - 721, 1967.
Introduces the Relational Data File, a system based on binary relations (see also Di Paola).

106. Levitt, G., Stewart, D. H., and Yormark, B. A Prototype System for Interactive Data Analysis. 1974 AFIPS NCC Proc. vol. 43, 63

- 69, 1974.
Describes an implemented system for analysis of measurement data relying on standard analytic procedures. It makes heavy use of graphics and statistical methods.

107. Lewis, P. A. W., and Shedler, G. S. Statistical Analysis of Transaction Processing in a Data Base System. IBM Research Report RJ 1629, August 1975.
Describes the modeling of a transaction stream as a Poisson process with a time varying rate.

108. Liu, S., and Heller, J. A Record Oriented, Grammar Driven Data Translation Model. 1974 ACM SIGFIDET Workshop, ACM, New York, 1974.
Grammars may be taken as mappings of a string to a tree. Two grammars mapping different strings to equivalent trees are used as a string to string mapping specification.

109. Lockemann, P. C., and Knutsen, W. D. A Multiprogramming Environment for Online Data Acquisition and Analysis. CACM 10, 758 - 764, 1967.
An earlier approach to the problem of measurement data. Prefabricated programs may be assembled communicating via data sets and parameters.

110. Lorie, R. A., and Symonds, A. J. A Schema for Describing a Relational Data Base. Proc. 1970 ACM SIGFIDET Workshop, ACM, New York, 1970.
Describes RAM - a data base management system based on binary relations (in some sense like LEAP of Feldman/Rovner).

111. Lorie, R. A. XRM - an Extended (n-ary) Relational Memory. IBM Scientific Center Report G 320 - 2096, Cambridge, Massachusetts, January 1974.
XRM implements homogeneous flat files on top of RAM (see Lorie/Symonds).

112. Lum, V. Y. Multi-attribute Retrieval with Combined Indexes. CACM 13, 660 - 665, 1970.

113. Lum, V. Y., Yuen, P. S. T., and Dodd, M. Key to Address Transform Techniques, a Fundamental Performance Study on Large Exist-

ing Formatted Files. CACM 14, vol. 4, 1971.
Contains a survey and evaluations of hashing techniques as applied to large data sets.

114. Lum, V. Y., and Ling, H. An Optimization Problem on the Selection of Secondary Keys. Proc. 1971 ACM Natl. Conf., vol. 26, 349 - 356, 1971.
One of the earlier investigations into the problem considered by Cardenas and others.

115. Lum, V. Y. General Performance Analysis of Key-To-Address Transformation Methods Using an Abstract File Concept. CACM 16, 603 - 612, 1973.

116. Lum, V. Y., Senko, M. E., Wang, C. P., and Ling, H. A Cost Oriented Algorithm for Data Set Allocation in Storage Hierarchies. CACM 18, 318 - 322, 1975.
A cost function combining the cost of storage, CPU, channel etc. is defined and an algorithm for data set allocation is outlined, which minimizes this cost.

117. Maruyama, K., and Smith, S. E. Analysis of Design Alternatives for Virtual Memory Indexes. IBM Research Report RC 5087, Oct. 1974.
A number of implementation alternatives for indexes organized as B-trees are analyzed resulting into formulas, which are numerically evaluated.

118. Maurer,W. D., and Lewis, T. G. Hash Table Methods. ACM Computing Surveys 7, 5 - 19, 1975.

119. McDonald, N., and Stonebraker, M. CUPID - the Friendly Query Language. ACM Pacific Conference, San Francisco, April 1975, ACM, New York, 1975.
CUPID is a grahic, data flow diagram-like language to the INGRES system. See also Held.

120. McGee, W. C. Generalized File Processing. Annual Review in Automatic Programming vol. 5, Pergamon Press, 1969.

121. McGee, W. C. File Structures for Generalized Data Management. Information Processing 68, 1233 - 1239, North Holland, Amster-

dam, 1968.
Introduces graphs as conceptual models for stored information.

122. McGee, W. C. A Contribution to the Study of Data Equivalence. Data Base Management. Proc. IFIP Work. Conf. Cargese, Corsica, April 1974, North Holland, Amsterdam, 1974.
The author presents a number of equivalent organizations in the class of homogeneous flat file (CRM) organizations and of data description language (DBTG) organizations.

123. McGee, W. C. File Level Operations on Network Data Structures. ACM SIGMOD 1975 Intl. Conference, Proc., ACM, New York, 1975.
The paper outlines requirements and a proposal for a data manipualtion language operating on network data structures.

124. Mealey, G. H. Another Look at Data. Proc. AFIPS 1967 FJCC 525 - 534, 1967.
One of the earlier papers proposing to view information as sets and relations between sets.

125. Mehl, J. W., and Wang, C. P. A Study of Order Transformations of Hierarchic Structures in IMS Data Bases. 1974 ACM SIGFIDET Workshop, ACM, New York, 1974.
A proposal to increase the data independence supported by IMS with the help of compiled routines, which intercept the communication between application program and data management.

126. Merten, A. G., and Fry, J. P. A Data Description Language Approach to File Translation. 1974 ACM SIGFIDET Workshop, ACM, New York, 1974.
Describes the idea and design behind the University of Michigan data translation project.

127. Merten, A. G., and Severance, D. G. Performance Evaluation File of Organizations through Modeling. Proc. ACM 1972 Natl. Conf., ACM, New York, 1972

128. Meyer, B., and Schneider, H. J. Predicate Logic and Data Base Technology. Course Notes, University of Berlin, available from the authors.
Reviews predicate logic and its use as a model for man-machine interface like in Codd's work and in natural language question-

answering systems.

129. Minsky, N. On Interaction with Data Bases. 1974 ACM SIGFIDET Workshop, ACM, New York, 1974.
The author discusses concepts, integrity rules, user views etc. He proposes a constructive approach to integrity by defining "consistent operators" to be used as primitives for more complex operations.

130. Mullin, J. K. An Improved Index Sequential Access Method using Hashed Overflow. CACM 15, 301 - 307, 1972.

131. Mylopoulos, J., Schuster, S., and Tsichritzis, D. A Multilevel Relational System. 1975 AFIPS NCC Proc. vol. 44, 403 - 408, 1975.
The mechanism used in the development of the prototype system ZETA/TORUS are described. ZETA is a relational data management system with a definition capability to define a high level query language on top of lower level primitives. TORUS is bulit on ZETA as an "intelligent" natural language interface.

132. Nakamura, F., Yoshida, I., and Kondo, H. A Simulation Model for Data Base System Performance Evaluation. 1975 AFIPS NCC Proc. vol. 44, 459 - 463, 1975.
Description of experiments simulating the processes within a data base management system in a conventional simulation package.

133. Navathe, S. B., and Merten, A. G. Investigation into the Application of the Relational Model to Data Translation. ACM SIGMOD 1975 Intl. Conf. Proc., 123 - 138.
The paper concludes that Codd's relational model "... poses serious problems when used in the context of data translation as a vehicle for more powerful restructuring".

134. Neuhold, E. J. Data Mapping: A Formal Hierarchical and Relational View. University of Karlsruhe, Forschungsberichte, Bericht 10, February 1973.
The paper compares hierarchical and relational data models in formal notation. In particular, it makes clear that the relational model is a special case of the hierarchical model.

135. Nievergelt, J. Binary Search Trees and File Organization. ACM Computing Surveys 6, 3, 1974.

136. Notley, M. G. The Peterlee IS/I System. IBM UK, Peterlee, Report UK-SC 0018.
Describes IS/I, one of the earlier Codd relational implementations.

137. Olson, C. A. Random Access File Organization for Indirectly Accessed Records. Proc. of 1969 ACM Natl. Conf. ACM, New York, 1969.

138. Owens, P. J. Phase II - a Data Base Management Modeling System. Information Processing 71, 827 - 832, North Holland, Amsterdam, 1972.
Phase II is a modeling tool designed specifically for data management evaluation.

139. Palermo, F. P. A Quantitative Approach to the Selection of Secondary Indexes. IBM Research Report RJ 0730, July 1970.
One of the earlier papers on index selection. See Cardenas for recent results.

140. Palermo, F. P. A Data Base Search Problem. IBM Research Report RJ 1072, July 1972.
The paper contains one of the earlier optimizing reduction algorithms for queries in predicate calculus form.

141. Petrick, S. R. Semantic Interpretation in the REQUEST system. IBM Research Report RC 4457, July 1973.
REQUEST is an experimental, natural language question answering system.

142. Ramirez, J. A., Rin, N. A., and Prywes, N. S. Automatic Generation of Data Conversion Programs using a Data Description Language. 1974 ACM SIGFIDET Workshop, ACM, New York, 1974.
Describes an implementation of a data definition language (due to D. P. Smith), which compiles data definitions into data translating programs.

143. Reisner, P., Boyce, R. F., and Chamberlin, D. P. Human Factors Evaluation of two Data Base Query Languages - SQUARE and SE-

QUEL. 1975 AFIPS NCC Proc. vol. 44, 447 - 452, 1975.
A psychological experiment with 64 subjects is described and analyzed. Only nonprogrammers show a slight but statistically significant dependency on the language, which differ primarily in syntax.

144. Reiter, A. Data Models for Secondary Storage Representation. University of Wisconsin, MRC Report no. 1554, May 1975.
The data models are designed with the objective to be used for the performance evaluation of different implementations.

145. Rodriguez-Rosell, J., and Hildebrand, D. A Framework for Evaluation of Data Base Systems. Proc. of ACM European Chapters International Computing Symposium 1975.
An implemented framework for the measurement and evaluation of sequences of events at different levels of a data base system is presented. The different levels involve commands issued in the application program at the hgih end, and disk address reference traces at the low end.

146. Rothnie, J. B., and Lozano, T. Attribute Based File Organization in a Paged Memory Environment. CACM 17, 63 - 69, 1974.
A combination of "multiple key hashing" and inverted file technique allowing for a reduction of the number of page faults for multi-key-retrieval.

147. Rothnie, J. B. Evaluating Inter-Entry Retrieval Expressions in a Relational Data Base Management System. 1975 AFIPS NCC Proc. vol. 44, 417 - 423, 1975.
The employed strategy attempts to utilize the information gained with every tuple-access for the purpose of optimization.

148. Sayani, H. H. Restart and Recovery in a Transaction Oriented Information Processing System. 1974 ACM SIGFIDET Workshop, ACM, New York, 1974.
Restart and recovery policies are defined and discussed. The author puts emphasis on performance.

149. Schauer, U. Ein System zur interaktiven Bearbeitung umfangreicher Messdaten. IBM Germany, Informatik Symposium 1975, Bad Homburg. To appear as Lecture Notes in Computer Science, Springer Verlag, Heidelberg.

Introduces an interactive measurement data base system combining interactive computational facilities (APL), a relational data storage, a graphics oriented data manipulation language (like "query by example", see Zloof) with access to an open ended library of PL/I or FORTRAN subroutines. See also /13/.

150. Schkolnick, M. Secondary Index Optimization. ACM SIGMOD 1975 Intern. Conf. on Mgmt. of Data, San Jose, 1975.
See also Cardenas for similar research.

151. Schmid, H. A., and Swenson, J. R. On the Semantics of the Relational Data Model. ACM SIGMOD 1975 Intl. Conf. on Mgmt. of Data, San Jose, 1975.
The authors are concerned with the gap between the pure formalism of Codd's relational model and the modelled part of the real world. The authors employ a kind of graph model to fill the gap.

152. Schmutz, H. Parenthesis Regular Languages and Relations. IBM Germany, Heidelberg Scientific Center, Technical Report 74.10.004, Oct. 1974.
A special form of context-free grammars is used to describe the schema to a hierarchical data model. Pair grammars are used to describe the mapping between conceptual and internal or external view. The described system is a model for a theoretical treatment of important problems in data base systems.

153. Schneider, G. M., and Deasautels, E. J. Creation of a File Translation Language for Networks. Information Systems 1, 23 - 31, 1975.
The authors propose a language for data translation in a network such as the ARPA network.

154. Senko, M. E., Lum, V. Y., and Owens, P. J. A File Organization Evaluation Model (FOREM). Information Processing 68, 514 - 519, 1968. North Holland, Amsterdam, 1969.
FOREM is an evaluation and simulation tool specifically designed to evaluate data management systems.

155. Senko, M. E., Altman, E. B., Astrahan, M. M., and Fehder, P. L. Data Structures and Accessing in Data Base Systems. IBM Systems Journ. 12, 30 - 93, 1973.

This paper describes the thoughts and ideas behind the DIAM system, one of the earlier comprehensive approaches to data base research systems.

156. Senko, M. E. Information Systems: Records, Relations, Sets, Entities and Things. Inform. Systems 1, 3 - 13, 1975.

157. Senko, M. E. Data Description Language in the Context of a Multilevel Structured Description - DIAM II with FORAL. IBM Research Report RC 5073, Oct. 1973.

158. Senko, M. E. An Introduction to FORAL for Users. IBM Research Report RC 5263, 1975.

159. Senko, M. E. Specification of Stored Data Structures and Desired Output Results in DIAM II with FORAL. Proc. of the Int. Conference on Very Large Data Bases, Boston, 1975, available from ACM.
The last three references introduce DIAM II, a proposed system, which is based on binary associations and has FORAL as its query language.

160. Severance, D. G. Identifier Search Mechanism: A Survey and Generalized Model. ACM Computing Surveys 6, 3, 1974.

161. Severance, D. G. A Parametric Model of Alternative File Structures. Inform. Systems 1, 51 - 55, 1975.
A scheme is described, which maps a "two dimensional space of parameters" to a set of data organizations including well-known conventional organizations as special case.

162. Shneiderman, B. Optimum Data Base Reorganization Points. CACM 16, 362 - 365, 1973.

163. Shneiderman, B., and Scheuermann, P. Structured Data Structures. CACM 17, 566 - 577, 1974.
The paper describes an approach to deal with integrity in case of certain classes of data structures.

164. Shneiderman, B. A Model for Optimizing Indexed File Structures. IJCIS 3, 93 - 103, 1974.
The paper is concerned with the selection of index size at dif-

ferent levels to improve performance.

165. Shu, N. C., Housel, B. C., and Lum, V. Y. CONVERT a High Level Translation Definition Language for Data Conversion. CACM 18, 557 - 567, 1975.
A companion paper to Housel et al.

166. Sibley, E. H., and Taylor, R. W. A Data Definition and Mapping Language. CACM 16, 750 - 759, 1973.
The paper discusses goals of a data definition language and illustrates data definition and mapping by examples.

167. Sibley, E. H. On the Equivalence of Data Based Systems. 1974 ACM SIGFIDET Workshop, ACM, New York, 1974.
The two philosophical directions, "relational" (Codd) and the "data structured" or "procedural" (DBTG) are compared. Also data translation with its connection to data restructuring and data independence is discussed.

168. Sibley, E. H., and Sayani, H. H. Data Element Dictionaries for the Information Systems Interface. NBS-Report, 1974.
A discussion of the need for and objectives of a Data Dictionary capability.

169. Smith, D. P. An Approach to Data Description and Conversion. PH. D. dissertation, University of Pennsylvania, 1971.
One of the earlier data definition and mapping languages. See also Ramirez.

170. Smith, S. E., and Mommens, J. H. Automatic Generation of Physical Data Base Structures. ACM SIGMOD 1975 Intl. Conf. San Jose, 1975.
A prototype design aid is described which generates from descriptive input IMS physical data structure definitions taking into account constraints and objective functions.

171. Stahl, F. A. A Homophonic Cipher for Computational Cryptograhy. AFIPS NCC Proc. vol. 42, 565 - 568, 1973.

172. Steel, T. B. Data Base Standardization - A Status Report. ACM SIGMOD 1975 Intl. Conf. on Mgmt. of Data, San Jose, 1975.

173. Steuert, J., and Goldman, J. The Relational Data Management System: A Perspective. 1974 ACM SIGFIDET Workshop, ACM, New York, 1974.
An introductory description of RDMS, a system being used at MIT and based on Codd's relational model.

174. Stonebraker, M. The Choice of Partial Inversions and Combined Indices. IJCIS 3, 167 - 188, 1974.
See also Cardenas for research on this topic.

175. Stonebraker, M. A Functional View of Data Independence. 1974 ACM SIGFIDET Workshop Proc., ACM, New York, 1974.
The paper first analyzes the problem with a promising formal approach, which unfortunately is not kept through up to the end. It describes the types of data independence to be provided in INGRES.

176. Stonebraker, M. Implementation of Integrity Constraints and Views by Query Modification. ACM SIGMOD 1975 Intl. Conf. Proc., San Jose, 1975.
Describes the INGRES approach to integrity in more detail. See also Held et al.

177. Su, S. Y. W., and Lam, H. A Semiautomatic Data Base Translation System for Achieving Data Sharing in a Network Environment. 1974 ACM SIGFIDET Workshop, ACM, New York, 1974.

178. Sundgren, B. Conceptual Foundation of the Infological Approach to Data Base. Data Base Management Proc. of IFIP Work. Conf. Cargese, Corsica, April 1974. North Holland, Amsterdam, 1974.
The infological approach is a kind of a conceptual data model philosophy. It may have a corresponding datalogical approach associated with it, which deals with internal data forms.

179. Taylor, R. W. Generalized Data Base Management System Data Structures and their Mapping to Physical Storage. Ph. D. dissertation, University of Michigan, Ann Arbor, 1971.
Contains a proposal for a data definition and mapping language, which is being used in the Michigan data translation experiments. See Merten/Fry.

180. Taylor, R. W. Data Administration and the DBTG Report. 1974 ACM

SIGFIDET Workshop Proc., ACM, New York, 1974.
Among others, the author proposes to use a preprocessor to obtain data independence at precompile time.

181. Taylor, R. W., and Stemple, D. W. On the Development of Data Base Editions. Data Base Management, Proc. of IFIP Work. Conf. Cargese, Corsica, April 1974. North Holland, Amsterdam, 1974.
The authors' concern is the evolution of a data base at a user installation and its impact on programs.

182. Teichroew, D. An Approach to Research in File Organization. Proc. of the 1971 SIGIR Symposium on Information, Storage and Retrieval, ACM, New York, 1971.
The essential message in this paper: there is no absolutely best representation of information. Changes as a function of knowledge about the future use of the data have to be made with assistance of the computer.

183. Thomas, J. C., and Gould, J. P. A Psychological Study of Query by Example. 1975 AFIPS NCC Proc. vol. 44, 439 - 445, 1975.
Reports the results of an experiment with 35 subjects, who were given questions in English to be translated into query by example (see Zloof).

184. Thompson, F. B., Lockemann, P. C., Dostert, B., and deverill, R. S. REL: A Rapidly Extensible Language System. ACM 1969 Natl. Conf. Proc., 399 - 417, 1969.

185. Todd, S. J. P. PRTV: A Technical Overview. IBM UKSC Peterlee, Technical Report UKSC 0075, 1975.
A new description of the experimental system IS/1.

186. Tsichritzis, P. A Network Framework for Relation Implementation. University of Toronto, Technical Report CSRG-49, February 1975.
Discusses how Codd's relational model can be implemented on top of physical networks (i.e. linked structures).

187. Turn, R., and Shapiro, N. Z. Privacy and Security in Data Bank Systems - Measures of Effectiveness, Costs and Protection-Intruder Interactions. AFIPS 1972 FJCC, vol. 41, 435 - 444.

188. Van der Pool, J. A. Optimum Storage Allocation for a File in

Steady State. IBM J. Res. Div. 17, 27 - 38, 1973.
Files with key-to-address transformations (hashing) and with overflow areas are analyzed. Storage utilization, overflow rate and other relevant factors are given for the steady state.

189. Vose, M. R., and Richardson, J. S. An Approach to Inverted Index Maintenance. Comp. Bull. 16, May 1972.

190. Wang, C. P., and Wedekind, H.H. Segment Synthesis in Logical Data Base Design. IBM J. Res. Dev. 19, 71 - 77, 1975.
The authors specify a minimal cover algorithm, which calculates a set of minimal covers to a given set of relations with transitive dependencies. Each minimal cover is again a set of relations without transitive dependencies. Given the minimum cover, a set of relations in Codd's third normal form can easily be constructed.

191. Wedekind, H. Datenorganisation. de Gruyter, Berlin, 1972.

192. Wedekind, H. Datenbanksysteme I. Bibliographisches Institut Mannheim, 1974.

193. Wedekind, H. On the Selection of Access Paths in a Data Base System. Data Base Management, Proc. of IFIP Work. Conf., Cargese, Corsica, April 1974. North Holland, Amsterdam, 1974.
The paper's concern is modeling and analysis for the determination of efficient access paths.

194. Wellis, M. E., Katke, W., Olson, J., and Yang, S. C. SIMS - an Integrated, User-Oriented Information System. AFIPS FJCC 1972, vol. 41, 1117 - 1131, 1972.
SIMS is interesting for a number of reasons. It offers a high level data definition, mapping and manipulation language. Data on normal files may be mapped to a conceptual high level hierarchical form and used in the query language. Particular attention has been paid to transferability of data and programs.

195. Wong, E., and Chiang, T. C. Canonical Structure in Attribute Based File Organizations. CACM 14, 593 - 597, 1971.
Each query is assumed to be a boolean expression over elementary queries. In this case the data base can be organized according to the elementary queries and access becomes essentially the

problem of putting a boolean expression into some standard form.

196. Yao, S. B. Evaluation and Optimization of File Organization through Analytic Modeling. Ph. D. dissertation, University of Michigan, 1974.

197. Yue, P. C., and Wong, C. K. Storage Cost Considerations in Secondary Index Selection. IBM Research Report RC 5070, to appear also in IJCIS.
For other recent results in this area of research see Cardenas.

198. Zloof, M. M. Query By Example. 1975 AFIPS NCC Proc. vol. 44, 431 - 437, 1975.
The basic features of query by example are illustrated. The user's perception of data processing in this query language is that of manipulating tables in a graphically pre-established frame of reference consisting of table skeletons, into which the user fills information.

Grundlegendes zur Speicherhierarchie

Claus Schünemann, IBM Böblingen

1. EINLEITUNG

Das Thema dieses Beitrags ist die konkrete Daten-Speicherung und -Adressierung unter Zugrundelegung eines hierarchischen Aufbaus des Speichersystems.

Soweit Datenbankaspekte dabei berührt werden, sind sie aus der Sicht der Hardware-Implementierung und vorwiegend unter Leistungsgesichtspunkten gesehen.

Heutige Computer-Speichersysteme sind bereits weitgehend hierarchisch strukturiert. Dabei soll unterschieden werden zwischen einer lediglich durch Kapazitätsabstufung gekennzeichneten und einer strengen Hierarchie, bei der auf jeder Stufe wahlfreier Zugriff möglich ist und der Datenfluß keine Stufe überspringt.

Die Kombination Hauptspeicher - Pufferspeicher stellt eine strenge Hierarchie dar, bei der der Hierarchiebegriff überhaupt erst ins Bewußtsein gerückt wurde [1]. Der Pufferspeicher (Cache) ist für die Maschinenarchitektur transparent und paßt die Geschwindigkeit des Hauptspeichers an die noch höhere des Prozessors an. Ebenso ist die Folge Hauptspeicher - Magnetplattenspeicher als strenge Hierarchie anzusprechen, auch wenn diese Betrachtungsseite (mit Ausnahme von Programm-Paging im Rahmen des virtuellen Speichers) bislang nicht im Vordergrund stand und der Plattenspeicher mehr als Ein/Ausgabegerät aufgefaßt und so von der Maschinenarchitektur behandelt wurde.

Der Magnetbandspeicher ist wegen seiner langen Zugriffszeit (incl. Bandladen) nicht mehr im strengen Sinne zur Hierarchie zu rechnen.

Ansätze, die große und billige Bandspeicherkapazität als echte oberste Datenfluß-Hierarchiestufe zu integrieren, sind mit der jüngeren Entwicklung von automatischen Bandtransportsystemen, wie z.B. beim IBM 3850-Kassettenspeicher, sichtbar geworden. Dabei könnte beispielsweise dem Bandspeicher die Funktion eines Archivs und dem Plattenspeicher die Funktion eines Arbeitsspeichers großer Kapazität zugeordnet werden, wobei der Inhalt ganzer virtueller Plattenstapel automatisch auf Verlangen auf das Plattensystem übertragen wird [2]. In Abbildung 1 ist das Schema dieses Hierarchiekonzepts skizziert.

Der schwache Punkt der gegenwärtigen Speicherhierarchie ist das Verhältnis der Zugriffszeiten des Hauptspeichers zum Plattenspeicher von mehr als 1:10000, die sog. Zugriffslücke. Auch ein Dazwischenschalten von Trommelspeichern bzw. Plattenspeichern mit festem Lesekopf ändert die Situation nicht wesentlich. Man versucht daher bekanntlich, das Mißverhältnis durch Programmumschaltung im Rahmen von Multiprogrammierung zu überbrücken. Mit fortschreitender Prozessor- und Hauptspeichergeschwindigkeit, aber gleichbleibender Zugriffszeit der mechanisch arbeitenden Massenspeicher, muß der Multiprogrammierungsgrad, die Hauptspeichergröße und die Zahl der Plattenspindeln immer größer werden. Damit entfernt man sich vom Kostenoptimum, außerdem steigen die Anforderungen an das steuernde Betriebssystem und seine Komplexität,bei abnehmender Effizienz.

Im Folgenden wird versucht, für das gesamte Hierarchiespektrum die Speicherparameter nach einheitlichen Gesichtspunkten zu klassifizieren und anhand solcher Parameter die Leistungsfähigkeit der Hierarchie zu diskutieren, mit besonderer Blickrichtung auf das Problem der Zugriffslücke. Die Anforderungen des Datenbankbetriebes werden kurz angesprochen.

2. TECHNOLOGIE- UND OPERATIONSPARAMETER

Es sind zahlreiche Technologien bekannt, die unter Ausnutzung verschiedenster physikalischer Effekte zu sehr unterschiedlichen Speichereigenschaften führen. Am verbreitetsten ist heute die Halbleitertechnologie für die schnellen elektronischen Matrix-Speicher mit wahlweisem Zugriff und die Magnetschichttechnologie für die langsameren und billigen Massenspeicher, hauptsächlich in den Ausführungen Platten- und Bandspeicher.

Eine weitere Gruppe, die aber noch nicht das Stadium breiter Produktreife erreicht hat, ist die der optischen und mit Elektronenstrahl operierenden

Speicher [3,4]. Auch die diversen Schieberegistertechnologien wie CCD (Charge Coupled Device) [5,6] oder Magnetblasen (Bubbles) [7] machen vorerst nur tastende Schritte im kommerziellen Einsatz. Die spezifischen Arbeitsweisen der einzelnen Speicherfamilien sollen hier nicht diskutiert werden, vielmehr wird das gesamte Speicherspektrum einheitlich durch einen Satz von invarianten technologischen und operativen Parametern beschrieben, Tabelle I.

Die beiden wichtigen Operationsparameter, mittlere Zugriffszeit und Bitkosten, stehen in einer gewissen reziproken Relation zueinander. Sie bestimmen den Standort einer Technologie innerhalb des Gesamtspektrums. Im Diagramm Abb. 2 sind heutige typische Werte in Abhängigkeit des gewichtigsten Technologieparameters, Bitzahl pro Schreib/Lesestation, dargestellt [8].

Die Zugriffszeit setzt sich zusammen aus der Zugriffszeit im engeren Sinne, einer Art Totzeit vor der Übertragung des ersten Bit, und der Datenübertragungszeit. Die Übertragungszeit ist abhängig von der Datenrate, gegeben durch Taktfrequenz und interne Bitbreite, und der gewählten übertragenen Blocklänge. Zusätzliche Verzögerungen durch den externen Übertragungskanal sind in der Übertragungszeit mitenthalten.

Unter Modularität ist die Unterteilbarkeit eines Speichers bzw. einer Hierarchiestufe in Module mit eigenem parallelen Zugriff verstanden. Dadurch wird die Zugriffsrate erhöht. Die Fähigkeit zur modularen Aufteilung nimmt im allgemeinen ab mit dem Technologieparameter "Bitzahl pro Schreib/Lesestation". Bei mechanischer Entkopplung zwischen Lesen/ Schreiben und dem Datentransport kann die Zugriffsrate durch Überlappung weiter erhöht werden. So wird beim Bandkassettenspeicher IBM 3850 die nächste Kassette schon transportiert, während die vorhergehende sich noch in der Lese/Schreibstation befindet.

Weitere Beispiele für asynchronen Parallelbetrieb sind die Konfiguration mehrerer Plattenspeicher in einer DV-Anlage wie auch die Unterteilung des Hauptspeichers in unabhängig und parallel arbeitende Module.

Auch die Bitkosten bestimmen sich in erster Linie aus der Bitzahl pro Lese/Schreibstation. Sie sind außer von den spezifisch technologisch-konstruktiven Faktoren vom allgemeinen Miniaturisierungsstand der Technik abhängig. Abb. 3 zeigt beispielsweise die historische Entwicklung der Bitdichte beim Magnetplattenspeicher. Entsprechend sind die Zahlenangaben in Abb. 2 nur zeitbezogen zu verstehen. Die relativen Zuordnungen dürften hingegen weitgehend invariant zum allgemeinen Stand der Technik sein, da fortschreitende Miniaturisierung allen Technologien zugute kommt. Die Speicherkapazität pro Hierarchiestufe ergibt sich in einer ausgewogenen Konfiguration nach einer Art reziproker Funktion der jeweiligen Bitkosten

Ein weiterer operativer Parameter ist die Zuverlässigkeit des Speichers, d.h. die mittlere Zahl von gelesenen Bits pro fehlerhaftem Bit. Dieses Merkmal ist eine Funktion der natürlichen Fehlerfreiheit des Mediums, des Sortierungsgrades nach guten Einheiten und des Aufwands an gezielter Redundanz mit nachfolgender Fehlerkorrektur. Die Fehlerdichte des Mediums nimmt naturgemäß mit der Homogenität ab. Typische Zuverlässigkeitswerte sind (nach entsprechendem Sortierprozess) z.B. beim fabrikneuen Plattenspeicher 10^9 und 10^{12} nach erfolgter Korrektur.

Die physikalische Natur der Speicherung bestimmt den Grad der Flüchtigkeit der eingeschriebenen Information. Bei einem Arbeitsspeicher kann man eine gewisse Flüchtigkeit mit periodischem Wiederauffrischen zulassen, bei einem Archiv- oder Journalspeicher muß natürlich ein dauerhaftes Speichern gefordert werden.

In gewisser Verwandtschaft zur Flüchtigkeit steht die Eigenschaft des ON-line oder OFF-line Einschreibens, letzteres auch allgemein unter ROM verstanden. Bei verschiedenen Anwendungen, z.B. Speicherung von Dokumenten mit geringer Änderungsfrequenz, kann der ROM-Speicher durchaus sinnvoll und, da entsprechend billig, von Interesse sein. Ein Übergang zwischen dem normalen schreibbaren Speicher und dem ROM stellt der PROM bzw. EAROM (Programmable bzw. Electrically Alterable Read Only Memory) dar. Der ROM-Speicher wird hier nicht weiter behandelt.

Der letzte Operationsparameter ist die adressierbare Einheit, die im Verein mit der eigentlichen Zugriffszeit die Komplexität der Zugriffsmethode und Effizienz des Datensuchens bestimmt.

Man unterscheidet zwischen Orts- und Inhaltsadressierung. Die Ortsadressierung ist auf Hauptspeicherebene die dominierende Adressierungsart: Die physische Lokation jedes Datenelementes ist vom Programm definiert und wird über die Adresse direkt gefunden. Dieses Konzept ist auf den höheren Speicherebenen für das Aufsuchen von Datensätzen nicht mehr zweckmäßig, wenn die Sätze z.B. in Form einer Datenbank organisiert, programmunabhängig und vielen Benutzern verfügbar sein sollen. Sie müssen also letztlich durch ihren Inhalt, gegeben durch ein oder mehrere Merkmale, gekennzeichnet sein. Innerhalb eines Satzes sind die Daten im allgemeinen wieder formatiert, d.h. ihre semantische Bedeutung ist durch ihren relativen Ort bestimmt.

Die heutige Suchtechnik bei inhaltsadressierten Datensätzen bedient sich Indextabellen, in denen z.B. die Hauptmerkmale numerisch oder alphabetisch geordnet und die reale Speicheradresse direkt zugeordnet ist. Beim Vorliegen weiterer (Neben-) Merkmale können diese in eigenen Tabellen gelistet werden, wobei die Speicheradressen aller Sätze, die dieses Merkmal enthalten, wieder zugeordnet werden. Mit diesen invertierten Listen kann bekanntlich der Prozess des Suchens nach mehrfachen Merkmalen schnell, d.h. ohne alle Sätze sequentiell prozessieren zu müssen, durchgeführt werden. Mit Hilfe der Indextabellen wird also die Inhaltsadresse eines Datensatzes in eine Ortsadresse umgewandelt. Letztere wird dann beim Speichern mit wahlfreiem Zugriff schnell und direkt angesteuert.

Das Durchsuchen der Indextabellen nach dem gewünschten Merkmal stellt in sich nun wiederum einen Prozeß mit sequentieller Schrittfolge dar. Ein weiteres Parallelisieren wäre das Abspeichern der Indextabellen in Assoziativspeichern, mit folgenden Vorteilen:

- Fortfall der numerischen oder alphabetischen Merkmalsordnung.
- Dadurch einfache Aufarbeitung durch direktes Zufügen/Entfernen neuer Indizes.
- Fortfall der invertierten Listen, da gleichzeitig auf mehrfache Merkmale assoziiert werden kann.
- Direktes gleichzeitiges statt sequentielles Suchen.

Die Eigenart des Assoziativspeichers, eine Formatierung der Daten zu verlangen, wäre in diesem Fall kein Nachteil.

Ein Sonderfall der Ortsadressierung ist die Adressierung mit Zeigern. Dabei wird auch eine Entkopplung von Benutzerprogramm und Datenadresse erreicht. Nachteilig ist das sequentielle Durchlaufen der Zeigerkette.

Die einzelnen Speichertechnologien unterscheiden sich nun hinsichtlich der Größe der hardware-mäßig adressierbaren Einheit. Diese ist z.B. ein

Byte beim (Halbleiter-) Matrixspeicher, ca. 10-20 KBytes beim Plattenspeicher und Millionen von Bytes beim konventionellen Bandspeicher. Wenn diese adressierbare Einheit nun gleich oder kleiner als die gewünschte zu übertragene Blocklänge ist, soll von wahlfreiem Zugriff gesprochen werden.

Der Plattenspeicher hat nur einen semi-wahlfreien Zugriff, da seine Adressiereinheit (die Spur) um ein Vielfaches größer als eine bequeme logische Satzlänge bzw. eine für diese Hierarchiestufe optimale Blocklänge ist. Der konkrete Block muß dann wieder sequentiell auf der Spur gesucht werden.

Die sogenannten Zugriffsmethoden, also die praktischen Prozeduren zum Aufsuchen von Datensätzen spiegeln die jeweils zugrundeliegenden technologischen Adressierparameter wider.

Ein Beispiel ist die index-sequentielle Zugriffsmethode für "direkten wahlfreien" Zugriff zum Plattenspeicher: Dabei sind die Hauptmerkmale der Datensätze in einer Indextabelle nach aufsteigender Ordnungszahl geordnet. Die Tabelle ordnet jeweils einer Gruppe von Sätzen die zugehörende Spuradresse auf der Platte zu. Auch die Sätze selbst sind nach der gleichen Ordnungszahl geordnet, um im Falle sequentiellen Zugriffs die große Zugriffszeit für jeden individuellen Satz zu eliminieren. Beim Rotieren der Platte werden die ausgelesenen Satzmerkmale mit dem Suchmerkmal verglichen, bis Übereinstimmung herrscht. Beim Aufarbeiten, z.B. Zufügen eines weiteren Satzes in die möglicherweise physisch lückenlose Satzfolge, weist ein Zeiger zu einer neuen Spuradresse auf einer Überlaufspur. Die Methode kombiniert also die Suchelemente Indextabelle, sequentielles Suchen und Zeigertechnik zu einer den spezifischen Plattenspeicherbedingungen angepaßten Prozedur, Abb. 4a.

Bei einem anderen Speicher mit auch homogenem Medium, dem Elektronenstrahl-Speicher, ist die Adressiereinheit frei wählbar zwischen einem und Zehntausenden von Bytes. Das Zugriffsverfahren kann rein indexorientiert und entsprechend einfach gehalten werden: Das sequentielle Suchen entfällt. Ein Überlaufproblem existiert nicht. Dank der kurzen eigentlichen (elektronischen) Zugriffszeit kann auf eine sequentielle Satzordnung verzichtet und der Satz an beliebiger Stelle gespeichert werden, Abb. 4b.

Die größere Adressiereinheit, d.h. die geringere "Wahlfreiheit", bei den kostengünstigen Technologien ist an sich kein prinzipieller Nachteil, da innerhalb einer Hierarchie ohnehin mit Blockübertragung gearbeitet wird. Ein gradueller Nachteil ist nur dann festzustellen, wenn wie beim Plattenspeicher optimale Blocklänge und technologische Adressiereinheit nicht übereinstimmen. Diese Diskrepanz schlägt sich dann in aufwendigen und zeitraubend ablaufenden "Zugriffsmethoden" nieder.

3. SPEICHERHIERARCHIE

Aufgabe eines Speichersystems ist neben der Speicherung, dem Prozessor die benötigten Daten in genügend kurzer Zeit und in der angeforderten Menge pro Zeiteinheit zur Verfügung zu stellen. Analog zu den System-Leistungsparametern Antwortzeit und Durchsatz läßt sich die Speicherleistung durch die Parameter Zugriffszeit und Zugriffsrate definieren. Wenn ein Speicher nur einen Zugriff gleichzeitig gestattet, kann die Zugriffsrate etwa gleich dem reziproken Wert der Zugriffszeit gesetzt werden. Bei gleichzeitig mehreren Zugriffen, d.h. Modularität größer als 1, erhöht sich die maximale Zugriffsrate entsprechend. Wie weit die maximale Zugriffsrate ausgenutzt werden kann, hängt von Parametern wie Systemsteuerung, Programmprofil, Multiprogrammierungsgrad und Zahl der Parallelprozessoren etc. ab.

In einer Hierarchie ist eine gewisse Grundmodularität der einzelnen Stufen schon im Interesse eines gleichzeitigen Datenverkehrs nach oben und unten wünschenswert. Dies wird steuerungsmäßig z.B. auf Hauptspeicherebene durch das unabhängige Operieren von Prozessor und Kanälen erreicht. Für effektive Multiprogrammierung ist ausreichende Modularität der Plattenspeicherstufe zwingend Voraussetzung. Zweck der Multiprogrammierung ist es, die resultierende Zugriffsrate - gemessen an der Schnittstelle zum Prozessor - und damit den Systemdurchsatz zu erhöhen.

Bekanntlich liegt dessenungeachtet der Engpaß für den Durchsatz heutiger DV-Systeme immer noch bei der Zugriffszeit und Zugriffsrate des Plattenspeichers. Da weitere Geschwindigkeitsfortschritte für Prozessor und Halbleiterspeicher in Zukunft durchaus erwartet werden dürfen, die Plattenspeicher-Zugriffszeit aber kaum noch verbesserungsfähig ist, wird dieses Problem immer drängender: Eine Lösung über weitere Erhöhung des Multiprogrammiergrades, d.h. der Zahl der gleichzeitig operierenden Programme, mit entsprechender Erhöhung von Hauptspeichergröße und Plattenspeichermodularität erscheint aus Kosten- und Komplexitätsgründen unpraktikabel. Außerdem leidet bei zu hohem Multiprogrammierungsgrad die Effizienz: Die Systemverwaltung nimmt relativ zur Wirkarbeit zu, die Chance, mit einer Plattenarmposition mehrfache Zugriffe abzudecken, nimmt ab usw.

Eine andere Lösung dieses Problems ist der weitere Ausbau des Speicherhierarchiekonzeptes, bei beschränktem Multiprogrammierungsgrad. Der (nicht realisierbare) ideale Speicher, d.h. der Speicher mit der Zugriffszeit des Pufferspeichers und den Kosten des Bandspeichers, läßt sich durch eine ausgewogene Hierarchie mit genügend feiner Stufung annähern.

Glücklicherweise verspricht die technologische Entwicklung Speicherprodukte, die leistungs- und kostenmäßig gerade das Gebiet der "Lücke" ausfüllen und sich so gut in das Spektrum einfügen. Mögliche Technologien für die "Lücke" sind z.B. der CCD-Schieberegisterspeicher, der Schieberegisterspeicher mit verschiebbaren magnetischen Blasen (Bubbles) sowie die Elektronenstrahlspeicherröhre, Abb. 5. Diese Technologien sollen im Folgenden elektronische Massenspeicher genannt werden.

3.1 Hierarchiemechanismus

Die Speicherhierarchie besteht also aus der Hintereinanderschaltung von Speicherstufen, wobei mit zunehmender Stufenordnungszahl die Zugriffszeit und Speicherkapazität zunimmt. Bei einem Speicherzugriff des Prozessors versucht dieser zunächst, die Daten auf der untersten schnellsten Ebene zu finden. Bei Mißerfolg wird zur nächsten Ebene zugegriffen und so fort. Bei einer Datenübertragung auf die jeweils niedere Ebene wird nun nicht nur das verlangte Wort oder Byte, sondern gleich ein ganzer Block übertragen. Auf jeder unteren Ebene wird ein Teil des Blocks abgelagert. Die Übertragungszeit ist bei den gewählten Blocklängen meist klein gegen die eigentliche Zugriffszeit. Das Wesen der Speicherhierarchie drückt sich also darin aus, daß unter Zulassung von geringfügig mehr Zugriffszeit (nämlich incl. Übertragungszeit) ganze Daten- oder Programmblöcke übertragen werden, in der Annahme, daß davon ein Teil in nächster Zukunft ohnehin zum Prozessieren angefordert wird. Es liegt also ein prophylaktischer Zugriff (look ahead) unter Ausnutzung der (gegen die eigentliche Zugriffszeit) kurzen Übertragungszeit vor. Unterstützt wird dieser Mechanismus dadurch, daß die Daten oftmals in kurzem Zeitraum mehrfach zugegriffen werden, z.B. bei Programmschleifen, aber auch beim Operieren auf häufig benutzte Arbeitsdaten wie Indextabellen, Kataloge usw.

Die Trefferrate, d.h. die Wahrscheinlichkeit, Daten auf der jeweils zugegriffenen Ebene anzufinden, nimmt zu mit der Speicherkapazität dieser Ebene, ferner im allgemeinen mit der Blocklänge. Davon unabhängig hängt sie natürlich vom jeweiligen Daten- und Programmprofil ab.

Das Freimachen von Speicherplatz auf einer gefüllten Hierarchiestufe erfolgt im einfachsten Fall selbstregelnd nach den gebräuchlichen Algorithmen wie FIFO oder LRU (Least Recently Used). Dieser Mechanismus kann selbstverständlich unterstützt werden durch residentes Einspeichern gewisser häufig gebrauchter Datenteile in untere schnelle Ebenen, z.B. Teile des Betriebssystems im Hauptspeicher usw. Auf den höheren Ebenen, bei denen jeder Zugriff in die Leistungsbilanz eingeht, ist die Steuerung software-implementiert und entsprechend "intelligenter".

Die Adreßsteuerung und das Suchen von Daten auf einer Ebene könnte konzeptuell am einfachsten über einen das Gesamtspeichersystem umfassenden Adressraum erfolgen.

Jede Hierarchiestufe enthielte dann eine Tabelle für die dynamische Zuordnung der virtuellen Gesamtspeicheradresse zur lokalen Ebenenadresse.

Aufgrund der historischen Entwicklung gibt es meist mehrere Adressräume in einer Speicherhierarchie: Auf Pufferspeicherebene wird die reale Hauptspeicheradresse einem bestimmten Platz im Pufferspeicher zugeordnet. Beim Hauptspeicher wird die heute meist virtuelle Adresse, die also bereits einen größeren Adressraum umfaßt, der realen Adresse zugeordnet. Bei den inhaltsadressierten höheren Hierarchiestufen übernehmen die vorerwähnten Indextabellen die Datenlokalisierung: Logisches und hierarchiespezifisches Suchen wird identisch.

Die Zuordnungstabellen werden entweder auf der gleichen oder auf unteren Ebenen gespeichert. Beim (schnellen) Pufferspeicher wird die Tabelle in einem eigenen mehr oder weniger assoziativ arbeitenden Speicher gehalten.

Man kann sich so das gesamte DV-System vorstellen als die Kombination eines Archivspeichers, der alle Daten im ON-line Zugriff enthält, beispielsweise einen magnetischen Bandspeicher mit automatischem Bandtransport, und einem Prozessorsystem, das wiederum aus dem eigentlichen Prozessor und einer Hierarchie von Arbeitsspeichern besteht. Die verschiedenen, teilweise im vorigen Abschnitt diskutierten Technologie- und Steuerungsparameter variieren entlang der Hierarchieachse wie in Abb. 6 skizziert.

3.2 Leistungsbetrachtung

Das wichtigste Kriterium der Speicherhierarchie ist die Gesamtzugriffszeit bzw. Gesamtzugriffsrate, absolut gesehen als auch kostenbezogen. Diese Zusammenhänge sollen im folgenden anhand eines sehr einfachen Modells diskutiert werden. Das Modell orientiert sich an "typischen" Werten für die verschiedenen Parameter und extrapoliert bei nicht bekannten Daten.

Wie das Technologiediagramm Abb. 2 bereits indiziert, scheint eine natürlich einfache Gesetzmäßigkeit zwischen den Bitkosten und der Spektrumsvariablen Zugriffszeit zu bestehen. Diese und die Zuordnung der Trefferrate und Speicherkapazität zur Zugriffszeit sind im Modellparameterdiagramm Abb. 7 aufgetragen. Die Kapazitätsverteilungskurve ist als Gerade (im log. Maßstab) angenommen, mit den Endpunkten Puffer- und Archivspeicher. Die gewählte Archivkapazität ist 10^{12} b, die Pufferkapazität 200 Kb. Die auf der Geraden liegenden Punkte für Haupt- und Plattenspeicher entsprechen etwa realen Werten. Die Kapazitätsverteilungskurve ist an sich natürlich innerhalb des technologisch verfügbaren Spektrums frei wählbar. Mit wachsender Prozessorleistung und Datenmenge wird sie nach oben verschoben werden.

Für die Trefferrate im multiprogrammierten Stapelbetrieb liegen als Funktion der Kapazität und Blocklänge einige Erfahrungsdaten im Bereich Puffer - Hauptspeicher vor [9]. Typische Werte dafür wurden der Modellkurve zugrundegelegt. Zu den oberen Hierarchieebenen hin wurde extrapoliert.

Das Modell berücksichtigt nicht die gegenseitigen Abhängigkeiten von Blocklänge, Zugriffszeit, Trefferrate, Multiprogrammierungsgrad usw., sondern nimmt starr typische Werte an.

Die Gesamtzugriffszeit ist

$$t_{ges} = t_1+(1-h_1)t_2+(1-h_2)t_3+....(1-h_{n-1})t_n \qquad \text{Gl. 1}$$

mit

t_n = Zugriffszeit der n-ten Stufe
h_n = Trefferrate der n-ten Stufe

Die maximale Gesamtzugriffsrate, d.h. der Zugriffsfluß an der Schnittstelle zum Prozessor ist

$$\text{max. } Z_{ges} = \frac{1}{\frac{t_1}{p_1} + \frac{1-h_1}{p_2} t_2 + \ldots \frac{1-h_{n-1}}{p_n} t_n} \qquad \text{Gl. 2}$$

mit

p_n = Zugriffsparallelität auf der n-ten Stufe.

Die Zugriffsparallelität entspricht in etwa der Modularität. Es wird angenommen, daß 50% der Zugriffsparallelität sich jeweils in echter Erhöhung der Zugriffsrate durch Multiprogrammierung niederschlagen, p_{eff} also 0,5 p. Ferner, daß unterhalb der Plattenspeicherebene Programmumschaltung nicht mehr lohnt (p=1) und schließlich, daß Einzel-Prozessorbetrieb vorliegt. Gl. 2 modifiziert sich dann entsprechend.

Einige Modellergebnisse auf der Grundlage realer Technologien sind in Tabelle II zusammengestellt. Unterschiedliche Speicherzugriffsraten schlagen sich in unterschiedlicher Prozessorauslastung nieder. Es wurde ein Modellprozessor mit 2 MIPS (Millionen Instruktionen pro Sekunde) und durchschnittlich 2 Zugriffen pro Instruktion gewählt. Dieser Prozessor kann seine volle Leistung nur entfalten, wenn das Speichersystem 4 Millionen Zugriffe pro Sekunde zuläßt.

Die schlechte Auslastung dieses 2-MIPS-Prozessors bei heutiger Konfiguration ohne Multiprogrammierung überrascht nicht. Auch mit Multiprogrammierung ist die Auslastung nur mäßig.

Erst die Einführung des elektronischen Massenspeichers erbringt eine Verbesserung auf eine vernünftige Größenordnung. Bei Multiprogrammierung verlagert sich jetzt der Engpaß für die Zugriffsrate vom Plattenspeicher (mit seiner hohen Modularität) zum Bandspeicher. Dieser Engpaß könnte überwunden werden durch weitere Erhöhung der Hierarchiestufenzahl, konkret durch Einbau einer Zwischenstufe zwischen Platten- und Bandspeicher.

Technologisch liegt eine solche Stufe im Bereich des Sichtbaren, nämlich über eine Modifizierung des konventionellen Plattenspeichers zu einem Satz von flexiblem Platten mit sehr hoher Bit-Volumendichte [9]. Die Zugriffsrate der Hierarchiekonfiguration liegt dann oberhalb von 4 Millionen pro Sekunde.

Die Ergebnisse aus Tabelle II werfen die Frage nach der optimalen Hierarchiestufung auf, bei festgehaltenen Endpunkten. Für diese Analyse wird ohne Bezug auf reale Technologien eine gleichmäßige Stufung vorgesehen und die Stufenzahl variiert. Multiprogrammierung wird jetzt nicht berücksichtigt. Ergebnisse sind in Abb. 8 aufgetragen: Bei ca. 16 Stufen stellt sich ein Sättigungswert für die Zugriffsrate ein (die in diesem einfachen Fall der reziproke Wert der mittleren Zugriffszeit ist). Diese Zugriffsrate ist nur etwa 2 mal kleiner als die der reinen Pufferspeicherstufe.

In Abb. 8 ist weiterhin die Preisleistungszahl, nämlich Zugriffsrate pro Gesamtbitkosten, aufgetragen.

Hier liegt das Optimum bei ca. 8-10 Stufen. Die Verbesserung gegenüber einer 4-stufigen Hierarchie ist größer als Faktor 6. Auf der Grundlage der realeren Daten in Tabelle II ist der Gewinn bei einem Schritt von heutigen 4 Stufen auf (die durchgespielten) 6 Stufen noch wesentlich höher, da dort nicht von einer gleichmäßigen Stufung ausgegangen wurde.

Ein weiterer Vorteil der feineren Hierarchiestufung ist die Verbesserung des Prozessor-"Wirkungsgrades": Die Zahl der Zugriffe zum Platten- und Bandspeicher nimmt ab. Damit nimmt auch die Zahl der prozessierten Instruktionen (der Zugriffsroutinen) pro Zugriff zur Speicherhierarchie ab, und der Prozessor-"Wirkungsgrad" nimmt zu. Schließlich kann das Betriebssystem einfacher gehalten werden.

In diesem Modell ist der Zuverlässigkeitsaspekt nicht enthalten, der mit wachsender Stufenzahl kritischer wird. Ebenso sind die Kosten der Steuerungen, Adresstabellen, etc. nicht berücksichtigt. Die Extrapolation der Trefferratenkurve ist völlig hypothetisch. All dessen ungeachtet dürfen die Modellergebnisse als Indiz dafür verstanden werden, daß eine feinere Hierarchiestufung noch erhebliches Leistungspotential enthält.

4. SPEICHERASPEKTE BEI DATENBANKBETRIEB

Auch der Datenbankbetrieb kann grundsätzlich in die bisherige Modellbetrachtung eingenordnet werden. Derjenige Parameter, der sich möglicherweise (in Richtung ungünstiger Werte) ändert, ist die Trefferrate, insbesondere auf den hohen Ebenen. Erfahrungen darüber müssen aber erst gewonnen werden, sodaß hier die Modellwerte beibehalten werden, zumal auch bei der Datenbank ein gewisses "Nachbarschafts"-Verhältnis von Anfragen festzustellen sein dürfte. Praktisch-anschaulich könnte man sich eine Funktionsverteilung auf die einzelnen Hierarchiestufen wie in Tabelle III skizziert, vorstellen. Datengruppen mit hoher professioneller Zugriffsrate müssen von der Archivstufe auf die Plattenspeicherstufe resident ausgelagert werden.

Der spezifische Datenbank-Leistungsparameter ist, neben der Datenmenge, die zulässige Anfragenrate. Diese sollte mit wachsender Datenbankkapazität auch ansteigen. Die folgende Überschlagsrechnung möge einige Veranschaulichung bringen:

Nach Tabelle II ist bei heutiger Hierarchie und Multiprogrammierung die Modellzugriffsrate .85 M/s. Wenn wir einen Programmablauf von durchschnittlich 100 K Instruktionen pro Datenbank-Anfrage annehmen, würde das System 4.25 Anfragen pro Sekunde erlauben. Dieser Wert dürfte bei einer Datenbank-Kapazität von 10^{12} b nicht ausreichen. Nach Einführung des elektronischen Massenspeichers erhöht sich die Anfragenrate auf 14 pro Sekunde. Mit einer zusätzlichen Zwischenstufe zwischen Platten- und Bandspeicher erhöht sie sich auf ca. 30 pro Sekunde - entsprechende Prozessorleistung von ca. 3 MIPS vorausgesetzt.

Die letzten Endes interessierende Frage, wieviele Terminals an eine Datenbank dieser Größe bei befriedigender Bedienung angeschlossen werden können, hängt natürlich von der mittleren Anfragelast pro Terminal ab. Bei einer angenommenen mittleren Last von einer Anfrage pro Terminal und Minute errechnet sich eine Terminalzahl von $30 \cdot 60 = 1800$. Diese Anschlußmöglichkeit pro 10^{12} b Datenbankkapazität erscheint ausreichend.

Als Schlußfolgerung aus diesen Betrachtungen soll die Feststellung getroffen werden, daß Organisation und Technologie zukünftiger Speichersysteme das Potential haben, den Leistungsanforderungen eines breiten Datenbankbetriebes gerecht zu werden.

Literatur

[1] C.W. Pugh, "Storage Hierarchies: Gaps, Cliffs and Trends", IEEE Transactions on Magnetics, Vol. Mag-7, No. 4, Dez. 1971

[2] C. Johnson, "IBM 3850-Mass Storage System", Nat. Comp. Conf. 1975, S. 509

[3] J. Kelly, "The Development of an Experimental Electron-Beam-Addressable Memory Module", Computer, Februar 1975

[4] W.C. Hughes et. al., "BEAMOS, A New Electronic Digital Memory", Nat. Comp. Conf. 1975, S. 5-41

[5] G.F. Amelio, "Charge-Coupled Devices for Memory Application", Nat. Comp. Conf. 1975, S. 515

[6] W.S. Boyle et. al., "Charge-Coupled Devices - A New Approach to MIS Device Structures", IEEE Spectrum, Juli 1971, S. 18

[7] A.H. Bobeck et. al., "A New Approach to Memory and Logic: Cylindrical Domain Devices", Proc. AFIPS Conf., Vol. 35, 1969

[8] R.R. Martin et. al., "Electronic Disks in the 1980's", Computer, Februar 1975, S. 24

[9] D.H. Gibson, "Considerations in Block-Oriented Systems Design", AFIPS Proc., Vol. 30, SJCC 1967, S. 75-80

TECHNOLOGIE PARAMETER	- SPEICHERMEDIUM (HOMOGENITÄT, BITDICHTE) - BITZAHL PRO SCHREIB-LESE-STATION (MATRIX-/SEQUENTIELLE ANORDNUNG) - DATENTRANSPORT
OPERATIONS-PARAMETER	- ZUGRIFFSZEIT - ÜBERTRAGUNGSZEIT = F(ÜBERTRAGUNGSBREITE, BLOCKLÄNGE, TAKTFREQUENZ) - MODULARITÄT → ZUGRIFFSRATE - BITKOSTEN → KAPAZITÄT - ZUVERLÄSSIGKEIT - FLÜCHTIGKEIT - ADRESSIERBARE EINHEIT (BYTE/BLOCK-ADRESSIERUNG)

TABELLE I

SPEICHERPARAMETER

KONFIGURATION	$t[\mu s]/p_{eff}$ P	H	E	SP	FP	B	t_{ges} $[\mu s]$	max. Z_{ges} $[10^6/s]$	Prozessor Auslastung [%]	Gesamt-Kosten $[10^6 \$]$	$\frac{Z_{ges}}{\$}$ $[\frac{1}{\$ \cdot s}]$
P+H+SP+B	0,03	0,04		9		0,3	9,37	0,11	2,8	1,27	0,084
P+H+SP+B Multiprogr.	0,03	0,04		0,9		0,2	(1,17)	0,85	21	1,27	0,67
P+H+E+SP+B	0,03	0,04	0,075	0,9		0,3	0,535	1,87	47	1,32	1,4
P+H+E+SP+B Multiprogr.	0,03	0,04	0,075	0,009		0,2	(0,354)	2,82	70	1,32	2,1
P+H+E+SP+F+B Multiprogr.	0,03	0,04	0,075	0,009	0,004	0,015	(0,17)	5,88	100	1,82	3,2

TABELLE II

Modellhierarchie-Leistungsparameter (Prozessor 2 MIPS, 2 Zugriffe/Instruktion)

P	Pufferspeicher
H	Hauptspeicher
E	Elektronischer Massenspeicher
SP	Starre Platte
FP	Flexible Platte
B	Band

HIERARCHIEEBENE NR.	TECHNOLOGIE	TYP. KAPAZITÄT	FUNKTION
1	BIP PUFFER-SPEICHER	4-16K BYTES	SCHNELLER ARBEITSSPEICHER FÜR VERKNÜPFUNG VON DATEN MIT PROGRAMMEN
2	FET HAUPT-SPEICHER	10^5-10^7B	BEREITSTELLUNG VON PROGRAMMEN UND DATEN FÜR ÜBERSCHAUBAREN OPERATIONSZEITRAUM
3	SCHIEBERE-GISTER- BZW. E-STRAHL-SPEICHER	10^7-10^9B	HALTEN VON HÄUFIGEN PROGRAMMEN Z.B. BETRIEBSSYSTEM UND AR-BEITSDATEN Z.B. INDEXTABELLEN, DESKRIPTOREN, KATALOGE, ZEIGER-NETZE USW.
4	PLATTEN-SPEICHER	10^8-10^{10}B	DATEIEN FÜR PROFESSIONELLE BENUTZUNG, DATENSICHERUNG
5	BAND-SPEICHER (AUTOMAT. BANDTRANS-PORT)	10^{10}-10^{13}B	DOKUMENTEN-DATENBANK DATENSICHERUNG, ARCHIVIERUNG

TABELLE III

FUNKTIONSVERTEILUNG BEI DATENBANKBETRIEB

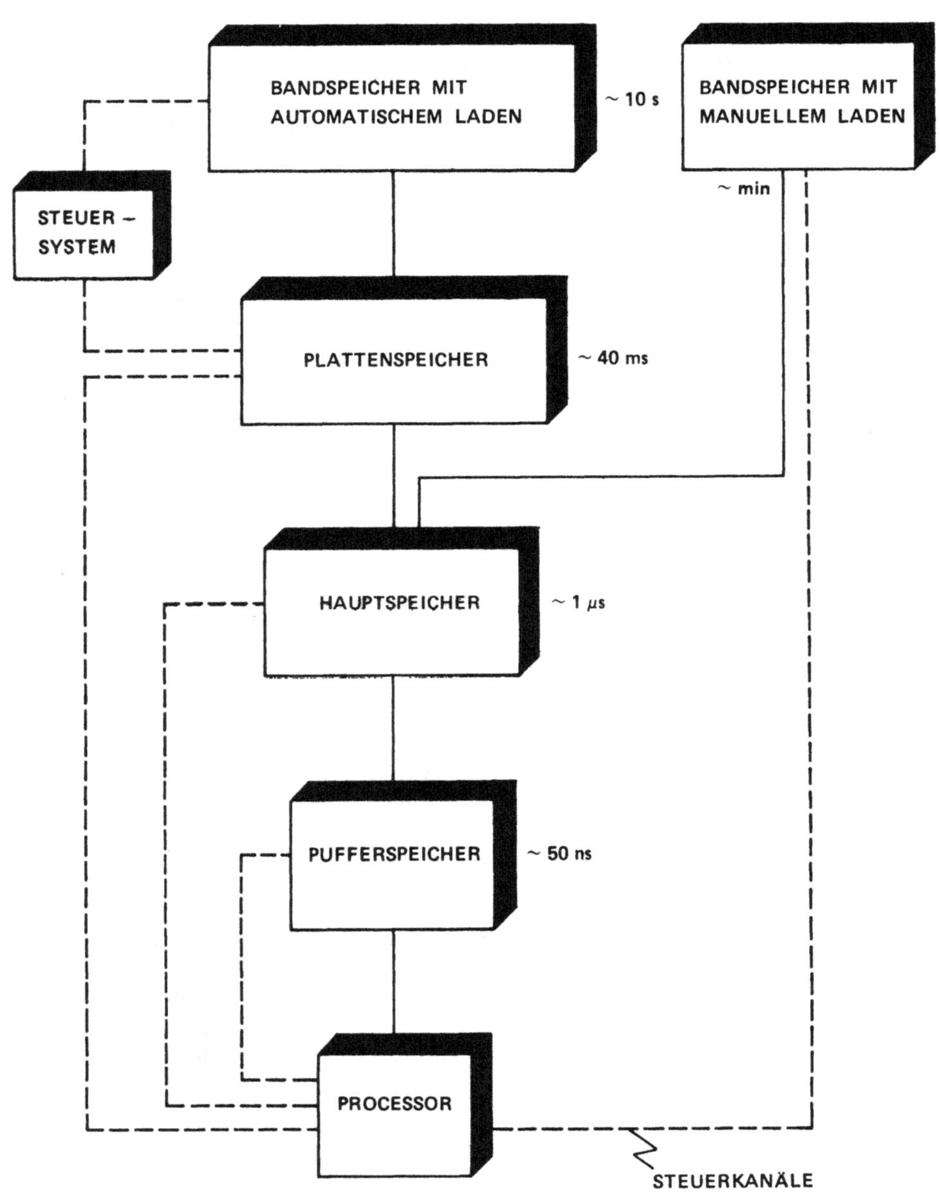

Abb. 1 SPEICHERHIERARCHIE HEUTE

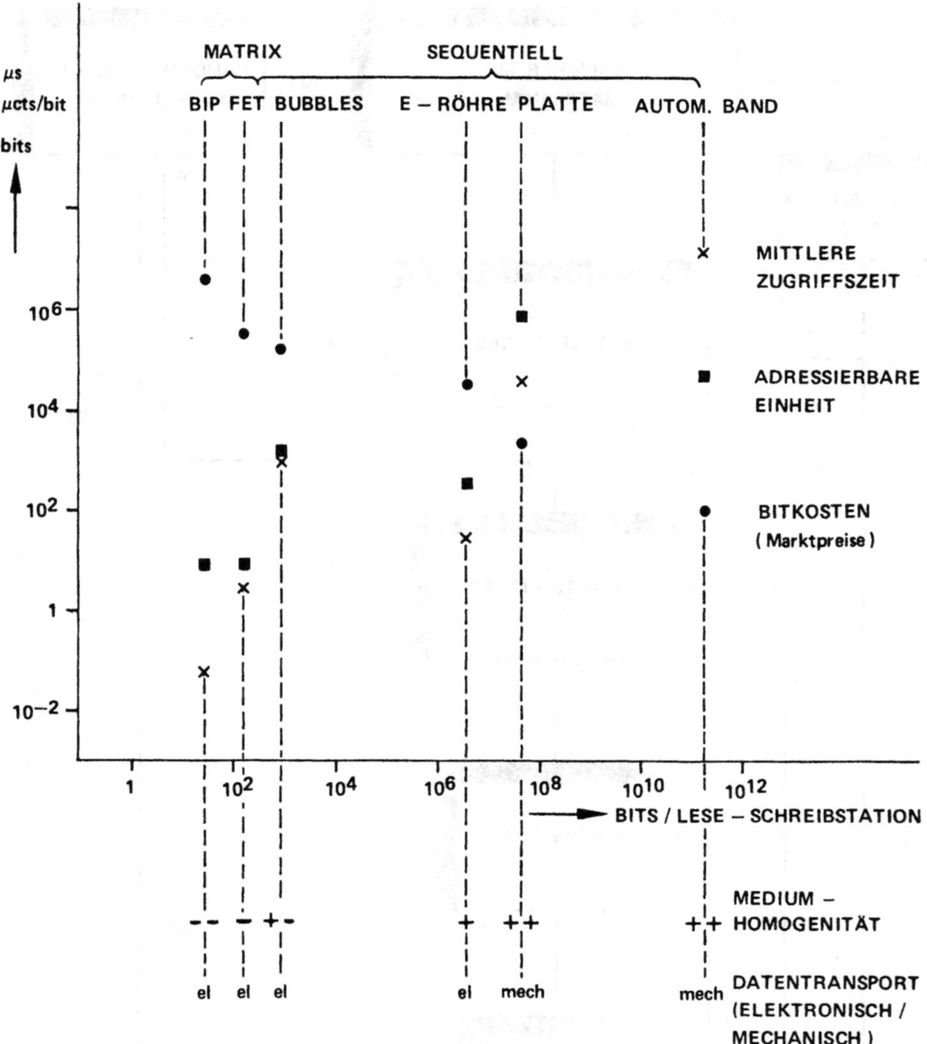

Abb. 2 OPERATIONSPARAMETER ALS FUNKTION DER TECHNOLOGIEPARAMETER

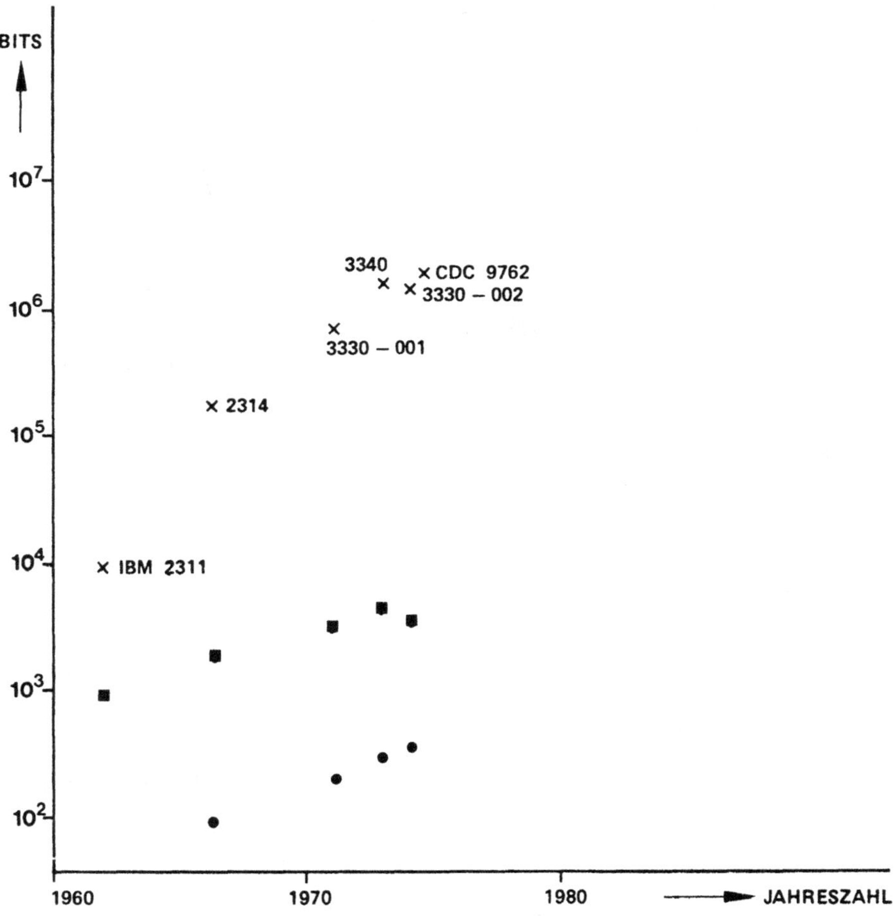

× BITFLÄCHENDICHTE BITS / INCH ^{2}

■ BITSPURDICHTE BITS / INCH

● SPURDICHTE SPUREN / INCH

Abb. 3 PLATTENSPEICHER – BITDICHTE

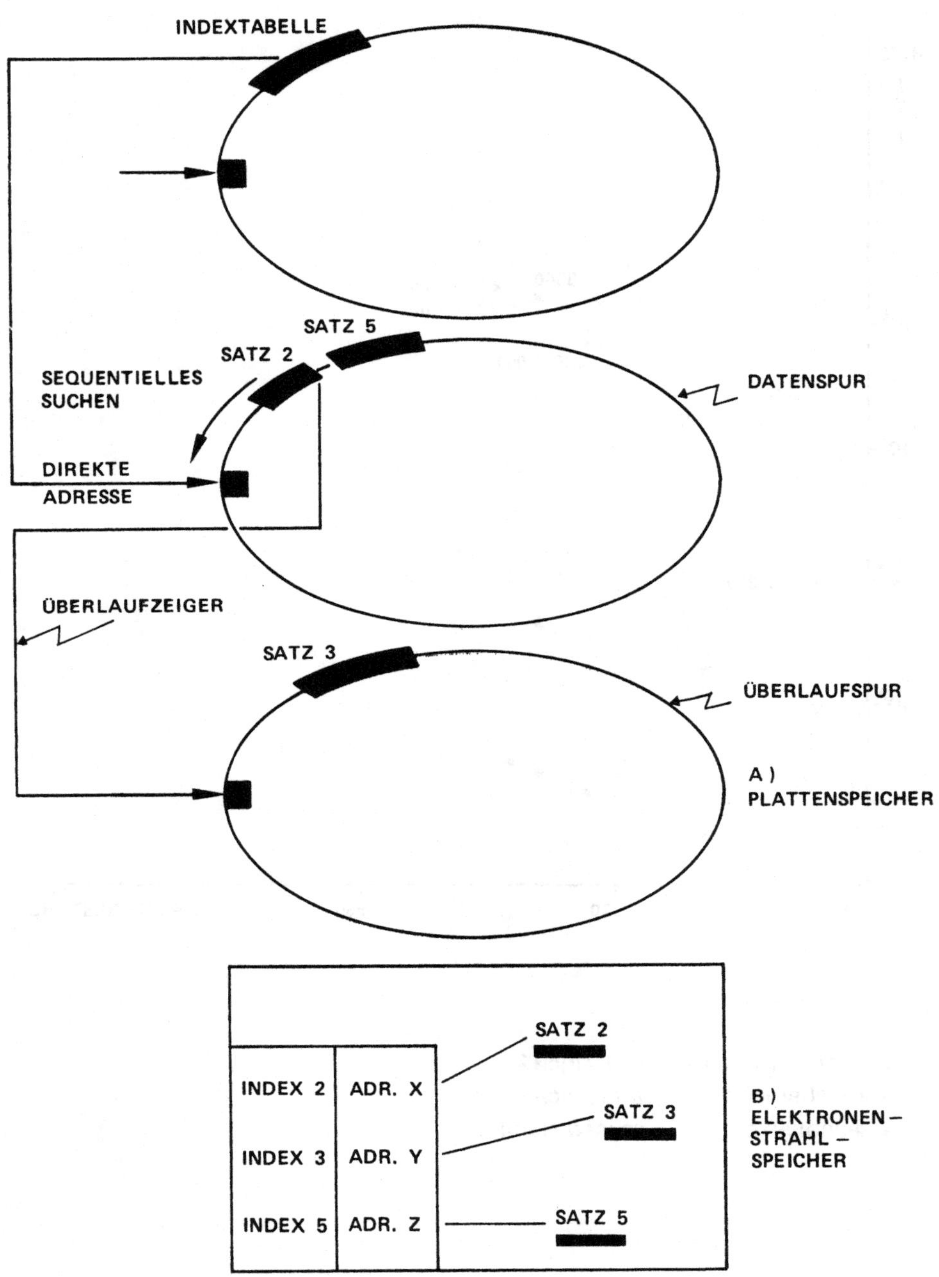

Abb. 4 ADRESSIERUNGSSYSTEME

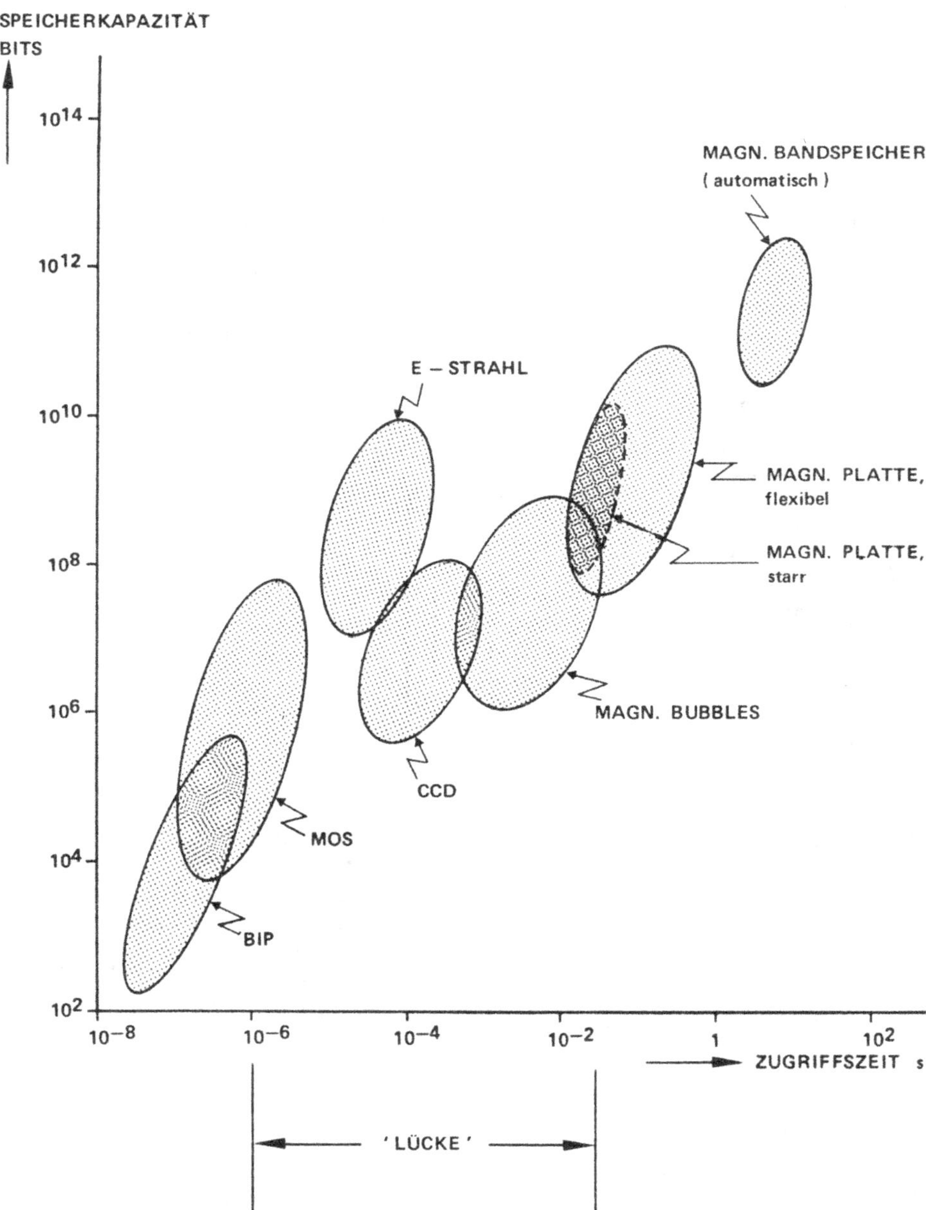

Abb. 5 TECHNOLOGIE – ÜBERSICHT (ohne opt. Techn.)

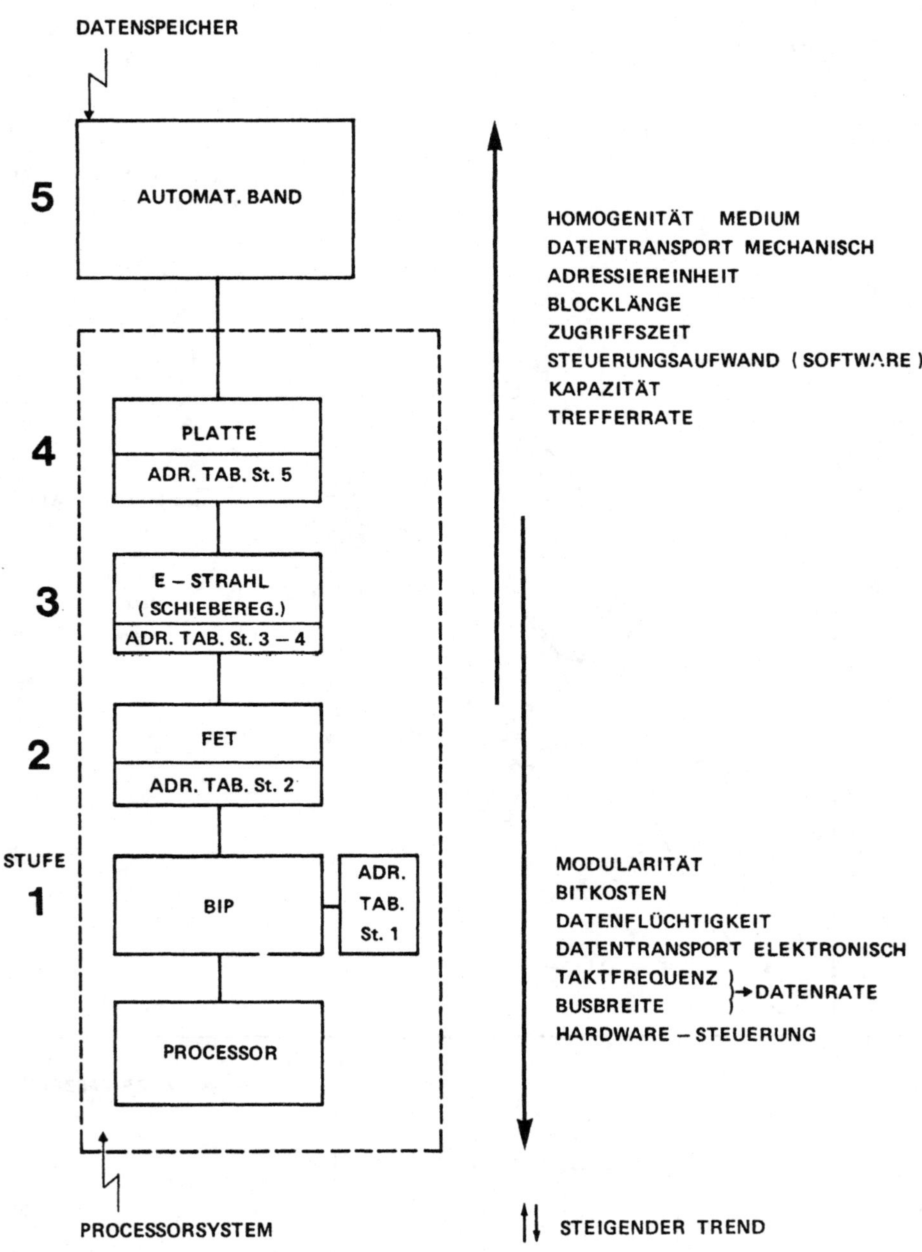

Abb. 6 PARAMETERTREND ÜBER HIERARCHIESPEKTRUM

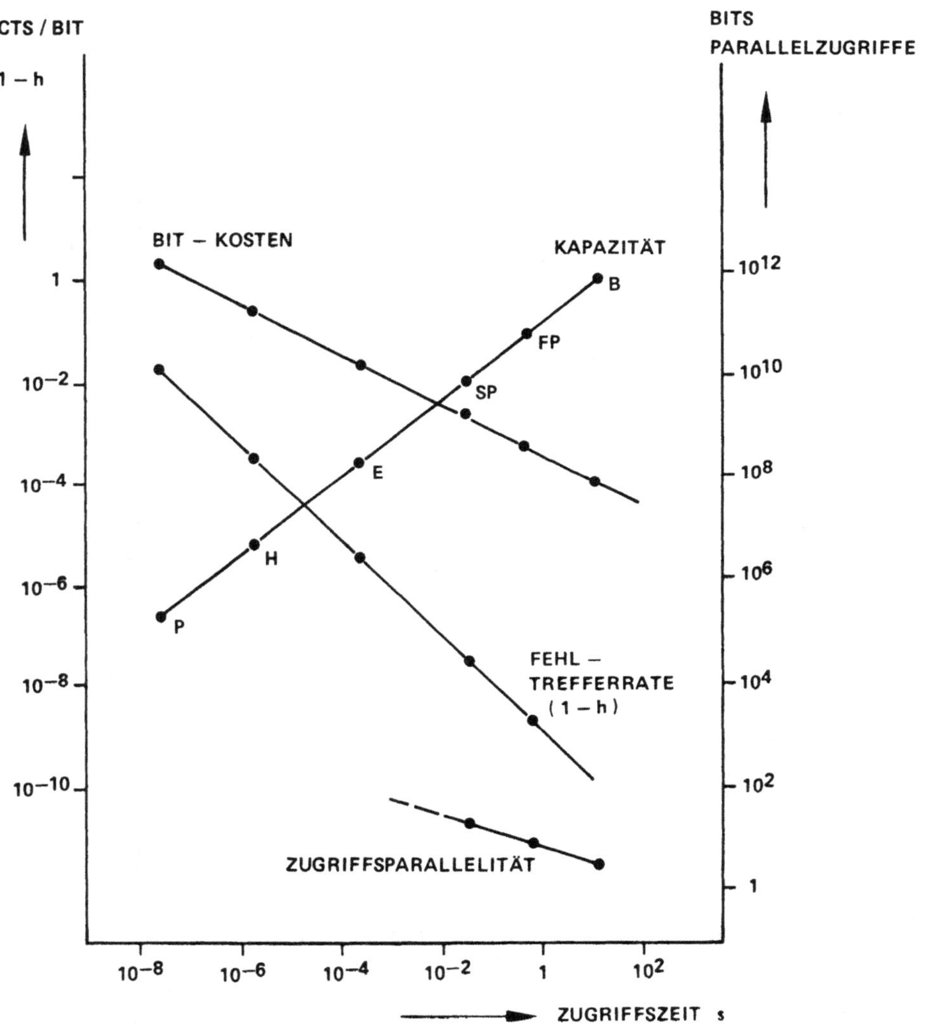

P	PUFFERSPEICHER
H	HAUPTSPEICHER
E	ELEKTRON. MASSENSPEICHER
SP	STARRE PLATTE
FP	FLEXIBLE PLATTE
B	BAND

Abb. 7 MODELLPARAMETER

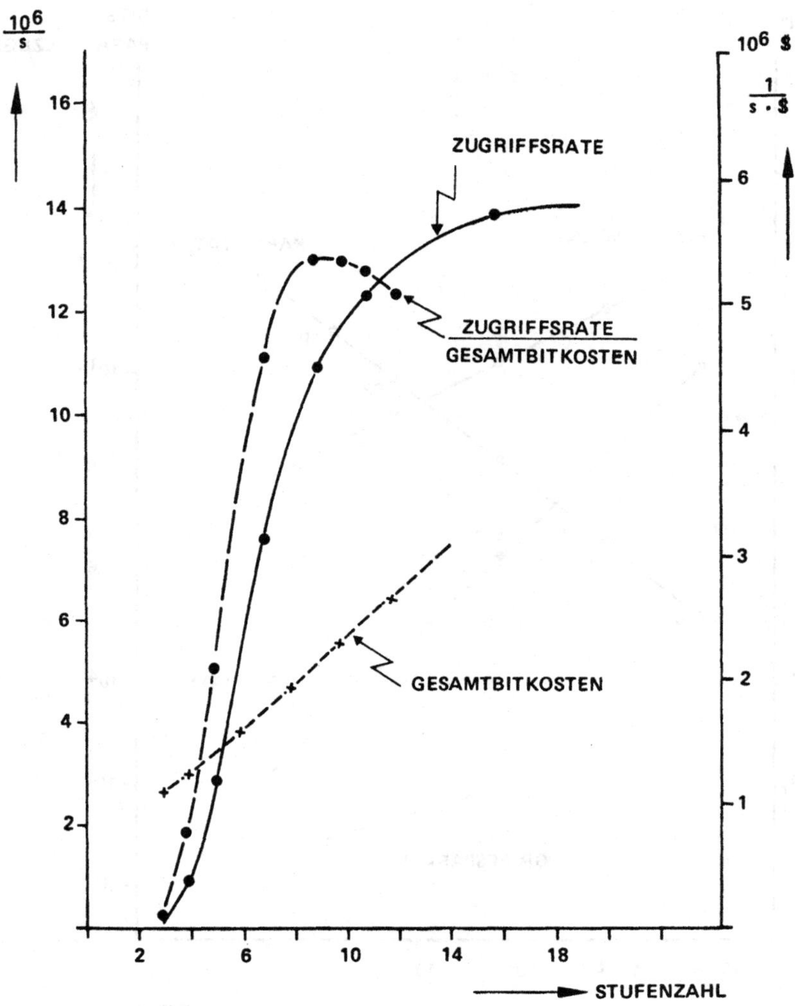

Abb. 8 MODELLERGEBNISSE
GLEICHMÄSSIGE STUFUNG (im log. Maßstab)

System R: A Relational Data Base Management System

Morton M. Astrahan, IBM Research Laboratory, San Jose, California
Donald D. Chamberlin, IBM Research Laboratory, San Jose, California
W. Frank King, IBM Research Laboratory, San Jose, California
Irving L. Traiger, IBM Research Laboratory, San Jose, California

INTRODUCTION

System R is a data base management system which provides a high-level, non-procedural relational data interface. The system provides a high level of data independence by isolating the end user as much as possible from underlying storage structures. The system permits definition of a variety of relational views on common underlying data. Data control features are also provided, including authorization, integrity assertions, triggered transactions, a logging and recovery subsystem, and facilities for maintaining data consistency in a shared-update environment.

The relational model of data was introduced by Codd [1] in 1970 as an approach toward providing solutions to the various outstanding problems of current data base management systems. In particular, Codd addressed the problems of providing a data model or view which is divorced from various implementation considerations (the data independence problem) and also the problem of providing the data base user with a very high-level, non-procedural data sublanguage for accessing data. It should be stressed here that the relational model is a framework or philosophy for finding compatible solutions to these and other problems in data base management; the relational approach is thought to make solutions more elegant and perhaps simpler but the approach by itself does not solve these problems. With this caveat in mind, our first purpose is to briefly describe a related set of data base problems which we are attempting to solve in a coherent way following the relational approach. Our solutions are embodied in an experimental prototype data management system called System R which is currently being designed, implemented, and evaluated at the IBM San Jose Research Laboratory.

We wish to emphasize that System R is a vehicle for research in data base architecture, and is not available as a product. Furthermore, the ideas discussed in this paper should not be considered as having product implications.

To a large extent, the acceptance and value of the relational approach hinges on the demonstration that a system can be built which is operationally complete (can actually be used in a real environment to solve real problems) and has performance at least comparable to today's existing systems. With the present state of systems performance prediction, the only credible demonstration is to actually construct such a system, and to evaluate it in a real environment. The point of this paper, then, is to describe the set of problems which are being studied in the System R framework, to discuss the objectives of the system (which amounts to a description or definition of the term <u>operationally complete</u>), and to describe the architecture of the system, including overall structure, interfaces, and functional design.

The System R project is not the first implementation of the relational approach; however, we know of no other system which is really aimed at an operationally complete capability. Other efforts have demonstrated feasibility in various of the related problem areas. For example, both the IS/1 system [2] and the Phase/0 SEQUEL prototype [3] were single-user systems. No concurrent sharing of data was permitted and hence data control, locking, and recovery issues were greatly simplified. The INGRES project [4] at U.C. Berkeley is also single-user oriented. In addition, each of these projects has an incomplete treatment of views, i.e., of providing various views of data to various users.

The next section describes the overall goals of System R and describes the list of capabilities which we believe to be necessary in an operational environment. The following section describes the architecture of the system, and describes in overview terms its major interfaces and the components which support these interfaces

SYSTEM OBJECTIVES

System R is focused on five main goals:

1. To provide a high level, non-procedural relational data interface.
2. To provide the maximum possible data independence for the basic data objects (base relations).
3. To support derived relational views.
4. To provide facilities for data control consistent with the high level of the data interface.
5. To discover the performance trade-offs inherent in this type of data base capability.

First, each of these goals will be discussed and illustrated.

1. <u>High Level Non-Procedural Relational Data Interface</u>

The trend toward higher level languages has long been evident in the programming domain. Set-oriented data sublanguages were introduced in 1962 in the CODASYL Information Algebra [5]. Codd's ALPHA language [6] and Relational Algebra [7] raised the level of data sublanguages by letting the user specify the properties of the data required without describing the access path or detailed sequence of operations to be used to obtain the data. This trend toward higher level non-procedural programming [8] is aimed at reducing the number of decisions the programmer must make in order to express his problem/solution, and at making the decisions more relevant to the solution (as opposed to being relevant to the programming of a specific computer). Halstead has examined two programs solving the same problem using his software physics techniques [9], one written in ALPHA and the other in DBTG-COBOL and for this case found that the ALPHA solution required 30 times fewer mental discriminations than the lower level solution. This observation should be directly translatable into increased programmer productivity and ease of maintenance. Thus, human productivity is one strong reason for the goal of supporting a high-level, non-procedural data interface.

The other reason for moving in the direction of non-procedural interfaces is related to the optimization of the execution of the program. If the data base were dedicated to a single application, its structure could be optimized for that application only, and the application could be written in terms of that optimized structure. However, in an integrated data base environment, such local optimization is likely to be inefficient. Hence, the system must itself optimize the execution of each application on a data base whose structure is a compromise among the various applications. The non-procedural, high-level specification better reveals the application intent and hence is easier for the system to use as a basis for optimization.

The available relational languages (ALPHA, Relational Algebra) were very formal and required rather much mathematical sophistication on the part of the user. In particular, the ALPHA language is based on the first order predicate calculus. The relational algebra introduces a collection of aggregrate operators (selection, projection, join, division, etc.) which have relational operands and produce relational results. The need to discover more user-oriented, non-mathematical relational languages became apparent and is currently being pursued by several research groups [11,12].

The principal external interface of System R is called the Relational Data Interface (RDI), and provides relationally complete [7] facilities for data manipulation, data definition, and data control. To support high-level, non-procedural, set-oriented applications, the RDI contains the SEQUEL data sublanguage in its entirety. SEQUEL is documented in [10].

Of course, not all requirements can best be met through a non-procedural approach and for this reason the RDI contains single-tuple-oriented operators (FETCH, INSERT, DELETE, REPLACE, etc.) in addition to the set-oriented capabilities of SEQUEL.

We have designed the RDI to be used in two modes:
(a) Directly by an application program (e.g., a COBOL program) which uses RDI operators to access the data base.
(b) As the target of a translator program (a special case of an application program) which is emulating some other type of user interface.

2. Data Independence

Date [13] has defined data independence as the immunity of applications to change in storage structure and access strategy. Often, however, the notion is associated with the ability of a data base system to provide various logical views of the data base; for example to make visible only selected records of a file, and selected attributes of each record. By view, informally we mean a relational window through which an application can access the data base. The term "window" is used to imply that changes to the data base which affect the view are visible to the application. We wish to distinguish these two notions of data independence. In this subsection we address the only first notion of data independence; the second, which we call the support of derived views, is discussed in the next subsection.

Typically, data management systems permit two levels of data definition. The lower level, or "schema", describes the primitive data objects being managed by the system. In System R, these primitive objects are called base relations. The description of a base relation includes the relation name, attribute names, description of the units of each attribute, the domain of each attribute, the order of the attributes within a relation, the order (if any) of the tuples within a relation, etc. In particular, the definition of a base table does not include any information about physical storage or available physical access paths to the data. However, each base relation has a very direct physical representation, i.e., each tuple of the relation has a stored representation. Data independence implies that the base relation can be supported by a variety of physical structures and access strategies.

Clearly data independence is important if a system is to allow growth and meet the changing requirements of various applications. System R provides a rich set of access structures. Any of these can be used to support a given base relation.

3. Support of Derived Views

The higher level of data independence consists of the ability to define alternative views in terms of the primitive data objects. This notion appears in most contemporary data management systems and the usefulness of such systems depends in large measure on the capability of the system to support derived views.

The inability to support views which differ from the primitive views often leads to programs which are complex, because they are warped to use views which are not natural but can be supported, and which require extensive maintenance as the system changes over time.

As an example of the usefulness of derived views, consider a data base containing the following two types of records: CATALOG (PARTNO,DESC,PRICE) and SALES (SALENO,PARTNO,QSOLD). The CATALOG file is ordered by part number, and gives the description and price of each part. The SALES file is ordered by sale number, and gives the part number and quantity sold for each sale. Suppose we wish to print out all the SALES records for parts which have a price greater than $1000.

We could write a program to scan through the CATALOG file, finding parts with PRICE> $1000; for each such part, a separate scan could be made through the SALES table to find all the corresponding records. This program would be highly procedural; it would require repeated scanning of the SALES table, and would give the system little opportunity to optimize the query by choosing among alternate access paths.

However, if our system permits the specification of derived views, the user might specify a view consisting of the join of the two files, as follows: SALES-CAT (SALENO,PARTNO, DESC,PRICE,QSOLD). The program could then consist of a single scan through the SALES-CAT view. Besides being easier to write, this program would give the system flexibility to take advantage of new access paths which may become available (such as a PARTNO index on the SALES file) without requiring changes in the program.

A major goal of the System R project is to develop and investigate the technology of derived views. This problem has three distinct aspects, each of which is being studied:

(a) Exactly what set of operations on derived views is supportable? As an example of this issue, imagine a request to delete a tuple from the SALES-CAT view described above. Since this view is a join of two underlying files, it is not obvious what actions should be taken on the files to support the deletion. (Should we delete the SALES record but retain the CATALOG record?) For some kinds of view modification requests, there may be several possible actions which would produce the desired result; for other kinds of requests, there may be no possible supporting action. Codd [18] has described some examples of the latter phenomenon.

(b) How should the view be bound to the available physical structures and access paths? This aspect of the binding problem concerns the optimization of the view and accesses on the view in terms of available access paths, e.g., indexes, sequential scan, etc.

(c) When should binding be performed? For dynamic view definition, the binding must also be dynamic. In System R, we are investigating various binding-time strategies; dynamic binding will occur for dynamically defined views but for certain often-used or very demanding views, the binding will be done statically with (hopefully) an increase in performance.

4. Data Control Facilities

Data Control includes those aspects of a data base system which control the access to and use of data. We distinguish four types of data control, each of which is being investigated in System R.

(a) Authorization. This form of control is the most common type, being present in almost all current systems. Authorization is the mechanism to permit or deny the creation and manipulation of data structures and views by various users. Any user of System R may potentially be authorized to create new tables and views, and to selectively grant authorizations for his objects to other users. The authorization mechanism of System R is described more fully in [14].

(b) Integrity. Integrity control provides a mechanism for enforcing that the data in the data base obeys certain rules or predicates which have been declared to the system. This form of control is typically not found in current data base systems but is left to protocols imbedded in various application programs. In System R, two main types of control facilities are provided: integrity assertions and triggers. Integrity assertions are expressed in the SEQUEL language as predicates about the data in the data base [15]. The system then guarantees the truth of these predicates. Exactly when the system checks an assertion is a function of both the type of assertion and the transaction boundary which caused the assertion to be checked.

Triggers are actions that are invoked when some triggering condition or action is detected. For example, suppose that the DEPT relation contains an attribute NEMPS which represents the number of employees in the department. To maintain the validity of this value, we can declare triggers to update this field whenever an employee is hired, fired, or transferred.

(c) Consistency. Integrity implies the static correctness of the data base and consistency is concerned with the dynamic correctness. Suppose that one application program is transferring a set of employees from Dept. 48 to Dept. 50, while simultaneously another application program is giving raises to all employees in Dept. 50. The interaction of these programs may have the undesirable result that some but not all of the transferred employees receive the raise. Even worse, if the transferring program encounters a failure and backs out its updates, it may develop that a raise has been given to someone in Dept. 48.

In current systems the application would contain specific statements (e.g., "LOCK DEPT 50") to avoid these problems. A major goal of System R is to eliminate such defensive coding which is not a part of the problem being solved but is related only to the fact that the solution is running in a certain environment. Since the user cannot know in advance the exact environment in which his application will run (perhaps no other users are currently updating employee records; in this case the lock is not needed), the system must provide the control needed to enforce consistency. The approach being pursued is to require that the user define the boundaries of a transaction, which is a sequence of statements to be executed as an atomic unit. The system then requests whatever resources it needs in the run-time environment to guarantee atomicity. Furthermore, this same atomic unit is used as the unit of integrity, i.e., integrity may be suspended within a transaction but it is guaranteed at the transaction endpoints. If a transaction violates integrity at its endpoint, then the transaction is backed out.

(d) Recovery. The fourth aspect of data control is concerned with preserving the integrity of the data if the system experiences a malfunction or if an application backs up either voluntarily or involuntarily, (e.g., as in the case of deadlock). The recovery capabilities of System R include the usual checkpoint/restart functions as well as the ability to back up an ongoing transaction to user-specified points. These capabilities are examples of functions which are required in order to have an operationally complete capability.

ARCHITECTURE AND SYSTEM STRUCTURE

We will describe the overall architecture of Sytem R from two viewpoints. First, we will describe the system as seen by a single transaction, i.e., a monolithic description. Second, we will investigate its multi-user dimensions. Figure 1 gives a functional view of the system including its major interfaces and components. The RDI, as described previously, is the external interface which can be called directly from a programming language, or used to support various other interfaces. The Relational Storage Interface (RSI) is the access-method-like level which handles the access to single tuples of base relations. This interface and its supporting system (Relational Storage System - RSS) is actually a complete storage subsystem in that it manages devices, space allocation, storage buffers (one level store), transaction consistency and locking, deadlock, backout, transaction recovery and logging. Furthermore, it maintains indexes on selected attributes of base relations.

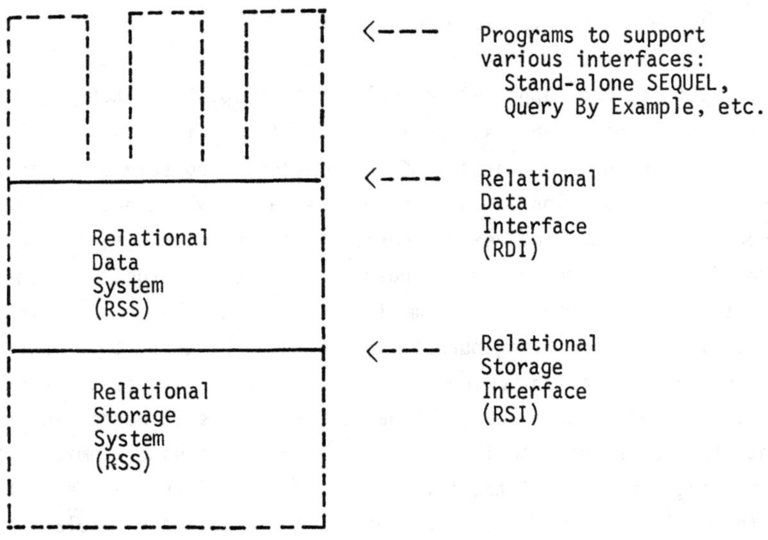

Figure 1

Architecture of System R

With this brief description of the RSS facilities, we can return to the RDI and its supporting system (Relational Data System - RDS). The major functions performed by the RDS are authorization, integrity enforcement, and nonprimitive view support which includes all the binding issues discussed previously. In addition, the RDS maintains the catalogs of external names, since the RSS uses only system-generated internal names. The RDS contains a sophisticated optimizer which chooses the best access path for any given request from among the paths supported by the RSS. The operating system enviornment for this system is VM/370 [16]. Several extensions to this virtual machine capability have been made [17] in order to support the multi-user environment of System R.

ACKNOWLEDGEMENT

The authors wish to acknowledge many helpful discussions with E. F. Codd, originator of the relational model of data, and with L. Y. Liu, manager of the Computer Science Department of the IBM Research Laboratory. We also wish to acknowledge the extensive contributions to System R of Paul L. Fehder, who has transferred to another location, and Raymond F. Boyce, who served as one of the project managers until his untimely death in June of 1974.

REFERENCES

[1] E. F. Codd. A Relational Model of Data for Large Shared Data Banks. Communications of the ACM, June 1970.

[2] M. G. Notley. The Peterlee IS/1 System. IBM UK Scientific Center Report UKSC-0018, March 1972.

[3] M. M. Astrahan and D. D. Chamberlin. Implementation of a Structured English Query Language. Presented at ACM SIGMOD conference, San Jose, California, May 1975; to be published in Communications of the ACM, October 1975.

[4] G. D. Held, M. R. Stonebraker, and E. Wong. INGRES: A Relational Data Base System. Proc. AFIPS National Computer Computer Conference, Anaheim, California, May 1975.

[5] CODASYL Development Committee. An Information Algebra. Communications of the ACM, April 1962.

[6] E. F. Codd. A Data Base Sublanguage Founded on the Relational Calculus. Proc ACM SIGFIDET Workshop, San Diego, California, November 1971.

[7] E. F. Codd. Relational Completeness of Data Base Sublanguages. Courant Computer Science Symposia, Vol. 6: Data Base Systems. Prentice Hall, New York, 1971.

[8] B. M. Leavenworth. Nonprocedural Programming. IBM Research Report RC4968, IBM Research Center, Yorktown Heights, New York., August 1974.

[9] M. H. Halstead. Software Physics Comparison of a Sample Program in DSL Alpha and COBOL. IBM Research Report RJ1460, IBM Research Laboratory, San Jose, California, October 1974.

[10] D. D. Chamberlin and R. F. Boyce, SEQUEL: A Structured English Query Language. Proc. ACM SIGFIDET Workshop, Ann Arbor, Michigan, May 1974.

[11] N. McDonald and M. Stonebraker. CUPID: The Friendly Query Language. Proc. ACM Pacific Conf., San Francisco, California,

April 1975. Available from Boole and Babbage, 850 Stewart Drive, Sunnyvale, California 94086.

[12] M. M. Zloof. Query By Example. Proc. AFIPS National Computer Conference, Anaheim, California, May 1975.

[13] C. J. Date. An Introduction to Data Base Systems. Addison Wesley, 1975.

[14] D. D. Chamberlin, J. N. Gray, and I. L. Traiger. Views, Authorization, and Locking in a Relational Data Base System. Proc. AFIPS National Computer Conference, Anaheim, California, May 1975.

[15] K. P. Eswaran and D. D. Chamberlin. Functional Specifications of a Subsystem for Data Base Integrity. IBM Research Report RJ1601, IBM Research Laboratory, San Jose, California, June 1975.

[16] Introduction to VM/370. IBM Publication No. GC20-1800. IBM, White Plains, New York.

[17] J. N. Gray and V. Watson. A Shared Segment and Inter-process Communication Facility for VM/370. IBM Research Report RJ1579, IBM Research Laboratory, San Jose, California, February 1975.

[18] E. F. Codd. Recent Investigations in Relational Data Base Systems. Proc. IFIPS Congress, Stockholm, Sweden, August 1974.

GEOGRAPHIC BASE FILES:
Applications in the Integration and
Extraction of Data from Diverse Sources

Patrick E. Mantey, Eric D. Carlson, IBM Research Laboratory, San Jose, California

Abstract
This paper addresses the development of integrated municipal data bases, with consideration given to political realities and to the sources of data now available in municipalities. First, the potential users and potential uses of a municipal data base are discussed, and an information system which would serve these users and uses is considered. Next, the "current" status of data bases in municipalities is reviewed and it is concluded that there is a large quantity of data available in many municipalities, but that integrated data bases for supporting an information system are not usually a reality. The problem of building an integrated data base from the variety of data sources presented by local agencies is then addressed. A central ingredient for an integrated data base is the Geographic Base File (GBF) which permits the construction of extracted data files from these multiple sources to support information system applications. The concept of extraction, for the integration of diverse source files via geographic references, is developed (and a prototype implementation is described in the Appendix). Using the GBF, and source data from various municipal functions, extracted data bases can be rapidly built to serve a variety of applications of an information system in the decision-making situations of municipalities.

I. APPLICATIONS OF A MUNICIPAL DATA BASE

Municipal governments are, in essence, created to deliver services to a geographical area. There is an unusual variety, in comparison to private industry, of services offered. Local government is often structured (or fractured) along functional lines into special districts, as well as by geography. Such structuring has precluded concentration of power, but it has increased the complexity of planning, resource allocation, or management.

Many of the problems in municipal government require decisions which are not routine. Rather, they require the professional insight and judgment of human decision makers who consider the specific conditions of each problem. Ideally, this insight and judgment would be aided and guided by appropriate information derived from a comprehensive data base. This is the objective of a municipal information system: to facilitate effective analysis and solution of specific problems by supporting human decision makers with data resources and analysis functions in readily usable form. Because a municipality provides services to a geographical area, much of the data relevant to decision making or problem solving in local agencies will have geographical attributes, and can be given spatial interpretation via maps. A key attribute of a municipal information system is the capability for displaying information in the form of maps. Another requirement for such systems to be effective is that they support ready use by decision makers who know very little about computers. The system must help the decision makers develop their precise objectives or decision criteria for solving a problem. The solution process in such decision making requires exploratory analysis, selection of relevant data, and meaningful data presentation in an interactive environment. A system which provides such capabilities, called GADS (Geo-data Analysis and Display System) has been developed and evaluated in several applications, such as police manpower allocation and analysis of urban development policies [1-4]. The evaluations of GADS indicate that interactive analysis and display systems have a great potential in the operations, management, and planning of municipalities.

As an example, consider a municipality which maintains a computerized property information file (via the tax assessor function). Such a file would have data on each parcel, possibly including:

- address
- owner
- zoning
- improvements
  - date constructed
  - type construction
  - size (area)
  - current use
- area
- centroid
- assessed value

If this data were accessed via an interactive information system, a decision maker could readily obtain, for example, the address and assessed value of all residences constructed between 1960 and 1962 and having floor area between 1600 and 1800 square feet, on lots with 6800 to 7200 square feet. If the user of the system were a real-estate appraiser, this information in tabular form might be of value in determining if a particular home is fairly appraised (Figure 1). A histogram giving the distribution of assessed value of these homes would provide additional insight

(Figure 2) and a map relating the average value of such homes in the city's planning areas to the city-wide average (Figure 3) would provide the appraiser with information in a spatial framework.

If the user of the information system were an assessor concerned with determining the neighborhoods which could be considered equivalent for purposes of computer-aided appraisal, additional data would be required. If recent sales records are the basis for calibrating the assessment model, it may be found that the assessor's data alone cannot be used to model variations in selling price of houses fitting the description above. Showing on a map the mean and variance of the selling price of such houses by neighborhood will offer the assessor a visual means for examining the quality of the assessment model. The display may cause the assessor to consider other factors to explain the variations; e.g. crime rate, level of public facilities and services (such as the influence of an adjacent regional park [5]) or the influence of other near-by land uses.

In making decisions related to residential zonings, pertinent questions and information displays would relate to adjacent land use, the effect that the proposed development would have on the mix of housing stock available in the community, or to the effect these new residents would make on the per-capita park acerage in the area. The school officials (and in some areas the local zoning authority) need to evaluate the impact such a development will have on the existing school facilities. Each of these questions, and many others, are of interest to different decision makers involved in the area of community development.

An example of the use of a municipal data base in resource allocation could relate to finding the best approach to the reduction of burglaries in a residential neighborhood. One group may advocate better street lighting. If the queries relating to these burglaries show they are day-time crimes, another approach probably offers greater promise. Certainly the level of police patrols would be examined. If the area is found to have a high percentage of two wage-earner families, and the majority of burglaries are during the week, then some suspicion will fall on the children. If a large number of burglaries occur on school days, it may appear that the school-age children are not the perpetrators. However, if the data base contains school information so that it can be determined that a school adjacent to the neighborhood has flexible scheduling and that school children are free to roam about off school grounds, the source of the trouble may have been identified.

As a last example, consider the application for a building permit for an automobile service station. With the recent wave of service station abandonments, many municipalities are reluctant to grant such permits. Similarly, financial institutions are probably wary about loaning money for such ventures. For all concerned, and for the public good, a careful analysis of such a proposal is required. Factors of interest would include location and number of existing stations, traffic access and traffic patterns at the proposed site, and an estimate of the automobile ownership and disposable income in the surrounding areas.

In these examples it has been assumed that the information system has access to a comprehensive municipal data base. However, such data bases are a rarity today. In the next section the current status of municipal data bases is discussed, and in Section III an approach toward the provision of integrated data is offered.

II. CURRENT STATUS OF MUNICIPAL DATA BASES

The importance of a comprehensive integrated data base to support decision-making in municipal government has been widely recognized. There have been several different approaches taken to the development of comprehensive municipal data bases.

One approach, which was popular in the 1960's, was the development of a comprehensive "data bank". This data bank was usually generated as a special collection or census, and often was carried out and funded as part of a comprehensive transportation and land use planning study. As a part of such studies, detailed field surveys of land use (at the parcel level) were conducted, and survey data also was gathered on employment, income distribution, and commercial activity (Figure 4). The data acquisition consumed a major portion of the study resources, and did not provide any information relating to many municipal services (e.g. public safety). Although accurate data was often gathered in the development of these data banks, their value was short-lived because they were at best a snap-shot of the state of a very dynamic system, and no means were provided for updating and extending these data banks. At about the same time, the computer was becoming a tool in the operations of local governments. The application of computers by municipalities beginning in the 1960's can be characterized as a function-by-function approach, with data processing introduced into tasks involving high-volume routine transactions. The computer is generally utilized in those functions which have previously been computerized in private industry: payroll, accounting, billing, budget status reporting, personnel records, etc. Also, the 1960's saw wide-spread use of computers in the processes associated with elections and in operations of law enforcement agencies. Usually these applications were isolated from each other, and no attempts were made to make this information available for use by other municipal functions.

The real property assessment function of local government in the late 1960's began to recognize the potential of computer applications. The court decisions in various locales requiring property to be appraised at current market value placed a significantly increased work load on assessment officials. In numerous areas, the assessor has turned to computer-aided appraisal to meet these demands. If a model is to be built and calibrated to reliably estimate fair-market value of residential properties, a comprehensive real property data base is a must. These data bases were constructed, often by computerizing the data contained on the assessor's file cards which were maintained on each parcel. Some property data bases, besides the usual references to assessor map, book and page and to situs address, also added geographic data such as a "centroid". Computerized real property systems required the field acquisition of very comprehensive data. A work sheet for field surveys by appraisers in a California county is shown in Figure 5. Note the detailed land and building attributes used in this system. There was a significant increase in the amount of data used and required by the introduction of this computerized appraisal system, but much of the data on this sheet would not change from year-to-year, and the appraiser in the field would only need to correct those data items which had changed.

An additional requirement for computer-aided appraisal is data relating to current selling price of residential properties. This data provides the calibration information for the regression models, and is available, depending upon the state or local laws, from the registrar of deeds, from the collector of transfer taxes, or from title companies. Assessors in some locales obtain this data by questionnaires which buyers are required by law to complete and return (Figure 6). These sources and/or others also can be used to obtain financial data (e.g. mortgage terms) for the property. Clearly this data base is an integral part of a municipal data base for applications such as illustrated by the examples in Section I.

Another approach related to the development of municipal data bases is characterized by the USAC projects [6], particularly those of Charlotte, North Carolina, and Wichita Falls, Texas. These cities were funded by the Federal USAC project to build Integrated Municipal Information Systems, (IMIS). The concepts of IMIS are [6]:

"(1) Integrated data processing systems should inter-relate municipal processes.
(2) A fundamental analysis of municipal operations and identification of related data processing components is a precondition to the effective use of computers.
(3) A systems approach is required throughout the development process.
(4) The automation of municipal operations must exploit the full range of computer technology.
(5) Automation of routine municipal processes is a fundamental condition to the realization of an IMIS.
(6) An IMIS views the municipality as a basic building block for intergovernmental information systems.
(7) Municipal information systems are by-products of computer-driven, operations-based systems.

(8) Adequately designed data processing systems can be transferred from one municipality to another.
(9) The integrated approach to municipal systems development must proceed on the basis of a plan within which incremental installation may be achieved in accordance with the priorities and resources of any particular city."

The USAC efforts involve city governments, and were the consequence of studies such as the IBM/New Haven project [7] and the USC/Burbank project [8]. These groups sought to develop a methodology, via a "systems approach", for the application of computers by municipalities [6] but did not result in system implementation of integrated municipal information systems.

The USAC approach wisely focused on operational sources to provide the current data required for municipal decision-making. In the implementations, which are still in progress, the cities have concentrated on building up operational uses of computers, and on implementing these applications on a central computer under an integrated data-base management system. The value of computers to these operational functions has been confirmed [9] but the applications of IMIS in the areas of management decision making are still to be demonstrated. One of the difficulties that must be overcome in providing a comprehensive municipal data base, (even in cities with a fully integrated and operational IMIS constructed according to the USAC philosophy), is that complete integration, where all municipal functions use the same computer and data base management system, is not a likely prospect with current local governmental structure and with the limited resources of local governments. For example the data pertinent to decision making in a city may be gathered by another agency, such as the tax assessor (and conversely), and may reside on different computers, under different data management schemes and in different file formats. In addition, problems of data security, compatibility of files, and high processing costs may make complete integration unrealistic for many municipalities.

Special data collections, such as the U.S. Census, and data available from state sources, must also be readily incorporated into a municipal data base. With census data gathered according to blocks, block groups and census tracts, with assessors property data coded according to assessor map, book and page, with public works data in state-plane coordinates, and school data gathered by school attendance area, the building and maintenance of a truly integrated municipal data base presents a formidable task.

III. APPROACHES PERMITTING DEVELOPMENT OF INTEGRATED FILES

A completely integrated data base would have all data relating to any functions of a municipality residing on the same computer system, under the same data management system and organized and indexed to facilitate correlation. This ideal is not attainable, given present organizational structures and computing capabilities in most municipalities. However, if the computerized files of various municipal functions are "properly structured", it will be possible to achieve the same benefits as if there existed a completely integrated municipal data base. In addition, such an approach will not require re-implementation of current applications, but rather leaves the application data base in the control of the function responsible for its primary maintenance and use.

The approach taken is to make use of data, when data files are "properly structured", to develop effectively the results as if there existed a completely integrated data base without requiring that complete integration take place. This should not be construed as an argument <u>against</u> integration. If integration is politically and technically possible, provides required data security, and is economically attractive, it should be implemented. Even with an integrated data base, there will always be decisions which require different groupings of data than those supported by the integrated data base. (There will also remain, in practice, data sources which cannot be integrated.) So, the problem of providing a comprehensive data base from multiple data sources is unavoidable and is not completely solved by an "integrated" data base.

The "proper structuring" required to make data integration possible can be illustrated by example. If one is interested in information about burglaries, and wishes to relate this information to neighborhood conditions, data sources could include police dispatch files, criminal justice arrest files, census data and tax assessor files. Suppose the police dispatch data is used for burglary incidence, and that such data is available in terms of police beats, e.g. the number of burglaries in each beat for each day. If one wishes to use census data for socio-economic information, and if the census tracts and beats have few common boundaries, no small area information is obtainable relating these data sources. Alternatively, if the police dispatch data is captured by the street address of the call, and if a directory exists for the city which will permit identification of the census tract for each street address, then burglaries and socio-economic data can be related at the census tract level.

"Proper structuring" of data files only has meaning with respect to potential uses of the data (i.e. data files are not an end in themselves). If the objective is to offer data to support decision making in a wide range of problem areas, then the data files must be as detailed as possible, within the constraints of economics, privacy and security. The detailed data can then make possible the development of the widest variety of data subsets and aggregations, and is more likely to permit development of the required set of integrated data for a particular decision-making context. An additional requirement is the existence of data elements in each file which will facilitate relating the data to that from different files. (In this paper, geographical references will be singled out as data elements serving this function in municipal files. Common references to account numbers, project numbers or personnel identifiers are other examples of data elements permitting the relating of data from different source files.) A set of files will be called "properly structured" if they contain information permitting the relating of data from different source files so that integrated subsets of data at the appropriate level of detail can be developed to support the requirements of problem solvers.

Because municipal government is a service delivery function, mutual references to geography can often be used to relate data from the diverse files available in municipalities. A powerful file in facilitating the relating of data, based on these common geographical references, is a Geographic Base File (GBF). Functionally, the GBF contains data to support the relating of data from other files to geographical location and also the display of this data on a map. The creation of a GBF for a municipality is a key requirement in the development of a municipal data base from source files. Several different approaches have been taken.

The simplest GBF is a file sometimes called a Property Location Index (PLI) which contains a list of the valid addresses in the municipality and an x,y coordinate for each. This approach is the one used in Lane County, Oregon, and by the Assessor in Santa Clara County , California. To make this more useful, a list of public place and street intersections and their x,y coordinates is appended. With such a GBF it is then possible to automatically convert addresses (in the police call file for example) to x,y coordinates. If the GBF also contains the police beat, census tract, and municipality for each address, then it is very simple computationally to count the number of calls in each beat. Evaluation of calls by census tract would also permit consideration of socio-economic data with the crime data (of course, police officers could also encode calls by beat and census tract, but this approach is liable to significant errors and seems to be a poor use of police manpower).

The most detailed GBF's contain digitized land parcel boundaries, easement locations, building outlines, utility placements, and even topographic information, along with street address information on all parcels and names of all public lands and buildings. This GBF is at the level of detail of surveyor's data, and is suitable for engineering applications and detailed map building. Ottawa, Canada's National Capital Commission [11] has pioneered in the development of this kind of GBF.

The most common GBF at the present time is the result of work by the U.S. Census Bureau in conjunction with the 1970 Census. Using the Metropolitan Map Series, a massive feature labeling and digitization was performed for 200 major metropolitan areas in the United States. The resulting computerized maps were called the DIME (Dual Independent Map Encoding) files [12]. Each entry (record) in the DIME file represents a line segment (a portion of a street segment, railroad, creek, city limit, etc.). Figure 7 shows a sample record and the map data from which the record is derived. The segment has a "From" node and a "To" node, as well as a Left and Right side. Thus, each entry describes its two ends and its two sides. The description of the nodes includes x,y coordinates, produced by the Census Bureau's map digitization. The nodes are labelled as falling on a particular map of the series, and given a sequential number within map and census tract. The other data on each entry is feature identification for the segment and its sides. Each feature is identified by a prefix, name, suffix, type (e.g., North Army Southwest Street); only name and type are required (e.g., Coyote Creek). The description of a side actually describes the adjacent land. The census tract number, the block number, and the place (city) code are included for each side. High and low address ranges for the street segment sides are also given. The records are ordered by feature name and low address (features without addresses have no secondary ordering). Administrative overlays (e.g. beats, census tracts) can be readily defined in terms of segments of this file. Used in combination with "point-in polygon routines", these computerized overlays facilitate development of counts of events in areas of any specified overlay map.

As in the development of any large machine readable file, high startup costs, data errors, and poor standardization have hindered development of GBF's. But the key problem in the development and use of a GBF is editing (corrections and additions).* Because of the startup cost, accuracy, and standardization problems, editing is a key aspect of development. It is particularly important to verify the topological and coordinate accuracy of the file. Even if there were no developmental problems, "geographic" changes, such as new streets or changing area boundaries, make file editing essential to a useful GBF.

The Census Bureau and related efforts have produced programs for off-line creation and batch editing of a DIME file [12-13]. These programs require a digitizer for data entry and take large amounts of computer and clerical time for editing. Although the procedures were used to create 200 GBF's, there has been little editing, and hence little use, of these files. Some cities (e.g., [14]) have developed their own GBF's similar to DIME. These efforts are also characterized by the use of a digitizer and batch computer programs for file creation, and by cumbersome file editing procedures. There have been a few efforts to develop on-line digitization systems, (e.g., [15], and there are experimental systems which could support on-line digitization with visual feedback [16-17]. Yet, none of these systems provide all of the capabilities required for effective GBF creation and editing.

*The Census Bureau uses the word "editing" to mean topological verification, and uses "update" for what we define as editing in this paper.

Conclusions drawn from the IBM study [10] regarding the requirements for interactive GBF editing and maintenance were:

1. There must be a capability for projecting hard copy maps and/or photographs onto the display screen. It must be possible to select arbitrary (contiguous) sections of the maps, and to produce a range of scales.
2. The display system must be able to handle multiple, non-rectangular geographic coordinate systems.
3. The display system must be able to produce both text and lines, with at least three colors for lines (in order to be able to distinguish two maps).
4. The display system must enable selection of any addressable point on the screen, whether or not anything is displayed at that point.
5. The creation and editing functions must include: digitization of base and overlay maps; labeling of points, lines, and polygons in the maps; moving and deleting points and lines; display of any section of the maps, and of specific points, lines and polygons; and checking for topological accuracy.

IV. DATA EXTRACTION

A. Philosophy and Operation

In the previous section, the combination of a GBF and properly structured source files containing geographic references were identified as the basis for offering a problem solver an effectively integrated data base to support decision making. Recent studies of interactive information systems applications in the solution of unstructured problems [4,18,19] have identified the need for reduced subsets of data for supporting the problem solving. Data reduction is required because:

a. the potentially useful data base will be much larger than the data actually used,
b. the user will want access to varying levels of detail in the data base,
c. the relevant subset of data will vary during the problem-solving process,
d. some data (e.g. census and event data such as police calls) may not be compatible at the detail level of the data captured in the source files.

Extraction is a process by which an integrated subset of data is developed from the source files relevant to a particular problem-solving application. Extraction thus provides the user with a capability effectively indistinguishable from a fully integrated data base, without requiring the development of such an integrated data base at the detail level of the source files, i.e. it provides a "virtually" integrated data base.

The extraction approach builds a data base subset from the source files according to a priori specifications for a particular application. Total integration of the source files, and dynamic aggregation and subsetting of the data at the time the data items are required is of course an alternative approach. This approach is not attractive in today's environment because:

a. for any application all the relevant source files would have to be on-line to support conversational interaction,
b. protection of the source files would be more difficult,
c. development of conversational information systems would require additional standardized data structures and codes for the dynamic aggregation and subsetting,
d. better conversational performance is possible when the problem solving accesses a smaller data base.

Clearly the development of a fully-integrated, on-line data base from the source files, solely for problem-solving applications, is not (currently) economical. Such an approach would also require special procedures for keeping the duplicate records current and consistent. With the extraction approach, the subset of data thought to be relevant to the particular problem is developed and made accessable to the problem-solving system in an extracted data base. The subset is an extract from the available source files at the level of detail desired by the decision maker for (that phase of) problem solving. This extracted data base may be thought of as a set of tables. Each table contains values for a set of variables extracted from the source files. For each variable there is one value in the table for each basic unit (e.g. zone, account, employee) used for the problem solving. New variables can be added directly to the extracted data base as an added column of the tables. An example of an extracted data base is shown in Figure 8, for use in crime analysis. The extracted data tables are formed from: source files containing 10 years' data on crimes, land use, and population; a special purpose map of police beat-building-blocks (basic zones); and an extraction specification for computing 20 crime categories and selecting population and number of houses by year. The result is 10 tables (one for each year) giving crime by category, population, and number of houses for each basic zone.

The extraction approach leaves control of the operational source files in the hands of the originating application. The extracted data bases are "snapshots" which are current at the time of their development. The problem solver can re-invoke the extraction process at any time to get a more current extracted data base. This process decouples the data base used in problem solving from the operational files, and assures the problem solver that the data base upon which he makes decisions is under his control. This user control of the extracted data base, and the potential performance advantages offered by access to the smaller extracted data set as compared to access to the total set of data, make the extraction approach attractive even in installations where an integrated data base exists (as with a complete IMIS as in the USAC approach described in Section II). Extraction is simplified with the existence of an integrated data base, because there are then no difficulties with file formats and data conversion.

B. Extraction System Architecture

The architecture of a municipal information system designed using the data extraction philosophy would have three major sets of programs and data bases (e.g. Figure 9). The first set would be the source data files and related programs for data entry, update, and other routine processing. These files should be "properly structured" as defined earlier in this paper. The data base management for these files may be an integrated system, such as IBM's IMS, or a more traditional system such as those provided by IBM's DOS. The second component includes accurate reference files (indices), such as the Geographic Base File, Programs for maintaining these files, and programs for providing the data extraction functions of data matching, subsetting, and aggregation. This component is the key to integrating the data base of source files. The GADS experience indicates that it is possible to develop general purpose programs for the data extraction functions. Essentially, these functions provide integration through user-invoked processing, rather than through the complicated data structures and accompanying processing overhead often found in integrated data base systems. The data extraction programs are the interface between the municipal data base and the third component of the architecture, the extracted data bases and associated decision support system. The GADS analysis and display functions are an example of a decision support system for non-programmer users. A data extraction interface can provide multiple extracted data bases for a single decision support system, or for multiple decision support systems. For example there might be decision support systems for cash management, budget preparation, urban planning, computer-assisted appraisal, crime analysis, etc., all supported by a common extraction interface. The data management techniques for the extracted data bases should be tailored for each decision support system. However, the data access techniques may be the same as those provided for the source data files.

The details of the data extraction architecture and the implementation requirements are beyond the scope of this paper and there will be installation-specific comments. (An extraction implementation is briefly described in the Appendix). There is, however, one general requirement for any data extraction system. This requirement pertains to the data aggregation functions of extraction and can be described by considering examples of the data sources encountered in municipal governments and the kinds of extracted data to be developed from these sources. Consideration here is limited to data which can be related to points or areas. Data related to networks, budget items, part numbers, etc., should be handled in an analogous fashion.

1. Compatible data

This is the easiest, and fortunately the most frequent situation, if data are captured as specified in Section III. The data in source files which can be identified with geographic points (x,y) can be directly related. If the extracted data base is to be relevant to a study of slum dwellings, for example, and if health cases, fire alarms and building code violations are all data sources which are available at the event level, (i.e. by address) then an extracted data table showing incidence of each of these events for specified address can be directly developed. Another frequently used extracted data base is the tabulation of such event data by geographical area, in terms of a specified map. (The extracted data base in Figure 8 is an example of this). Extracted data bases in such cases are obtained by matching coordinates of events to the corresponding map areas (via point-in-polygon processing of the event coordinates against the map boundaries specification). Figure 10 illustrates the extraction and aggregation to relate property (assessment) data and census data to support inquiries at compatible levels (e.g.) blocks or block groups), and further aggregation to support transit planning models.

2. Non-compatible area data

If data is available by areas in the source files, and these areas are not compatible (i.e. one map is not a subset of the other), then the extraction process is more complicated. For a chosen set of variables from the source files, there is a minimum level of aggregation at which an extracted data base is possible. For example, school attendance areas and police beats (and therefore the associated data) may only be compatible at the census tract level, i.e. they may both be (different) finer partitions of census tracts. The extraction process should alert the user to the non-compatibility and display for the user the minimum level of aggregation necessary for compatibility of the data sources of interest, in the form of a map, and permit the user to specify further aggregation from this map as desired.

If the user desires an extracted data base at a detail level finer than is compatible with the data sources given, the user must supply additional information. For example, suppose the user is studying property values vs age distribution of inhabitants, with the age data on citizens available from the census only at census tract levels of aggregation. Compatability exists at the census tract level. Any finer detailed extracted data base, at the city block level for example, could only be developed if the user is willing to make assumptions (such as homogenity of the distribution of population ages in the census tract).

V. SUMMARY AND CONCLUSIONS

The development of information for decision-making in municipalities requires integration of data from the various operational files which are generated in local government. Even when an integrated municipal data base does not exist, it is possible to develop integrated data from properly structured source files in conjunction with a well-maintained Geographic Base File. The current sources of information developed in municipalities, in particular the property data of the tax assessor function and the operating files of various service delivery functions, provide a rich source of information, augmented by special collections such as the U.S. Census.

Data Extraction is the process of developing integrated data subsets from diverse source files to support interactive problem solving. Extraction provides the interface to large data bases of source files and provides data description, subsetting and aggregation functions. Our experience with GADS has shown that data extraction is useful when the user or problem characteristics require access to varying amounts, detail, and selection of data, and conversational (rapid response) interaction with a decision support system. These characteristics are likely to be encountered when designing decision support systems for nonprogrammer, professional users working on unstructured problems. The data extraction interface matches the functional and response time requirements of interactive decision support, can be implemented on a variety of computer system configurations, and can reduce the operating costs of the decision support system.

Because data extraction operations can produce multiple extracted data bases, with different structures, a single data extraction interface can support multiple decision support systems. In addition, existing decision support systems can be supported and enhanced by data extraction without major program revisions.

APPENDIX: An Extraction System Implementation

A project in the IBM Research Division has developed an interactive Geo-data Analysis and Display System (GADS as a vehicle for studying interactive problem solving [1-4]. GADS supports nonprogrammer users solving unstructured problems where the relevant data can be related to a geographic location. Examples of the problems for which GADS has been used include: land use planning, police manpower allocation, school districting, and commercial site location. The need for data extraction was recognized during the first studies of the use of GADS. In particular, the need for data aggregated to a variety of geographic levels (e.g., block, police beat, census tract, neighborhood), and changing data needs expressed by users indicated the inadequacies of the static, special purpose data base and the one-level, integrated data base approaches.

GADS data extraction is configured essentially as shown in Figure 9. The extraction implemented in GADS is limited to compatible event data. There is a requirement that each record of each file in the large data base contain a geographic code (such as an address, x,y coordinates or block number) so that extracted data can be related to points, lines, and polygons on a map. A utility program is provided to transform geographic codes into x,y coordinates if necessary for data extraction or display. A data base developed by extraction is a table; an example is shown on Figure 8. Adding another crime type, acres of commercial land use, or re-aggregating by census tracts would take only a few minutes.

In the GADS implementation the large data base management system is a special purpose one designed to handle fixed format files with no hierarchies or repeating groups. Simultaneous access to multiple files, and shared access to single files are not supported. Multiple file extractions are handled by consecutive extractions from the individual files. Sequential and direct access I/O are provided. Character, fixed binary, packed decimal, and floating point (binary) data representations can be used. The entire large data base is stored on disk, and there is a utility for loading files from tapes.

Figure 11 gives examples of the data description and subsetting capabilities. The data description implementation allows different formats to be used for the same file or the same formats to be used for different files (Figure 11a). Seven data types are allowed. The subsetting language includes constructs for: subsetting based on any arithmetic or logical combination of the items in a file, creating of new items, conditional subsetting or creation (IF, THEN, ELSE), and function calls (Figure 11b.). Results from subsetting can be displayed as lists (Figure 11c) or as locations on a map (Figure 11d). Using the display capabilities, two dimensional subsetting is possible. That is, the user can draw a polygon on the screen, and select only those elements of a file whose location is within that polygon. This facility is much more user-oriented than algebraic specifications for subsetting, and other graphic subsetting operators would be useful (e.g., display all the crimes of the same type as the one being pointed at).

The aggregation operations in the implementation are restricted to forming the extracted data base for the GADS analysis and display functions. This data base is aggregated by areas of a map. It is stored on disk, and is accessed by column name.

GADS is implemented in FORTRAN, but the data extraction components were implemented in PL/I because of its larger set of data types, and better functional suitability for the extraction tasks. The combination system runs on the IBM S/360 or S/370 series under the Time Sharing Option (TSO). The combination requires 220K bytes of main storage. Separating extraction reduces the main storage requirement to about 120K. The user terminals may be IBM 2250s or storage tube display terminals. The I/O time from the large data base, and the data rate to the terminal are the limiting facotrs in extraction response times (i.e. selection and aggregation times are negligible compared to I/O times). Although five minutes may be required to list or display an entire file, the user can see the results unfolding (e.g. the selected items are listed as they are selected). Thus users seem willing to wait during extraction. After all, the batch mode equivalent capabilities have response times of days, and manual methods have response times of weeks or months.

REFERENCES

[1] P. E. Mantey, J. L. Bennett, E. D. Carlson, Information for Problem Solving: The Development of an Interactive Geographic Information System. IEEE Int. Conf. on Communication, Vol. II. Seattle, Wash. June 1973.

[2] E. J. Cristiani, R. J. Evey, R. E. Goldman, P. E. Mantey. "An Interactive System for Aiding Evaluation of Local Government Policies," IEEE Transactions on Systems, Man & Cybernetics, Vol. SMC-3, No. 2, March 1973, pp. 141-146.

[3] E. D. Carlson, J. L. Bennett, G. M. Giddings and P. E. Mantey. "The Design and Evaluation of an Interactive Geo-data Analysis and Display System," Proceedings of the IFIP Congress 74, International Federation for Information Processing, Stockholm, August 1974. North Holland Publishing Company, Amsterdam, 1974.

[4] E. D. Carlson and J. A. Sutton, A Case Study of Non-programmer Interactive Problem-Solving, IBM Research Report, RJ 1382, IBM Research Laboratory, San Jose, California, April 1974.

[5] T. R. Hammer, R. E. Coughlin, E. T. Horn IV, "The Effect of a Large Urban Park on Real Estate Values," Journal of the American Institute of Planners, Vol. 40, No. 4, July 1974, pp. 274-277.

[6] "City Hall's Approaching Revolution in Service Delivery," Nation's Cities, January 1972.

[7] Concepts of an Urban Management Information System," a Report to the City of New Haven, Connecticut, by Advanced Systems Development Division, IBM Corporation, Yorktown, January 1967.

[8] A Municipal Information and Decision System. University of Southern California, School of Public Administration, 1968.

[9] R. L. Stickrod and L. C. Martin. Data Processing: Analysis of Costs, Benefits, and Resource Allocations. Lane County, Oregon, Management Report, February, 1973.

[10] G. M. Giddings and E. D. Carlson, An Interactive System for Creating, Editing and Displaying a Geographic Base File. IBM Research Report, IBM Research Laboratory, San Jose, California, 1973.

[11] D. C. Symons, A Parcel Geocoding System for Urban and Rural Information, Ottawa, Ontario, National Capital Commission, 1970.

[12] U. S. Bureau of the Census, Census Use Study, The DIME Geocoding System Report No. 4, Washington D.C., 1970.

[13] U. S. Bureau of the Census, Census Use Study, The DIME Editing System Washington D.C., 1970.

[14] R. Jull, Geo-modeling: A Local Approach, Eugene, Oregon, Lane Council of Governments, 1972.

[15] R. D. Hogan, Remote Graphic Terminal and Urban Geographic Information System Demonstation, Gaithersburg, Maryland, IBM Federal Systems Center, 1968.

[16] R. D. Merrill, "Representation of Contours and Regions for Efficient Computer Search," Communications of the ACM, Vol. 16, No. 2, February 1973, pp. 69-82.

[17] B. V. Saderholm, "Paper 'Keyboard' Runs Experimental IBM System," IBM Research Division Press Release, Yorktown Heights, N. Y., March 8, 1973.

[18] R. M. Cyert, H. A. Simon, and D. B. Throw. Observation of a Business Decision. Journal of Business, 29, (1956), 237-248.

[19] D. M. S. Peace and R. S. Easterby. The Evaluation of User Interaction with Computer-based Management Information Systems. Human Factors, 15, April 1973, pp. 163-177.

PARCEL NUMBER	ADDRESS	YEAR CONST	LOT SIZE	FLOOR AREA	ASSESSED VALUE
123-06-174	100 ABBYWOOD CT.	1962	7145	1675	28000
123-06-175	102 ABBYWOOD CT.	1962	6965	1650	29000
123-06-176	104 ABBYWOOD CT.	1962	6500	1600	27000
123-06-177	106 ABBYWOOD CT.	1961	7125	1650	25000
123-06-150	112 ABINATE LN	1960	7200	1800	35000
123-06-151	114 ABINATE LN.	1960	7185	1800	37000
123-06-152	116 ABINATE LN.	1960	6995	1700	30000
123-06-153	117 ABINATE LN.	1960	6955	1850	31000
123-06-154	120 ABINATE LN.	1860	7095	1900	32000
123-06-158	132 ABINATE LN.	1961	7155	1750	29000
123-06-160	111 ABINATE LN.	1960	7005	1975	34000
123-06-161	113 ABINATE LN.	1960	6885	1650	27000
123-06-162	115 ABINATE LN.	1960	7100	1750	30000
123-06-163	117 ABINATE LN.	1960	7055	1780	30000
123-06-184	31 AFTON CT.	1960	7020	1650	29000
123-06-185	33 AFTON CT.	1960	7165	1600	27000
123-06-186	35 AFTON CT.	1961	7190	1775	29000

Figure 1. Tabular display of assessment data

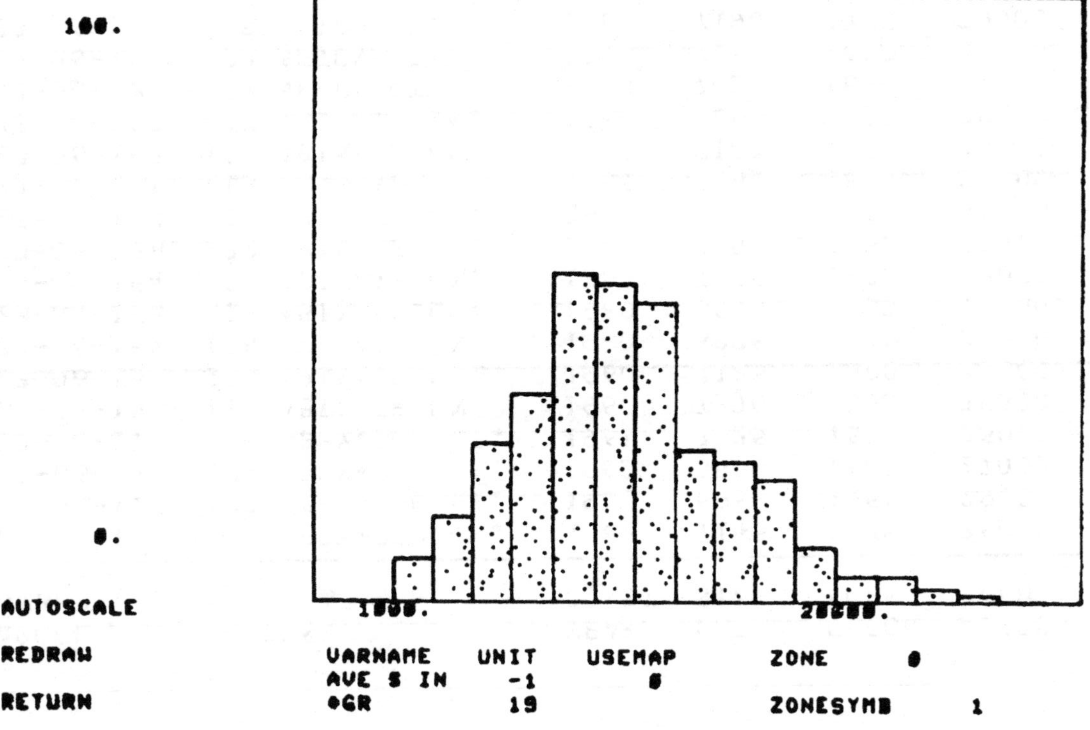

Figure 2. Histogram display of housing values

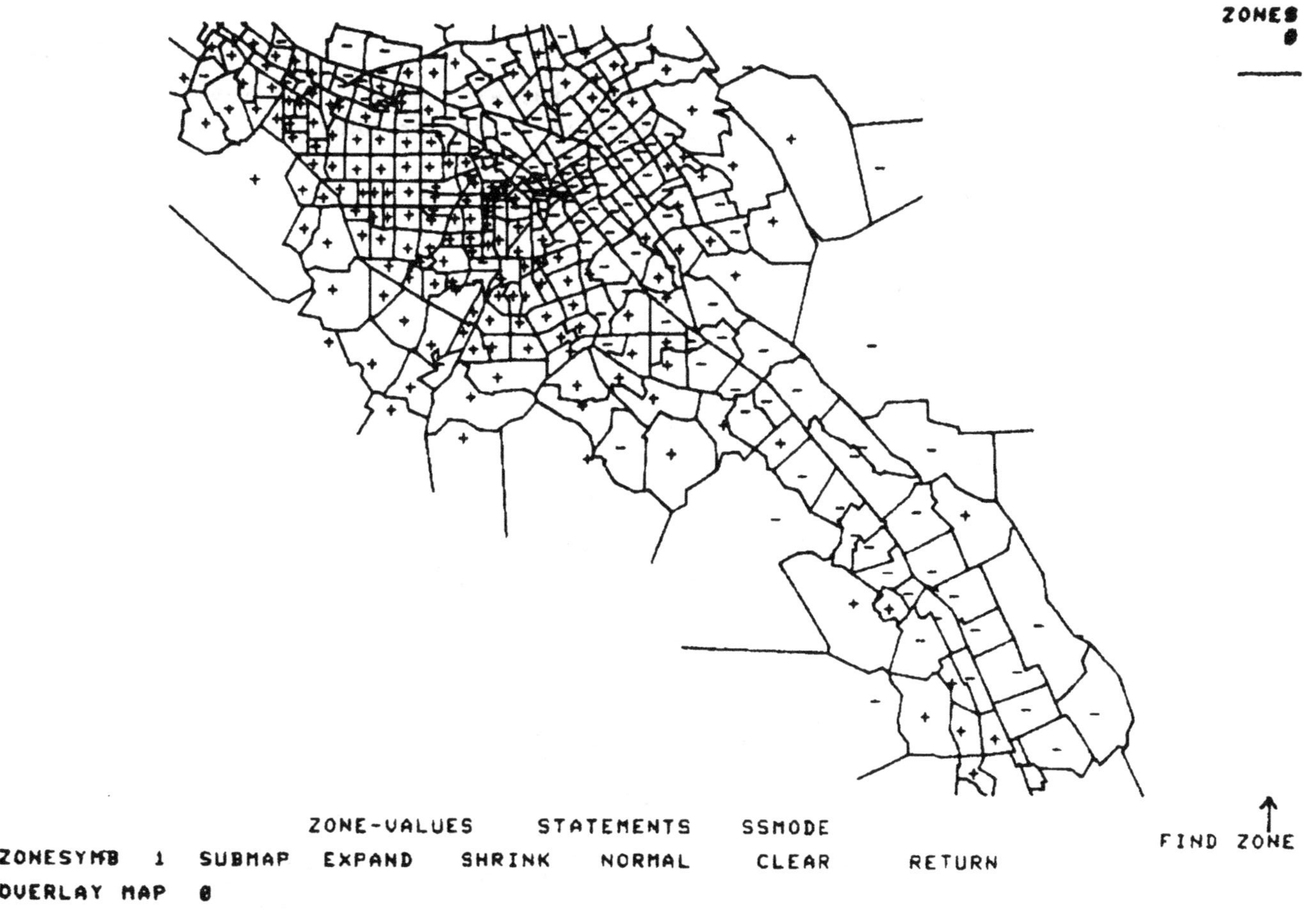

Figure 3a. Map display of relative housing values

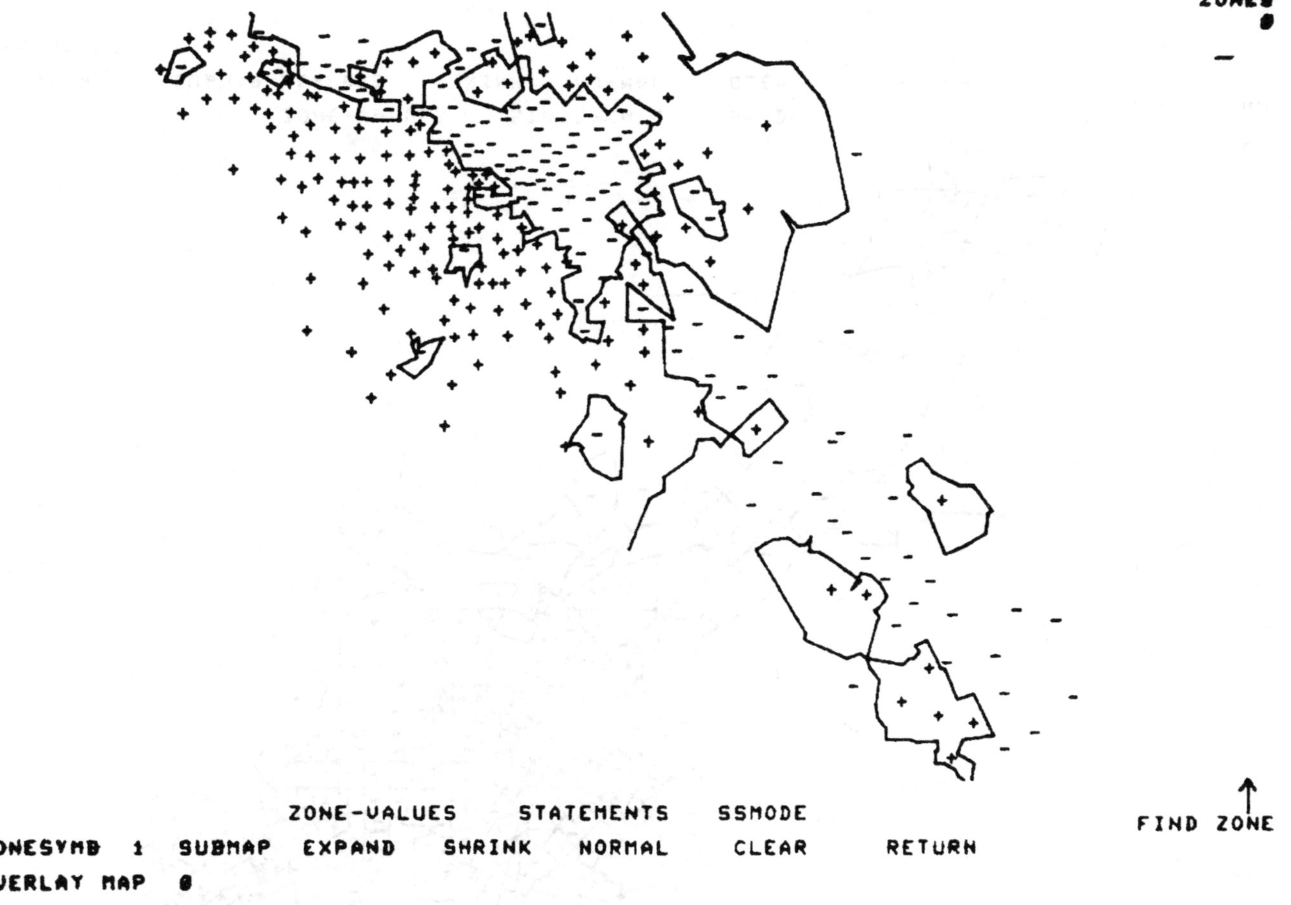

Figure 3b. Simplified display of housing values

AVE $ IN   AVERAGE INCOME PER HOUSEHOLD

ACCESS $ ACCESSABILITY TO DISPOSABLE INCOME

ACCESS   ACCESSABILITY TO EMPLOYMENT

AVLAND-S   ACRES AVAILABLE FOR SINGLE FAMILY DEVELOPMENT
AVLAND-M   ACRES AVAILABLE FOR MULTIPLE FAMILY DEVELOPMENT
AVLAND-C   ACRES AVAILABLE FOR COMMERCIAL DEVELOPMENT
AVLAND-I   ACRES AVAILABLE FOR INDUSTRIAL DEVELOPMENT

GROW NXS   GROWTH FACTOR IN SINGLE FAMILY
GROW NXM   GROWTH FACTOR IN MULTIPLE FAMILY

ODWU/A-S   NO SINGLE FAMILY DWELLING UNITS PER RESIDENTIAL
ODWU/A-M   NO MULTIPLE FAMILY DWELLING UNITS PER RESIDENTI
ODWU/A-T   TOTAL NO DWELLING UNITS PER ACRE OF RESIDENTIAL

EMP-MFG   NO. OF EMPLOYEES WORKING IN MANUFACTURING
EMP-WHOL   NO. OF EMPLOYEES WORKING IN WHOLESALE AND TRUCK
EMP-COMM   NO. OF EMPLOYEES WORKING IN COMMERCIAL(RETAIL)
EMP-TC&U   NO. OF EMPLOYEES WORKING IN TRANS, COMMUN,AND U
EMP-GOVT   NO. OF EMPLOYEES WORKING IN GOVERNMENT
EMP-TOTL   TOTAL NO OF EMPLOYEES

EMPDEN-C   NO. COMMERCIAL EMPLOYEES PER ACRE OF COMMERCIAL

HHOLD0-6   NO. OF HOUSEHOLDS WITH INCOME: 0- 6000
HHLD6-10   NO. OF HOUSEHOLDS WITH INCOME: 6000-10000
HHLD1015   NO. OF HOUSEHOLDS WITH INCOME:10000-15000
HHLD15+   NO. OF HOUSEHOLDS WITH INCOME:15000+

ISHOPCTR   ZONES OF ANTICIPATED SHOPPING CENTERS
IBAY   ZONES TREATED AS BAYLANDS

OCDWUN-S   NO. OF EXISTING SINGLE FAMILY DWELLING UNITS
OCDWUN-M   NO. OF MULTIPLE FAMILY DWELLING UNITS
OCDWUN-T   TOTAL NO. OF SINGLE AND MULTIPLE FAMILY DWELLIN

OCLAND-S   ACRES OCCUPIED BY SINGLE FAMILY DWELLINGS
OCLAND-M   ACRES OCCUPIED BY MULTIPLE FAMILY DWELLINGS
OCLAND-C   ACRES OCCUPIED BY COMMERCIAL DEVELOPMENT
OCLAND-I   ACRES OCCUPIED BY INDUSTRIAL DEVELOPMENT

PRODEN-S   PROJECTED DENSITY FOR SINGLE FAMILY DEVELOPMENT
PRODEN-M   PROJECTED DENSITY FOR MULTIPLE-FAMILY DEVELOPME

POPUL-S   TOTAL POPULATION IN SINGLE FAMILY DWELLINGS
POPUL-M   TOTAL POPULATION IN MULTIPLE FAMILY DWELLINGS
POPUL-T   TOTAL POPULATION

POP/HH-S   POPULATION PER HOUSEHOLD FOR SINGLE FAMILY DWEL
POP/HH-M   POPULATION PER HOUSEHOLD FOR MULTIPLE FAMILY DW
POP/HH-T   POPULATION PER HOUSEHOLD FOR ALL DWELLINGS

RES-LAND   RESERVED LAND-NOT AVAILABLE FOR CURRENT DEVELOP

SLOPE   PERCENT OF LAND WITH LESS THAN 10% SLOPE

TSKTR   CHANGE FACTOR IN INTRAZONAL TRAVEL TIME

DISP $IN   DISPOSABLE INCOME PER HOUSEHOLD

SEWER   SEWER SERVICE DISTRICT
FLOOD   FLOOD CONTROL AREA

Figure 4. Land use/transportation planning data base [2]

RESIDENTIAL FACT SHEET

DISTRICT (AC16)______ NEIGHBORHOOD (AC17)______ APN (AA01)____________

TRACT (AC06)______ LOT______ BLOCK______ SITUS (AA10)____________________ SHEET______ OF______ SHEETS

RECORD DATA			LAND ATTRIBUTES			BUILDING DATA			COST DATA		
App'l. Date	AC10		Width Ft.	AI01		Year Built	AJ01		Quality Class	AC18	
Appraiser No.	AB02		Depth Ft.	AI02		Eff. Year	AC19		Total Living Area	AC05	
Site Use Code	AB01		Sq. Ft. (Actual)	AC04		REL.	AJ02		1st Flr. Area	AK01	
Zone	AC01		Sq. Ft. (Useable)	AI04		Dining Room	AJ03		2nd Flr. Area	AK02	
Total Prop. Val.	AE01		Typical	AI07	N^1 Y^2	Fam.-Den-Rumpus	AJ04		2nd Flr. Factor	AK03	
Land Value	AB04		Irregular	AI08	N^1 Y^2	No. of Bedrooms	AJ05		3rd Flr. Area	AK04	
Imp. Value	AB06		Cul-De-Sac	AI09	N^1 Y^2	No. of Baths	AJ06		3rd Flr. Factor	AK05	
New Lot Value	AE02		Non-Thru-St.	AI10	N^1 Y^2	Util. Rooms	AJ07		Bsmt. Area	AK06	
SALES DATA			St.-Frontage	AI11	N^1 Y^2	Total Rooms	AC21		Bsmt. Factor	AK07	
Rec'd. Date	AA13		Corner	AI12	N^1 Y^2	Funct. Plan	AJ08	P^1 A^2 G^3	Addn. Area	AK08	
Sales Price	AC12		Alley	AI13	N^1 Y^2	Condition	AJ09	P^1 A^2 G^3	Addn. Factor	AK09	
Confirmed	AE03	N^1 Y^2	Util. U./G.	AI14	N^1 Y^2	Workmanship	AJ10	P^1 A^2 G^3	Gar. Area	AK10	
TEMPORARY VALUE			Curbs & Gutters	AI15	N^1 Y^2	Stg. Space	AJ11	P^1 A^2 G^3	Carport Area	AK11	
Part Compl.	AC20	N^1 Y^2	Sidewalks	AI16	N^1 Y^2	Heating (Ducted)	AJ12	N^1 Y^2	Carport Factor	AK12	
Board Action	AF02	N^1 Y^2	St. Lights	AI17	N^1 Y^2	Cooling (Ducted)	AJ13	N^1 Y^2	Pch. Area	AK13	
Other	AF03	N^1 Y^2	Common Green	AI18	N^1 Y^2	Gar.	AJ14	N^1 Y^2	Pch. Factor	AK14	
IMMEDIATE AREA			Common Rec.	AI19	N^1 Y^2	Gar. Conv.	AJ15	N^1 Y^2	Fireplace Cost	AK15	
Mkt. Demand	AG01	P^1 A^2 G^3	H. & B. Use	AI20	N^1 Y^2	Carport	AJ16	N^1 Y^2	A. C. Cost	AK16	
Trend	AG02	P^1 A^2 G^3	Sewer	AI21	N^1 Y^2	Patio	AJ17	N^1 Y^2	Patio Area	AK17	
Trans.	AG03	D^1 S^2 G^3	View	AI22	N^1 Y^2	Decking	AJ18	N^1 Y^2	Patio Factor	AK18	
Res. Area	AG05	N^1 Y^2	View Qual.	AI23	P^1 A^2 G^3	Pool	AJ19	N^1 Y^2	Pool Area	AK19	
Single Fam.	AG06	N^1 Y^2	Traffic Flow	AI24	H^1 A^2 L^3	Fence	AJ20	N^1 Y^2	Pool Extras	AK20	
TOTAL PROPERTY			Water Front	AI25	N^1 Y^2	Guest House	AJ21	N^1 Y^2	Misc. Cost	AK21	
Arch. Attr.	AH01	P^1 A^2 G^3	Beach Front	AI26	N^1 Y^2	Fireplace	AJ22	N^1 Y^2	Misc. Struct. Cost	AK22	
Prop. Improved	AH02	N^1 Y^2	Docking Rights	AI27	N^1 Y^2	Built-Ins	AJ23	N^1 Y^2	TOPOGRAPHY		
Prop. Lot Util.	AH03	N^1 Y^2	Horses	AI28	N^1 Y^2	Stru. Failure	AJ24	L^1 M^2 H^3	Grade	AL01	B^1 A^2 E^3
Landscape	AH04	P^1 A^2 G^3				Tile Roof	AJ25	N^1 Y^2	Bank	AL02	N^1 Y^2
Nuisance Infl.	AH05	N^1 Y^2	FIELD USE ONLY - DO NOT ENCODE						Slope	AL03	N^1 Y^2
Condominium	AH06	N^1 Y^2	% Base Lot	A130					Other	AL04	N^1 Y^2

AO-225 Ventura County Assessor

Figure 5. Field work sheet for appraisal data

Office of the County Assessor
201 County Administration Building
70 West Hedding Street
San Jose, California 95114
299-3941 Area Code 408

County of Santa Clara

California

Date Recorded ________________

Recorder's Deed #________________

Property Description #________________

1. Our records indicate you purchased this property.

   What was the full price? ________________

   a. Amount of cash down payment: $________________

   b. Please enter details concerning any balance:

      (1) 1st Deed of Trust $________________ at____________% interest
          Duration of Loan________years

      (2) 2nd Deed of Trust $________________ at____________% interest
          Duration of Loan________years

   c. Was a trade involved? Yes__________ No__________

   d. Outstanding Improvement Bonds against property $________________

   e. Did price include personal property? Yes__________ No__________
      If yes, please estimate value of such property $________________

   f. If this is income property, please enter the monthly gross income as if it were 100% occupied $________________

2. Remarks: Please enter on the reverse side or by attachment any information you feel may help us to make a fair appraisal of your property.

3. If you would like mail concerning this property sent to a different address from the one above, please indicate below.*

4. If there are questions regarding this questionnaire please contact the Assessment Standards Division at 299-3941.

5. See Reverse Side.

____
Signature of Owner

____
Telephone Number

____
Date

*________________
Address

____
City, State, Zip

7047 REV. 11/71

Figure 6. Assessor's questionnaire for financial data

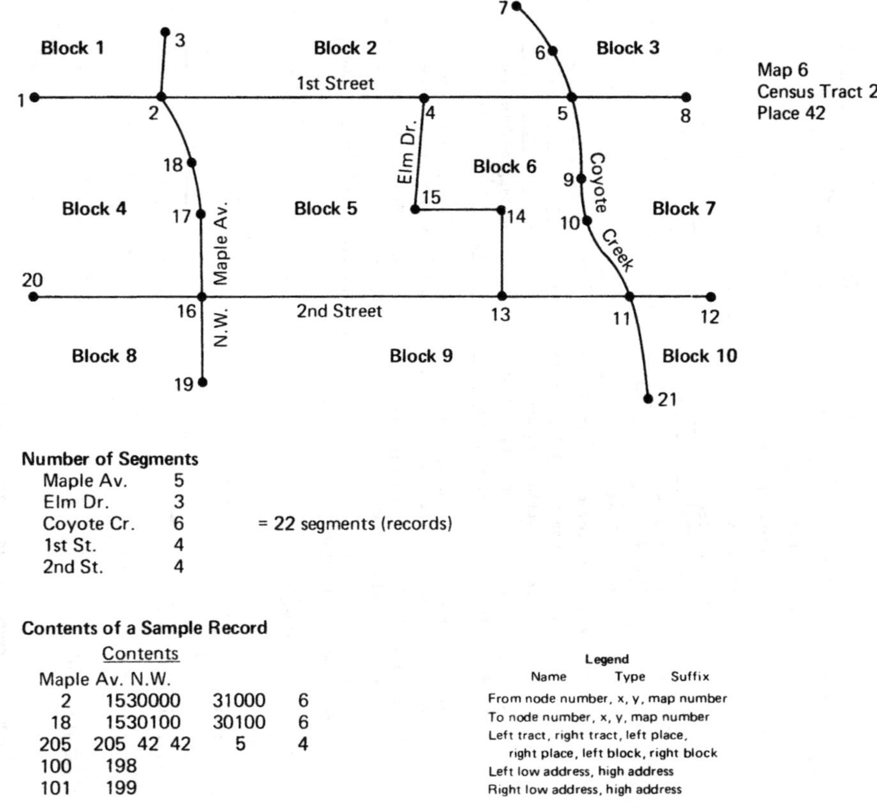

Figure 7. 'DIME' geographic base file structure

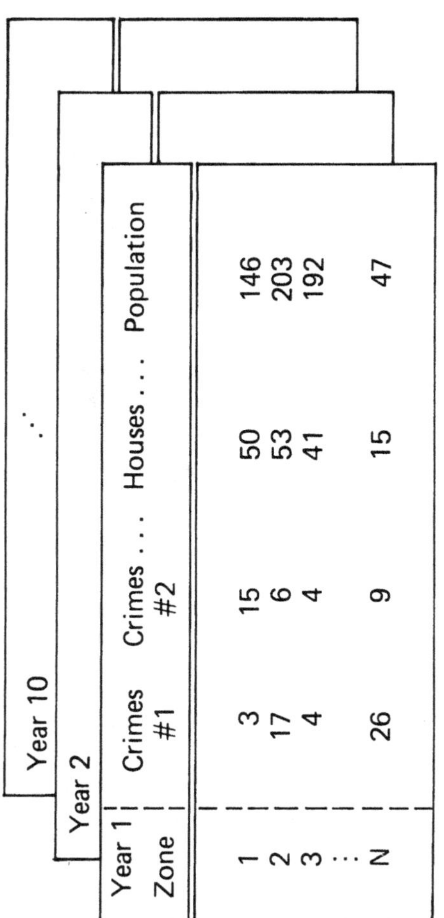

Zone	Crimes #1	Crimes . . . #2	Houses . . .	Population
1	3	15	50	146
2	17	6	53	203
3	4	4	41	192
⋮				
N	26	9	15	47

Figure 8. Example of tables in extracted data base

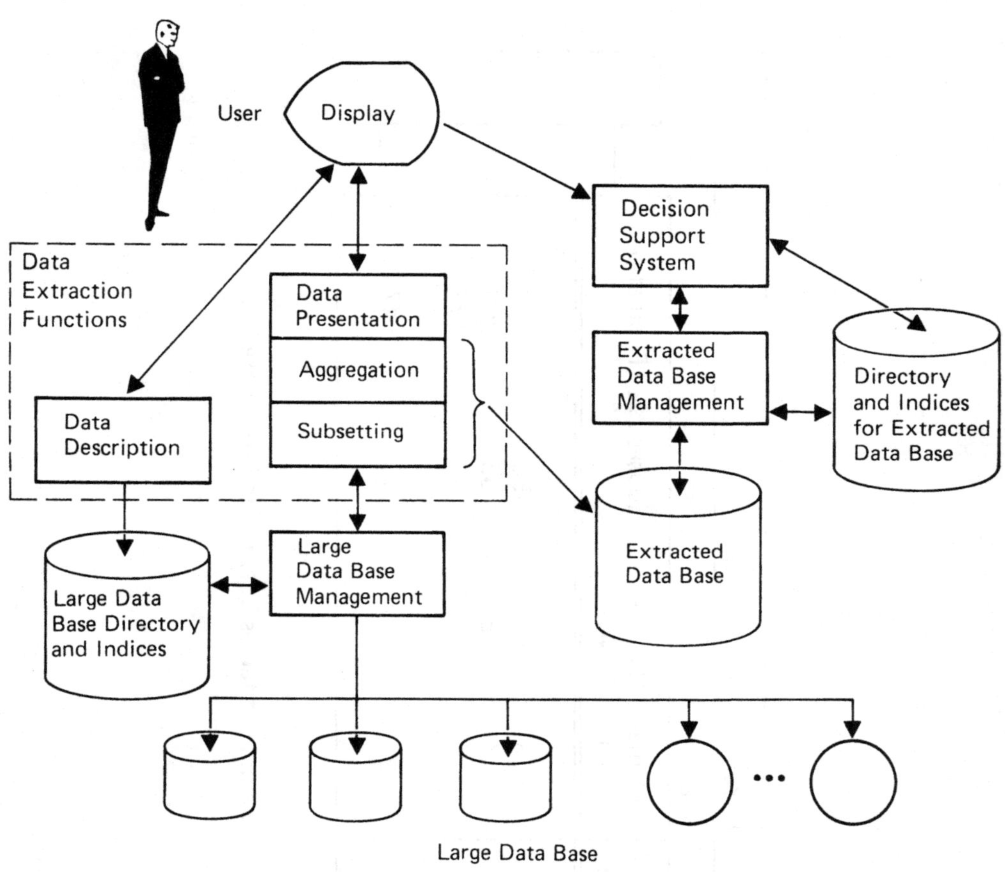

Figure 9. Interactive data extraction and problem solving system

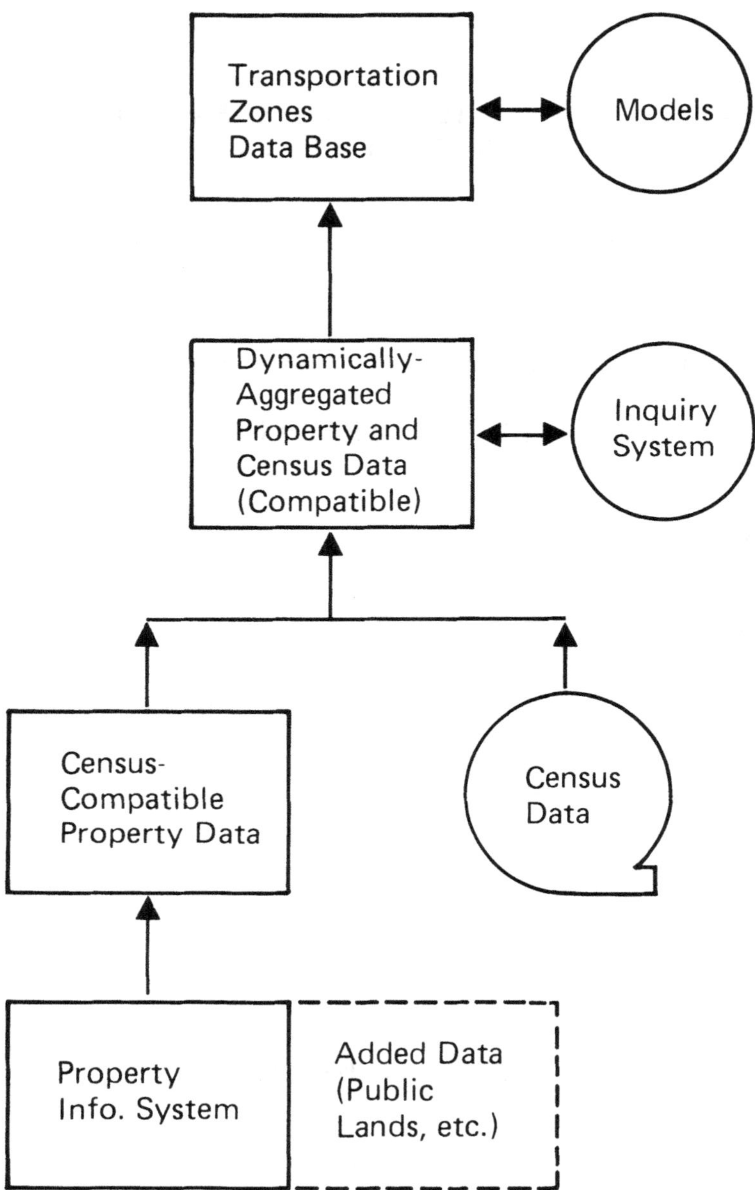

Figure 10. Extraction and aggregation relating property and census data

FUNCTIONS AVAILABLE FOR EXTRACTING
DATA FROM EVENT FILE

CREATE AND EDIT

DATA FORMAT DESCRIPTIONS

SELECTION SPECIFICATIONS

BUILD-UNIT SPECIFICATIONS

VIEW EVENTS ON MAP

LIST EVENTS

BUILD GADS UNITS

RETURN (TO GADS MAIN MENU)

Figure 11. Extraction system functions

```
                    CREATE AND EDIT DATA DESCRIPTIONS

EMP 82     IBM EMPLOYEE FILE WITH X,Y
MATCH CH 13 1       MATCH KEY FROM UNIMATCH
STNO CH 5           STREET NUMBER
BLANK1 CH 1
STNAME CH 16        STREET NAME
STTYPE CH 2         STREET TYPE
CITY CH 16          NAME
ZIP CI 5            CODE
BLANK2 CH 1
X CI 7              COORDINATE
BLANK3 CH 1
Y CI 6              COORDINATE
-
-
-
-
-
-
-
-
-
                          SCRATCHPAD

INPUT MODE          GET PAGE    6       RESTORE      DELETE LINE
REPLACE MODE =ON    VIEW TITLES                      INSERT BLANK LINE
CHECK               SAVE PAGE  ___                   COPY LINE DOWN
RETURN              REDRAW            ERASE             PRINT
```

Figure 11a. Data description function

```
                    CREATE AND EDIT SELECTIONS

EMP
_
_
_
IF X<=0 OR X>2000000 THEN X=0 ;

IF Y<=0 OR Y>1000000 THEN Y=0;

SELECT WHERE ZIP = 95125
_
_
_
_
_
_
_
_
_
_
                              SCRATCHPAD

INPUT MODE    =ON   GET PAGE    15        RESTORE      DELETE LINE
REPLACE MODE        VIEW TITLES                        INSERT BLANK LINE
CHECK               SAVE PAGE   15                     COPY LINE DOWN
RETURN              REDRAW              ERASE             PRINT
```

Figure 11b. Data selection function

```
MT000002      00100   GLENEYRIE            SANJOSE   95125   1591723   298204
MT000004      01245   GLENEYRIE         AV SANJOSE   95125   1590839   297581
MT000004      01600   GLENFIELD         DR SANJOSE   95125   1592561   285700
MT000004      01631   GLENFIELD         DR SANJOSE   95125   1592377   285847
MT000004      01161   GLENN             AV SANJOSE   95125   1591593   296320
MT000004      01148   GLENN             AV SANJOSE   95125   1591758   296376
MT000004      01487   GLENPINE          DR SANJOSE   95125                  0
             0
MT000004      01538   GLENPINE          DR SANJOSE   95125                  0
             0
MT000004      01499   GLENPINE          DR SANJOSE   95125                  0
             0
MT000004      01754   GLENUNA           AV SANJOSE   95125   1596140   293698
MT000002      01930   GLENUNA              SANJOSE   95125   1596628   292822
MT000004      01742   GLENUNA           AV SANJOSE   95125   1596140   293698
MT000002      01348   GLENWOOD             SANJOSE   95125   1592291   293314
MT000004      01551   GRACE             AV SANJOSE   95125   1587514   293085
MT000004      01482   GRACE             AV SANJOSE   95125   1587719   294182
MT000004      01623   GRACE             AV SANJOSE   95125   1587514   293085
MT000004      01500   GRACE             AV SANJOSE   95125   1587687   293232
MT000204      01550   GUADALAJARA       AV SANJOSE   95125   1592633   267304
MT000004      01460   HAMILTON          WY SANJOSE   95125   1591109   292471
MT000004      01880   HARMIL            WY SANJOSE   95125   1596290   293944
MT000004      01024   HAZELWOOD         AV SANJOSE   95125   1596056   292681
MT000004      01479   HERVEY            LN SANJOSE   95125   1596632   297004
MT000004      01514   HERVEY            LN SANJOSE   95125   1597340   296305
MT000004      01502   HICKS             AV SANJOSE   95125   1591625   293923
MT000004      02243   HICKS             AV SANJOSE   95125   1592833   289482
GRADDRESS 00  01656   HILLSDALE         AV SANJOSE   95125                  0
             0
MT000004      00947   HUMMINGBIRD       DR SANJOSE   95125   1599186   289507
MT000004      00910   HUMMINGBIRD       DR SANJOSE   95125   1599225   289352
MT000004      00870   HUMMINGBIRD       DR SANJOSE   95125   1599225   289352
MT000004      00910   HUMMINGBIRD       DR SANJOSE   95125   1599225   289352
MT000004      01674   HUSTED            AV SANJOSE   95125   1591335   285412
MT000004      01436   HUSTED            AV SANJOSE   95125   1594501   287659

 LISTING: FILE = EMP      SELECTION = EMP              RETURN
 USING P1P2: NO                                        PAGE FORWARD
                                                           PAGE     5
```

Figure 11c. Listing of data selected

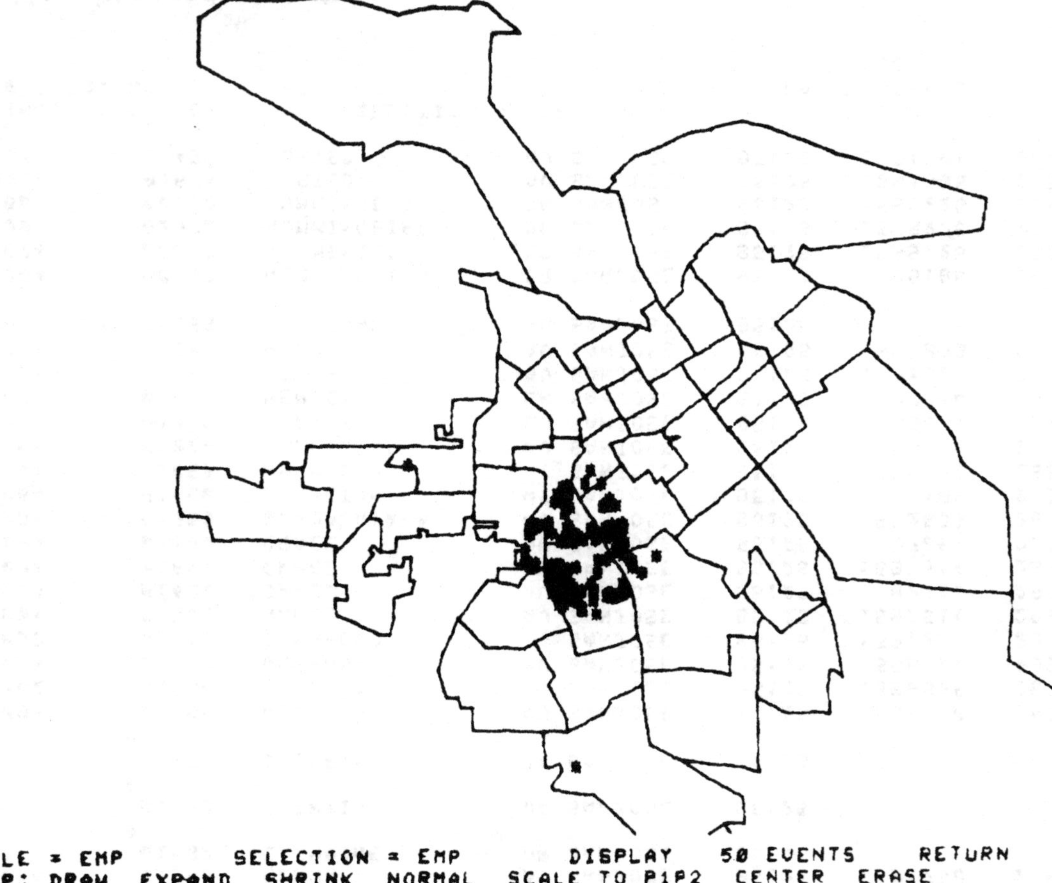

Figure 11d. Map showing location of selected data

DATA BASE USER LANGUAGES FOR THE NON-PROGRAMMER

Peter C. Lockemann
Fakultaet fuer Informatik, Universitaet Karlsruhe
D-75 Karlsruhe 1

Abstract

In light of the necessary investments, commercially available data base systems usually offer comparatively general-purpose interfaces. These are suitable only for the data base specialist. In order for a data base system to attract non-programmer users, interfaces must be provided that approximate the special user terminology and conceptualizations. If, in particular, these users form a heterogeneous group, a variety of interfaces will be required. Questions of interest are then the extent to which user interfaces should be standardized, the techniques which allow rapid implementation of new more specialized interfaces, or the procedure for selecting the most suitable interface for a given problem. Based on the concept of hierarchy of abstract machines, the paper presents a possible approach to the solution of these questions. Three examples will be introduced to critically examine the concept and demonstrate some of its merits and shortcomings.

1 Introduction

The success or failure of a data base system, no matter how well-conceived it may appear to the author's mind, is ultimately decided by the users the system is supposed to serve. This aspect is often overlooked by system planners who devote almost their entire effort towards organizational problems such as analyzing the informational needs of an institution or organization, the current status of information flow within the organization and the necessary improvements to it. From the analysis a number of requirements are derived such as the extent of information integration, time characteristics, information system structure, adaptation of the organizational structure, relinquishment of old resources and provision of new ones. All too often, much less attention is being paid to the individuals who must use the system. They are simply expected to appreciate the needs of the organization and to adapt most willingly to the new environment.

Human nature, however, is conservative. Human individuals will cling to the same terminology and methodology and try to solve the same problems unless and until one can make a most convincing point for reorientation. In many cases data base systems are not even introduced to solve new kinds of problems. Rather they are supposed to improve the solution to existing and already well-understood problems, or at least use these problems as a point of departure. Under these circumstances there is no reason why users should be burdened with radical changes in style.

Unfortunately, for the manufacturer of a data base system this is just one side of a coin. For him, the development and implementation of a data base system represents a large investment which he can only justify by corresponding sales figures. This precludes him from attending to each of a large variety of individual user needs but compels him to offer general-purpose interfaces. On the other hand it is these general-purpose interfaces that prove repugnant to many a potential user who has his own special terminology, conceptualizations and application problems.

In order to resolve the dilemma, techniques must be developed that permit the adaptation of a data base system to various user needs. In particular, the solutions should address themselves to the following questions.

(i) How can user language interfaces be separated from the operational and management characteristics of the data base system?

(ii) Are there any techniques that allow, in a systematic way, for the rapid implementation of a user language according to given specifications?

(iii) To which extent is it economically feasible to construct and stockpile "off-the-shelf" user languages?

(iv) Given a set of language specifications, under which conditions can one build upon an already existing user language? Can one define a relation on user languages that formalizes these conditions and determines the amount of effort required?

To answer these questions we shall define a hierarchical relationship between user languages. The nature of the relationship will be discussed in some detail. A number of examples will be introduced to explicate the approach and to point out its merits as well as some of its present shortcomings. The discussion is intended basically for non-procedural interactive languages.

2 Hierarchies of user languages

2.1 Concepts

The hierarchy of language interfaces shall be defined as follows [Kr 75]:

- Each interface is defined in terms of a ("lower") interface, and may itself serve as the basis for definition of a ("higher") interface.
- There is exactly one interface which cannot be defined in terms of another interface and hence serves as the ultimate basis for all other interfaces.

Such a hierarchy of interfaces may be graphically represented in the form of a tree where each node corresponds to a particular interface.

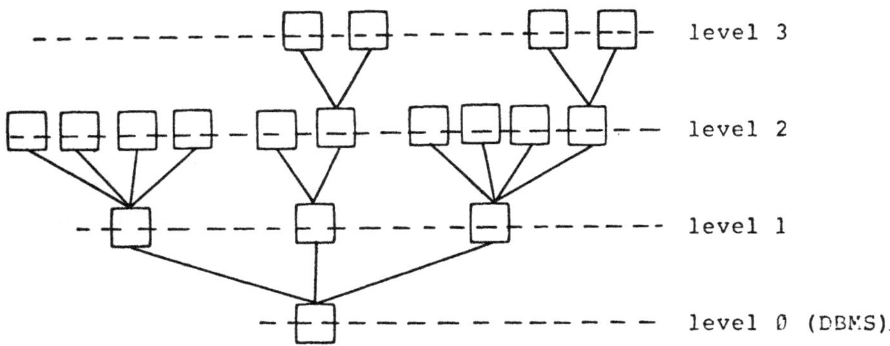

figure 1

The hierarchy must be chosen such that it reflects a hierarchy of users. Level 0 corresponds to the data base specialist, while level 3 might cater to a user completely untrained in computer affairs.

The previous questions can now be restated with a little bit more precision.

(i) Can all fundamental operational and management functions be solved underneath the basis on level 0?

(ii) What are the formal criteria that allow to construct a hierarchy by defining new languages in terms of existing ones?

(iii) Up to which level in the tree should interfaces be standardized?

(iv) Suppose a given language specification is represented as a node. Can a path to an existing node be constructed, and the length of the path be "measured"? Can one determine the path with minimum length? If the path is too long, should intermediate nodes be introduced, and what would be their specifications?

At this point in time, "length" is no more than an intuitive notion for which a formal measure does not exist. However, a rough outline of the definition of one node in terms of another one may often give some insight into the amount of effort necessary and thus provide an estimate of the length.

Language hierarchies have long been mentioned in connection with programming languages, e.g. Assembler - Low-level programming languages (e.g. PL 360 [Wi 68], ESPOL [Bu 72]) - High-level programming languages - Very high level languages (e.g., set oriented languages [SI 74]). However, except for macro languages these do rarely conform to the strict definition given above (e.g. COBOL is not defined in terms of a lower-level programming language), the reason being that this would entail inefficient compilation. The same argument does not hold for data base languages where language analysis is but a minor part of query processing [Kr 75].

2.2 Explications

The notion of hierarchy as introduced above is still vague and should be made more precise. Below several concepts known from the literature are introduced. Their usefulness as well as some of their deficiencies will be discussed in the remainder of the paper.

(1) Characteristics of the root.

There exist several schools that claim to provide the just and only basis for data base concepts. Before one may pass any judgment on these claims one ought to agree on the criteria that a basis would have to meet. It is commonly accepted that a data base is to be considered as the model of a certain reality. Hence a basis should be such that it provides concepts so primitive that any reality, be it physical or conceptual, could be adequately covered by it. Some authors [Ab 74, Su 74] have attempted to enumerate certain primitives: elementary objects, properties, relations, orderings, categories (or types), names, as well as sets of operators for creating, accessing, manipulating and deleting these. In addition, one might consider organizational questions such as parallelism and sharing of models by various users.

(2) Dependencies between successive nodes.

Since it is extremely general, the root is of little practical value to the average user. Users are invariably concerned not with all possible realities but with certain classes of realities, and wish their models to reflect the corresponding limitations. In other words, the modeling tools on level 1 will differ from those on level 0 by defining certain restrictions on the way the primitives may interact. The same obviously is true for level 2 vis-a-vis level 1, etc. These restrictions relate mainly to the manner in which objects may be composed into new objects, relations into new relations, and/or operations into new operations.

(3) Characterization of a node as an abstract machine.

Basically, the restrictions defined on the permissible compositions determine the dependencies between successive nodes. To make this a little bit more precise, the concept of abstract machine is introduced. An abstract machine is a set of object types, a set of operators for manipulating objects and defined on object types, together with a control mechanism that allows to construct and execute sequences of operations. Each node is then described in terms of an abstract machine.

(4) Dependencies between abstract machines.

By assigning an abstract machine to each node, the following properties must hold between two successive nodes A_i and A_{i+1} [Go 73]:

a) The resources and the functions provided by A_i form the complete basis on which to build A_{i+1}. There is no way to use properties of A_{i-1} in building A_{i+1}. Hence every A_i is a complete interface description in the hierarchy.
b) Resources of A_i used in defining new resources of A_{i+1} can no longer be present in A_{i+1} (i.e. they may become resources of A_{i+1} only if they are not part of a definition for another resource of A_{i+1}).

Keeping these rules in mind I shall attempt, as a matter of illustration, a tentative classification of some results discussed in the literature [Ab 74, Co 70, We 74, Kr 75, Wo 68, Wo 73, Gr 69, Col 68].

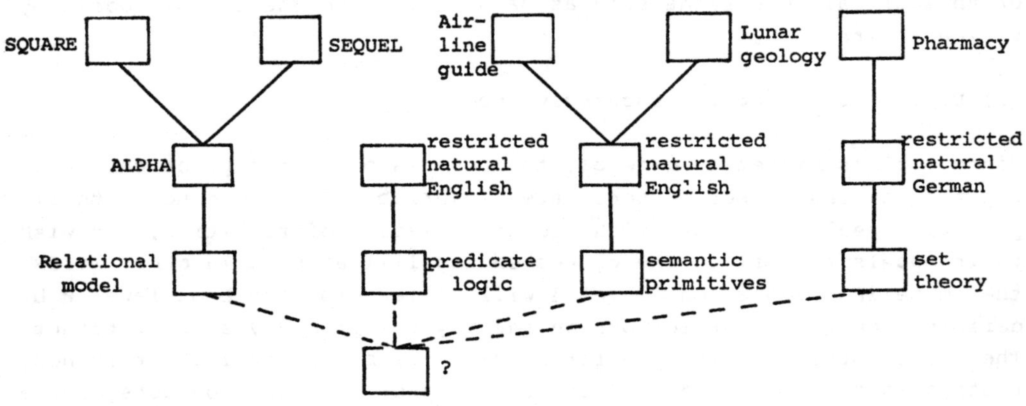

figure 2

2.3 Consequences

The concepts and rules introduced above impose a certain discipline on the design of user languages, on their application, and on the transition between them. Some of the consequences are outlined below.

(1) If we strictly keep to the rules above, a new interface must be defined in terms of its immediate predecessor and not any arbitrarily chosen predecessor, i.e. immediate predecessors must not be bypassed ("stepwise abstraction"). On the other hand, given certain specifications and a suitable node in a tree, intermediate nodes that hopefully are of general usefulness should be introduced on the intervening path whenever the path proves too "long" ("stepwise refinement").

(2) Given a path to the root, a user should be put into position - at least in principle - to formulate his requests in any of the languages that correspond to the nodes on the path. As a matter of fact, we found this an essential prerequisite for efficient system testing since system activities may be observed and controlled to any desired level of detail [Kr 75].

(3) Queries are stated on some level and must successively be translated between levels until the root has been reached. Definition (of an abstract machine) and translation reciprocate each other: The definition of the next higher level from a given one determines the rules that govern the translation of statements on the higher level to those on the lower level.

(4) Results are produced on the lowest level but must be presented to the user on a higher level. As a consequence, following the evaluation of a query a second ("reverse") translation must be invoked in order to propagate the results to higher levels.

3 Set theoretic basis

3.1 Motivation

The rules of ch.2 have been applied to the construction of the KAIFAS question-answering system and have proven highly useful there. Hence this system will be chosen as the first example to demonstrate the practicability of the rules. For a more detailed description of the system the reader is referred to the literature [Kr 75].

Restrictions with regard to the general basis are motivated by the realities one wishes to consider. In the case of KAIFAS we presume that relations are exclusively of the property type (sets) or are binary relations and, more important, that objects are selected exclusively on the basis of given properties or relations which they meet or undergo, perhaps in logical combination. Indeed one can show that the set theoretic approach may be viewed as a generalization of the inverted file technique [Kr 75].

3.2 Set theoretic machine

Object types

I Elementary objects (individuals), e.g. Hans Maier, Bonn, Aspirin

M Sets, e.g. city, medication
List of individuals.

R Relations, e.g. father, contraindication
List of ordered pairs of individuals.

Z Numbers

D Measures, e.g. 2 years, 4 tablets/day
Ordered pairs (number, unit expression).

F Measure functions, e.g. age, dosage
Lists of ordered n-tuples whose last components are measures.

B Truth values

Operators

On retrieval the machine is supposed to function in the following way. Set, relation, and function names refer to objects in permanent storage. In order to manipulate the objects they must be transferred into unnamed registers of which an unlimited number is thought to exist. Hence all operations except for the load operations are register-to-register operations.

Load operators

Mw, ev, en, ef	Load a set, a relation (ev, en), and a measure function, respectively.

Set operators

MU:	$M \times M \to M$	Union
M∩:	$M \times M \to M$	Intersection
Km:	$M \times M \to M$	Relative complement $\{x \mid x \in M_1 \wedge x \notin M_2\}$
Kz:	$M \to Z$	Cardinality

Binary relation operators

Ko:	$R \to R$	Converse relation
Rb:	$R \times M \to R$	Restriction $\{(x,y) \mid (x,y) \in R \wedge x \in M\}$
Rp:	$R \times R \to R$	Product $\{(x,y) \mid \exists z: (x,z) \in R_1 \wedge (z,y) \in R_2\}$
R∪:	$R \times R \to R$	Union

Reduction of binary relations

Vo:	$R \to M$	Domain $\{x \mid \exists y: (x,y) \in R\}$

Na: R->M Range $\{x|\exists y:(y,x)eR\}$
Vg: RxI->M Individual domain $\{x|(x,I)eR\}$
Ng: RxI->M Individual range $\{x|(I,x)eR\}$
VgU: RxM->M Restricted domain $\{x|(x,y)eR \wedge yeM\}$

Reduction of measure functions

Fw: FxI->D (n=2)

Logical operators

e: IxM->B Test on set membership
c: MxM->B Test on set inclusion

In addition, the standard logical operators are available as well as the standard arithmetic and comparison operators for numbers and measures.

Control mechanism

Sequencing of operations

"Programs" for the set theoretic machine are expressed in a functional notation. Operations are performed from left to right and, for each nested argument, from inside out.

Example: A question such as "Are cities birthplaces of engineers?" would take the following form in the set theoretic machine

$c(Mw(M_{city}), VgU(en(R_{birthplace}), Mw(M_{engineer})))$

Loops

Loops are introduced by the use of bounded quantifiers which have three arguments:

1) An expression resulting in a set of objects (range).
2) An expression for the condition resulting in a truth value (scope); it may be regarded as the loop body.
3) The name of a bound variable; each of its substitutions defines an invocation of the loop.

Important quantifiers are

AL: MxB ->B all, every
EI: MxB ->B some
DB: MxB ->M which

ZB: MxB →Z   how many
with the left-hand M the bounding set and the left-hand B the condition.

Examples:

DB (x,Mw(M_{city}), e(x,VgU(en($R_{birthplace}$),Mw($M_{engineer}$))))

with the meaning of "Which cities are birthplaces of engineers".

DB (x_1,
  Mw(M_{manuf}),
  ZB(x_2,
    Vg(en(R_{prod}),x_1),
    DB(x_3,
      Mw($M_{ailment}$),
      e(x_2, Vg(en(R_{medic}),x_3)))))

with the meaning of "How many products of which manufacturers are medications for which ailments?"

Expressions in the data base

Set membership of an arbitrary kind is expressed by including, in the representation of a set, arbitrary set expressions. Example (in German):

$M_{rezeptpflichtig}$	
$I_{Spasmocibalgin}$	
Vg(en($R_{Derivat}$), $I_{Oxazolidin}$)	①
$I_{Morphin}$	
Mw(M_{Opiate})	②
Mw($M_{Hypnotika}$)	
$I_{Methadon}$	
Vg(en($R_{Derivat}$), $I_{Succinimid}$)	
Vg(en($R_{Heilmittel}$), $I_{Agitiertheit}$)	

where ① indicates all derivates of Oxazolidin to be prescription drugs, ② all opiates, etc.

This concept is extended to relations and measure functions. Two of its advantages are:

- Since all objects are evaluated on request only, changes to the data base may be made locally without regard to any interrelationships that may exist.

- Expressions may be stored without regard for the existence of any individuals for it. Hence one could construct a data base consisting exclusively of higher-order relationships.

One consequence, however, is that the control mechanism must itself be defined recursively since it may be invoked on any load operation.

3.3 Natural language

Few users will feel at ease with the highly stylized language introduced in sec. 3.2. One possible step of abstraction, therefore, is the definition of a new abstract machine accepting natural language input. By necessity this is a highly restricted form of natural language since its semantics, and hence its syntactic forms, can be no more than what may ultimately be reduced to a set theoretic interpretation. Moreover, it must be considered more restrictive than the set theoretic interface because while one may nest set theoretic expressions to an arbitrary depth, those beyond a certain depth simply cannot be stated in natural language in any comprehensible fashion.

To speak of objects, operators and control mechanism in connection with natural language turns out to be highly unnatural, or rather impossible. It is possible, however, to define an abstract machine on that level in terms of the syntax of the interface which in turn may still be based on object types. This is in striking similarity to Very High Level languages vis-a-vis High Level programming languages: Very High Level languages are loosely described as languages used to specify what is to be done, rather than how it is to be done [SI 74].

In accordance with sec.2.2, the object types must relate to the ones of the set theoretic machine. In this case the relationship is straightforward as indicated by the following list:

N proper names for the objects of the universe.
A attributes (properties of an object of the universe).
R references from one object of the universe to a second one (e.g. Thebacon is referred to by Morphium as its derivate).
M references to measures.
D numbers or measures.
S sentences. These are of two kinds: sentences to be answered by yes or no, and sentences to be answered by counting or enumerating proper names.

Some examples from KAIFAS in which German was chosen as natural language interface.

```
Ist Psyquil rezeptpflichtig?
      N          A
Betraegt die Tagesdosis von Chinidin 2 Gramm?
                M          N       D
Welche Derivate von Morphium sind rezeptpflichtig?
          R          N               A
```

The syntax of the interface is described by a grammar with the following general properties:

(1) Syntactical variables must relate to the object types, hence they cannot be based on the traditional grammatical categories such as noun, noun phrase, adjective, etc. but on categories that are essentially semantical in nature. The variables are IN(names), ME (attributes), RE(references), MF(references to measures), ZA (numbers), SA (sentences), QU (quantifiers).

(2) On the other hand, the traditional categories must be accounted for in some way, e.g. in order to reject incorrect inflections. As a consequence, each syntactical variable is indexed by a number of features. Examples:

```
MAS masculine )               NOM nominative  )
FEM feminine  )gender         GEN genitive    ) case
NEU neuter    )               DAT dative      )
STR strong declension         ACC accusative  )
ATT attribute apposition      ADJ word class(adject./noun)
NUM number (singular/plural)
```

(3) Even for restricted natural language, grammars are known to be extremely complex because of the multitude of syntactic aspects to be observed. The application of features simplifies the grammar insofar as it can be arranged in two levels,

a) a context-free grammar in terms of the variables from (1);

b) a feature program to be associated with each production on level a).

Example: Typical productions of level a) are

```
ME -> ME ME                ME -> QU ME
ME -> RE                   SA -> ME sind ME?
ME -> RE ME                SA -> Sind ME ME?
ME -> RE IN
```

The production

$ME_1 \rightarrow ME_2\ ME_3$

refers to the following feature program (syntactic variables are numbered for reference).

Part 1: Test of right-hand features for acceptance (reduction takes place only if the condition is true).

<u>test</u> (ME_2,+ADJ+ATT) ∧ <u>test</u> (ME_3, -ADJ-ATT)

∧ <u>meq</u> (MAS,FEM,NEU,ME_2,ME_3) ∧ <u>meq</u> (NOM,GEN,DAT,ACC,ME_2,ME_3)

∧ <u>equ</u> (NUM,ME_2,ME_3)

Part 2: Assignment of features to the syntactic variable on the left-hand side.

-ADJ-ATT, <u>cop</u> (NUM,ME_2),

<u>and</u> (MAS,FEM,NEU,ME_2,ME_3), <u>and</u> (NOM,GEN,DAT,ACC,ME_2,ME_3)

Feature operators are underlined. For example, <u>test</u> is true when the features of the first argument meet the condition specified by the second argument. <u>meq</u> is true whenever at least one of the listed features agree in both syntactic variables specified. <u>cop</u> copies the features of the syntactic variable specified.

3.4 Pharmacology

The natural language level is supposed to serve a variety of application areas. We postulate that these application areas are all served by the same natural language grammar since each must be explainable in terms of set theory. Consequently, these areas differ only in the vocabulary they assign to the object types. Level 3 is reached from level 2 simply by introducing names, and relating them to the object types. Below a few typical examples of assignment are given in the area of pharmacology.

proper names	medications, substances, companies, ailments, e.g. Thebacon, Morphium, CIBA, Angina pectoris
attributes	properties e.g. Tablette, rezeptpflichtig
references	e.g. Indikation and Kontraindikation (from ailment to medication), Hersteller (from company to medication)
references to measures	e.g. Preis, Dosis, Haltbarkeit
numbers or measures	e.g. 5 DM, 2 Tabletten/Tag, 4 Wochen
sentences	e.g. Welche Preise haben Praeparate, die bei Angina Pectoris indiziert sind und deren Kontraindikation nicht Glaukom ist?

3.5 Translations

The path between adjacent nodes is traversed by translation (sec.2.3, (3) and (4)). We shall briefly illustrate this for the passage between natural and set language. In this case translation consists of the three traditional phases: lexical analysis, syntactic analysis and code generation. The sentence
"Welche Firmen sind Hersteller tablettenfoermiger Medikamente?"
shall serve as an example.

Lexical analysis

Lexical analysis includes the mapping from the pharmacological to the natural language level, and for each word encountered, with a few exceptions, proceeds in three steps:

(i) reduction of a word to its word stem;

(ii) dictionary lookup resulting in a syntactical variable, values of some of its features, and a morphemic class, as well as the set level name for the word.

(iii) assignment of further features on the basis of the morphemic class and the actual morphemic ending.

The lexical analysis of the entire sentence results in

word	syn. var	features	int.name
Welche	QU	+MAS+FEM+NEU -NUM+NOM+ACC	DB
Firmen	ME	FEM-NUM+NOM+GEN+DAT+ACC	M26
sind	-	-	-
Hersteller	RE	+MAS+NUM+NOM+DAT+ACC	R23
	RE	+MAS-NUM+NOM+GEN+ACC	
tabletten-	ME	+MAS+NUM+NOM+ATT+STR+ADJ	
foermiger	ME	+FEM+NUM+GEN+DAT+ATT+STR+ADJ	M9
	ME	+MAS+FEM+NEU-NUM+GEN+ATT+STR+ADJ	
Medika-mente	ME	+NEU-NUM+NOM+GEN+ACC	M22
?	-	-	-

Note the syntactic ambiguities due to the different feature combinations for 'Hersteller' and 'tablettenfoermiger'. Note also that lexical analysis by itself cannot always determine the case (as for 'Firmen', all four cases are still possible), or the gender (as for 'tablettenfoermiger').

Syntactic analysis

Syntactic analysis includes three phases: reduction (level a)), feature analysis (level b)), final code manipulation. For each production applied, reduction and feature analysis follow each other immediately. Hence a production is applied in three steps:

(i) Matching of input string and right-hand side.

(ii) Test of right-hand features for acceptance.

(iii) If true, reduction to left-hand side and assignment of features.

For example, the production and feature program from sec.3.3 result in the following when applied to the phrase "tablettenfoermiger Medikamente":

ME2 ('tablettenfoermig'):
1) +MAS+NUM+NOM+ATT+ADJ (rejected on meq)
2) +FEM+NUM+GEN+DAT+ATT+ADJ (rejected on meq)
3) +MAS+FEM+NEU-NUM+GEN+ATT+ADJ
ME3 ('Medikamente')
1) +NEU-NUM+NOM+GEN+ACC
ME1 (result):
1) +NEU+GEN-NUM-ADJ-ATT
(note the disambiguation)

The syntactic analysis of the entire sentence is illustrated in figure 3. Because of the possibility of ambiguities the result is a parsing graph rather than a tree (in this case the ambiguity of the sentence is due to 'Hersteller'). The numbers adjacent to the syntactic variables refer to an associated list of features.

Final code manipulation is left to the final stages of code generation, but must be considered part of the syntactic analysis because without it context-sensitive or transformational rules could not be avoided.

Code generation

Whenever a production is applied, a semantic action associated with it generates a functional set expression. Its arguments point to other such expressions unless they are individuals.

Example:

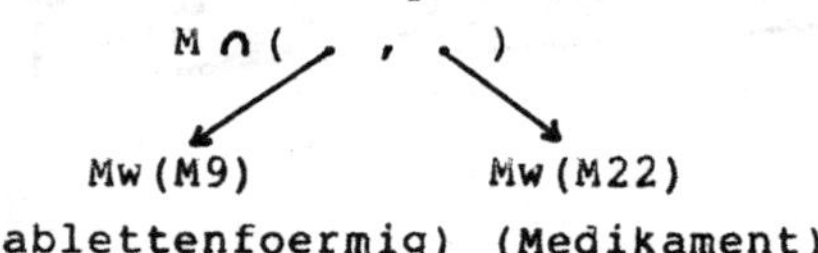

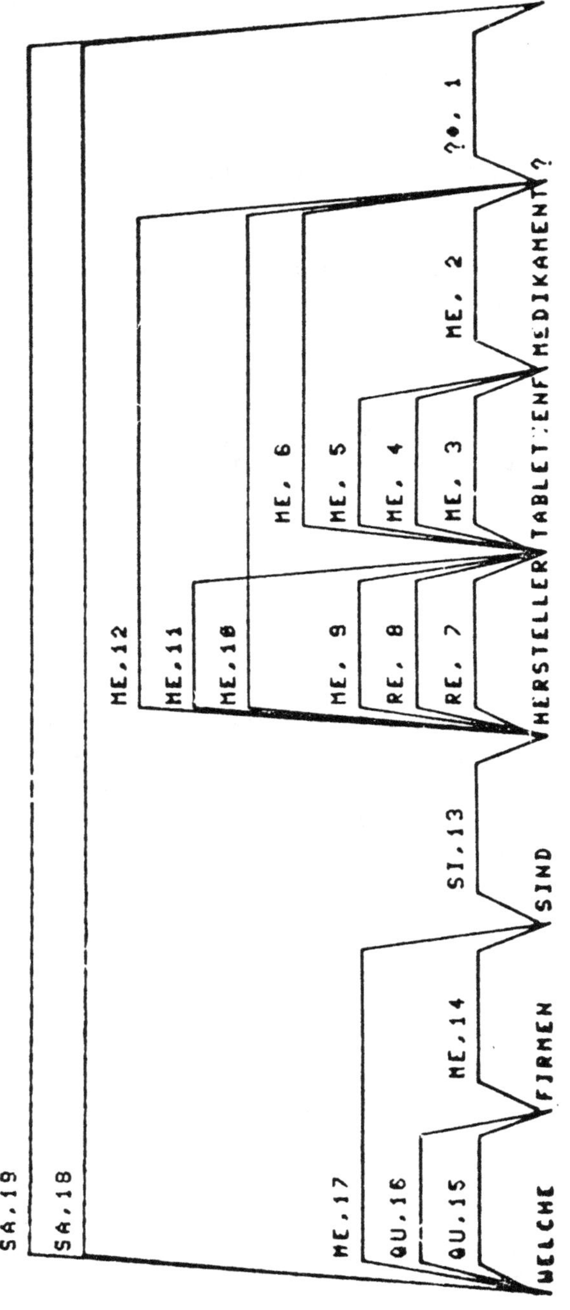
SA,19
SA,18
ME,17
QU,16
QU,15
ME,14
SI,13
ME,12
ME,11
ME,10
ME,9
RE,8
RE,7
ME,6
ME,5
ME,4
ME,3
ME,2
?•,1
WELCHE
FIRMEN
SIND
HERSTELLER
TABLETTEN
MEDIKAMENT
?
=SEND=

Figure 3

WELCHE FIRMEN SIND HERSTELLER TABLETTENFOERMIGER MEDIKAMENTE ?

```
02300047  15000000  DB          (
10000001  01100025  X1          AA
15000000  14000005  (           M-T ( 5)
01100033  15000000  MW          (
04000032  16000000  M26         )
16000000  01200001  )           E
15000000  10000001  (           X1
01100025  15000000  AA          (
14100026  01100045  M-T (22)    MV*
15000000  01200040  (           VG*
15000000  01100030  (           EN
15000000  05000027  (           R23
16000000  01200044  )           MD
15000000  01100033  (           MW
15000000  04000033  (           M27
16000000  01100033  )           MW
15000000  04000026  (           M22
16000000  16000000  )           )
16000000  16000000  )           )
16000000  16000000  )           )
26000000  00000000  EWIRBE      --------
```

Figure 4

On completion of the parse, the pointer structure corresponding to the syntactic variable SA is transformed into a linear string. This string must be submitted to a further string manipulation for two reasons.

(1) Completion of the syntactic analysis.
Quantifiers do not yet appear in front of the expression. Moving them there is subject to a number of rules that govern their sequence.

(2) Optimization.
In many cases quantifiers (whose evaluation may be time-consuming) can be replaced by standard set or relation operators, e.g. DB by M∩.

The code resulting from translation of the sentence above is shown in the printout in figure 4.

<u>Reverse translation</u>

Set level names may immediately be translated into the pharmaceutical level simply by again invoking the dictionary. However, under certain conditions (empty sets) set expressions may themselves be part of a result. This requires a translation into both level 2 and level 3.

Examples:

Vg(R12, I14)	->	Heilmittel fuer Psychosen
Mw(M9)	->	tablettenfoermig
I2	->	Verophen

4 Semantic primitives as a basis

4.1 Motivation

In order to study the adequacy of the rules of ch.2 and to determine whether they must be further refined or augmented it is helpful, short of constructing systems, to examine existing systems that are arranged in the form of layers. One of the oldest systems of this kind (though it was not conceived that way) is Woods' question-answering machine [Wo 68, Wo 73]. Like the set theoretic approach, Woods' universe is composed of objects and interrelationships between them. Unlike the previous approach, these are not collected into mathematical sets and relations but treated as propositions to which a procedural approach is taken. This is probably due to an orientation towards explaining the semantics of natural language rather than manipulating concrete data bases.

4.2 Semantic primitives

Object_types

O Elementary objects, e.g. Boston, AA-57, DC-9, 8:00 a.m.

F^n n-ary functions (n>1), e.g. departure time (of flight x_1 for place x_2). These need not be functions in the strict sense. If a function may yield more than one value (e.g. officer of a ship) it is defined as a successor function such that

(start) officer(x,O) = a_1
officer(x,a_1) = a_2
. . . .
(end) officer(x,a_n) = END

R^n n-ary relation (predicate) (n≥1), e.g. jet (flight x_1 is a jet), arrive (flight x_1 goes to place x_2).

D Designators are either names of elementary objects or of the form $F^n(x_1,\dots,x_n)$ where x_i is a designator; e.g. departure time (AA-57, Boston) for 8:00 a.m.

P Propositions $R^n(x_1,\dots,x_n)$ where x_i is a designator; e.g. jet (AA-57), place (Boston), arrive (AA-57, Chicago).

B Truth values

Example: A set of semantic primitives for the flight schedules table (from [Wo 68]):

Primitive Predicates

CONNECT (X1, X2, X3)	Flight X1 goes from place X2 to place X3
DEPART (X1, X2)	Flight X1 leaves place X2
ARRIVE (X1, X2)	Flight X1 goes to place X2
DAY (X1, X2, X3)	Flight X1 leaves place X2 on day X3
IN (X1, X2)	Airport X1 is in city X2
SERVCLASS (X1, X2)	Flight X1 has service of class X2
MEALSERV (X1,X2)	Flight X1 has type X2 meal service
JET (X1)	Flight X1 is a jet
DAY (X1)	X1 is a day of the week (e.g.Monday)
TIME (X1)	X1 is a time (e.g. 4:00 p.m.)
FLIGHT (X1)	X1 is a flight (e.g. AA-57)
AIRLINE (X1)	X1 is an airline (e.g.American)
AIRPORT (X1)	X1 is an airport (e.g. JFK)

CITY (X1)	X1 is a city (e.g. Boston)
PLACE (X1)	X1 is an airport or a city
PLANE (X1)	X1 is a type of plane (e.g. DC-3)
CLASS (X1)	X1 is a class of service (e.g. first-class)
AND (S1, S2)	S1 and S2 (where S1 and S2 are propositions)
OR (S1, S2)	S1 or S2 (where S1 and S2 are propositions)
NOT (S1)	S1 is false (where S1 and S2 are propositions)
IFTHEN (S1, S2)	if S1 then S2 (where S1 and S2 are propositions)

Primitive Functions

DTIME (X1, X2)	the departure time of flight X1 from place X2
ATIME (X1, X2)	the arrival time of flight X1 in place X2
NUMSTOPS (X1,X2,X3)	the number of stops of flight X1 between place X2 and place X3
OWNER (X1)	the airline which operates flight X1
EQUIP (X1)	the type of plane of flight X1
FARE (X1,X2,X3,X4)	the cost of an X3 type ticket from place X1 to place X2 with service of class X4 (e.g. the cost of a one-way ticket from Boston to Chicago with first-class service)

Operators

To every function and relation there exists a programmed subroutine (procedure) which determines a value of a function or the truth of a proposition.

Examples (procedure names are capitalized):

JET (AA-57) -> true

ARRIVE (AA-57,Chicago) -> true

ARRIVE (AA-57, Boston) -> false

DTIME (AA-57, Boston) -> 8:00 a.m.

Whereas the abstract machine of ch.3 was based on object types but specific operators, the abstract machine in this case is defined in terms of both object and operator types. Specific instances must be supplied by the user for both of them. However, with the advent of microprogramming, computer scientists should have little problems in adjusting to this kind of notion.

Control mechanism

As in the preceding example, programs are expressed in functional notation, e.g.

TEST(CONNECT (AA-57, BOSTON, CHICAGO))
would stand for "Does AA-57 go from Boston to Chicago?". Likewise, queries of any appreciable degree of complexity are based on the notion of bounded quantifier as a representative for loops.

The format for a quantified expression is

FOR <quant> <var>/<class>:<pvar>; <qvar>
where

<quant>	a type of quantifier (EACH,EVERY,SOME,THE, nMANY).
<var>	a bound variable.
<class>	class of objects over which quantification is to range. The specification is performed by special enumeration functions, e.g. SEQ,DATALINE,NUMBER,AVERAGE. Besides enumeration these functions may perform searches or computations.
<pvar>	restriction on the range } may both be quantified
<qvar>	scope } expressions.

Unlike KAIFAS where the result of the evaluation of an expression is automatically retranslated and displayed, this must be explicitly requested by commands such as TEST (test truth of a proposition), PRINTOUT (print the representation for a designator).

Examples:
(FOR EVERY X1 / (SEQ TYPECS):T; (PRINTOUT (X1))
prints the sample numbers for all the lunar samples which are of type C rocks, i.e. breccias (T stands for "true").
(TEST (FOR 30 MANY X1 / (SEQ FLIGHT):JET(X1); DEPART (X1,BOSTON)))
"Do 30 jet flights leave Boston?"

4.3 Natural language

As a general rule, the introductory remarks to sec.3.3 apply here as well: The level of the "English-like" query language provided on level 2 is influenced by the range of expressions possible on the previously discussed level 1. In contrast to KAIFAS, inspection of the data base is not limited to the evaluation of level 1 expressions but may take place during translation from level 2 into level 1, too. The semantic actions associated with a rule of grammar impose further restrictions, e.g. they make sure that the first argument of CONNECT is indeed an instance of the class FLIGHT.

This is illustrated by the following example. In a first step a syntactic analysis is performed and a phrase marker is derived, e.g.

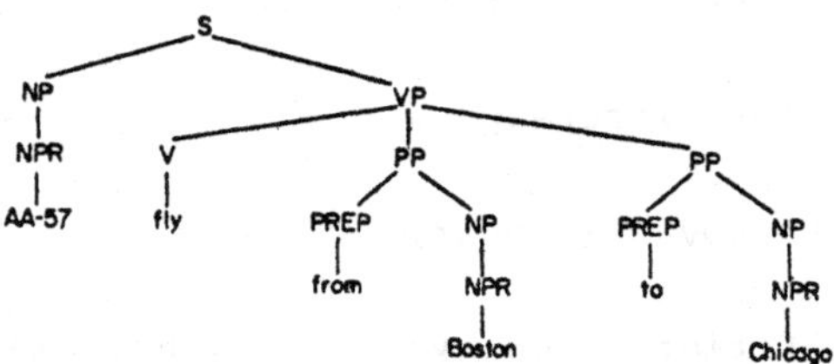

Since verbs in English correspond roughly to predicates, and noun phrases are used to denote the arguments of the predicate, the verb in the phrase marker will be the primary factor in determining the predicate. In the example, the predicate will be CONNECT. For this it is necessary that the subject be a flight and that there be prepositional phrases whose objets are places representing origin (from) and destination (to). The grammatical relations among elements of a phrase marker are defined by partial tree structures, e.g.

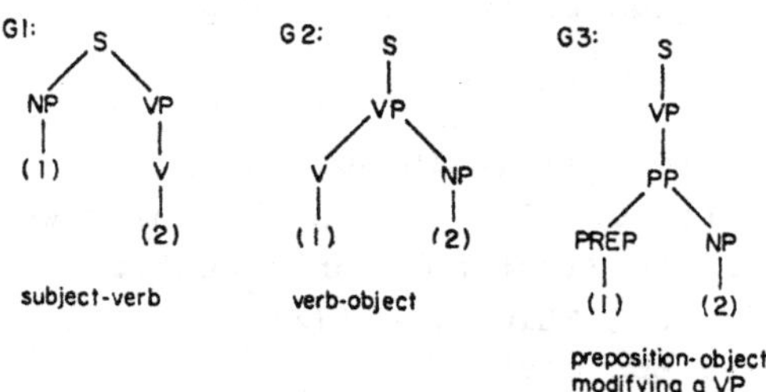

Among the three structures, G1 and G3 both match subtrees in the phrase marker. Which of these is acceptable depends on the additional rules, e.g.

(G1:FLIGHT(1) and(2) = fly).

((1) and (2) are positional variables in the partial tree structure). This rule obviously is satisfied. More complex rules are possible; for example, the topmost S-node of the phrase marker is matched by the rule

1-(G1:FLIGHT((1)) and (2) = fly) and
2-(G3:(1) = from and PLACE ((2))) and
3-(G3:(1) = to and PLACE((2)))
==> CONNECT(1-1,2-2,3-2)

4.4 Airline guide

The system under discussion was first applied to a flight schedules table. To illustrate the application interface, a few examples of queries shall be given below (from [Wo 68]).

Does American Airlines have a flight which goes from Boston to Chicago?
What is the departure time from Boston of every American Airlines flight that goes from Boston to Chicago?
What American Airlines flights arrive in Chicago from Boston before 1:00 p.m.?
How many airlines have more than 3 flights that go from Boston to Chicago?

4.5 Lunar geology

More recently the system has been applied to access, compare and evaluate the chemical analysis data on lunar rock and soil composition that was accumulating as a result of the Apollo missions [Wo 73]. Examples:

What is the average concentration of aluminum in high alkali rocks?
Give me all analyses of S10046!
How many breccias contain olivine?
Do any samples have greater than 13 percent aluminum?
What is the average model concentration of ilmenite in type A rocks?

4.6 Critique

(1) The possibility of inspecting the data base both on level 1 and during translation from level 2 to level 1 introduces a note of confusion. Since, according to sec.2.3, translation is directly related to definition, the translation process must make no reference to the data base. The lack of separation will have practical repercussions: Either certain changes on level 1 will necessitate changes in the rules of grammar, or parts of the control mechanism for level 1 must be duplicated for translation purposes.

(2) In Woods' system the subroutines do not appear to verify that their arguments are of the proper kind (e.g. ARRIVE does not check whether AA-57 is indeed a flight or Chicago a place), since this

is done on translation. If one left this (correctly) to level 1 then primitive predicates and functions are related to each other. These interdependencies may be expressed by a set of axioms, or in the parlance of data structures by types or categories corresponding to those unary predicates that restrict ranges of arguments. As a consequence, the concepts of abstract machine and relationships between abstract machines must account not only for primitive terms but for axioms as well. (Note that the KAIFAS machine circumvents this problem only by prescribing all operators.)

(3) Operators (subroutines) and objects are interdependent as well, albeit in a one-to-one fashion. In order to make sure that the requirements governing the relationship between abstract machines are met it suffices to treat a predicate or function and its corresponding procedure as two instances of the same resource.

5 Relational model

5.1 Motivation

One of the most widely discussed approaches to data bases is Codd's relational model [Co 70,Co 72, We 74] which lends itself particularly well to an interpretation by abstract machines. Codd supposes his users to explain their universe in terms of table-like structures. Intuitively speaking, a table consists of a number of entries that are formatted in exactly the same way: a sequence of fields ordered on certain headings or field names or, as they are called here, attributes. More formally, a entry is an ordered n-tuple and, consequently, a table is a relation that may be named. Entries are not named but are uniquely identified by a key, i.e. the contents of particular fields.

A certain familiarity with the relational model is assumed on the reader's part. Only its interpretation by a machine will be examined here.

5.2 Relational algebra

Objects

A attributes naming a set of objects (domain)
R^n relations

$R^n (A_1, A_2, \ldots, A_n) \subseteq A_1 \times A_2 \times \ldots \times A_n$
Example: SUPPLIER (SUPPLIERNR, NAME, LOC), KEY=SUPPLIERNR

SUPPLIER:	SUPPLIERNR	NAME	LOC
	1	Jones	New York
	2	Smith	Chicago
	3	Connors	Boston
	4	Thompson	New York

Key attributes are indicated; keys may be composite. Hierarchical and other relationships are usually eliminated by normalization. Hence all relations can be assumed to be normalized.

$T^n \in R^n$ n-tuple.

Operators [We 74]

Standard relation operators

$R^{n_1} \otimes R^{n_2} \rightarrow R^{n_1+n_2}$ Direct Product:
$\{(T^{n_1} \frown T^{n_2}) \mid T^{n_1} \in R^{n_1} \wedge T^{n_2} \in R^{n_2}\}$
($\frown$ Concatenation operator)

$R^n \cup R^n \rightarrow R^n$ Union
$R^n \cap R^n \rightarrow R^n$ Intersection
$R^n - R^n \rightarrow R^n$ Difference
} attributes must be "compatible"

Special operators

$R^n[A] \rightarrow R^m$ Projection: Relation R^n restricted to the attributes $A=\{A_1,\ldots,A_m\}$.

$R^{n_1}[A\theta B]R^{n_2} \rightarrow R^{n_1+n_2}$ Join:
$\{(T^{n_1} \frown T^{n_2}) \mid T^{n_1} \in R^{n_1} \wedge T^{n_2} \in R^{n_2} \wedge T^{n_1}[A]\theta T^{n_2}[B]\}$
where A,B sets of attributes, θ one of $\{=,\neq,<,\leq,>,\geq\}$.
(Slight modifications, e.g. natural join, are possible).

$R^n[A\theta B] \rightarrow R^n$ Restriction: $\{T^n \mid T^n \in R^n \wedge T^n[A]\theta T^n[B]\}$
where A,B,O as above.

$R^n\ [A \div B] R^n \rightarrow R^m$ Division: [Co 71], p.74.

Control mechanism (Relational algebra)

Since all operators have been defined as infix operators, "programs" are formed by linear sequences of operators and operands rather than by nested expressions. For an example see sec. 5.3.

5.3 Relational calculus (ALPHA)

In place of relation algebra Codd proposes an applied predicate calculus (relational calculus), and proceeds to show that any expression in the relational calculus (alpha-expression) may be reduced to an equivalent relation algebraic expression.

Alphabet for the calculus:

Individual constants, $a_1, a_2, a_3, \ldots$

Index constants, 1, 2, 3, 4, ...

(attributes are indexed per relation instead of named)

Tuple variables, $r_1, r_2, r_3, \ldots\ldots$

Predicate constants, monadic, $P_1, P_2, P_3, \ldots;$

dyadic, $=, \neq, <, \leqslant, >, \geqslant$

Logical symbols, $\exists, \forall, \wedge, \vee, \neg$

Delimiters.

Simple alpha-expressions have the form

$(t_1, t_2, \ldots, t_k) : w$

where - w a well-formed formula,

- t_i distinct terms consisting of an indexed or non-indexed tuple variable,
- the set of tuple variables occurring in $t_1, \ldots, t_k$ is precisely the set of free variables in w.

Example: Alpha-expression for "Find the name and location of all suppliers each of whom supplies all projects":

$(r_1[2], r_2[3]):$

$$P_1 r_1 \wedge \forall P_2 r_2 \exists P_3 r_3 ((r_1[1]=r_3[1]) \wedge (r_3[3]=r_2[1]))$$

After reduction to relation algebra:

$S_1 = R_1$

$S_2 = R_2$

$S_3 = R_3$

$S = S_1 \otimes S_2 \otimes S_3$

$T_3 = S[1=6] \cap S[8=4]$

$T_2 = T_3\ [1,2,3,4,5]$

$T_1 = T_2\ [(4,5) \div (1,2)] S_2$

$T = T_1[2,3]$

ALPHA is a language for alpha expressions that is slightly more appealing to the user than the predicate form shown above. The example may be reformulated in ALPHA as

<u>RANGE</u> SUPPLIER L
<u>RANGE</u> PROJECT P
<u>RANGE</u> SUPPLY K
<u>GET</u> <u>W</u> (L.NAME, L.LOC):
(∀P)(∃K) ((L.SUPPLIERNR=K.SUPPLIERNR) ∧ (K.PROJNR=P.PROJNR))

or, equivalently (order of quantifiers must be maintained!),

<u>RANGE</u> SUPPLIER L
<u>RANGE</u> PROJECT P <u>ALL</u>
<u>RANGE</u> SUPPLY K <u>SOME</u>
<u>GET</u> W (L.NAME, L.LOC):
(L.SUPPLIERNR = K.SUPPLIERNR) ∧ (K.PROJNR = P.PROJNR)

5.4 Higher levels

For reasons similar to the ones in chs. 3 and 4 languages have been devised that do not have to rely on a user's formal training. One language of this kind is SQUARE [Bo 74] which has been shown to be reducible to the relational calculus. However, the view of relations offered by SQUARE is different from that offered by ALPHA:

(i) Scan a column or columns of a table looking for a value or a set of values (as opposed to inspecting one row after another).
(ii) For each such value found examine the corresponding row and elements of given columns in this row.

SQUARE statements are of a form such as ("disjunctive mapping")

$_B R_A(S)$

(read: "find B of R where A is S") that defines a mapping such that R is a relation, A and B are sets of attributes (domain and range, respectively), S is an argument that may itself be an expression. Other forms, e.g. for projection, conjunctive and n-ary mappings, have a similar appearance.

Example: $_{NAME}EMP_{DEPT}$('TOY')
stands for "Find the names of employees in the toy department".

More recently attempts have been reported that allow a user to engage a relational data base system in a dialog founded on natural English [Co 74]. The approach differs drastically from the ones discussed in chs.3 and 4 in that a truly two-way communication is envisioned.

5.5 Comment

It has been shown that both ALPHA and SQUARE are equivalent to the relational algebra, i.e. any query expressible in relation algebra is expressible in ALPHA and in SQUARE, and vice versa. Hence ALPHA and SQUARE are themselves equivalent. Equivalence is a symmetric relation. The condition on the succession of abstract machines does not preclude equivalence, the definition of the hierarchy by restriction however does. From the point of user sophistication a hierarchy could still be given as relational algebra - ALPHA - SQUARE (in the direction of increasing level). This indicates that further refinement on the notion of hierarchy is necessary.

6 Conclusions

There are some striking similarities between the examples of chs.3,4 and 5:

- In each the lowest level has been well formalized.
- All rely on quantification as a means for building complex expressions.
- All tend towards natural language on their higher levels.
- All three systems have been implemented and found some application.

On the other hand, only one of them (ch.5) so far attempted to provide a less formal but still stylized language on an intermediate level. Experiences indicate that, at least in some well-defined situations, this may be necessary with the KAIFAS system (ch.3) as well.

While a few examples do not constitute proof, at the very least they do suggest that hierarchies of user languages could meet the objectives mentioned in the introduction. Of course, the relationship between successive levels will have to be made much more precise, as has been indicated before. Furthermore, higher levels imply a number of successive translations, and techniques must be explored to measure and perhaps raise the efficiency of higher levels. Finally, the paper did not attend to the critical question what form the root should take; this appears to be a largely unsolved problem.

Acknowledgement. The author is grateful to G.Goos for carefully reading the manuscript and making helpful suggestions.

References

[Ab 74] J.R.Abrial, Data Semantics, in [Kl 74], 1-59

[Bo 74] R.F.Boyce, D.D.Chamberlin, W.F.King, M.M.Hammer, Specifying Queries as Relational Expressions, in [Kl 74], 169-176

[Bu 72] Burroughs Corp., B6700/7700 Executive System Programming Language (ESPOL), Information Manual, 1972

[Co 70] E.F.Codd, A Relational Model for Large Shared Data Banks, Comm.ACM 13(1970), No.6, 377-387

[Co 72] E.F.Codd, Relational Completeness of Data Base Sublanguages, in: R.Rustin (ed), Data Base Systems, Courant Computer Science Symp., Prentice-Hall, Inc. 1972, 65-98

[Co 74] E.F.Codd, Seven Steps to Rendezvous with the Casual User, in [Kl 74], 179-199

[Col 68] L.S.Coles, An Online Question-Answering System with Natural Language and Pictorial Input, Proc. 23rd Natl. ACM Conf. (1968), 169-181

[Go 73] G.Goos, Hierarchies, in F.L.Bauer (ed), Advanced Course on Software Engineering, Lecture Notes in Econ. and Math. Systems, vol.81, 29-46

[Gr 69] C.C.Green, The Application of Theorem Proving to Question-Answering Systems, Tech. Rep. No. CS138, Stanford Univ. 1969

[Kl 74] J.W.Klimbie, K.L.Koffeman (eds), Data Base Management, North-Holland Publ. Co. 1974

[Kr 75] K.D.Kraegeloh, P.C.Lockemann, Hierarchies of Data Base Languages: An Example, Information Systems (in print)

[Su 74] B.Sundgren, Conceptual Foundation of the Infological Approach to Data Bases, in [Kl 74], 61-94

[SI 74] ACM SIGPLAN Symposium on Very High Level Languages, March 1974, ACM, New York 1974

[We 74] H.Wedekind, Data Base Systems I, BI-Wissenschaftsverlag, Reihe Informatik, vol.16, 1974 (in German)

[Wi 68] N.Wirth, PL360, A Programming Language for the 360 Computers, <u>Journ.ACM</u> 15(1968), No.1, 37-74

[Wo 68] W.A.Woods, Procedural Semantics for a Question-Answering Machine, <u>Proc. AFIPS Fall Joint Comp.Conf.</u> 33(1968), 457-471

[Wo 73] W.A.Woods, Progress in Natural Language Understanding - An Application to Lunar Geology, <u>Proc. AFIPS Natl.Comp.Conf.</u> 42(1973), 441-450

Ein System zur interaktiven Bearbeitung umfangreicher Meßdaten

Ulrich Schauer, IBM Deutschland GmbH, Wiss. Zentrum Heidelberg

Zusammenfassung

Bei der Bearbeitung von Meßdaten muß man unterscheiden zwischen einer Standardauswertung der Messungen, bei der eine bestimmte Modellvorstellung zugrunde liegt und einer Analyse mit dem Ziel, logische Zusammenhänge zu erkennen und ein erklärendes Modell zu finden. Während die Standardauswertung durchaus im Stapelbetrieb ablaufen kann mit einem Datenmodell, das abgestimmt ist auf die im Modell ablesbaren Verknüpfungsmöglichkeiten, ist für die Analyse ein interaktives System wünschenswert mit einem Datenmodell, das beliebige Verknüpfungen ermöglicht und mit einer Datenmanipulationssprache, die möglichst deskriptiv sein sollte, aber komplexe Auswahlkriterien erlaubt. Verfügbare Systeme werden den Anforderungen der Analyse nur teilweise gerecht, meist mangelt es der Datenmanipulationssprache an Fähigkeiten zur rechnerischen Datenbearbeitung.

Im folgenden wird ein experimentelles System für die Bearbeitung von Meßdaten beschrieben, an dem im Wissenschaftlichen Zentrum der IBM in Heidelberg gearbeitet wird.

1. EINFÜHRUNG

Umfangreiche Sammlungen von Meßdaten können erst in vollem Maße nutzbar gemacht werden, wenn die für die Analyse zuständigen Fachleute (z. B. Wissenschaftler, Techniker - meist ohne große Programmiererfahrung) in die Lage versetzt werden, ohne Zuhilfenahme von Programmierern selbst die Bearbeitung vorzunehmen. Dazu ist ein interaktives System erforderlich, das erlaubt, Teilmengen der Daten unter komplexen Auswahlkriterien zu bilden und in vorhandene oder neu zu schreibende Bearbeitungsprogramme zu stecken und die Ergebnisse tabellarisch oder graphisch darzustellen.

Schon bei den Auswahlkriterien können recht verwickelte Berechnungen anfallen, die zweckmäßig mit Bausteinen aus einer Programmbibliothek durchgeführt werden. Anpassung des Systems an bestimmte Fachgebiete ist damit möglich durch Anpassung der zugrundeliegenden Programmbibliothek.

Da nur eine begrenzte Anzahl von vorgefertigten Programmen zur Verfügung stehen kann, wird häufig noch Datenmanipulation durch eine Trägersprache (host language) notwendig sein. Als Trägersprache ist APL für die angestrebte Zielsetzung besonders geeignet durch ein hohes Maß an Interaktivität, durch Anpassungsfähigkeit an die Programmiererfahrung des Benützers und eine Vielzahl von Operationen zur Datenmanipulation.

Figur 1 vermittelt einen Überblick über den Systemaufbau.

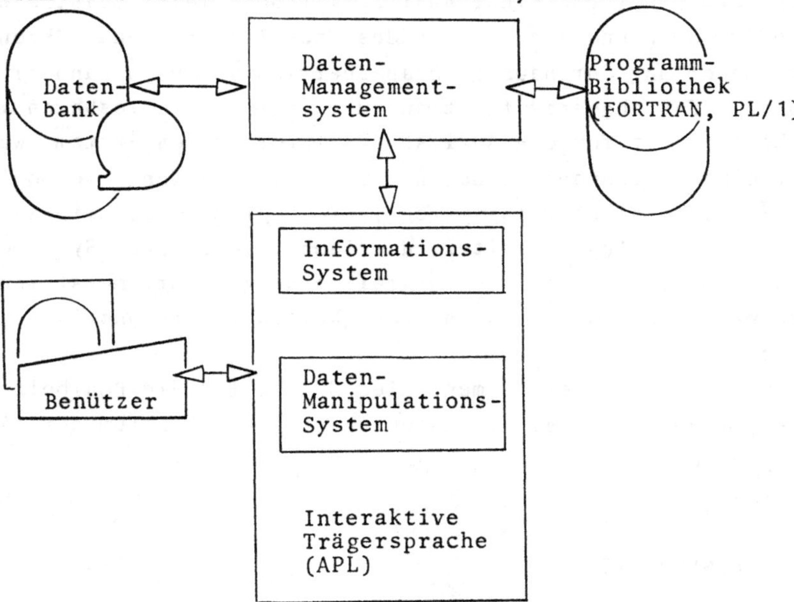

FIGUR 1: System-Aufbau

Die Datenbank enthält sowohl Problemdaten als auch beschreibende Daten. Programmbibliothek steht symbolisch für eine Sammlung von Programmen, die in PL/1, FORTRAN oder Assembler geschrieben sein können und die von APL aus mit Daten aus dem APL-Arbeitsspeicher oder der Datenbank angestoßen werden können und ihre Ergebnisse wieder im APL-Arbeitsspeicher abliefern. Die Benützer-Kommunikation erfolgt mit APL oder mit einem der in APL eingebetteten Systeme zur Manipulation von Meßdaten, Programmen und zugehöriger Dokumentation. Als Benützerstation (Terminal) kommen in erster Linie Bildschirm und Schreibmaschine in Frage.

Einen Überblick über die Datenkomponenten, die vom System zu verwalten sind, gibt Figur 2.

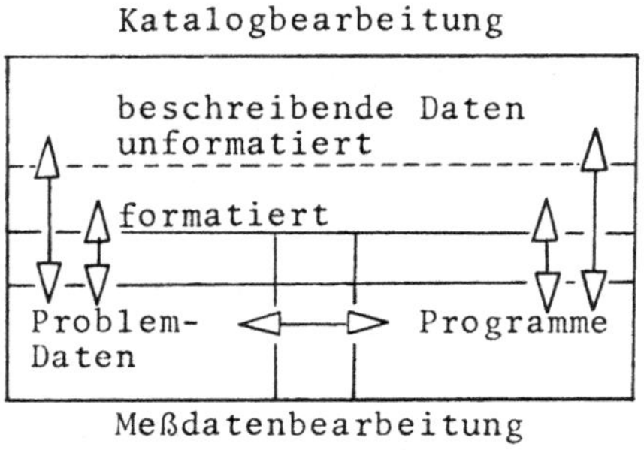

Katalogbearbeitung

beschreibende Daten
unformatiert
formatiert
Problem-
Daten
Programme

Meßdatenbearbeitung

FIGUR 2: Datenkomponenten

Das System muß drei in Wechselbeziehung stehende Klassen von Daten verwalten:

a) Algorithmen (Programmbibliothek)
b) Problemdaten (Meßdaten)
c) Beschreibende Daten (Katalog der Daten und der Programme)

Im allgemeinen wird der Benützer bei einem konkreten Bearbeitungsfall erst anhand der Kataloginformation feststellen, aus welchen Datenaggregaten (Tabellen) seine Problemdaten auszuwählen sind und welche Programme bei der Bearbeitung eingesetzt werden können, und erst dann die vollständige Problemlösung festlegen mit Hilfe des Datenmanipulationssystems.

2. ÜBERBLICK ÜBER DIE SYSTEMKOMPONENTEN

2.1 Algorithmen

Die verfügbaren Hilfsmittel zur Bearbeitung der Meßdaten und zur Darstellung von Resultaten und Zusammenhängen zwischen den Daten lassen sich in drei Klassen einteilen:

a) Arithmetische und logische Operationen zum Ausdrücken von logischen Beziehungen (z. B. $a > 5$) und zur Datenmanipulation (z. B. $x \leftarrow y \div z-100$) für numerische und abgesehen von arithmetischen

Operationen auch für nicht numerische Daten. Die Verwendung von APL als Trägersprache erlaubt insbesondere auch bequeme Manipulation von Rechtecksstrukturen von numerischen und von Textdaten (Vektoren, Matrizen).

b) Unterprogramme zur Lösung von standardisierten Problemen aus Gebieten wie Mathematik (z. B. numerische Integration und Differentiation) und Statistik (z. B. lineare Regression, Testverfahren, Darstellung von Häufigkeitsverteilungen etc.).

c) Anwendungsbezogene Standardverfahren (z. B. Analyse von EKG-Aufzeichnungen, Klassifizierung von Fingerabdrücken etc.).

Die Trägersprache APL mit einer Vielzahl von verfügbaren APL-Bibliotheksprogrammen und der Möglichkeit, von APL aus graphische Darstellungen zu initiieren, bietet schon alle Möglichkeiten zur Datenmanipulation. Trotzdem sind die Klassen b) und c) notwendige Bestandteile des Systems. Die Klasse b) erlaubt Ausweichen auf FORTRAN, PL/1 oder Assembler geschriebene Unterprogramme, was besonders bei großen Datenmengen bessere Rechenzeiten bringen kann. Programme der Klasse c) existieren vorwiegend in FORTRAN oder PL/1, weil sie meistens für Anwendung im Stapelbereich entwickelt werden.

2.2 Problemdaten

Das System benützt ein relationales Datenmodell; die Datenbank besteht aus einer Sammlung umfangreicher Tabellen, die mit leicht verständlichen Operationen manipuliert werden können (Codd /1,2,3/). Datenattribute sind den Spalten einer Tabelle fest zugeordnet wie beim SEQUEL-System (Boyce, Chamberlin /4,5/). Spezifikation von Teilmengen von Daten aus einer oder mehreren Tabellen erfolgt mit einer an Beispieleintragungen in die fraglichen Tabellen orientierten deskriptiven Sprache, die sich gleichermaßen für den Einbau von Unterprogrammaufrufen in den Programmablauf eignet (Zloof /6/).

Die Datenelemente in einer Tabellenspalte können dimensionierte Daten sein (z. B. Vektoren, die eine Meßreihe darstellen oder Matrizen, die mehrere Meßreihen oder eine Funktion von zwei Veränderlichen darstellen können etc.). Die offensichtliche Mehrdeutigkeit wird durch eine der Tabellenspalte zugeordnete Interpretierung behoben.

a) Interpretierungsattribut: Regelt die Deutung einer Matrix, z.B. als Werte einer Funktion von zwei Veränderlichen in den Punkten eines gleichabständigen Gitters. Die Definition der Gitterpunkte

$$(x_o + i.h,\ y_o + j.k) \quad \begin{array}{l} i = 0, 1, \ldots, m-1 \\ j = 0, 1, \ldots, n-1 \end{array}$$

erfolgt durch Angabe von x_o, y_o, h, k und m, n.

b) Darstellungsattribut: Erlaubt Spezifikation von Verdichtungsmechanismen für Datendarstellungen in Ergänzung zu beispielsweise 1, 2, 4 byte integer.

c) Speicherungsattribut: Die meisten Daten werden in der XRM-Datenbank gespeichert (Lorie /7/). Umfangreiche Datenelemente (z. B. digitalisierte Bilder) können jedoch auch in von CMS (Conversational Monitor System) verwalteten Band- oder Platten-Dateien abgelegt und in XRM nur durch Angabe ihres Dateinamens und einer Zugriffsroutine bekannt gemacht werden.

Das System besorgt automatische Umwandlung physikalischer Einheiten und automatische Datenkonversion entsprechend Interpretierungs-, Darstellungs- und Speicherungsattribut sowie Beachtung von durch logische Bedingungen definierten Konsistenzregeln bei neuen Eintragungen oder Änderungen in einer Tabelle.

2.3 Beschreibende Daten

Das System zur Manipulation der unformatierten Kataloginformation ist eine selbständige Komponente mit Fähigkeiten für Generierung, Wartung und für rechnerunterstütztes Auffinden der relevanten Katalogeintragungen über Daten und Algorithmen (Erbe, Walch /8/). Formatierte Datenbeschreibung wird in der XRM-Datenbank gespeichert und umfaßt jeweils ein Verzeichnis von:

a) Umwandlungstabellen für physikalische Einheiten.

b) Methoden mit Programmidentifikation.

c) Datenattributen mit Tabellen und Spaltenbezeichnern.

Mittels b) und c) können Programme und Tabellen rasch identifiziert werden, wenn die Bezeichnung der Methode bzw. der Attribute der fraglichen Tabellenspalte bekannt sind.

3. DIE DATENMANIPULATIONSSPRACHE

Zunächst sind zwei Sprachebenen vorgesehen.

3.1 Prozedurale Sprachebene

Die folgenden Eigenschaften kennzeichnen die prozedurale Datenmanipulation:

a) Der Datenzugriff erfolgt durch APL-Befehle (Lorie, Symonds /9/).
b) Umwandlungen zwischen der externen Datendarstellung in der XRM-Datenbank und der internen Datendarstellung erfolgen automatisch (z. B. Darstellung und Speicherung).
c) Konsistenzregeln werden automatisch kontrolliert bei Datenzugängen oder Veränderungen.
d) Die Daten werden tabellenweise oder zeilenweise verarbeitet.
e) Der Benützer ist verantwortlich für korrektes Verarbeiten der Daten hinsichtlich physikalischer Einheiten und Interpretation.

3.2 Deskriptive Sprachebene

Die nicht prozedurale Sprache EQBE stellt eine Erweiterung dar von QBE (Query by Example, Zloof /6/). Sie eignet sich auch für Benützer mit geringen Kenntnissen in APL (Erfahrung im Umgang mit APL als Tischrechner genügt) und ohne Programmiererfahrung. Die Sprache ist in hohem Maße deskriptiv. Relationen und in der Programmbibliothek verfügbare Unterprogramme werden als Tabellen dargestellt, und der Benützer formuliert seine Datenauswahl, indem er entsprechende Zeileneintragungen vornimmt, die Ausgabewerte bezeichnet und Auswahlkriterien - soweit erforderlich - durch APL-Statements definiert. EQBE läßt sich am besten anhand von Beispielen erklären.

3.3 Beispiele zu EQBE

R	R1	R2
r	x	y

ist ein Schema für eine Tabelle mit dem Namen R und zwei Spalten mit den Bezeichnern R1 und R2.

Die Werte x, y stellen eine Tabellenzeile dar, r ist ein Bezeichner für diese Zeile.

r, x, y werden vom Benützer eingetragen in das Schema

R	R1	R2

, das vom System geliefert wird, wenn man Tabelle R anfordert. Die Datenvariablen x, y können alle in R gespeicherten Tupelwerte annehmen.

$$\{(x, y) \mid (x, y) \in R\}$$

1. Auswahl einer Spalte (Projektion)

R	R1	R2
u	x	

⎕← x

Die Angabe eines Zeilenbezeichners ist nicht notwendig.
□ ist als Symbol für Ausgabe zu verstehen.
Die Abfrage lautet:
Gesucht ist die Menge der x Werte aus R1.
Eine mögliche Formulierung im Prädikatenkalkül wäre

$$\{x \mid \exists_{y} (x, y) \in R\}$$

Selbstverständlich erstreckt sich der Definitionsbereich von y nur auf Werte aus der R2-Spalte von R.
Im folgenden schreiben wir dafür auch kürzer

$$\{x \mid u(x,)\}$$

und fassen u(x,) als Prädikat auf, das wahr ist, wenn ein Tupel in R existiert, dessen erste Komponente gleich x ist.

2. Einfache Abfrage mit einschränkenden Bedingungen, die in der Trägersprache formuliert werden.

R	R1	R2	R3
u	x	y	z

x > 5 + y × y
(z < 25) ∨ (z > 50)
□← x

$$\{x \mid \exists_{y}\exists_{z} u(x,y,z) \wedge (x > 5 + y \times y) \wedge ((z < 25) \vee z > 50)\}$$

3. Schnittmenge

R	R1	R2
r	x	y

S	S1	S2
s	x	z

x > y
z = 10
□← x

Trägt man in S anstatt z den konstanten Wert 10 ein, so entfällt das APL-Statement z = 10.

$$\{x \mid \exists_{y}\, r(x,y) \wedge (x > y)\} \cap \{x \mid \exists_{z}\, s(x,z) \wedge (z=10)\}$$

oder

$$\{x \mid \exists_{y}\exists_{z}\, r(x,y) \wedge s(x,z) \wedge (x > y) \wedge (z=10)\}$$

4. Vereinigungsmenge

R	R1	R2	R3
u	x1	y	
v	x2		z
w	x:x1		
w	x:x2		

x1 > y

z = 10

□ ← x

$$\{ x \mid \exists_y\, u(x,y,) \wedge (x > y) \} \cup \{ x \mid \exists_z\, v(x,,z) \wedge (z=10) \}$$

oder

$$\{ x \mid (\exists_y\, u(x,y,) \wedge (x > y)) \vee \exists_z\, v(x,,z) \wedge (z=10) \}$$

5. Differenzmenge

R	R1	R2
r	x	y

S	S1	S2
~s		x

□ ← x

$$\{ x \mid \exists_y\, r(x,y) \wedge \sim s(,x) \}$$

Selbstverständlich muß jede Datenvariable, die in einer negierten Tupelvariable auftritt, auch in einer nicht negierten Tupelvariablen auftreten (oder als globale Variable bekannt sein).

6. Kartesisches Produkt

R	R1	R2
r	x	y

S	S1	S2
s	x1	z

□ ← x,y,x1,z

$$\{ (x,y,x1,z) \mid r(x,y) \wedge s(x1,z) \}$$

7. Equijoin (Restriktion im Kartesischen Produkt)

R	R1	R2
r	x	y

S	S1	S2
s	x	z

□ ← x,y,z

$$\{ (x,y,z) \mid r(x,y) \wedge s(x,z) \}$$

8. Verallgemeinerter Join mit nachfolgender Projektion

R	R1	R2
r	x	y

S	S1	S2
s	x1	z

x ≥ y

□ ← z

$$\{z \mid \exists_x \exists_{x_1} \exists_y \; r(x,y) \wedge s(x_1,z) \wedge (x \geq y)\}$$

Anstelle des ≥ Operators könnte eine beliebige Boolsche Funktion stehen.

9. Division

R	R1	R2
r	x	y

S	S1	S2
s	x	z

T	T1	T2
t	.y	z

□ ← x

$$\{x \mid \exists_z \forall_{y \in r} \; r(x,y) \wedge s(x,z) \wedge t(y,z)\}$$

.y steht für $\{y \mid \dashv_x \exists_z \; r(x,y) \wedge s(x,z)\}$,

wobei $\dashv_x$ bedeuten soll, daß x fest zu wählen ist, und das Auftreten von .y in t ist so zu verstehen, daß gilt $\forall_{y \in .y} \; t(y,z)$

10. Gruppierung

$\{x \mid \forall_y \exists_z \; r(x,y) \wedge s(x,z) \wedge t(y,z)\}$

kann bis jetzt noch nicht formuliert werden. Man braucht ein Hilfsmittel, um Abhängigkeit zwischen Variablen anzugeben. Mit der Vereinbarung, daß y.z bedeuten soll $\dashv_y \exists_z$, sind die entsprechenden Eintragungen:

R	R1	R2
r	x	y

S	S1	S2
s	x	z

T	T1	T2
t	.y	y.z

□ ← x

Wir sind jetzt in der Lage, jede Operation der Relationenalgebra auszuführen. Die Vollständigkeit von QBE in der vorgestellten erweiterten Form ist damit für einfache Abfragen, die nur eine Operation der Relationenalgebra umfassen, erwiesen.

Sie folgt auch für beliebig zusammengesetzte Operationen: Jede Abfrage von QBE etabliert bei ihrer Definition eine logische Datensicht, die der Resultattabelle entspricht. Erst bei Ausführung eines APL-Programmes, das von einem Abfrageprozessor aus der logischen Datensicht erzeugt wird, entsteht die Resultattabelle. Eine neue Abfrage kann auf der logischen Datensicht von schon definierten Abfragen aufgebaut werden, und damit kann eine komplexe Abfrage in Einzelschritte aufgelöst werden.

3.4 Diskussion der Erweiterungen von QBE

Die nachfolgend beschriebenen Erweiterungen erlauben die Behandlung von recht komplexen Abfragen, wie sie bei Meßdaten zu erwarten sind, ohne die Einfachheit für elementare Abfragen zu beeinträchtigen.

a) In einer Programmbibliothek erfaßte Algorithmen (APL-Funktionen, FORTRAN-Unterprogramme, PL/1-Prozeduren oder Assemblerroutinen) können für Datenauswertung oder Datenselektion innerhalb einer Abfrage eingesetzt werden.
b) Beliebige APL-Befehle können innerhalb einer Abfrage zur Datenselektion und Auswertung verwendet werden. QBE erlaubt außer den Vergleichsoperationen nur eine begrenzte Anzahl eingebauter Funktionen wie COUNT, SUM etc.
c) Die Resultattabelle einer Abfrage kann durch Angabe von formatbeschreibenden Formularen auf verschiedenste Art dargestellt werden, auch in graphischer Form und wiederholt mit wechselnden Formularen.
d) Durch jede Abfrage wird eine logische Datensicht definiert, die zur Entkoppelung komplexer Abfragen in einer Folge von einfacheren Abfragen verwendet werden kann.
e) Jede Abfrage kann zu wiederholten Malen ausgeführt werden. Dabei können von Mal zu Mal die Werte globaler Variablen geändert werden. Für APL-erfahrene Benützer eröffnen sich dadurch interessante Möglichkeiten zur Datenbearbeitung mit anpassungsfähigen Bausteinen.
f) Der Entkopplungseffekt von QBE, daß die Zeileneintragungen in beliebiger Reihenfolge möglich sind, wurde noch verstärkt (Verwendung der Gruppierungsmöglichkeit).
g) Durch die Gruppierungsmöglichkeit können auch Abfragen ohne Zerlegung in aufeinanderfolgende Schritte bearbeitet werden, die sich der Behandlung durch QBE entziehen.
h) Als Gegenstück des ALL D-Operators (all different) von QBE dient in EQBE ein vorgesetzter Punkt, entsprechend beim ALL-Operator (alle mit Wiederholungen) ein vorgesetzter Punkt <u>und</u> Angabe des Tupelbezeichners in Klammern gesetzt. Eine Pseudovariable wie .y oder .x (r) kann in APL-Befehlen verwendet werden und steht stellvertretend für einen Bereich gleichartiger Werte.

4. MESSDATENBEARBEITUNG

4.1 Das Datenbearbeitungssystem

APL ist zur interaktiven Analyse von Meßdaten, die im APL-Arbeitsspeicher Platz finden, hervorragend geeignet (Schatzoff /10/). Bei großem Datenumfang verliert APL an Attraktivität, weil Datenselektion aus Tabellen dann aus Platzgründen nicht im APL-Stil durch eine Operation über einen dimensionierten Bereich dargestellt werden kann, sondern nur durch eine Rekursionsvorschrift über alle Tabellenzeilen. Eine prozedurale Sprachebene mit APL als Trägersprache ist daher noch nicht voll zufriedenstellend.

Ein weiterer Gesichtspunkt bei Meßdaten ist, daß Messung häufig für die Zusammenfassung von vielen Einzelwerten steht (z. B. digitalisierte Meßkurve). Für die Bearbeitung solcher Messungen ist es wünschenwert von der Trägersprache APL aus, Programme, die in einer anderen Sprache (FORTRAN, PL/1, Assembler) entwickelt wurden, aufrufen zu können.

Andere experimentelle Datenbanksysteme, die APL als Trägersprache verwenden, sind meist nur für geringen Datenumfang konzipiert (Palermo /11/), Klebanoff, Lochovsky, Tsichritzis /12/) und erlauben den Einsatz von Programmen, die nicht in APL geschrieben wurden, entweder gar nicht oder nur mit ineffizienter Datenkommunikation (über externe Dateien).

Bei der in Figur 3 beschriebenen Architektur erhalten wir ein System zur Problemlösung mit

- Datenbankzugriff auf zwei Sprachebenen (prozedural und deskriptiv)
- Einsatzmöglichkeit von vorgefertigten Programmen aus einer leicht erweiterbaren Programmbibliothek (FORTRAN, PL/1 oder Assemblerprogramme)
- Hilfsmitteln zur Verwaltung der Dokumentation über Daten und Programme
- Automatischer Datenumwandlung in gewünschte physikalische Einheiten
- Automatischer Datenkonversion, soweit durch Implementierung, Darstellung und Speicherung erforderlich
- Unterstützung graphischer Ein/Ausgabegeräte
- Verfügbarkeit von Programmen zur graphischen Darstellung
- einer Schnittstelle für leichte Substitution von Ein/Ausgabegeräten

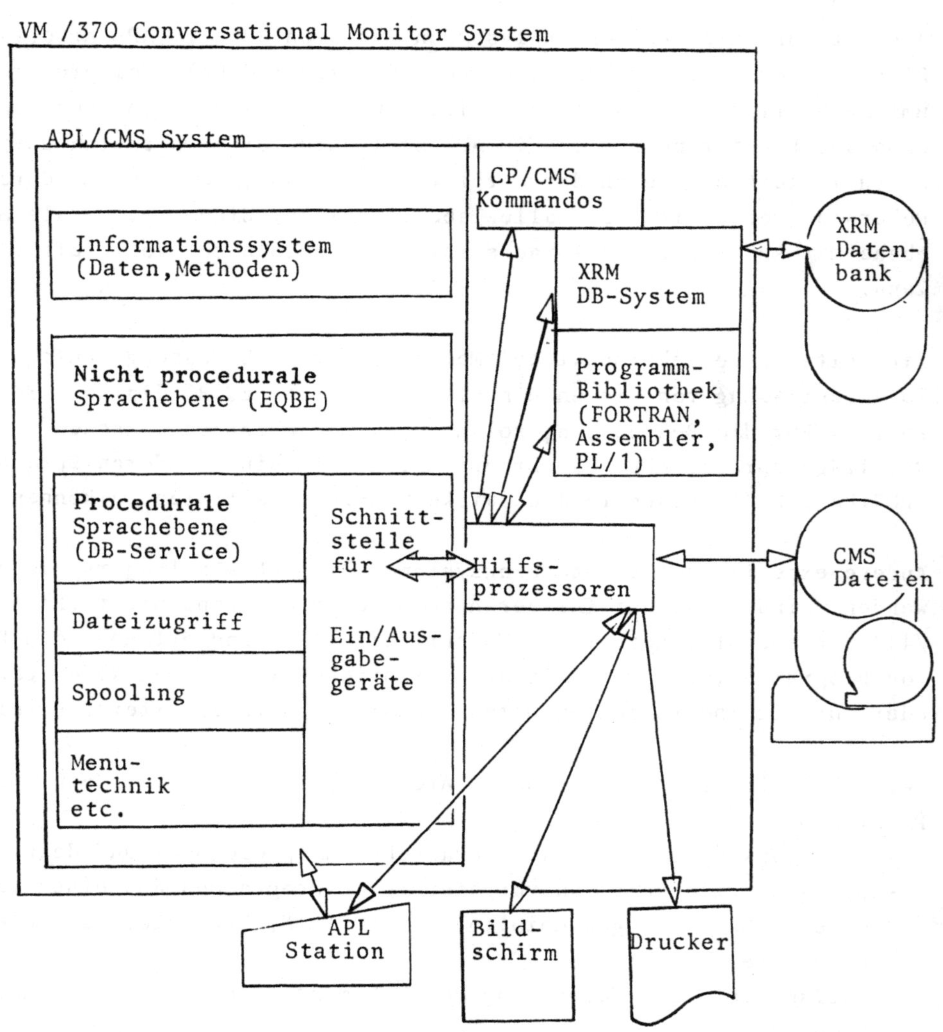

FIGUR 3: Systemarchitektur

4.2 Beispiele zur Datenbearbeitung

Die folgenden zwei Beispiele sollen die Fähigkeiten zur Problemlösung illustrieren. Im ersten Beispiel wird die Verbindung mit Programmen aus einer Programmbibliothek gezeigt, im zweiten Beispiel unter anderem die Benützung von globalen Variablen.

1. Welches in der Datenbank erfaßte Material hat einen mittleren Reflexionsbeiwert (zwischen 250 und 300 nm) größer als 60?

MATERIAL-SPEKTREN	MATERIAL-NAME	REFLEXIONSSPEKTRUM	
		STARTWERT	SCHRITTWEITE
		150 NM	5 NM
	material	reflexion	

SIMPSON-REGEL	AUSGABE	EINGABE				
	INTEGRALWERT	INTEGRAND			GRENZEN	
		x_o	Δx	y(x)	von	bis
	integral	150	5	reflexion	x1	x2

```
x1  ←  250
x2  ←  300
60 <integral ÷ (x2-x1)
⎕← material
```

Die obigen Eintragungen in das Tabellenschema der Materialspektren und eine schematische Darstellung des Programmes SIMPSON-REGEL zusammen mit einigen APL-Befehlen definieren die Ergebnisliste der gesuchten Materialien.

Kommt als zusätzliche Bedingung hinzu, daß für das gesuchte Material das Produkt aus spezifischem Gewicht $\gamma[kg/dm^3]$, spezifischer Wärme c [cal/(grad.g)] und Wärmeleitfähigkeit λ[cal/(cm.grad.sec)] größer als 0.5 sein muß, so ist das obige Schema wie folgt zu ergänzen:

MATERIAL-WERTE	SPEZ. GEWICHT	SPEZ. WÄRME	WÄRME LEITFÄHIGKEIT	MATERIAL-NAME
	gamma	c	lambda	material

0.5 > gamma[KG÷DM*3]×c[CAL ÷GRAD × G] ×lambda [CAL÷CM× GRAD ×SEC]

Bei dieser Formulierung ist die Existenz einer Eintragung in der Tabelle MATERIALWERTE gesichert. Eine widersprechende Eintragung könnte außerdem existieren (falls MATERIALNAME nicht Schlüsseleigenschaft hat). Bei der folgenden Abänderung ist entweder die zusätzliche Bedingung erfüllt oder nicht entscheidbar (weil keine Eintragung der Materialwerte existiert):

MATERIAL-WERTE	SPEZ. GEWICHT	SPEZ. WÄRME	WÄRME-LEITFÄHIGKEIT	MATERIAL-NAME
~	gamma	c	lambda	material

0.5 ≤ gamma [KG÷DM*3]×c[CAL÷GRAD×G]×lambda [CAL÷ CM×GRAD×SEC]

2. Die Datenbank möge Aufzeichnungen enthalten über die Wirkung verschiedener Behandlungsarten sowie Daten über die behandelten Personen.

   Um einen ersten Überblick zu bekommen, ist eine Häufigkeitstabelle gewünscht, die den Zusammenhang zwischen Wirkung und Behandlungsart für ein bestimmtes Kollektiv von Versuchspersonen (Raucher, männlich, älter als 40 und mit Übergewicht) wiedergibt.

BEHANDLUNG	ART	WIRKUNG	PERSON
b	x	y	name

PERSON	NAME	MÄNNLICH	GRÖSSE	GEWICHT	ALTER	RAUCHER
	name	1	h	g	a	1

40 < a [JAHR]

1 < g [KG] ÷ (h[CM]-100)

```
I ← x(b)
J ← y(b)
P[I;J] ← P[I;J] + 1
```

Durch das Anhängen von (b) an x und y wird bewirkt, daß alle in b vorkommenden Paare x,y berücksichtigt werden (auch Wiederholungen). Die globale Variable P, welche mit den Werten x(b), y(b) gebildet wird, muß vor Ausführung der Abfrage initialisiert werden, z. B. durch P ← 5 10 ρ 0, wenn zwischen 5 Behandlungsarten und 10 Wirkungsstufen unterschieden wird.

Würden kontinuierliche Werte für Kennzeichnung von Behandlungsart und Wirkung vorliegen, so müßte noch eine Intervalleinteilung vorgegeben werden für x und y,

z.B.: $x < x_1$, $x_1 \leq x < x_2$, ..., $x_3 \leq x < x_4$, $x_4 \leq x$

$y < y_1$, $y_1 \leq x < y_2$, ..., $y_8 \leq y < y_9$, $y_9 \leq y$

durch Angabe der Zahlenfolgen IX ← x_1, ..., x_4 und IY ← y_1, ..., y_9.

IX und IY können gleichfalls als globale Variable übergeben werden. Anstelle von I ← x(b) und J ← y(b) tritt dann I ← IX INDEX x(b) und J ← IY INDEX y(b). Dabei ist INDEX eine APL-Funktion, die die Intervallnummer feststellt:

```
∇I  IX INDEX X
[1]I ← 1 + +/X ≥ IX ∇
```

Durch Abänderung der globalen Variablen IX, IY, P kann eine völlig neue Resultattabelle erzeugt werden, ohne neuerliche Kompilation der Abfrage.

4.3 Einsatzmöglichkeiten

Das vorgestellte System ist in erster Linie für die Bearbeitung von Meßdaten in Wissenschaft und Technik konzipiert. Sicher finden sich auch im kommerziellen Bereich Einsatzmöglichkeiten, z. B. für interaktive Datenanalyse mit dem Ziel, Zusammenhänge zu erkennen, die sinnvolle Vorhersagen ermöglichen.

Computerunterstütztes Entwerfen (CAD) als spezielles Anwendungsgebiet dieses Systems wird am Wissenschaftlichen Zentrum Heidelberg untersucht (Kantorowitz /13/).

Wie Figur 4 zeigt, läßt sich das System - je nach Benutzerstandpunkt - charakterisieren als:

- Erweiterung von APL (Datenbankzugriff, Einsatzmöglichkeit von kompilierten Programmen, Auskunftssystem über Methoden, Programme und Daten),
- Erweiterung eines Datenbanksystems zum Problemlösungssystem (Interaktive Datenmanipulationssprache mit Einsatzmöglichkeit für eine Sammlung von Programmen, Auskunftssystem über Methoden, Programme und Daten),
- Erweiterung einer Sammlung von Programmen zum Problemlösungssystem (Datenbankzugriff, interaktive Datenmanipulationssprache, Auskunftssystem über Methoden, Programme und Daten),
- Erweiterung eines Auskunftssystems über Methoden, Programme und Daten zum Problemlösungssystem (Datenbankzugriff, interaktive Datenmanipulationssprache mit Zugriff zu Programmbibliothek).

Funktion	Komponente
Datenmanagementsystem	XRM (Extended Relational Memory)
Interaktive Träger- sprache	APL
Prozedurale Sprachebene (Interface zu XRM)	APL-Funktionen
Deskriptive Sprachebene (mit Übersetzung nach APL)	EQBE (Extended Query by Example)
Programmbibliothek	Scientific Subroutine Package (Benützerprogramme)
Programmdokumentation	Methodenbank (in APL implementiert)
Kommandosprache für Programmausführung	EQBE
Interaktive graphische Datenmanipulation	GRAPHPAK
Sequentielle Dateien	CMS/APL
Schnittstelle APL - PL/1	Hilfsprozessor
Unterstützung von Ein/Ausgabegeräten	APL-Funktionen

FIGUR 4: Komponenten zum Problemlösungssystem

Keine der oben erwähnten Komponenten stellt allein gesehen ein Novum dar, ausgenommen vielleicht das Auskunftssystem über Daten, Methoden und Programme. Im Zusammenwirken entsteht ein System zur interaktiven Bearbeitung umfangreicher Meßdaten, bei dem der Problemlöser selbst (ohne Zwischenschaltung von Programmierern) die für ihn wichtige Information aus einer Datenbank unter anwendungsspezifischen Auswahlkriterien abrufen und für gleichfalls anwendungsbezogene Berechnungen nutzbar machen kann. Bei unserem experimentellen System wird APL als Implementierungs- und Trägersprache verwendet, um entsprechend implementierte Teilsysteme leicht einfügen zu können.

Durch die Wahl der Komponenten bedingt bleiben manche Aspekte eines Datenmanagementsystems zunächst unberücksichtigt. Dennoch kann das System helfen, Erfahrung zu sammeln über die Forderungen, die für die Bearbeitung von Meßdaten an Datenbanksystem, Datenmanipulationssprache und Auskunftssystem zu stellen sind, um ein Problemlösungssystem zu erhalten, das auch für Nichtprogrammierer attraktiv ist.

Literatur

[1] E.F. Codd, "A Relational Model of Data for Large Shared Data Banks", CACM, Vol. 13, No. 6, June 1970, pp. 377-387

[2] E.F. Codd, "Normalized Data Base Structure: A Brief Tutorial", Proc. 1971 ACM SIGFIDET Workshop

[3] E.F. Codd, "Interactive support for Non-Programmers: The Relational and Network Approaches", Proc. 1974 ACM SIGFIDET Workshop

[4] R.F. Boyce, D.D. Chamberlin, "SEQUEL: A Structured English Query Language", Proc. 1974 ACM SIGFIDET Workshop

[5] R.F. Boyce, D.D. Chamberlin, "Using a Structured English Query Language as a Data Definition Facility", IBM Research Report RJ 1318, Dec. 1973

[6] M.M. Zloof, "Query by Example", IBM Research Report RC 4917,July 1974

[7] R.A. Lorie, "XRM an Extended (n-ary) Relational Memory", IBM Technical Report 320-2096, Jan. 1974

[8] R. Erbe, G. Walch, "An Interactive Guidance System for Method Libraries", IBM Germany, Wissenschaftliches Zentrum Heidelberg, Technical Report 75.04.001, April 1975

[9] R.A. Lorie, A.J. Symonds, "A Relational Access Method for Interactive Applications", Courant Computer Science Symposia 6, "Data Base Systems", 1971, Prentice Hall

[10] M. Schatzoff, "Interactive Statistical Data Analysis - APL Style", IBM Technical Report 320-2079, April 1972

[11] F.P. Palermo, "An APL Environment for Testing Relational Operators and Search Algorithms", Proc. APL 75

[12] J. Klebanoff, F. Lochovsky, D. Tsichritzis, "Teaching Data Base Concepts Using APL", Proc. APL 75

[13] E. Kantorowitz, "A Computer Aided Design Front End for the Measurement Data Base", IBM Germany, Wissenschaftliches Zentrum Heidelberg, Technical Note 75.07, July 1975

DATENBANKORGANISATION BEI DER HOECHST AKTIENGESELLSCHAFT

Otmar Saal, Diplom-Volkswirt, HOECHST AKTIENGESELLSCHAFT

Zusammenfassung

In einem generellen Rahmen wird zunächst aufgezeigt, von welchen Bedingungen und Überlegungen HOECHST bei der Planung von Datenbanksystemen ausgeht. Am Beispiel von Anforderungen seitens stark integrierter Abrechnungs- und Abwicklungssysteme werden dann ausgewählte Fragen aus der praktischen Anwendung von Datenbank- und Datenkommunikationssystemen erörtert.

DATENVERARBEITUNG IM SYSTEMVERBUND

Um den Rahmen der späteren Ausführungen verständlich zu machen, erscheint es zweckmäßig, zunächst einen kurzen Überblick über die Struktur unseres Unternehmens zu geben.

Die HOECHST AG legte für das Geschäftsjahr 1974 einen Weltabschluß vor, in dem über 400 in- und ausländische Gesellschaften konsolidiert sind, an denen das Unternehmen mit mindestens 50 % beteiligt ist. Weltweit wurde ein Umsatz von 20,2 Mrd. DM erzielt. Die Produktionspalette deckt mit etwa 50.000 verschiedenen Erzeugnissen fast vollständig das gesamte Gebiet der Chemie ab.

Das Gesamtunternehmen HOECHST wird in 3 Gruppen betrachtet, nämlich HOECHST Welt, HOECHST Konzern und HOECHST AG, wobei sich die nachfolgenden Ausführungen überwiegend auf die Muttergesellschaft mit insgesamt 13 inländischen Werken und einem Umsatzvolumen im Jahre 1974 von 9,7 Mrd. DM beziehen werden.

Betrachten wir das Zusammenwirken der einzelnen Unternehmenseinheiten der HOECHST AG (Werke, Konzerngesellschaften, Auslandsgesellschaften) mit den Funktionsbereichen (Ressorts, Bereiche, Unternehmensleitung) hinsichtlich der dabei anfallenden Aufgaben für die Datenverarbeitung, dann wird offensichtlich, daß die notwendigen

Daten für Abrechnungssysteme, Abwicklungs- und Dispositionssysteme sowie Informations- und Planungssysteme nur durch umfassende Systeme der Datenverarbeitung erfaßt, zugeführt, einheitlich aufbereitet, gespeichert und ausgewertet werden können.

Dementsprechend trägt ein den jeweils zentralen und/oder dezentralen Aufgaben entsprechendes System von Datenverarbeitungseinrichtungen in einem quasi hierarchisch organisierten Zusammenwirken dazu bei, die benötigten Daten zu erfassen und zu verarbeiten und/oder für eine weitere Stufe der Verarbeitung im Gesamtsystem bereitzustellen.

Unter der Bezeichnung Systemverbund HOECHST arbeiten wir an der Realisierung einer Konzeption, die die Probleme einer zentralen und dezentralen oder lokalen Datenverarbeitung in einer möglichst effizienten und betriebssicheren Weise lösen helfen soll. Unser Mehrrechnerverbundsystem von 3 Großrechnern in der Zentrale wird sinnvoll ergänzt durch einen Verbund angepaßter dezentraler Rechner- oder Terminalintelligenz, wobei weniger eine System-Distribution im Vordergrund steht, sondern vielmehr die Verwendung der jeweils geeignetsten Einrichtungen für die Aufgaben der lokalen Datenerfassung und Verarbeitung mit einer möglichst direkten Kommunikationseinrichtung zum zentralen System. Soweit möglich und sinnvoll werden vom lokalen Rechner aus auch die zentralen Ressourcen mittels "Remote-Job-Processing" genutzt, wofür ein entsprechendes Workstationprogramm zur Verfügung steht. Die Werke und Geschäftsstellen werden durch dieses Verbundsystem außerdem in die Lage versetzt, eigene werksbezogene Informationsbedürfnisse zu befriedigen, die normalerweise dort nur durch eine die wirtschaftlich sinnvolle Größenordnung übersteigende Datenverarbeitungsanlage erfüllt werden könnten.

Dieses Gesamtsystem der Datenverarbeitung in unserem Unternehmen kann sich aber nicht allein auf eine Weitergabe von Daten für die übergeordneten zentralen Datenverarbeitungsaufgaben durch die jeweils örtlich oder funktional getrennten Teileinheiten erstrecken, sondern verlangt gerade im Bereich der Datenspeicherung und Informationsauswertung eine einheitliche Architektur.

Damit ergab es sich fast zwangsläufig, daß die Datenverarbeitung bei HOECHST in konsequenter Verfolgung des Konzeptes einer integrierten Datenverarbeitung zu einer Datenbankorganisation kommen mußte, die eine Allgemeinverwendbarkeit der Datenbestände sowohl über die einzelnen Anwendungsbereiche als aber auch über die physischen Grenzen eines einzelnen Rechenzentrums hinaus sicherstellen kann.

Wie bei jedem Unternehmen, das schon sehr frühzeitig mit dem Einsatz der Datenverarbeitung begonnen hat, strebte auch HOECHST anfangs vorwiegend die Integration der Datenerfassung und einen effizienten Datenfluß zwischen den Anwendungsgebieten an.

Das soll aber keineswegs bedeuten, daß beim Aufbau der zentralen Dateien die Ganzheitlichkeit der Planung und die Beachtung der Gesamtzusammenhänge vernachlässigt worden ist. Es standen eben anfangs überwiegend Projekte der Massendatenverarbeitung in den Abrechnungs- und Administrationsbereichen an, die zuerst einmal primär für den eigentlichen Fachbereich aufgebaut wurden und die aufgrund der stapelorientierten Datenverarbeitung auch meist in der Dateiorganisation überwiegend auf die Belange der unmittelbaren Fachbereiche hin organisiert waren. Darüber hinausgehende, nicht fachbereichstypische Daten dienten vorwiegend der integrierten Datenerfassung und der zweckmäßigsten Weitergabe möglichst umfassend geprüfter Daten. Schon rein technisch gesehen hatten wir damals keinerlei Möglichkeiten hinsichtlich einer umfassenden, aber dennoch möglichst anpassungsfähigen und leicht zu handhabenden integrierten Datenbankorganisation.

Erst die technologischen Entwicklungen der Datenverarbeitung ließen uns etwa ab 1967 durch geeignete externe Speicher mit wahlfreiem Zugriff und durch die neuartigen Kommunikationsformen im Rahmen einer Echtzeitverarbeitung an die Planung und Realisierung von umfassenderen und dateiorganisatorisch stärker integrierten Anwendungssystemen herangehen.

AUFGABEN DER DATENBANKEN IM GESAMTINFORMATIONSSYSTEM

Seit etwa 6 - 7 Jahren befinden sich Art und Struktur unserer Anwendungen in einem starken Wandel. Die reinen Abrechnungs- und Administrationssysteme konnten jetzt durch Datenbankkonzeptionen und direkten Zugriff über Datenfernverarbeitungseinrichtungen zu Dispositions- und Informationssystemen ausgebaut werden. Die Datenspeicherung kann von dem bisher überwiegend inaktiven Zustand auf den Magnetbändern in eine aktive, jederzeit von den Benutzern ansprechbare Speicherungsform auf Magnetplattenspeicher überführt werden. Die Datenerfassungs- und Administrationssysteme für die Fachbereiche selbst wurden dadurch sowohl im Hinblick auf die Art der maschinellen Durchführung durch die Echtzeitverarbeitung viel rationeller gestaltet als aber auch durch die direkte Verknüpfbarkeit zu anderen Datenbanken aussagefähiger. Denn nun konnten die für den Fachbereich notwendigen Informationen durch Zugriff auf die Datenbankorganisation anderer Fachbereiche oder auf zentral geführte Datenbanken leichter zu wirksamen Teilinformationssystemen ausgebaut werden. Zusätzlich ermöglicht die integrierte Datenbankorganisation einen direkten Abruf von Daten aus fachbereichsbezogenen Teilsystemen zur Bearbeitung in Schwerpunktsystemen mehrerer Funktionsbereiche oder gar in zentralen Informationssystemen.

Wenn wir den Begriff "zentrales Informationssystem" oder auch "zentrales Berichtssystem" anstatt der vielfach üblichen Bezeichnung "Management Information System" benutzen, dann hat das seinen Grund.

Uns scheint MIS zu stark auf eine Informationsgewinnung nur für höhere Führungsebenen festgelegt, wodurch der Eindruck erweckt wird, daß das entsprechende System der Datenverarbeitung und Datenspeicherung primär unter diesem Gesichtspunkt konzipiert wurde. Wir sind vielmehr der Ansicht, daß die Informationsbedürfnisse von der operativen Ebene bis hin zur höchsten Führungsebene unbedingt aus jeweils gemeinsamen, zentral geführten Datenbanken abgedeckt werden müssen. Diese Datenbanken selbst können dann durch verschiedene Teilinformationssysteme erstellt werden und dienen zunächst einmal primär zur Bewältigung der Aufgaben in Systemen, die für die operative Ebene erstellt wurden. Daß diese Datenbanken darüber hinaus auch in der Lage sein müssen, die Anforderungen von übergeordneten Informationssystemen abdecken zu können, das ist im wesentlichen eine Frage einer planvollen und flexiblen Datenbankstruktur.

Eine planvolle und auf die Erfüllung aller zentralen Informationsbedürfnisse ausgerichtete Datenspeicherung erfordert aber zunächst einmal ein einheitliches System der Datendefinition und Datenverschlüsselung. Dementsprechend wird auch bei HOECHST vom Beginn der Datenverarbeitung an ein sehr großer Wert auf die zentrale Definition, Entwicklung und Pflege aller Schlüsselbegriffe und Ordnungskriterien gelegt, die in einem zentralen Schlüsselbuch der Datenverarbeitung für das gesamte Unternehmen verbindlich festgelegt und ergänzt werden.

Unter der Voraussetzung einer klaren Datendefinition und Verschlüsselung ist es dann prinzipiell kein allzu schwieriges Problem mehr, die Daten den jeweiligen Anforderungen der Informationssysteme entsprechend bereitzustellen, zu verdichten, zu verknüpfen und auszuwählen. Wenn man ein geeignetes Datenbank-Management-System zur Verfügung hat, kann durch einen universellen Aufbau der Datenbanken viel elastischer und unmittelbarer auf wechselnde Informationsbedürfnisse des Managements reagiert werden als dies bei dem starren Rahmen eines einmal vorgedachten und im Dateieninhalt festgelegten MIS möglich wäre.

Damit gehen wir bei HOECHST eindeutig den Weg, zunächst einmal sehr umfassende Teilinformationssysteme aufzubauen und das eigentliche MIS als ein quasi übergeordnetes "zentrales Berichtssystem" durch die gemeinsame, zentrale Organisation der Datenbanken jederzeit aussagefähig zu halten.

DATENBANKEN IN EINEM INTEGRIERTEN TEILINFORMATIONSSYSTEM

Durch praktische Beispiele möchte ich die bisherigen generellen Aussagen etwas konkreter werden lassen. Um aber auch hierfür zunächst den Gesamtzusammenhang verständlich zu machen, werde ich einen Überblick über ein umfangreiches und stark verzahntes System im Bereich des Verkaufs und der Produktion geben, das seinerseits aus einer Anzahl für sich allein wirksamer Teilsysteme besteht.

Die derzeit engste Verzahnung im Datenverbund haben wir zwischen den Teilsystemen im Bereich der Auftragsabwicklung, der Lagerbestandsführung und Disposition, der Produktionsdatenerfassung, der Versanddisposition und -Abwicklung, der Einkaufsdisposition sowie der Kontokorrentführung. In den wesentlichen Bestandteilen arbeiten alle diese Teilsysteme im Echtzeitbetrieb und greifen dabei weitestgehend auch auf zentrale Datenbanken zurück.

Eine Auftragsabwicklung von der Auftragsannahme über die verschiedenen Dispositions- und Abwicklungsstufen bis hin zur Rechnungsverbuchung im Kontokorrent läßt sich nur voll automatisiert durchführen, wenn auch die jeweils relevanten und wirklich aktuellen Daten aus den tangierten anderen Teilsystemen im direkten Zugriff zur Verfügung gestellt werden können.

Dementsprechend benötigt bereits das Teilsystem der Auftragsabwicklung und Rechnungsschreibung umfassenden Zugriff auf Informationen aus den Bereichen Kunden, Produkt, Lagerbestandsführung, Produktionsplanung, Transportmittel und andere. Aber diese gegenseitige Bereitstellung von Daten von und für andere Arbeitsgebiete darf keineswegs nur im engen Rahmen eines lokal orientierten Systems erfolgen, sondern muß dem Gesamtverbund der Abwicklung und Abrechnung über einzelne Unternehmenseinheiten hinweg Rechnung tragen.

So kann die Definition der Kundenaufträge sowohl in dem Stammhaus als auch in den Geschäftsstellen erfolgen, und die Auslieferung ist von Außenlägern, von Zentrallägern oder von den verschiedenen Betriebsstätten in Deutschland aus möglich.

Anhand einiger stark vereinfachter Frage- und Aufgabenstellungen aus diesem Bereich der Auftragsabwicklung bei HOECHST werde ich nun versuchen, Überlegungen, die zur entsprechenden Datenbankorganisation geführt haben, zu verdeutlichen. Dazu stelle ich drei stark integrierte Datenbanken heraus, nämlich für:

A = Aufträge (Lager, Werke, interne Lieferungen)

B = Bestände (Istbestand, Dispositionsbestand, Prod.-Plan, Bestellung)

C = Kunden und Lieferanten (Offene Posten, Bestellungen)

Zunächst soll durch Auftragsdefinition in dem Bestand der Datenbank A ein Neuzugang gebildet werden. Dazu bedarf es aber bereits bei der Auftragsannahme folgender Feststellungen:

- Kann die Ware zur Zeit überhaupt geliefert werden und zu welchen Konditionen, oder wenn nicht, wann und von welchem Lager oder Produktionsbetrieb kann wieder geliefert werden?

- Ist der Kunde bezüglich seines Kreditlimits noch belieferbar, oder aber, falls der Kunde gleichzeitig auch als Lieferant vorkommt, wie sieht die Differenz zwischen Kundenobligo und unseren Verbindlichkeiten oder Bestellwerten aus?

Um diese Fragestellungen beantworten zu können, müssen für die erste Frage Informationen aus der Datei B und für die andere Frage Daten aus der Datenbank C zur Verfügung stehen.

Die Veränderungen der Bestandsdatei (B) werden, soweit es sich um Betriebsbestände handelt, durch Aktivitäten bewirkt, die nicht allein durch das Verkaufsgeschehen verursacht werden, sondern ebenso durch Zu- oder Abgänge im Produktionsprozeß, denn bei der Auftragsabwicklung in den Produktionslägern ist der Kundenauftrag nur einer von vielen statusverändernden Vorgängen. Eine ständige Dispositionsbereitschaft erfordert nämlich noch eine Reihe anderer Daten. Je nachdem, ob die Produktion auftragsorientiert, lagerorientiert, kontinuierlich oder diskontinuierlich abläuft, müssen die entsprechenden Dispositionssysteme auch auf aktuelle Bestandsdaten, Auftragsdaten, Produktionsplandaten, Anforderungen aus Produktion und Bestelldaten zugreifen können.

Ausgehend von einer einfachen Fragestellung nach der Lieferbereitschaft für ein Produkt können wir jetzt bereits eine beachtliche Verknüpfung verschiedener Teilsysteme erkennen, die alle einen gemeinsamen Integrationspunkt in der Bestandsdatenbank haben.

Auch bei der Beantwortung der anderen Frage nach der Bonität des Kunden erkennen wir Abhängigkeiten vom Zahlungseingang, von der Auftragsannahme durch Disponenten anderer Verkaufsbereiche und schließlich von den eigenen Bestellanforderungen sowie der Begleichung unserer Lieferantenrechnungen, falls dieser Kunde auch gleichzeitig uns gegenüber Lieferant ist.

In meinen bisherigen Ausführungen wurde absichtlich diese organisatorische Umgebung und andeutungsweise auch die funktionalen Zusammenhänge der Teilsysteme mit aufgezeigt, um klar erkennen zu lassen, daß die Dateiorganisation vor allem unter dem Aspekt der Gesamtzusammenhänge gesehen werden muß. Datenbankorganisation muß sich nämlich von der früher vorherrschenden Dateiorganisation dadurch unterscheiden, daß eine universelle Verwendbarkeit der Daten für eine Vielzahl von Anwendungen auch über den primären Anwendungsbereich hinweg erreicht werden kann.

Wenn man zusätzlich die bekannten Postulate für den Einsatz von Datenbanken erfüllen will, nämlich Aktualität der Daten für alle Benutzer, Redundanzfreiheit und Zugriff zu den Daten nach verschiedenen Kriterien, dann war dies genau die Ausgangssituation unserer Überlegungen, als wir etwa Anfang 1968 an die Systemplanung für unser erstes Auftragserfassungs- und -Abwicklungssystem im Echtzeitbetrieb herangingen und uns nach einer geeigneten Datenbank-Software umsahen. Unsere Anforderungen an die einzusetzende Datenbank-Software betrafen aber nicht nur ein Instrument für die eigentliche Datenbankverwaltung, sondern wir suchten ein insgesamt flexibles und ausbaufähiges, aber auch in seiner weiteren Entwicklung abgesichertes System.

Da auch unsere ersten Datenbank-Anwendungen nur als Teilssysteme konzipiert werden konnten und selbst innerhalb der Einzelsysteme lediglich in Entwicklungsphasen zu realisieren sind, mußte das einzusetzende Datenbanksystem ebenfalls in seiner Struktur recht anpassungs- und ausbaufähig sein und im Datenbankverwaltungsteil leicht und sicher die Integration weiterer Anwendungsprogramme ermöglichen.

IMS als Datenbank-Software

Noch bevor uns IMS bekannt wurde, haben wir unter dem Stand der Erkenntnisse und Möglichkeiten Anfang 1968 versucht, einen eigenen Datenbankprozessor zu entwickeln. Ausgehend von der Dateiorganisation des Stücklistenprozessors sollte die notwendige Strukturierung der Dateien möglichst und über entsprechende Makros der universelle Zugriff zu den Datenelementen realisiert werden.

Doch noch während der Entwicklung dieses eigenen Datenbankprozessors erhielten wir Vorabinformationen über das Information Management System (IMS) und entschlossen uns nach einem umfangreichen Systemtest zum Einsatz dessen Datenbankteiles (DL1).

Für die Datenbankorganisation mit IMS sprach vor allem der aufgrund der Baumstruktur gegebene flexible Aufbau mit maximal 256 Segmenttypen und einer variablen

Segmentanzahl auf 15 verschiedenen Stufen. Darüber hinaus bot das IMS, durch die programmunabhängigen Datenbankbeschreibungen und durch die Einrichtung, für die einzelnen Benutzerprogramme nur jeweils erforderliche Segmente als sensitiv zugängig machen zu können, eine uns ideal erscheinende Möglichkeit, programmunabhängige und dem wachsenden Integrationsgrad gut anpaßbare Datenbanken aufzubauen.

Konnten wir uns in den beiden ersten Anwendungsjahren noch mit der stark linearen Struktur unserer IMS-Datenbanken zufrieden geben, so brachte der wachsende Integrationsgrad durch unterschiedliche Anwendungssysteme und das ansteigende Informationsbedürfnis die Notwendigkeit, die Datenbanken unabhängig von ihrer physischen Speicherung auch logisch strukturieren zu können, wie dies dann ab IMS Version 2 auch möglich wurde.

Ebenfalls mit Version 2 wurde auch der Datenkommunikationsteil des IMS zu unserem zentralen System für die Nachrichtenannahme, -Steuerung- und Verwaltung von inzwischen 140 Datenstationen übernommen, so daß heute schon ein System /370-168 fast nur für den IMS-Betrieb eingesetzt werden muß. Darüber hinaus wird IMS aufgrund seiner zentralen Datenbankverwaltung und Nachrichtensteuerung jetzt auch in Verbindung mit GIS eingesetzt und außerdem mit STAIRS verknüpft. Somit wird IMS heute von HOECHST als ein umfassendes Datenbankverwaltungs- und Nachrichtensteuerungssystem angesehen.

Aufgrund der zentralen Bedeutung der mit IMS organisierten Datenbanken und eines recht hohen Nachrichtenaufkommens mit einem starken Anteil änderungswirksamer Vorgänge in den Datenbanken mußten wir besonders beim Datenbankdesign sowie bei der Programmstruktur und bei der Wahl der Zugriffsbefehle einen großen Wert auf Schnelligkeit und Sicherheit legen.

IMS läßt dem Benutzer einen großen Spielraum bei der Organisation und Strukturierung der Datenbanken. Deren Design aber beeinflußt ganz entscheidend die Verarbeitungsgeschwindigkeit der zugehörigen Anwendungsprogramme und kann sich auch im Hinblick auf den Gesamtdurchsatz im IMS-System spürbar bemerkbar machen.

Da zu Beginn der Anwendung von IMS weder Erfahrungen vorlagen noch in irgendeiner Weise ein Verfahren zur Simulation des Zeitverhaltens der Datenbanken bei unterschiedlicher Strukturierung zur Verfügung stand, mußten viele grundlegende Erkenntnisse von uns zuerst einmal im Rahmen spezieller Testuntersuchungen gesammelt und dann im praktischen Betrieb ergänzt und angepaßt werden. Allerdings mußten im Laufe der Zeit manche unserer dabei gewonnenen Regeln infolge wesentlicher Änderungen von Hard- und/oder Software wieder neu überdacht und verändert werden.

So hat die Verfügbarkeit über preiswertere Plattenspeicher mit erheblich verbesserter Speicherkapazität einerseits und die immer aufwendiger werdende Kommunikation zwischen Benutzer- und Verwaltungssystem bei den neuen Betriebssystemen andererseits dazu geführt, vom Konzept der tieferen Strukturierung mit feiner Segmentierung wieder abzugehen. Es wird dabei zwangsläufig mit größeren Informationseinheiten (Segmenten) gearbeitet, die jedoch oft nicht voll genutzt werden und entsprechend mehr externen Speicherplatz benötigen. Der Mehraufwand bei der Datenbereitstellung im Anwenderprogramm zwischen einem größeren und einem kleineren Segment ist verschwindend gering gegenüber dem zweimaligen Kommunizieren zwischen Anwender- und Kontrollprogramm.

Ähnliche Einsparungen erlauben die im Laufe der Weiterentwicklung von IMS eingeführten Syntaxverbesserungen. Während früher im Regelfall mehrere Segmente angefordert wurden und die Auswahl im Anwenderprogramm erfolgen mußten, erlauben es jetzt die booleschen Verknüpfungen verschiedener Kriterien in den Suchanweisungen, die gewünschten Informationen mit weniger Aufrufen vom System auswählen zu lassen.

In der Organisationsform der IMS-Dateien streben wir heute überwiegend Verfahren an, bei denen zum Auffinden des Satzes nicht mehr das aufwendige Durchsuchen der Indextafeln erforderlich ist, sondern durch ein Umrechnungsverfahren aus dem Sortierschlüssel eine direkte Adresse ermittelt werden kann. Allerdings ist es oft schwierig ein Verfahren zu finden, das gleichmäßig über den gegebenen Bereich verteilt. Dies gilt besonders für sogenannte sprechende Schlüssel, die keinerlei Rücksicht auf eine Speicherorganisation nehmen. Obwohl bei diesen Umrechnungsverfahren in der Regel die Sortierfolge verloren geht, interessiert uns der schnellere Zugriff für die Echtzeitverarbeitung erheblich mehr als der vermehrte Aufwand für ein gelegentliches sequentielles Verarbeiten dieser Datenbestände.

Heute sind bei HOECHST ca. 60 % aller online-Dateien nach direkten Zugriffsverfahren organisiert. Die restlichen Dateien konnten wegen ihrer Schlüsselstruktur und häufigen sequentiellen Verarbeitung noch nicht umgestellt werden. Problematisch bei den indexorientierten Verfahren sind Neuzugänge, da IMS für sie Überlaufketten bildet, was die Performance ganz erheblich senkt. Gerade bei einem online-System werden die neuen Sätze in mehreren Phasen geprüft, verarbeitet und weitergeleitet, wobei jeweils ein aufwendiges Lesen erforderlich ist. In jeder Nacht reorganisieren wir die meisten dieser Dateien, wobei benötigte Auswertungen und Statistiken erstellt werden und als Datensicherung eine Kopie anfällt.

VSAM als verbesserte indexorientierte Zugriffsform des Betriebssystems wird zur Zeit bei uns getestet. An einen produktiven Einsatz ist aber erst zu denken, wenn wir vom sicheren fehlerfreien Funktionieren im Zusammenspiel mit IMS überzeugt sind.

Durch praktische Erfahrungen wurde auch ein gewisser Wandel bei der Gestaltung umfangreicher zentraler Datenbanken ausgelöst; speziell dann, wenn von verschiedenen Benutzern oft recht unterschiedliche Anforderungen hinsichtlich Inhalt und Umfang aufzunehmender Daten gestellt werden. Die in solchen zentralen Stammdatenbanken, wie beispielsweise der Kunden- und Lieferantendatenbank, für einzelne spezielle Abwicklungs- oder Abrechnungsprogramme zu speichernden Informationen, können häufig über das hinausgehen, was für die restlichen Benutzer jemals von Bedeutung sein kann.

Wir hatten dieses Problem vor allem bei typischen branchenbezogenen Daten in unserer Kundendatei, die beispielsweise bei Arzneimittelkunden zu einer völlig anderen Ausfüllung des einheitlichen Strukturrahmens führte als bei Kunden des Industriebereichs. Hinzu kommen häufig abweichende Anforderungen hinsichtlich Aktualisierung der Informationen, Zuständigkeit im Änderungsdienst und Aufnahme neuer Daten, wodurch trotz allen Komforts der Datenbankverwaltungssysteme doch immer wieder Unruhe auch in diejenigen Benutzergruppen solcher Datenbanken getragen wird, die primär von der Erweiterung oder einer kleineren Änderung in der Struktur nicht betroffen sind.

Aus überwiegend pragmatischen Gründen haben wir uns daher in einigen Fällen weniger an die reine Theorie eines universell verwendbaren und redundanzfreien Datenbankkonzeptes gehalten und mehr die flexible und benutzerfreundliche Handhabbarkeit sowie ein sicheres Verhalten der Datenbank in der Systemumwelt in den Vordergrund unserer Überlegungen gestellt.

Darum wurden einige bisher schon recht komplexe Datenbanken nicht mehr in dem an und für sich durch neu hinzukommende Anwendungsgebiete erforderlich werdenden Umfang erweitert. Wir gingen nun verstärkt auf das Prinzip der Auslagerung spezieller Daten in dedizierte Dateien über. Diese Subdateien bleiben logisch in gewissem Umfang noch von der Mutterdatenbank abhängig, weil der Stammteil der Informationen von dorther eingespeist wird. Auf der anderen Seite müssen veränderte Daten aus der Subdatei völlig unabhängig von der Mutterdatenbank übernommen werden können. Physisch werden diese Subdateien völlig unabhängig von der Mutterdatenbank geführt und erhalten dort im Rootsegment lediglich Vermerke über Eröffnung, Änderungshinweise oder Löschungen. Logisch bleiben sie dadurch voneinander abhängig, denn ohne einen bereits eröffneten Stammteil in der Mutterdatei kann auch die Subdatei nicht eröffnet werden. Ebenso dürfen Basisdaten in der Mutterdatei nicht gelöscht werden, solange entsprechende Daten in den Subdateien noch benötigt werden.

Derartige Aufteilungen einer Datenbank in Mutterdatei und Subdateien können nicht nur aus organisatorischen Gründen erfolgen, sondern müssen auch durch die

Verhaltensweise der Hard- und Softwaresysteme in Erwägung gezogen werden; denn bei sehr viele Anwendungsgebiete umfassenden Datenbanken kann es schon allein durch die Zugriffshäufigkeiten auf den gleichen Plattenstapel zu erheblichen Engpässen kommen. Andererseits bereitet uns die temporäre Sperrung der Datenbanken während der Update-Vorgänge einige Zeitprobleme, vor allem dann, wenn die Datenbankänderungen sinnvollerweise im Stapelbetrieb auf einem anderen Rechner durchgeführt werden.

Durch die Aufteilung in dedizierte Subdateien ermöglichen wir es jedoch, daß im Bereich der voneinander unabhängigen Daten einer logischen Gesamtdatenbank verschiedene Anwendungsprogramme weitgehend ungestört und gleichzeitig arbeiten können. Synchronikationspunkte und ein aufeinander abgestimmtes System von Hinweisvermerken in den Einzeldateien sorgen dann dafür, daß der Gesamtzusammenhang der Datenbank erhalten bleibt.

Ein anderer in der praktischen Arbeit nicht zu unterschätzender Vorteil von dedizierten Subdatenbanken liegt in der erheblich besseren Reaktionsfähigkeit bei Fehlersituationen oder sonstigen Störungen im System. So nehmen wir ggf. innerhalb dieses Subdatenbanksystems lieber eine gewisse Datenredundanz in Kauf, als daß wichtige Programme im Falle eines Ein-/Ausgabefehlers oder anderer technischer Behinderungen im Zugriff zu lange auf die Durchführung umfangreicher Wiederherstellungsmaßnahmen für die Gesamtdatenbank warten müssen. Dies gilt im Prinzip auch dann, wenn die nachts im Stapelbetrieb durchzuführenden Änderungs- und Reorganisationsläufe zentraler Datenbanken eine Störung im Ablauf erfahren und nicht mehr rechtzeitig bis zum Anlaufen des Echtzeitbetriebs bereitgestellt werden können. Zugehörige Subdatenbanken hingegen bleiben von diesen Störungen oft völlig unberührt oder können auch ohne die anstehenden Datenbankänderungen weiterhin benutzt werden.

Andererseits können aber auch Auswirkungen von Programmzusammenbrüchen auf ein Gesamtdatenbanksystem durch dedizierte Subdateien geringer gehalten werden. Man muß dann nicht unbedingt die Gesamtdatenbank und damit alle tangierten Anwendungsprogramme stoppen, sondern kann wegen geringer gegenseitiger Abhängigkeiten viel gezieltere Maßnahmen zur schnellen Behebung der Fehlersituation einleiten.

Gerade dem Problem der Vermeidung einer gewissen Anfälligkeit gegenüber Störeinwirkungen, sowohl durch die Benutzersysteme als aber auch nach wie vor durch Soft- und Hardware, wird heute vom Hersteller noch viel zu wenig Aufmerksamkeit geschenkt; denn welche Vorteile soll eine theoretisch sehr sinnvoll strukturierte und auf alle Informationsbelange eingerichtete Datenbankorganisation bringen, wenn diese nicht absolut benutzungsfreundlich und zuverlässig angelegt ist? Das Ziel integrierter Datenbank- und Informationssysteme muß es vielmehr sein, daß, bei aller wünschenswerten Bewahrung der Gesamtzusammenhänge, die Teilsysteme in ihrer speziellen Funktion von Störungen verbundener Systeme unbeeinträchtigt und soweit wie nur möglich operationsfähig erhalten bleiben.

Da Auswirkungen durch Aufbau und Anwendungen von Datenbanken sowohl hinsichtlich des Systemverhaltens einzelner Anwendungsprogramme als auch im Hinblick auf die Belastung für das Gesamtsystem und die grundsätzlichen Verfügbarkeitsaspekte nur noch aus übergeordneter Sicht beurteilt werden können, wurde bei HOECHST eine spezielle Koordinationsstelle eingerichtet. Diese hat zur Aufgabe, bereits während der Planungsphase sowohl die datenbanktechnischen Gesamtaspekte zu beachten und auf das einzelne Datenbankdesign entsprechend einzuwirken, als auch durch Empfehlung geeigneter Strukturierungen der Anwendungsprogramme zu einem zeitlich und sicherheitsmäßig günstigen Ablauf im Gesamtsystem rechtzeitig beizutragen.

Darüber hinaus werden von diesen Spezialisten allgemein gültige Normen und Anwendungsbeispiele für Datenbankdesign erarbeitet und in jeweils geeigneter Form durch Merkblätter und Informationsseminare den Anwendern von Datenbanksystemen zugänglich gemacht.

HILFSMITTEL FÜR DATENBANKDESIGN UND -VERWALTUNG

Während wir uns in der Vergangenheit sehr tastend und mit teilweise recht aufwendigen Testversuchen an eine endgültige Struktur einer Datenbank heranbewegt haben, bemühen wir uns heute beim Design sowohl mehr um die Anwendung generell gesicherter Erkenntnisse aus der praktischen Erfahrung als auch um den Einsatz geeigneter Hilfsmittel für eine wirksame Datenbankmodellierung.

Einerseits helfen uns zur Erreichung dieses Zieles eine Reihe von Hilfsprogrammen, die rein organisatorisch die Struktur der Datenbank und deren Inhalt transparenter gestalten und als Modellierungshilfe sehr einfach notwendige Veränderungen im Design ermöglichen; andererseits können zusätzlich noch Programme zur Simulation der Datenbanken eingesetzt werden, die eine geeignete Struktur unter dem Gesichtspunkt der Mengengerüste, der Zugriffshäufigkeit und der Kombinationsfähigkeit der Datenelemente herausfinden helfen.

Allerdings möchte ich einschränkend sagen, daß wir umfassende Simulationen wegen der sehr aufwendigen Vorarbeit für die Beschaffung der quantitativen Angaben und wegen des Aufwandes für die Beschreibungen der vielfältigen Zugriffsfunktionen seitens der Benutzerprogramme bisher noch nicht durchgeführt haben. In der Zukunft jedoch werden zuverlässigere Planungen unter Anwendung verbesserter Simulationsverfahren schon deshalb unerläßlich werden, weil die Datenverarbeitung nicht nur wegen des allgemeinen Kostendrucks, sondern auch wegen der überhöhten Systembeanspruchung durch spezielle Anwendungsprogramme nicht ständig das Gesamtsystem erweitern kann.

Andere, ganz dringend notwendige Hilfsmittel, sowohl für die Design-Phase als auch für die laufende Verwaltung der Datenbanken, sind geeignete Dokumentationsprogramme. Ohne derartige, im englischen Sprachraum mit "Data Dictionary and Directories" bezeichnete Systeme kann man eine effektive Datenbankplanung und einen laufenden Überblick über Struktur, Querverbindungen im Daten- und Benutzerbereich sowie über den jeweiligen Status der Datenbank nicht mehr zuverlässig erreichen.

Umso mehr müssen wir es als Anwender komplexer Datenbanksysteme bedauern, daß bisher vom Anbieter der Datenbanksysteme dieses schwierige Problem der Datenbank-Dictionary-Systeme so sehr schleppend bearbeitet wurde und die Benutzer meist eigene und wegen des hohen Aufwandes oft unzureichende Teillösungen für ihre Datenbankdokumentation und Administration erarbeiten mußten. In dieser, für eine weitere und gesicherte Fortentwicklung von Anwendungen mit Datenbanken so entscheidenden Frage müssen wir an IBM die dringende Aufforderung richten, die Kunden in ihrer Datenbankverwaltungsarbeit durch ein umfassenderes und benutzerfreundliches "Data Dictionary System" zu entlasten und zu einer weitgehend maschinellen Dokumentation der eingesetzten Datenbanken beizutragen.

Neben diesen Administrationshilfen für eine leichtere Gestaltbarkeit und Verwaltung von Datenbanksystemen ist auch der permanente Einsatz von Hilfsprogrammen zur Beobachtung des arbeitenden Systems und zur Auswertung statistischer Kenngrößen unerläßlich, um dadurch sowohl die Arbeitsweise einzelner Programme als auch das gesamte Systemverhalten beurteilen und anpassen zu können. Hierfür können wir aber auf ausreichende Daten aus IMS und SMF zurückgreifen und geeignete Monitoren zu deren Auswertung einsetzen.

Geringe Belastung durch einzelne Anwender führt bei IMS wegen der Verzahnung der Abläufe innerhalb der online-Kontrollregion zu einem insgesamt besseren Performance-Verhalten. Es ist daher erforderlich, sowohl das Verhalten einzelner Programme als auch ihr Zusammenspiel miteinander zu überprüfen. Dazu benutzen wir Programme, die auf der Auswertung von Logbandsätzen basieren. Die Tagesstatistik zeigt die Aktivitäten eines Programmes während eines ganzen Tages. Daraus kann man erkennen, ob einzelne Programme im Verhältnis zu den verarbeiteten Nachrichten eine überdurchschnittliche Rate von Datenbankzugriffen haben.

Die Tagesstatistik ermittelt keinen Eindruck vom Verhalten eines Programms innerhalb einer gewissen Umgebung (z. B. zu Spitzenzeiten), von der Reihenfolge der Aktivitäten innerhalb eines Programmdurchlaufs sowie von der Dauer einzelner Datenbankzugriffe. Für diese Zwecke gibt es den DC-Monitor, der auf besondere Anforderung entsprechende Informationen mitschreibt. Systemspezialisten werten die damit gewonnenen Listen aus und können den verantwortlichen Programmierer zu geschickteren Datenbankaufrufen veranlassen bzw. allgemeine Richtlinien herausgeben. Wir haben auf diesem Wege schon wesentliche Verbesserungen im Ablauf der Programme erreichen können. Es ist bei einem online-System, in dem ca. 40 Anwendungsprogramme miteinander konkurrieren, natürlich kaum möglich, gleiche Konstellationen oder Ablaufreihenfolgen zu wiederholen. Der Einfluß von kleinen Änderungen kann daher meist nicht in exakten Zahlen ausgedrückt werden. Bewertungsmaßstäbe sind daher allenfalls Gesamtzahl der Zugriffe, insgesamt verbrauchte Rechnerzeit, Durchsatzrate von Nachrichten zu bestimmten Tageszeiten usw.

GEGEBENE UND NOTWENDIGE KOMMUNIKATIONSFORMEN

Aus den bisherigen Ausführungen war zu erkennen, daß die entscheidende Notwendigkeit zum Aufbau einer umfassenden Datenbankorganisation durch die Echtzeitprojekte ausgelöst wurde. Echtzeitverarbeitung mit Öffnung der Datenverarbeitung unmittelbar hin zum Arbeitsplatz des eigentlichen Systembenutzers, der in einer interaktiven Betriebsweise mit dem System und seinen Datenbanken kommunizieren soll, erfordert aber die Anwendung eines umfassenden Nachrichtensteuerungs- und Verwaltungssystems.

Die wesentlichen hier vorgestellten Anwendungen sind von ihrem Typ her sogenannte Teilhabersysteme, bei denen in einem vorgegebenen Anwendungssystem aufgrund der einzelnen vom Benutzer ausgelösten Transaktionen fest zugeordnete Prozeduren aktiviert werden. Für diesen Typ der Nachrichtensteuerung und Programmkontrolle bietet IMS mit seinem Datenkommunikationsteil die für ein Informationssystem notwendige Ergänzung des Datenbankteils. Auch die für das Gesamtsystem des IMS vorhandenen Sicherheitseinrichtungen mit einem umfangreichen Logging sowohl der Nachrichten als auch der datenbankwirksamen Aktivitäten und einem wirksamen Prüfpunkt und Wiederanlaufverfahren, bestärken uns zusätzlich in der Ansicht, daß wir mit IMS im Prinzip das richtige Softwareprodukt für unsere Informationssysteme zur Verfügung haben.

Richtigerweise ist die Systemsteuerung von IMS recht umfassend ausgelegt, so daß wir inzwischen unter dessen Kontrollprogramm nicht nur die transaktionsbedingten "Message Control Programme" laufen lassen, sondern auch stapelorientierte Datenfernverarbeitungsprogramme, das GIS und das "Information Retrieval System" STAIRS mit umfangreichen Dokumentationsdatenbanken zur Anwendung bringen.

Das erwähnte GIS hat allerdings zur Zeit noch eine völlig untergeordnete Bedeutung und soll erst nach Ablauf einer erfolgreichen Erprobungszeit in zukünftige Planungen einbezogen werden. Trotzdem können wir schon aufgrund der ersten Probeanwendungen erkennen, daß es eine interessante Ergänzung zu den Datenbanksystemen darstellen kann. Ob es allerdings voll geeignet ist, um unmittelbar vom Endbenutzer sporadisch auftretende Anfragen an bestehende Datenbanken schnell formulieren zu lassen, scheint noch ungewiß. Es wäre unseres Erachtens besser, für die Endbenutzer eine einfachere und in deutscher Sprache formulierbare Abfragesprache zu haben und dafür GIS für erfahrene Benutzer noch weiterhin auszubauen, um beispielsweise auch durch Feld- und variable Indizierung noch bequeme Anfragen an IMS-Datenbanken richten zu können. Dabei wäre es ebenfalls von Vorteil, wenn aus den vorhandenen IMS-Datenbankbeschreibungen auch automatisch die IMS-Dateibeschreibung erzeugt würde, oder aber durch ein übergeordnetes Datenbankmanagement IMS und GIS gemeinsam bedient würden.

Das hier ebenfalls erwähnte STAIRS wird bei HOECHST als umfassendes Dokumentations- und Information Retrieval System eingesetzt. Unter der Nachrichten- und Programmsteuerung von IMS wird STAIRS bisher für umformatierte Datenbanken im Bereich der medizinischen Literaturdokumentation, der Forschungsdokumentation und zur Patentdokumentation eingesetzt. Sämtliche Fragestellungen und Suchvorgänge in zur Zeit auf 16 Magnetplattenspeicher IBM 3330-11 gespeicherten Dokumenten erfolgen in Echtzeitverarbeitung über Bildschirmterminals unmittelbar im System-Benutzerdialog.

Die bisher erläuterte umfassende Nutzung des IMS als Gesamtsteuerungssystem bringt allerdings ein überproportionales Ansteigen der CPU-Belastung durch vermehrten systeminternen Verwaltungsaufwand mit sich, so daß wir uns jetzt Gedanken machen, bis zu welchem Zeitpunkt das IMS bei unserer geplanten Vermehrung der Datenstationen - selbst bei einer /370-168 - noch in der Lage sein kann, alle Anforderungen in einem System zu bedienen.

Sollte demzufolge die Leistungsfähigkeit und die jetzige Arbeitsweise des IMS seitens IBM nicht entscheidend geändert werden, dann bliebe nur eine verhältnismäßig unwirtschaftliche Aufteilung der IMS-Anwendungen auf zwei Systeme. Dem sind allerdings sowohl durch die Datenbankverwaltung des IMS als auch durch die Anwendungssysteme eindeutige Grenzen gesetzt. Ein wesentlich sinnvoller Weg scheint uns hingegen in der Realisierung einer Konzeption zu liegen, die eine Auslagerung geeigneter Funktionen in intelligente und mit dedizierten Dateien ausgestattete Datenstationen ermöglicht. Dadurch kann das Zentralsystem sowohl von vermeidbaren Transaktionen entlastet werden als aber auch die Funktionsfähigkeit des Systems durch eine zumindest temporär mögliche unabhängige Arbeit an den peripheren Datenstationen verbessert werden.

In diese Richtung weisende Konzeptionen wurden ja auch beispielsweise mit den SNA-Systemen IBM 3790 oder auch 3770 angekündigt. Allerdings erwarten wir dann auch im IMS sowohl hinsichtlich seiner Datenbankkonzeption als auch bei der Nachrichtensteuerung eine volle Integration der Möglichkeiten dieser Terminalcomputer im Sinne eines echten hierarchisch gegliederten Systemverbundes. Wünschenswert wäre dann nämlich ein voller Einbezug der vom Vorrechner geführten Datenbestände in das Datenbankverwaltungssystem des IMS, so daß alle entsprechenden Dateiveränderungen in der Mutter-Datenbank auch sofort für die dedizierte Datei mit ausgelöst würden und umgekehrt.

Wenn wir die übliche Definition eines Teilhabersystems, bei dem verschiedene Teilhaber am System voneinander abhängig sind und über ein gemeinsames Informationssystem miteinander verbunden sind, hinsichtlich einer umfassenden Datenbankorganisation in unserem Unternehmen betrachten, dann sind viele Arbeiten, die im Remote Job Processing von den Werken aus im Rahmen des Systemverbundes betrieben werden, eher Teilhaber als Teilnehmersysteme. Obwohl die Datenübertragung stapelorientiert erfolgt und in der Regel auch völlig unabhängige Programme aufgerufen werden, gibt es doch auch im RJE-Betrieb viele Anwendungen, die auf gemeinsame zentrale Prozedur- und Datenbanken zugreifen.

Diese Arbeiten können derzeit aber nur im Rahmen der RJE-Prozeduren auf unserem ASP-System abgewickelt werden, das einerseits auf einer ganz anderen Anlage gefahren wird als das IMS, andererseits aber auch eine völlig andere Übertragungstechnik benutzt, so daß nicht einmal eine gemeinsame Leitungsbenutzung von IMS und RJE möglich ist, obwohl beide Systeme Bestandteile des gleichen Gesamtinformationssystems und der gemeinsamen Datenbankorganisation sind. Hier ist es sowohl aus wirtschaftlichen als auch aus organisatorischen Gründen dringend erforderlich, umgehend eine gemeinsame Leitungssteuerung und möglichst auch Datenbankverwaltung für IMS und RJE herbeizuführen.

Ein solches Paket von Verfahren für eine einheitliche Datenübertragungssteuerung ist ja inzwischen von IBM als "System Network Architecture" angekündigt. Allerdings scheint uns diese Bezeichnung wenigstens bisher noch ein vielversprechendes Schlagwort zu sein, das vor allem hinsichtlich des Wortes "Network" noch mit sehr viel Inhalt ausgefüllt werden muß; denn wir benötigen in unserem Unternehmen im Rahmen des Systemverbundes nicht nur das einheitliche Konzept für die Datenübertragungssteuerung und die hierarchisch geordnete Kommunikation zwischen Rechner und untergeordneten Datenstationen, sondern wir erwarten vor allem aus Gründen einer erhöhten Sicherheit und Verfügbarkeit ein Netzwerksystem zwischen gleichberechtigten Systemen mit gemeinsam benutzbaren Programmbibliotheken und Datenbanken.

Ich hoffe, daß ich trotz des überwiegend allgemein gehaltenen und nur auf praktische Erfahrungen oder konkrete Planungsansätze bei HOECHST ausgerichteten Referates auch den anwesenden Wissenschaftlern und Software-Architekten einige Bestätigungen ihrer Auffassungen oder auch einige Anregungen zum Thema Datenbanken und Datenkommunikation geben konnte.

Nutzung von Datenbanken im nicht-wissenschaftlichen Bereich einer Hochschule

Eckhard Edelhoff, Universität Dortmund

Zusammenfassung

Ziel des Vortrages ist es darzustellen, in welchem Umfang und zu welchem Zweck Datenbanken in Verwaltung und Bibliothek einer Hochschule eingesetzt werden können. Genauer eingegangen wird auf die datenverarbeitungsrelevanten Fragen im Bereich einer Hochschulbibliothek, insbesondere auf die Auswirkung unterschiedlicher Datenverarbeitungstechniken.

Inhaltsverzeichnis

1. DER GESAMTHOCHSCHULBEREICH DORTMUND

Der Gesamthochschulbereich Dortmund besteht aus

der Universität Dortmund,
der Pädagogischen Hochschule Ruhr,
der Fachhochschule Dortmund,
der Fachhochschule Hagen.

Nach der Absicht des Gesetzgebers sollen die genannten Hochschulen zu einer Gesamthochschule integriert werden.

Das Rechenzentrum an der Universität Dortmund versorgt seit 1973 mit Hilfe einer IBM/370-158 die Hochschulen des Gesamthochschulbereiches Dortmund, die Universität Bielefeld und seit 1975 die Fernuniversität in Hagen mit Datenverarbeitungskapazität und den dazugehörigen Dienstleistungen.

Die Bibliotheken im Gesamthochschulbereich werden ab 1976 - nach Einzug in einen Neubau - zu einer Einheit zusammengefaßt sein. Das bedeutet, daß ab 1976 das Bibliothekssystem in Dortmund aus einer Zentralbibliothek und ca. 25 Bereichsbibliotheken besteht.

Die einzelnen Hochschulen im Gesamthochschulbereich haben eigenständige Verwaltungen.

2. PROJEKTE IM BEREICH DER BIBLIOTHEKEN UND VERWALTUNGEN

In den Jahren 1971/72 wurde entschieden, die Bibliotheken und Verwaltungen des Gesamthochschulbereiches Dortmund in die Versorgung durch den zu beschaffenden Großrechner einzubeziehen. Hierfür sprachen folgende Gründe:

- Es bestand keine Aussicht neben einem Großrechner einen für Bibliotheken und Verwaltungen dedizierten Rechner zu beschaffen.
- Bei entsprechender Leistungsfähigkeit eines Großrechners führen die Anwendungen der Bibliotheken und Verwaltungen zusammen mit den Anwendungen aus Forschung und Lehre zu einer ausgewogenen Ausnutzung.

Als Konsequenz zu dieser Entscheidung wurde

- 1972 eine Projektgruppe zur 'Organisation der Arbeitsabläufe in den Bibliotheken unter Berücksichtigung der Datenverarbeitung' gemeinsam von den Bibliotheken und dem Rechenzentrum unter Einbeziehung von Mitarbeitern der Firma IBM und
- 1974 eine Projektgruppe mit entsprechendem Auftrag gemeinsam von den Verwaltungen, dem Rechenzentrum unter Einbeziehung von Mitarbeitern der Firma IBM und der Hochschulinformationssysteme GmbH gegründet.

3. DAS BIBLIOTHEKSPROJEKT

Die Aufgabenstellung 'Organisation der Arbeitsabläufe unter Berücksichtigung des Einsatzes der Datenverarbeitung' bedarf der Erläuterung:

Die Bearbeitung bibliothekarischer Objekte zum Zwecke der Nutzung in einer Hochschule erfolgt über zahlreiche Stufen

- Literaturauswahl,
- Bestandskontrolle,
- Bestellung,
- Eingangsbearbeitung,
- Rechnungsbearbeitung,
- Sachkatalogisierung,
- alphabetische Katalogisierung,
- Einbandbearbeitung,
- Schlußkontrolle,
- Auskunft,
- Ausleihe.

Für eine geordnete Bearbeitung und eindeutige Identifikation der bibliothekarischen Objekte ist in konventionellen Bibliotheken die Führung zahlreicher Kataloge, Karteien, Register und Listen für Statistiken am Arbeitsplatz erforderlich. Die Redundanz der jeweils abgelegten Daten ist erheblich. Ziel der Einführung der Datenverarbeitung in die Bibliotheken muß deshalb u.a. sein:

- die einzelnen Arbeitsgänge miteinander zu verknüpfen,
- die manuelle Führung der verschiedenen Auskunftsmittel überflüssig zu machen, deren Redundanz zu beseitigen und den im Zusammenhang mit deren Unterbringung stehenden Wegeaufwand zu verringern,

- die Kommunikation der Bibliothek mit den Lieferanten und den Nutzern zu erleichtern bzw. zu verbessern und
- die Nachhaltung der erforderlichen Statistiken, das Drucken von Belegen, Meldungen u.ä. zu automatisieren.

Für diesen Zweck wurden folgende Datenverarbeitungsmöglichkeiten in Aussicht gestellt:

- Magnetplattenspeicher zur Aufnahme und Rückgewinnung aller während der Literaturbearbeitung anfallenden Daten.
- Sichtgeräte mit der Möglichkeit, die gespeicherten Daten online am Arbeitsplatz jederzeit verfügbar zu machen bzw. zu ergänzen.
- Nutzung des Monitors CICS der Firma IBM.

Bei dieser Entscheidung wurden folgende Gesichtspunkte berücksichtigt:

- Zu dem durch Lehre und Forschung bestimmten Aufgabenprofil des zu beschaffenden Großrechners sind Anwendungen aus dem Bereich der Bibliotheken und der Verwaltungen einfügbare ein/ausgabeintensive Komplemente.
- Die Aufgaben der Bibliothek fallen verteilt über deren gesamte Öffnungszeit an.
- Die genannten Ziele der Einführung der Datenverarbeitung in die Bibliothek sind nur dann erreichbar, wenn als Auskunftsmittel der Rechner am Arbeitsplatz jederzeit zur Verfügung steht.

3.1 Stand der Automatisierung im Bibliotheksbereich

Versuche, bibliothekarische Arbeiten mit Hilfe der elektronischen Datenverarbeitung zu rationalisieren, haben eine über 10-jährige Geschichte. Zu nennen sind u.a. die auf Batch-Verfahren sich stützenden Systeme (Off-line-Systeme):

- der Bibliothek der Universität Bochum,
- der Bibliothek der Washington University School of Medicine,
- der Bibliothek der University of Illinois

und in neuerer Zeit die auf Realzeit-Verfahren sich stützenden Systeme und Versuche (On-line-Systeme):

der Bibliothek der Stanford University,
des Ohio College Library Centers,
der Bibliothek der Universität Bielefeld,
des IBM Labors in LOS GATOS.

Es handelt sich hierbei, abgesehen von der Datenverarbeitungstechnik, um im Ansatz und Umfang sehr unterschiedliche Systeme - Systeme, die auf die Automatisierung eines Teils der Arbeitsgänge ausgelegt sind, bzw. Systeme, die alle Arbeitsgänge umfassen. Das Dortmunder Bibliothekssystem ist in Anlehnung an die mit dem in dem IBM-LABOR entwickelten System gemachten Erfahrungen aufgebaut worden.

Off-line-Systeme

Off-line-Systeme sind unabhängig von der verwandten Technologie nicht in der Lage, die Handhabungen einer konventionellen Bibliothek grundsätzlich zu verändern bzw. zu erleichtern. Mit dieser Technik können wesentlich nur jene Arbeitsgänge rationalisiert werden, deren Ablauf an die turn around time des jeweiligen Rechners angepaßt werden kann:

- Die Führung der Kataloge, Karteien und Register kann bezügl. der jeweils notwendigen Veränderungen erleichtert werden. Am Arbeitsplatz sind sie für den Bibliothekar nach wie vor erforderlich.
- Die Wiederverwendung einmal erhobener Daten ist grundsätzlich möglich, jedoch in der Regel an die Ausnutzung externer Datenträger, wie Lochstreifen, Lochkarten u.a. gebunden. Korrekturen, Ergänzungen und umfangreiche Kategorienschemate führen zu Umständlichkeiten und Schwierigkeiten und doppelten Arbeitsvorgängen.
- Es gibt keine über die konventionelle Handhabung hinausreichende Möglichkeit, Informationen über den Stand der jeweiligen Bearbeitung eines Objekts verfügbar zu halten.

On-line-Systeme

On-line-Systeme sind in der Lage, die komplizierten konventionellen Handhabungen des Buchlaufes abzubauen:

- Der Bibliothekar benötigt an seinem Arbeitsplatz physisch keine Karteien, Register und Kataloge.
- Die Wiederverwendbarkeit von einmal erfaßten Daten ist sichergestellt, ebenso deren Änderungen und Ergänzungen.
- Es gibt eine einfache Möglichkeit der Information über den Stand der Bearbeitung eines bibliothekarischen Objektes. Informationslücken sind nicht vorhanden.

Beide Systeme nutzen die Technologie des jeweils zur Verfügung stehenden Rechners in völlig unterschiedlicher Weise aus. Während On-line-Systeme wegen ihres größeren Softwarekomforts einen Großrechner als Träger benötigen, können Off-line-Systeme prinzipiell auch auf für diesen Zweck spezialisierten Rechnern der mittleren Datentechnik gefahren werden.

3.2 Buchlauf in einer konventionellen Bibliothek

Es sollen hier als Grundlage für die nachfolgenden Abschnitte, die während eines Buchlaufes erforderlichen Arbeitsvorgänge in einer konventionellen Bibliothek dargestellt werden. Es handelt sich hierbei jedoch notwendig um eine unvollständige, auf Monographien beschränkte Schilderung:

o Buchauswahl

- Die Literaturauswahl erfolgt durch die Fachreferenten anhand von Bibliographien, Prospekten, wöchentlichen Verzeichnissen der Deutschen Bibliothek u.ä. unter Berücksichtigung der Benutzerwünsche und der Ausleihstatistik.
- Neben den jeweils von den Fachreferenten vorzugebenden bestelltechnischen Daten, wie

  Bestellart,
  Anzahl der Exemplare,
  Standort,
  Fachgruppe,

  gehen im Regelfalle die oben genannten gekennzeichneten Unterlagen an die Abteilung Erwerbung.

o Buchbestellung

- In der Abteilung Erwerbung werden die Anschaffungsvorschläge der Referenten geprüft. Hierbei sind unter Umständen bibliographische Recherchen durchzuführen und anschließend ist am alphabetischen Katalog, an der Interimskartei und an der Bestellkartei eine Bestandskontrolle durchzuführen.
- Entsprechend dem Ergebnis der Bestandskontrolle wird die Bestellung durchgeführt. Folgende Daten sind u.a. erforderlich:

  Verfasser (bei Verfasserschriften)
  Titel
  Verlag
  Ort, Erscheinungsjahr
  Auflage
  Bestellart
  Serientitel } (bei Serien)
  Bandangabe }
  Haushaltstitel
  Lieferant
  Quelle

- Kopien der Bestellung werden in die Bestellkartei und in die Buchhändlerkartei eingelegt.

o Bucheingang

- In der Abteilung Erwerbung wird das Buch auf Beschädigung oder Fehldruck hin überprüft. Ein Laufzettel zum Zweck der Kontrolle des Geschäftsganges und der Eintragung von Daten, die während des Geschäftsganges anfallen, wie z.B. Signatur und Sachkatalogisierungsdaten, wird beigegeben.
- Es wird eine Bestandskontrolle für unverlangte zur Ansicht-Sendungen durchgeführt. Unverlangte Sendungen und zur Ansicht-Bestellungen werden den Fachreferenten zur Kaufentscheidung vorgelegt.
- Für alle Bücher mit positiver Kaufentscheidung werden die Buchhändlerkartei, die Bestellkartei und die Interimskartei auf den neuesten Stand gebracht. Die Bücher werden inventarisiert.
- Die Referenten erhalten die Bücher zur weiteren Bearbeitung.

o Sachkatalogisierung

- Die Referenten klassifizieren die Bücher nach ihrem Inhalt und legen den Inhalt der Neuerwerbungsliste fest.
- Die Bücher werden zur Titelaufnahme für die alphabetischen Kataloge weitergeleitet.

o Titelaufnahme

- Entsprechend den Regeln für die alphabetische Katalogisierung werden die zur Identifizierung der Bücher relevanten Daten erfaßt. Es handelt sich hierbei um eine erneute Aufnahme jener Daten, die z.T. bereits während des Bestellvorgangs angefallen sind.
- Die Zettel für die alphabetischen Kataloge und den Sachkatalog werden erstellt und in

  den zentralen alphabetischen Katalog,
  den zentralen Sachkatalog und
  den Standortkatalog

  eingefügt. Bei Büchern mit Sonderstandort sind zusätzlich Zettel für

  die alphabetischen Kataloge der Abteilungen,
  den Lesesaalkatalog,
  den Katalog der Lehrbuchsammlung und
  den Katalog der Handapparate

  erforderlich.

  Sonderstandorte verfügen im wesentlichen ausschließlich über einen aktuellen Buchbestand. Auslagerungen von Büchern in die Zentralbibliothek sind in umfangreichem Maße erforderlich. Bei Änderungen des Standortes eines Buches sind die entsprechenden Korrekturen in allen Katalogen vorzunehmen.

- Die Bücher werden an die Einbandstelle weitergegeben.

o Einbandbearbeitung

- Soweit notwendig, werden die Bücher zum Buchbinder weitergeleitet. Hierfür ist eine Buchbinderkartei erforderlich.
- Die Bücher werden nach Durchführung der Buchbinderarbeiten an die Beschriftungsstelle weitergeleitet.

o Beschriftung

- Es werden die Signaturen und die Rückentitel aufgebracht und die Stempelungen gemacht.
- Die Bücher werden der Schlußkontrolle zugeführt.

o Schlußkontrolle

- Die Schlußkontrolle ist eine formale Kontrolle zum Zweck der Überprüfung des Geschäftsganges anhand des Laufzettels und zur Überprüfung von Buchdaten und Daten auf den Katalogzetteln.

o Benutzung

- Die Bücher werden in den Standorten aufgestellt.
- Für die Zwecke der Ausleihe werden Benutzerkartei und ein Couponregister geführt.

3.3 Buchlauf unter Ausnutzung eines On-line-Systems

In diesem Abschnitt sollen - beschränkt auf Monographien - mögliche Veränderungen in der Handhabung des Buchlaufes unter Einsatz eines On-line-Systems dargestellt werden. Hier, ebenso wie im vorangegangenen Abschnitt, bleibt die Darstellung wegen des möglichen Detailierungsgrades unvollständig.

Wesentliche Merkmale organisatorischer Veränderungen sind:

- Einmal erfaßte Daten können aufbereitet jederzeit zurückgewonnen werden.
- Das System hält jederzeit Informationen über den Bearbeitungsstand aller erfaßten Objekte bereit.
- Merkmalsgebundene Überwachungen und Überprüfungen können automatisch durchgeführt bzw. unterstützt werden.

Die Auswirkungen dieser Veränderungen auf den Buchlauf sind nachfolgend an einigen Beispielen dargestellt:

- Daten, die in der Erwerbungsabteilung für zu bestellende bibliothekarische Objekte ermittelt werden, können für die alphabetische Katalogisierung genutzt werden. Hierdurch ergibt sich eine Verlagerung der Katalogisierungsarbeiten in die Erwerbungsabteilung. Dies wird zusätzlich begünstigt durch die Möglichkeit, für die

Erwerbung und die Katalogisierung Fremdleistungen, wie z.B. die Magnetbänder der Deutschen Bibliothek, auszunutzen.

- Nicht gleichzeitig eintreffende Anforderungen eines Titels für die verschiedenen Bereichsbibliotheken führen im konventionellen System regelmäßig zur mehrfachen manuellen Ausfertigung von Bestellunterlagen. Mit Hilfe eines On-line-Systems können die einmal erhobenen Daten in der Regel ohne zusätzlichen Aufwand wiederverwendet werden. Konventionell ist dies aus technischen Gründen nicht möglich.
- Die Bearbeitung von unverlangten zur Ansicht-Sendungen kann nach der Kaufentscheidung durch den Fachreferenten von der Katalogisierung vorgenommen werden. Eine zusätzliche Bearbeitung durch die Erwerbung zur Vermeidung von Dubletten ist überflüssig. Der Vorgang der Katalogisierung kann wiederum unterstützt werden durch die automatisierte Ausnutzung von Fremdleistungen.
- Die Mahnungen bzgl. vorgenommener Bestellungen, Buchbinderaufträge u.ä. können automatisch und individuell entsprechend den vorliegenden Gegebenheiten durchgeführt werden.
  Auf den Buchlauf bezogenen Erinnerungslisten (von u.a. aufgrund beabsichtigter Katalogdatenübernahme von Fremdbändern nicht durchgeführter Katalogisierungsarbeiten)können automatisch erstellt werden.
- Zusammen mit der Verlagerung von Katalogisierungsarbeiten in die Erwerbungsabteilung führt die vollkommene Durchsichtigkeit des Buchlaufes zu einer schnelleren Verfügbarkeit des bibliothekarischen Objektes.
- Im Bereich der Auskunft können Aussagen über das Vorhandensein und die Verfügbarkeit bibliothekarischer Objekte unter Einschluß des jeweils aktuellen Standes vorgenommen werden.
- In der Ausleihe sind Reservierungen, Sperrungen, Mahnungen, Gebührenerhebungen lokal und nicht-lokal aufgrund des jeweils aktuellen Standes vornehmbar.

3.4 Die Bildschirme von DOBIS

Das Dortmunder Bibliothekssystem (DOBIS) ist mit dem Ziel entwickelt worden, den Rechner als Speicher für alle in der Bibliothek während des Buchlaufes anfallende und für diesen verwendbare Daten einzusetzen. Zum Absetzen und zur Wiedergewinnung von Daten stehen Sichtgeräte zur Verfügung. Es sind drei Arten von Bearbeitungsvorgängen zu unterscheiden:

- Vorgänge ohne Nutzung der Möglichkeiten der Datenverarbeitung. Hier sind u.a. bibliographische Recherchen zu nennen.
- Vorgänge unter Ausnutzung der On-line-Funktionen des Systems. Das sind:

  Registersuche
  Bestellung
  Zugang
  Zeitschriftenbearbeitung
  Katalogisierung
  Rechnungsbearbeitung
  Einbandbearbeitung
  Ausleihe
  Fernleihe

- Vorgänge unter Ausnutzung der Off-line-Funktionen des Systems. Diese sind Drucken u.a. von:

  Bestellungen
  Katalogen
  Mahnungen
  Überwachungslisten und Statistiken

Die Verfügbarkeit von Datenstationen ersetzt dem Bibliothekar am Arbeitsplatz die bisher benutzten manuell erstellten Kataloge, Register und Karteien. Die in Bildschirmdialoge umgesetzten Arbeitsabläufe erfordern allerdings eine große Anzahl verschiedenartiger Bildschirmanzeigen. Schwierigkeiten, die sich hieraus ergeben, werden dadurch vermieden, daß alle Anzeigen einem einheitlichen Aufbau folgen:

Daten desselben Typs erscheinen stets an der gleichen Stelle auf dem Schirm. Dieser ist in drei Teile unterschiedlicher Funktion gegliedert:

Kopfteil
Raum für wechselnde Informationen
Anweisungsteil

Der Kopfteil umfaßt Angaben über die angesprochenen DOBIS-Funktionen, deren gerade ablaufende Unterfunktion und eine Charakterisierung der angezeigten Bildschirmmaske

Der Raum für die wechselnden Informationen enthält entsprechend dem jeweiligen Arbeitsschritt innerhalb der ablaufenden Funktion unterschiedliche Angaben, z.B. Teile eines Registers, Informationen über einen Lieferanten oder ein bestimmtes Dokument usw.

Der Anweisungsteil enthält Hinweise darüber, in welcher Weise der Bearbeiter den Dialog fortsetzen kann. In einer Textzeile wird der Bearbeiter zur nächsten Aktion aufgefordert, z.B. zur Eingabe bestimmter Daten oder zum Aufruf einer weiteren Bildschirmausgabe.

Wie bereits mehrfach betont, müssen Daten nur einmal eingegeben werden. Von da an stehen sie an allen Arbeitsplätzen zur Verfügung. Dieses Prinzip hat zur Folge, daß alle Angaben, die zur Wiederauffindung eines bibliothekarischen Objektes im System wesentlich sind, wie:

ISSN, ISBN
Titel
Personen, Körperschaften
Signaturen
Nummern, Abkürzungen
Sachkatalogdaten

sorgfältig auf Fehler überprüft werden müssen. Hierdurch werden eine Speicherung gleicher Daten in verschiedenen Versionen und daraus folgende Bearbeitungsfehler vermieden. Der Bearbeiter wird deshalb bei jeder Angabe, die zur Änderung eines Registers - in diese sind die oben genannten Daten gespeichert - führt, zur Einsichtnahme in das betreffende Register gezwungen. Das geschieht entweder dadurch, daß das System automatisch die Eingabe zur Registersuche benutzt, oder der Bearbeiter zur Eingabe eines Suchwortes aufgefordert wird.

Bei zahlreichen bibliothekarischen Angaben sind bestimmte Abkürzungen oder standardisierte Formen zu verwenden. Um dem Bearbeiter den Umgang mit den Formvorschriften zu erleichtern, sind diese im System gespeichert und können vom Bibliothekar benutzt werden.

3.5 Die Datenbank im Dortmunder Bibliothekssystem

Unter den bereits im Kapitel 3 'Bibliotheksprojekt' genannten Prämissen

- Ersetzen aller Kataloge, Karteien usw.
- Wiederverwendung einmal erhobener Daten
- Durchsichtigkeit des Buchlaufes

ist es erforderlich, den gesamten Buchbestand d.h. den Inhalt sämtlicher konventioneller Informations- und Dokumentationsmittel integriert on-line verfügbar zu machen. Bei einem Buchbestand von 1 Mio. Bände bedeutet dies, daß Sekundärspeicher in der Größenordnung von 6-8 x $1o^8$ Bytes erforderlich wird.

Dem hohen Speicherbedarf auf der einen Seite stehen sehr komplexe, durch vielfältige Regeln und Zwänge festgelegte Datenstrukturen und Abfrageerfordernisse gegenüber. Da zwischen den Bibliotheken ein enger Datenaustausch national und international stattfindet, kann hiervon nicht ohne eigenen Schaden abgewichen werden.

Die Datenbank im Dortmunder Bibliothekssystem kennt die nachfolgend nach ihren Inhalten unterschiedenen Dateien:

- Hauptdateien zur Aufnahme von u.a.:

  bibliographischen Informationen
  Bestellinformationen
  Ausleihinformationen
  Rechnungsinformationen
  Druck- und Terminwarteschlangen.

  Die bibliographischen Informationen sind in zwei Hauptdateien gespeichert. Die logischen Sätze in diesen Dateien werden fortlaufend numeriert. Die einander entsprechenden Sätze sind miteinander verknüpft. Jeder physischen bibliographischen Einheit entspricht mindestens je ein logischer Satz in beiden Dateien. Entsprechend der Komplexität der bibliographischen Gebilde sind auch die logischen Sätze innerhalb einer Datei miteinander verbunden. Es sind zu unterscheiden:

  Monographien
  Monographien mit beigefügten Werken
  Mehrbändige Werke mit und ohne eigenen Stücktitel
  Schriftenreihen
  Zeitschriften

Monographien stellen den Normalfall dar. Jedem Exemplar kann in den beiden Hauptdateien je ein logischer Satz ohne Verknüpfungen zu anderen Sätzen zugeordnet werden. In allen anderen Fällen sind je physische Einheit mehrere logische Sätze bzw. Verknüpfungen zu anderen logischen Sätzen erforderlich. Im Nachfolgenden ist ein Beispiel für eine komplexe Struktur aus dem Bereich der Schriftenreihen abgebildet:

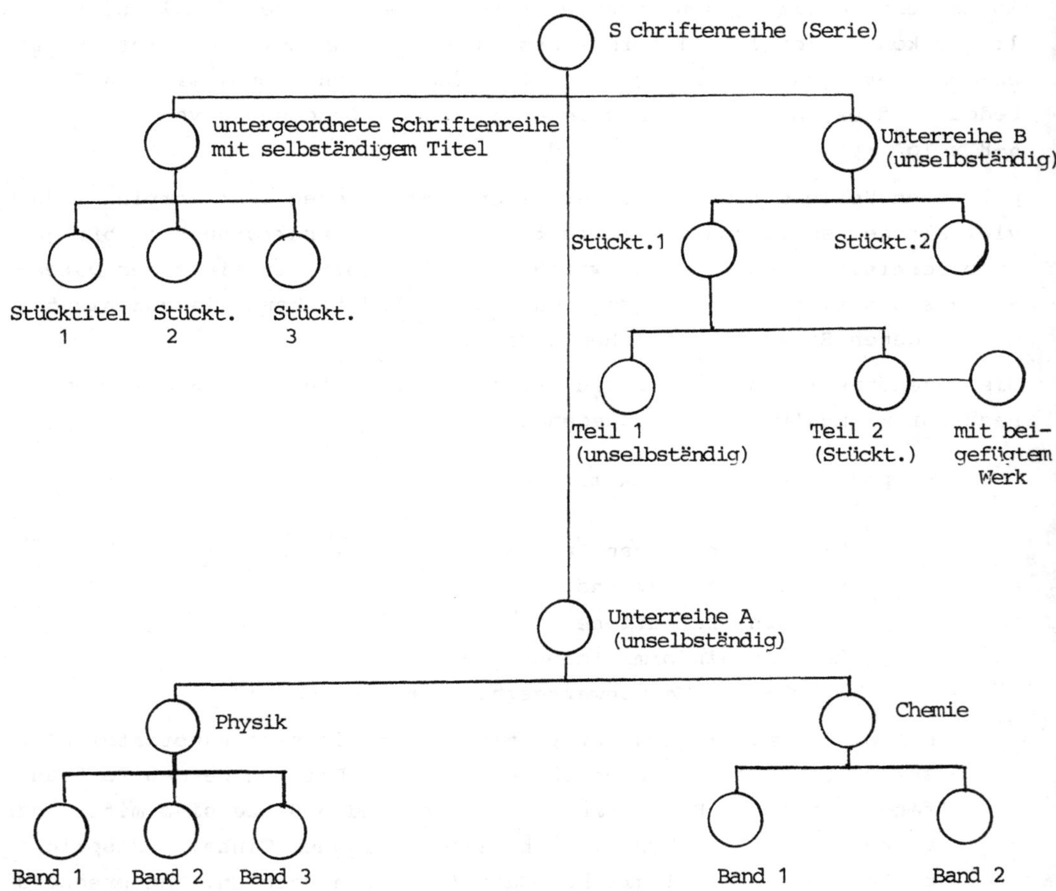

Anm.: Gekürztes Beispiel aus der unter Ziffer 12 zitierten Schrift.

- Zugriffsregister zur Aufnahme von u.a.:

  Personen/Kooperationen
  Titeln
  Schlagwörtern
  Signaturen
  Verlagen
  ISBN/ISSN
  Benutzername
  Lieferanten

  Die Zugriffsregister dienen auf der einen Seite dem Wiederauffinden der bibliographischen Einheiten. Sie bieten aus dieser Sicht wesentlich mehr Möglichkeiten als die konventionellen Informationsmittel aufgrund der großen Vielfalt und z.B. der Möglichkeit, das Titelregister um permutierte Titel mit entsprechenden Verweisungen zu erweitern. Andererseits dienen die Zugriffsregister zur Datenaufnahme. Z.B. sind in den ersten beiden Registern neben der Ansetzungsform (ordnend) auch die Vorlageform (beschreibend) gespeichert. Beide Register zusammen dienen weiterhin als Hilfsmittel, aufgrund deren Sortierung der alphabetische Katalog erstellt werden kann.

  Alle Hauptdateien und Zugriffsregister besitzen einen VSAM-ähnlichen Index, der mehrere Indexstufen umfassen kann. Auf diese Weise ist ein schneller Zugriff auf den jeweils benötigten physischen, bzw. variabel langen logischen Satz gewährleistet.

- Dateien zur Aufnahme von Code-Tabellen.

  Diese Tabellen dienen u.a. der Platzersparnis in den Hauptdateien.

4. Das Verwaltungsprojekt

Wie bereits eingangs gesagt, wurde 1974 eine Projektgruppe mit dem Auftrag der 'Organisation der Arbeitsabläufe in den Verwaltungen unter Berücksichtigung der Datenverarbeitung' gegründet. Zu dem Bibliotheksprojekt bestehen folgende Unterschiede:

- Wegen des Arbeitsumfanges können die verschiedenen Funktionen der Hochschulverwaltungen nicht gleichzeitig organisiert werden. Ihr schwächerer innerer Zusammenhang macht darüber hinaus eine nachträgliche Integration, soweit ein entsprechender Rahmen geschaffen wurde, möglich.
- Aufgrund der Hochschulsituation sollen nach Fertigstellung des Systems, bzw. dessen Teile, die einzelnen Verwaltungen unabhängig voneinander arbeiten können.
- Die Organisationsarbeit wird erschwert durch die unterschiedlichen Handhabungen von Verwaltungsvorgängen in den einzelnen Hochschulen.

Als erste Funktion wurde der Personal- und der Studentenbereich in Angriff genommen. Hierbei wurden die von der Firma Hochschulinformationssysteme GmbH und den Statistischen Ämtern entwickelten Normungen von Begriffen und Schlüsseln berücksichtigt.

Folgende Möglichkeiten der Datenverarbeitung stehen der Projektgruppe zur Verfügung:

- Die Datenbank IMS der Firma IBM.
- Plattenspeicher in dem benötigten Umfang.
- Der Einsatz des Rechners ist in den einzelnen Funktionen so zu planen, daß die Anwendungen vorwiegend in der zweiten und dritten Schicht gefahren werden können.

Literaturangaben

1 Elektronische Datenverarbeitung in der Universitätsbibliothek Bochum. Hrsg. von Günther Pflug u. Bernhard Adams. Bochum 1968.

2 Alexander, R.W.: Library Management System (LMS): Descriptive specifications for an on-line, real-time integrated system. Los Gatos, Cal.: IBM o.J.

3 Experimental Library Management System (ELMS): Librarian's User Manual. Los Gatos, Cal.: IBM 1972.

4 Datenerfassung und Datenverarbeitung in der Universitätsbibliothek Bielefeld. Hrsg. von Elke Bonneß u. Harro Heim. Pullach bei München 1972. (Bibliotheksstudien. Bd. IA.)

5 Bibliographic Automation of large library operations using a time-sharing system (BALLOTS): Phase 1. Final Report. Stanford, Cal. 1971.

6 Bibliographic Automation of large library operations using a time-sharing system (BALLOTS): Phase 2, part 1. Final Report. Stanford, Cal. 1972.

7 First annual report of the BALLOTS project to the National Endowment for the Humanities. Stanford, Cal. (1973).

8 The Shared Cataloging System of the Ohio College Library Center. Frederick G. Kilgour, Philip L. Long u.a. in: Journal of Library Automation. Vol. 5, No. 3, 1972.

9 An automated on-line circulation system. Ed.: Irene Braden Hoadley and A. Robert Thorson. The Ohio State University Libraries 1973. (Proceedings and Papers of an Institute Held at The Ohio State University Sept. 13-14, 1971.)

10 Ohio College Library Center. Annual Report 1973/1974.

11 Bibliotheksautomatisierung in den USA und in Kanada. Hrsg. von Walter Lingenberg. Pullach bei München 1973. (Bibliothekspraxis. Bd. 10.)

12 Deutsche Forschungsgemeinschaft. Bibliotheksausschuß. Maschinelles Austauschformat für Bibliotheken (MAB 1). Berlin 1974.

13 Empfehlungen für den Einsatz der Datenverarbeitung in den Hochschulbibliotheken des Landes Nordrhein-Westfalen. Hrsg. von der Planungsgruppe Bibliothekswesen im Hochschulbereich NRW. Düsseldorf 1974.

14 Jedwabski, Barbara: DOBIS - ein integriertes On-line-Bibliothekssystem. in: 10 Jahre Universitätsbibliothek Dortmund. Zum 1.6.1975 hrsg. von Valentin Wehefritz. Dortmund 1975.

15 DOBIS. Anwendungsbeschreibung. (GAP. Application Guide.) IBM 1975. (Erscheint Ende 1975)

16 DOBIS. Systembeschreibung. (GAP. Systems Guide.) IBM 1975. (Erscheint Ende 1975)

Einsatz eines Datenbanksystems beim Hessischen Landeskriminalamt

Rolf Heitmüller, 62 Wiesbaden, Am Hochfeld 12

1. DIE HESSISCHE POLIZEI

Die Hessische Polizei ist seit 1. Januar 1974 eine staatliche Polizei, d.h. alle polizeilichen Einrichtungen werden vom Land Hessen unterhalten.

Bis zum 31. Dezember 1973 gab es neben der staatlichen Polizei kommunale Polizeidienststellen in bestimmten Städten.

Im Bereich der Verbrechensbekämpfung hat das Hessische Landeskriminalamt den besonderen gesetzlichen Auftrag, die zur Verbrechensbekämpfung notwendigen Informationen zu sammeln, auszuwerten und gewonnene Erkenntnisse allen interessierten und berechtigten Stellen mitzuteilen. Neben dieser Funktion hat das Hessische Landeskriminalamt auch Exekutivaufgaben und unterhält für bestimmte Spezialaufgaben Zentralstellen (so z.B. zur Bekämpfung und Aufklärung von Wirtschaftskriminalität, zur Brandursachenermittlung). Darüberhinaus hat das Hessische Landeskriminalamt den Auftrag, die Datenverarbeitung der Hessischen Polizei zentral zu betreiben.

2. RÜCKBLICK IN DIE ENTWICKLUNG

Die Einführung der EDV bei der Hessischen Polizei kann nicht losgelöst von den entsprechenden Überlegungen in anderen Bundesländern und bei der Bundesverwaltung gesehen werden. Bereits 1964 und, wenn auch sehr vage, schon vorher wurden erste Überlegungen angestellt, wie polizeiliche Information sich mit dem modernen Arbeitsmittel EDV verarbeiten lassen könne. An Ende der Überlegungen stand die Forderung, zunächst müsse die Täterermittlung automatisiert werden. Diese Forderung wurde in den folgen den Jahren geradezu zur Voraussetzung zur Einführung der EDV bei der Polizei in der BRD hochstilisiert. Eine Analyse polizeilicher Arbeit war bisher noch nicht erfolgt; an ihre Stelle traten eben Forderungen, Einzelbereiche zu automatisieren. Eine auf Bundesebene eingesetzte Arbeitsgruppe erarbeitete erste Ansätze einer Analyse. Der Wert einzelner Informationsbereiche, zum Teil auch einzelner Begriffe, wurde diskutiert.

Für die Hessische Polizei fielen in diesen Zeitraum die ersten Gespräche mit Herstellern von EDV-Anlagen und wissenschaftlichen Institutionen. Das Ergebnis war eher entmutigend. Nach der groben Beschreibung der zu lösenden Aufgabe erklärten alle Befragten, eine allgemeingültige, fertige DV-Lösung zur Realisierung polizeilicher Aufgaben sei nicht vorhanden und lasse sich auch nicht ohne weiteres aus vorhandenen Verfahren entwickeln.

Im Vordergrund der Überlegungen standen damals bereits die Probleme der Speicherung von Massendaten im direkten Zugriff, der schnellen Wiedergewinnung gespeicherter Daten, der schnellen Aktualisierung der Information und nicht zuletzt das Problem der hohen Verfügbarkeitsforderung der Polizei an die DV-Einrichtungen.

Als Ergebnis dieses Zeitabschnittes bleibt festzuhalten, daß als Voraussetzung zur Einführung der EDV bei der Polizei zunächst eine intensive Analyse der polizeilichen Arbeitsabläufe erforderlich war und, auf dieser Analyse basierend, ein polizeiliches DV-System zu entwickeln sein würde.

Dieser Erkenntnis wurde auf verschiedenen Ebenen Rechnung getragen: Beim Bundeskriminalamt wurde zum 1.1.1968 eine "Arbeitsgruppe EDV" eingerichtet, zu der alle Bundesländer einen geeigneten Mitarbeiter entsenden sollten. Aufgabe dieser Arbeitsgruppe sollte es sein, ein einheitliches polizeiliches DV-System für die gesamte Polizei der BRD zu entwickeln. Die Arbeitsgruppe sollte alle bisher in der Bundesrepublik angestellten Überlegungen zur polizeilichen Datenverarbeitung sammeln und auswerten, um auf dieser Basis ein einheitliches System zu entwickeln. Die Arbeitsgruppe EDV war bis Anfang 1970 in wechselnder personeller Zusammensetzung tätig. Als Ergebnis ihrer Arbeit bleibt festzuhalten:

- Die Arbeitsgruppe war mit zu geringer Kompetenz ausgestattet, um den Auftrag auch nur annähernd zu erfüllen.

- Das geforderte Verfahren zur automatischen Täterermittlung war in dem gegebenen personellen und zeitlichen Rahmen nicht zu erstellen.

- Sinnvoller, weil einfacher und in zeitlich und sachlich überschaubaren Grenzen zu lösen, schien nach Auffassung der Arbeitsgruppe zunächst ein System, das die zum bekannten Täter vorhandene Information auf Anfrage möglichst schnell und umfassend zur Verfügung stellen konnte.

Die dazu erforderlichen Informationsbereiche und -mengen wurden in systematischer Form zusammengestellt. In dieses System sollte auch ein Teil der Personenfahndung, die sog. Bürofahndung, einbezogen werden. Hierbei handelt es sich um ein Verfahren, Suchanträge so aufzubereiten, daß in einer Druckerei Karteikarten zur täglichen Aktualisierung von Fahndungskarteien hergestellt werden und ein monatlicher Fahndungsbuchdruck erfolgen konnte.

Die parallel zu den Arbeiten der "Arbeitsgruppe EDV" durchgeführte Erhebung und Analyse des IST-Zustandes im Hessischen Landeskriminalamt brachte interessante Ergebnisse. Obwohl immer wieder behauptet wurde, das Karteisystem zur Tätetermittlung sei die wichtigste polizeiliche Informationssammlung, stellte sich heraus, daß von ca. 60 Karteien lediglich 20 ohne das Ordnungsmerkmal "Personalien" auskamen. Demnach wurde die Informationswiedergewinnung in der Hauptsache über die Personalien der Täter, nicht aber über andere Beschreibungsmerkmale betrieben. Diese Erkenntnis stimmte mit den Überlegungen der Arbeitsgruppe EDV beim BKA im wesentlichen überein.

Für den Aufbau eines Informationssystems der Hessischen Polizei ergaben sich nun grundsätzlich neue Denkansätze, die sich wie folgt zusammenfassen lassen:

- Mittelpunkt aller polizeilichen Tätigkeit im Bereich der Verbrechensbekämpfung ist der Fall als Anlaß zum Tätigwerden überhaupt. Daraus folgte, daß ein System ohne Berücksichtigung von Fallinformation nicht nur lückenhaft, sondern auch falsch aufgebaut sein würde.

- Da die Personalien des Täters eine wesentliche Rolle bei der Informations-Wiedergewinnung spielen, sollten sie an hervorragender Stelle, aber - und das war neu - nur einmal für eine Person in dem System Platz finden.

- Das Verhältnis Fall / Person sollte durch Verknüpfungen darstellbar sein.

- Das System sollte die Möglichkeit bieten, zu jedem beliebigen Zeitpunkt Erweiterungen sachlicher Art anzubringen.

Die genauere Betrachtung der vorstehenden Forderungen zeigte, daß sich das gesamte Problem nicht in einem Entwicklungsgang lösen lassen würde. Die Auswirkungen auf die polizeiliche Tätigkeit wären wahrscheinlich so schwer geworden, daß es zumindest fraglich schien, ob die Arbeit nicht gelähmt worden wäre. Dies war Grund genug, das Hessische Polizeiinformations-System (HEPOLIS) stufenweise aufzubauen und in der ersten Stufe nur das zu realisieren, was am wenigsten einschneidende Folgen für die polizeiliche Tätigkeit haben würde.

Zur Aktualisierung der gespeicherten Information wurden verschiedene Möglichkeiten in Betracht gezogen. Die beste Lösung schien, Datenaufbereitung und Datenerfassung zu dezentralisieren. Untersuchungen der Leistungsfähigkeit eines zunächst grob geplanten Datenübertragungsnetzes ergaben, daß die Kapazität neben dem Auskunftsdienst auch die dezentrale Aktualisierung des Bestandes zulassen würde.

Die grundsätzlichen Anforderungen an das aufzubauende System waren zusammengefaßt:

- Im Mittelpunkt der ersten Ausbaustufe soll die Personenauskunft stehen;

- Die Informationsübermittlung soll mittels Datenfernübertragung erfolgen;

- Die Information soll an zentraler Stelle gespeichert, aber dezentral aufbereitet und eingegeben werden;

- Die Aktualisierung des Bestandes soll jederzeit vom Ort der Informationsgewinnung aus möglich sein und

- die folgenden polizeitaktischen Forderungen sollen erfüllbar sein: Information muß auf Wunsch, ganz oder teilweise, schnell und jederzeit zur Verfügung stehen; sie muß von möglichst jedem Ort erreichbar, einfach zu handhaben und möglichst umfassend sein.

Aufgrund dieser Forderung erfolgte eine Ausschreibung mit der Aufforderung, Angebote zu Hardware und Software abzugeben. Die Firma IBM erhielt den Zuschlag, weil sie neben dem günstigsten Preis/Leistungsverhältnis das ausgewogenste Verhältnis zwischen Hardware und Software bieten konnte.

3. DIE REALISIERUNGSPHASE

Nachdem die Vertragsverhandlungen mit der Firma IBM abgeschlossen waren, wurde zunächst intensiv an der Konfiguration der DV-Anlagen gearbeitet. Die Forderung nach hoher Verfügbarkeit der Einrichtung führte dazu, zwei Rechner einzusetzen, (IBM /370-145 mit 768 KB Hauptspeicher) die beide in ihrer Ausstattung und ihren Fähigkeiten gleich sind, damit sie wahlweise einzeln den Betrieb von HEPOLIS aufrechterhalten können.

Die angeschlossenen externen Einheiten (Magnetplattenspeicher - 16 Plattenlaufwerke IBM 3330 mit insgesamt 2,2 Mrd. Zeichen im direkten Zugriff -, Magnetbandmaschinen, Schnelldrucker, Lochkartenleser und Datenübertragungssteuereinheiten) sind technisch so ausgelegt, daß jeder Rechner auf jede dieser Einheiten zu jeder gewünschten Zeit Zugriff haben kann. Die Datenübertragungssteuereinheiten sind, genau wie die Rechner, doppelt installiert. Alle anderen Einheiten sind in genügend großer Anzahl vorhanden, um auch hier Ausfälle im technischen Bereich möglichst ohne größere Wartezeiten überbrücken zu können.

Als Betriebssystem werden OS MFT II, derzeit im Release 27.7, und OS-VS eingesetzt.

Zur Verwaltung der gespeicherten Daten und zum Betrieb der Datenfernverarbeitungseinrichtungen wird IMS 2 Level 4 eingesetzt.

Als Datenstationen werden ausschließlich IBM 3270 Terminals verwendet. Diese sind als Einzelstation oder Mehrfachstationen - je nach Bedarf - vorhanden und alle mit einem Puffer für 1.920 Zeichen ausgelegt. Die Wahl fiel auf diese relativ großen Bildschirme, weil HEPOLIS, soweit irgend möglich, benutzerfreundlich aufgebaut werden sollte und kleinere Bildschirme automatisch zu Restriktionen in der Organisation des Bildschirmaufbaus geführt hätten.

Nur mit dem großen Bildschirm ist es gelungen:

- fast in allen Fällen eine Informationseinheit in einem Bildschirm aufzubauen, ohne an Übersichtlichkeit zu verlieren,

- jedes einzelne Datenfeld mit einer Feldbezeichnung von 10 Zeichen zu adressieren und so in den meisten Fällen Aussagen ohne Abkürzungen zu machen und, was für den Benutzer sehr wichtig ist,

- die Bildschirmformate für Auskunftsdienst und Änderungsdienst nahezu gleichförmig aufzubauen.

Es mag als Raumverschwendung angesehen werden, wenn fast jede Zeile des Bildschirms nur ein Datenfeld enthält. Dennoch dient ein solcher Aufbau der Übersichtlichkeit und macht das System benutzerfreundlich.

Der Datenbestand unter IMS-Steuerung gliedert sich zur Zeit in drei Bestanddatenbanken. Dies sind:

- Personenbezogene Daten
- Falldaten
- KFZ-Daten.

Der Bereich KFZ-Daten ist programmtechnisch noch nicht realisiert, jedoch im IMS-System bereits abgebildet.

Alle Informationen zu einem Objekt (Person, Fall, KFZ) werden innerhalb dieser Dateien in nur einem Datensatz abgebildet. Jeder Datensatz ist mit einem Ordnungsbegriff, einer satzspezifischen Nummer, adressierbar. Auf diese Weise kann die Information zu einem Objekt bei Kenntnis der entsprechenden Nummer wiedergewonnen werden. Da in der polizeilichen Praxis diese Nummer nicht immer und in jeder Situation bekannt ist, war es notwendig, auch auf anderen Wegen an die gewünschte Information heranzukommen. Dies ist im allgemeinen nur durch Invertierung möglich. Da IMS 2 keine Möglichkeit der automatischen Invertierung bietet, wurde das IMS-Konzept der "logischen Datenbank" aufgegriffen und die erforderlichen Invertierungslisten durch Anwendungsprogramme erstellt.

So bestehen nunmehr die folgenden Möglichkeiten, mit Identifizierungsmerkmalen auf Datensätze zuzugreifen, ohne die satzspezifische Nummer zu kennen:

- mit Name und Geburtsdatum oder
- mit dem phonetisierten Namen oder
- mit einem Deliktschlüssel auf die personenbezogenen Daten;

- mit der Angabe Behörde und Aktenzeichen auf fallbezogene Daten;
- mit dem amtlichen Kennzeichen oder
- mit der Fahrgestellnummer oder
- mit einer Kombination aus beiden oder
- mit der Motornummer auf KFZ-bezogene Daten.

Daneben sind Verbindungen hergestellt worden zwischen

- personenbezogenen Daten und fallbezogenen Daten,
- personenbezogenen Daten und KFZ-bezogenen Daten, jeweils in beiden Richtungen sowie innerhalb der personenbezogenen Daten zwischen
- den Personalien und den Personenfahndungsdaten.

Diese weitreichenden Verbindungen erlauben nahezu jede polizeilich interessante Auswertung des gesamten Datenbestandes. Es versteht sich von allein, daß in der ersten Ausbaustufe, die nunmehr realisiert ist, bei weitem nicht alle theoretischen Möglichkeiten genutzt werden können.

Ein weiteres Problem polizeilicher Datenverarbeitung, das sich mit IMS 2 nicht ohne weiteres lösen ließ, waren die variabel langen Datenfelder. Unter Ausnutzung des Verfahrens der abhängigen Segmente konnte auch das Problem zufriedenstellend gelöst werden, indem einem Segment eine Größe gegeben wurde, die die zu erwartenden Daten in einer statistisch vernünftigen Menge aufnehmen kann. Falls die tatsächliche Datenmenge größer ist als die Aufnahmefähigkeit des angesprochenen Segment-Typs, werden die nicht mehr unterbringbaren Daten in einem ersten abhängigen Segment untergebracht. Reicht auch das nicht aus, können beliebig viele Segmente dieses abhängigen Typs gefüllt werden.

Eine kurze Beschreibung von Auskunftsdienst und Änderungsdienst soll zeigen, wie das System in der Praxis genutzt wird:

- Auskunftsdienst

  Der Polizeibeamte benötigt Information über eine Person, die er gerade überprüft. Er wendet sich mit dem der Situation angepassten Kommunikationsmittel an die nächstgelegene Datenstation, gibt dem Bediener die erforderlichen Identifizierungsmerkmale und erklärt, er möchte wissen, ob die so beschriebene Person gesucht wird. Der Bediener tastet den Nachrichtenschlüssel AF02 sowie die ihm übermittelten Identifizierungsmerkmale in die erste Zeile des leeren Bildschirms ein und betätigt eine Funktionstaste. HEPOLIS teilt ihm aufgrund dieser Werte innerhalb von 10 Sekunden mit, ob diese Person gesucht wird oder nicht. HEPOLIS gibt dazu die gesamten Personalien einschließlich der Alias-Daten, besondere Hinweise zur Person und alle Fahndungsdaten aus. Mit einem anderen Nachrichtenschlüssel könnten entsprechende andere Daten abgerufen werden. Der jeweils angezeigte Bildschirminhalt kann, falls erforderlich, ausgedruckt werden.

- Änderungsdienst

  Das Aufgabengebiet Änderungsdienst umfaßt neben den Funktionen Verändern und Löschen vorhandener Daten und der Funktion Zufügen weiterer Daten in vorhandene Datensätze auch die Funktion Einbringen neuer Daten. Letzteres ist immer mit dem Eröffnen eines neuen Datensatzes verbunden. Mit dieser Funktion wird die Forderung nach dezentralisierter Datenerfassung erfüllt, da alle Funktionen des Änderungsdienstes grundsätzlich über alle Datenstationen ausgeübt werden können.

Im Änderungsdienst sind zwei Prinzipien angewendet worden:

- Die Funktionen sind - mit Ausnahme des Einbringens neuer Daten - nur mit dem entsprechenden Nachrichtenschlüssel und der satzspezifischen Nummer möglich. Dies ist notwendig, um sicherzustellen, daß eine Änderung genau an dem Datensatz durchgeführt wird, an dem sie durchgeführt werden soll.

- Alle Funktionen erfolgen formatgesteuert, d.h. jeder Funktion geht die Anforderung eines entsprechenden Änderungsformates voraus.

Handelt es sich um die Funktionen "Verändern" oder "Löschen", wird das Ausgabeformat mit den Daten gefüllt, die durch die satzspezifische Nummer adressiert werden. Bei der Funktion "Ergänzen in bereits vorhandene Daten" kann eine Formatanforderung vorausgehen, in der Anzahl, Art und Umfang der zuzufügenden Datenfelder spezifiziert werden können. Ist dies nicht gewünscht, gibt das System ein Standardformat aus, in dem jedes Datenfeld, das zugefügt werden darf, einmal Platz hat. Die Funktion "Einbringen neuer Datensätze" weicht etwas von den anderen Änderungsdienst-Funktionen ab. Der Benutzer kann sich auf jeden Fall so verhalten, als ob er der erste wäre, der Daten zu einem bestimmten Objekt einbringen will. Die dazu erforderliche Formatanforderung erfolgt mit dem Nachrichtenschlüssel und den entsprechenden Identifizierungsmerkmalen. Findet das System unter diesen Merkmalen keinen Bestand, wird ein Leerformat ausgegeben; ist Bestand vorhanden, wird er vollständig angezeigt. Der Benutzer kann nun entscheiden, ob er seine Daten einem vorhandenen Datensatz zuordnen will oder nicht. Über eine Sonderfunktion kann die Eröffnung eines neuen Datensatzes erzwungen werden.

Die Funktionen des Änderungsdienstes sind schwieriger zu handhaben, als die des Auskunftsdienstes. Das liegt daran, daß dem Benutzer im Bereich des Änderungsdienstes so viel wie möglich Formalismen von der DV-Anlage abgenommen werden sollen, gleichzeitig aber ein hohes Maß an Sicherheit erreicht werden muß. Alle Programme des Änderungsdienstes haben eine Kontrollfunktion, über die eine Prüfung der Änderungsberechtigung vorgenommen wird. So kann erreicht werden, daß nur der Besitzer der Daten - dessen Kennzeichen im Bestand gespeichert ist - Änderungen vornehmen kann. Änderungsversuche von Nichtbesitzern werden programmgesteuert abgewiesen.

Auskunftsdienst und Änderungsdienst können von derselben Datenstation aus jederzeit und in beliebiger Reihenfolge durchgeführt werden. Die dazu erforderlichen Programme und Datenbestände sind in HEPOLIS jederzeit verfügbar.

4. DER VERBUND ZUM INFORMATIONS-SYSTEM DER POLIZEI (INPOL)

Unter INPOL wird der Zusammenschluß polizeilicher Datenverarbeitungssysteme verstanden. INPOL ist erforderlich, um die auf Länderebene aufgebauten Polizeiinformationssysteme untereinander und mit dem System des Bundeskriminalamtes zusammenzuschließen. Das Bundeskriminalamt übernimmt dabei neben seinem eigenen Informationssystem die Funktion einer zentralen Nachrichtenvermittlungsstelle. Der Datenaustausch findet in einem Sternnetz über festgeschaltete Leitungen statt. Da Rechner verschiedener Hersteller mit unterschiedlicher Hardware und Software in INPOL betrieben werden, waren zum Verbundbetrieb bestimmte Absprachen erforderlich.

- Datenübertragungsprozedur
  Hier wurde eine auf den DIN-Normen basierende Absprache getroffen, die von allen Beteiligten realisierbar war. Die Prozedur erweist sich im täglichen Betrieb als durchaus zufriedenstellend.

- Datenaustauschsatz
  Zum Datenaustausch wurden bestimmte Nachrichtenformate festgelegt, die die Verbundteilnehmer beim Empfang und beim Senden von Nachrichten einheitlich anzuwenden haben. Weiterhin wurde ein Quittungsverfahren entwickelt, mit dem die Verbundpartner Daten über die Art des Nachrichtenempfangs austauschen. Auf diese Weise ist es möglich, den Sender einer Nachricht auf Fehler im Übermittlungsdatensatz aufmerksam zu machen. Fehlerquittungen können sowohl auf den unrichtigen Inhalt eines Datensatzes als auch auf einen falschen Zustand der Datenbank hinweisen.

- Nachrichtenkopf
  Jedem Austauschdatensatz ist ein Nachrichtenkopf vorangestellt, der von Anwendungsprogrammen verarbeitet wird. In diesem Nachrichtenkopf sind Informationen über den Sender und Empfänger der Nachricht ebenso enthalten wie Angaben über ihre Art und Länge. Der Nachrichtenkopf wird dem Sender in der Quittungsnachricht vom Empfänger der Nachricht zurückgesandt. Die zur Zuordnung erforderlichen Daten sind ebenfalls im Nachrichtenkopf enthalten.

Die Verbundsteuerung sowie die Aufbereitung der Sende- und Empfangsdaten in das jeweils nötige Format erfolgen im HEPOLIS in einem besonderen Programm, das unter IMS-Steuerung permanent im Rechner vorhanden ist. Zur Umsetzung der Daten in das erforderliche Format dient in diesem Programm ein Tabellen-Modul, der in beiden Richtungen wirksam ist. D.h. mit nur einem Tabellenglied erfolgt die Übersetzung vom HEPOLIS-Format in das Sendeformat oder vom Empfangsformat in das HEPOLIS-Format.

Über den Verbund werden in beiden Richtungen täglich zusammen ca. 2000 Nachrichten zuzüglich der erforderlichen Quittungen ausgetauscht. Hierbei handelt es sich ausschließlich um Update-Nachrichten.

Bestimmte Datenbereiche werden aus Sicherheitsgründen und zur Beschleunigung der Auskünfte in den an INPOL angeschlossenen Systemen parallel gespeichert. Um sicherzustellen, daß diese Bestände auch tatsächlich identisch sind, werden in bestimmten Zeitabständen Bestandsabgleiche durchgeführt. Hierzu werden die Datenbestände zu einem bestimmten Zeitpunkt vom Update ausgeschlossen und entladen. Nach Beendigung dieses Vorganges werden diese (entladenen) Bestände miteinander verglichen. Unstimmigkeiten werden protokolliert, auf ihre Ursache hin untersucht und beseitigt.

Es versteht sich von selbst, daß das vorher erwähnte Sicherungsverfahren zur Verhinderung von unberechtigten Updates auch im Verbund gilt.

5. HEPOLIS IM TÄGLICHEN BETRIEB

Das System wurde im Frühjahr 1974 mit den Erstdaten geladen. Dabei wurde der Ladeprozeß nicht in Form eines "initialload" durchgeführt, sondern die einzelnen Datensätze wurden programmgesteuert in das System eingebracht. Dabei wurde jeder Zugang über die parallel aufgebauten Suchlisten am jeweils vorhandenen Bestand vorbeigeführt. Dieses Verfahren diente dazu, Mehrfachbestände aus den bis dahin nicht bereinigten handgeführten Karteien zu erkennen und nicht in das System zu bringen. Bei diesem Erstladen wurden ca. 390.000 Personendatensätze eingespeichert und in ca. 15.000 Fällen Mehrfachbestand erkannt. Der so aufgebaute Bestand wurde alsbald für den Auskunftsdienst freigegeben.

Im November 1974 wurde der aktuelle Personenfahndungsbestand zur Parallel speicherung vom Bundeskriminalamt übernommen und nach dem oben beschriebenen Verfahren in den Bestand eingefügt. Von 150.000 übernommenen Datensätzen trafen ca. 12.500 bereits auf Bestand. In diesen Fällen wurden dem vorhandenen Datensatz lediglich die noch fehlenden Daten zugefügt.

Seit Januar 1975 läuft HEPOLIS voll im 24-Stundenbetrieb mit online-update und online-Auskunftsdienst. Die über die Datenstationen abgewickelte Menge von Arbeitsaufträgen liegt derzeit bei durchschnittlich 9.500 täglich mit Spitzen um 12.200 täglich. Da im Änderungsdienst zu jedem Arbeitsauftrag 2 IMS-Transaktionen gehören, liegt die Zahl der abzuwickelnden Transaktionen bei durchschnittlich 12.000, in Spitzen bei 16.000 täglich zuzüglich der Transaktionen des Verbundes. Die derzeit stärkste Belastung lag bei 1.200 Arbeitsaufträgen oder etwa 1.600 Transaktionen in einer Stunde.

Das System bewältigte diese Arbeitslast bei einer mittleren Antwortzeit von 3 Sekunden im Auskunftsdienst und 5 Sekunden im Änderungsdienst, wobei der Betrieb in 3 IMS-Regions abgewickelt wird. Die Arbeitsaufträge des Änderungsdienstes erfordern 2 IMS-Transaktionen, weil der Aufbau der Eingabemaske und das danach erfolgende Update von verschiedenen Programmen erledigt werden. Dies wurde so geplant, um die auch mögliche Conversational-Programmierung zu vermeiden. Im Betrieb sind derzeit 78 TP-Programme und 8 BMP-Programme mit insgesamt 172 Transaktionscodes.

Alle Programme benutzen denselben Plausibilitäts-Prüfungsmodul und dieselben Fehlerbehandlungsroutinen. Dadurch wird erreicht, daß der Datenbestand einen möglichst hohen Grad an Richtigkeit hat und dem Benutzer Fehler einheitlich auf dem Bildschirm angezeigt werden. Die Prüfungslogik ist so angelegt, daß alle eingehenden Nachrichten bis zum Ende auf Fehler geprüft werden. Am Ende der Prüfung werden festgestellte Fehler in einem Fehlerformat angezeigt. Ist trotz der Fehler eine Verarbeitung möglich, wird sie durchgeführt und das Ergebnis angezeigt. Ist eine Verarbeitung nicht möglich, erfolgt ein entsprechender Hinweis in der Fehleranzeige.

Das System wird aus Sicherheitsgründen einmal in 24 Stunden terminiert. Dies ist erforderlich, um die Restartzeiten bei abnormalem Ende so kurz wie möglich zu halten.

Die mittlere Ausfallzeit des Systems liegt unter Einschluß der o.g. geplanten Abschaltungen derzeit bei 2,2% der Verfügungszeit (bezogen auf 24 Stunden täglich). Die Restartzeiten bei abnormalem Ende liegen je nach Schwere des Fehlers zwischen 45 Minuten und 2 Stunden. Wesentlich zur Beschleunigung des Restarts hat beigetragen, daß jede Woche eine komplette Fassung der Datenbank auf Magnetplatten gesichert wird, so daß lange Restoreläufe von den ebenfalls vorhandenen Sicherungsbändern entfallen. Zur Fehlerbehebung allgemein ist zu sagen, daß die Restart- und Recovery-Routinen des IMS sich in der Praxis voll bewährt haben.

Eine Reorganisation der Datenbank war bisher erst einmal erforderlich. Sie dauerte insgesamt 92 Stunden und verlief nach anfänglichen Schwierigkeiten reibungslos. Da während dieser Zeit der Änderungsdienst unterbrochen werden mußte und der Auskunftsdienst in seinen Aussagen mit fortschreitender Zeit immer inaktueller wurde, wird zur Zeit mit Vorrang an der Erstellung eines Programmsystems gearbeitet, das den Änderungsdienst auch während der Dauer der Reorganisation erlaubt.

Im allgemeinen kann gesagt werden, daß HEPOLIS trotz der kurzen Dauer seines Einsatzes von den Benutzern bereits akzeptiert ist und den weiteren Ausbaustufen erwartungsvoll entgegengesehen wird.

6. AUFWAND

Zum Abschluß einige Bemerkungen zum Aufwand, der geleistet werden mußte, HEPOLIS in der ersten Ausbaustufe zu erstellen. Dabei sollte nicht verkannt werden, daß mit dem Aufbau von HEPOLIS erstmals EDV bei der Hessischen Polizei zum Einsatz kam. Das bedeutet, daß das EDV-Personal geworben und ausgebildet werden mußte. Dieser Prozeß dauert noch an.

Da das System mit eigenem Personal in der zur Verfügung stehenden Zeit nicht erstellt werden konnte, mußte externes Personal in erheblichem Umfang eingesetzt werden. In den letzten Wochen des Jahres 1974 waren zeitweise 26 externe Organisatoren und Programmierer beschäftigt. Insgesamt liegt der Aufwand bisher bei 75 - 80 Mann-Jahren. Darin sind enthalten Planung, Analyse, Programmierung, Schulung und Datenerfassung, nicht aber die Datenaufbereitung.

Gemessen am Erreichten scheint der Aufwand im vernünftigen Rahmen zu liegen.

Relational Data Dictionary Implementation

I A Clark, IBM United Kingdom Scientific Centre, Peterlee, UK

Abstract

The paper presupposes a team of application developers using an application generator served by a relational database (RDB). The application grows by including not only routines for input/output, but by accumulating new relations, the latter representing data-definition activity by the developers.

A data dictionary (DD) is needed

(1) to interrelate relations,

(2) to relate these to routines, input streams and reports,

(3) to produce auditing reports and clerical procedures manuals.

The benefits and technical problems of maintaining the DD itself as a RDB are treated.

INTRODUCTION

This paper assumes a development team using an application generator served by a relational database (RDB). The application grows not only by adding I/O and processing routines, but also by accumulating new relations. Such relations may be derived from already existing relations in the database, as well as being inserted independently as a set of tuples.

We do not want to argue here why we consider an application generator together with a relational data base. Suffice to say that we believe this combination to be an attractive one for use by a team of non-data-processing professionals. By 'non-DP professionals' we shall mean a group of highly skilled individuals who wish to innovate within their own discipline by making use of the computer, without being diverted from their true purpose by considerations of a purely technical nature to do with data-processing. In particular such individuals will not wish to be deflected by questions of choosing data pathways or the best data structure for their particular purpose (hence the relational database), nor get involved with the wide choice of techniques for doing essentially standard programming operations (hence the application generator).

We shall consider a relational database similar to a research prototype developed and used at the IBM UK Scientific Centre, Peterlee, called PRTV (1). The chief feature of PRTV is that of deferred operation, that is, a new relation derived from existing relations is not materialised into a set of tuples until these tuples are explicitly called for; eg, to open the relation as a read-only file, or to find out how many tuples it contains. A new relation can be defined during a terminal session by entering an expression which contains names of existing relations, acted on by the relational operations:

UNION	PROJECTION
INTERSECTION	SELECTION
DIFFERENCE	JOIN

The result is a named entity within the user's workspace which we shall call a '(relational) value'. It is not our purpose to describe how this entity is implemented. Suffice to say that it is a character string which specifies briefly but conveniently to the routines which materialise the tuples just how to go about doing so. Within this relational value there exist, as intact substrings in fact, either the names, or the values, of the relations from which it was derived.

However, note that by the term: 'derived relation', we shall mean specifically one whose relational value contains the <u>name</u> of another relation, say 'A', rather than just the value of A. This is because, in PRTV, there is no way of effectively recognising that, say, B has been obtained from A in the latter case. If for instance relation A were bulk-loaded from cards, next relation B created and simply assigned the value of A, there would be nothing inherently different about A and B. Indeed, in PRTV as it stands there would be no way of telling which came first! Moreover either A or B could be reassigned another value, leaving the other unchanged. This is clearly not the case if B were derived from A. Then whenever A changed its value, B would change correspondingly.

Since relational values are relatively small entities compared with the large sets of tuples they can potentially represent, one must not think that a computer process which forms new relations at run time out of existing relations is necessarily going to be extravagant. Thus PRTV allows one to formulate as much of one's application as one cares to in a relational algebra, which on the face of it performs set-theoretic operations upon whole sets of tuples. However, the operations are really performed on the relational values we have just described, with the result that the operation of forming the union, say, of two large sets of tuples is deferred until one actually lists a relation, or opens a sequential file based on that relation and scans the file. We are going to formulate, in a relational algebra, processes which experienced programmers would not consider handling in terms of elementary operations which combine entire sets of tuples, or as they would see them, sets of records.

Instead of a relational algebra, a relational calculus may of course be used instead, eg the ALPHA language of E F Codd (2). PRTV does not yet support ALPHA, nor any such relational calculus. However, as Codd has shown elsewhere, it is in principle feasible to translate from one to the other in a natural way. An ALPHA expression resembles a theorem in the Propositional Calculus. To a logician, this represents a natural and general way of making an assertion about a given computer process. Other professionals have their own languages within their own disciplines. Whether or not they can understand a Propositional Calculus expression does not matter: their own languages are likewise amenable to machine translation into the relational algebra.

Consider an application which accepts a batch of input and produces reports (invoices, cheques, etc). It is conceivable in principle to load the input straight into a number of relations, then print out the reports directly from relations derived from the input relations. How far one progresses towards this limit depends in practice on whether it appears easier to implement a given step using the relational algebra, or a conventional programming language. A non-DP professional is unlikely to be predisposed towards the programming solution, particularly if provided with an application generator which constructs the relational algebra for him out of more familiar specifications.

The main problems which the application generator will have to handle are those of making the work of one team member available to another in an orderly fashion, and to stop them unsuspectingly cutting the ground away from under each others' feet.

This can so easily happen if the result of one individual's work, embodied in a relation, is passed to another, who incorporates it into a derived relation which is in turn passed on. It becomes a heavy administrative task to keep track of what changes to the original relation are safe, permissible, or are nonsense in terms of the real-world application.

Note that with this remark we do not distinguish between application development and operational running of the application.

One possible way of coping with this task is for the application generator to administer a data dictionary. Since the task involves much cross-indexing, and the application generator is already served with a relational database, it is attractive to investigate maintaining the data dictionary itself as a relational database.

A range of tasks may be undertaken by the data dictionary, from the simplest to the most ambitious. Examples are:

(1) reporting upon all relations which are affected by updating a given relation,

(2) preventing or otherwise qualifying an order to destroy a relation upon which further relations are defined,

(3) enforcing semantic constraints imposed by the nature of the application at either application development time, eg, to prevent the insertion of 'nonsense' relations into the database, or at run-time, eg, to ensure that tuples are not inserted into a given relation without corresponding tuples being present in another relation.

(4) producing listings of all routines and reports relating to a given database relation, for auditing purposes,

(5) maintaining an up-to-date clerical procedures manual. This often requires cross-referenced lists of fields on input documents, reports, and domains in the database.

These tasks are represented in order of increasing severity. We shall treat the first three only, discussing some theoretical and technical problems which the data dictionary has to face. The remaining two topics, although ambitious in practice, are theoretically much simpler than the first three.

(1) REPORTING UPON UPDATE DEPENDENCIES

For the moment we are primarily concerned with update dependencies between relations in the course of application development. The other sort of update dependency, that between records, or tuples in our case, will be treated later under the heading of 'semantic constraints'.

This facility is straightforwardly achieved by maintaining a DD-relation, call it RDEPEND, on the domains RELID1, RELID2, DEPTYPE. By 'DD-relation', we mean 'data dictionary' relation, to distinguish it from the relations belonging to the application itself. DD-relations may or may not be kept in the same database as application relations: for research convenience the former is recommended due to the facility for bootstrapping the data dictionary, the latter advisable however for security.

Note that we require some means of referring to distinct occurrences of the same domain within the component list of a relation. We do this here by postfixing 1, 2, etc, to the <u>domain</u> name (eg, RELID1, RELID2, etc, for the domain name RELID). RDEPEND contains a tuple for each derived relation, stating what relation it depends on (RELID2) and in what capacity (DEPTYPE). Where a relation is derived from a number of other relations, that number of tuples is present in RDEPEND. Furthermore, if the relation uses another in more than one capacity, more than one tuple for that pair of 'RELIDs' occurs.

Now comes the advantage of using a relational database for the data dictionary. The relation RDEPEND is transitive in a logical sense. Thus by joining it to itself repeatedly we recover a relational value which carries a tuple for all the implicit dependencies, as well as those appearing explicitly in RDEPEND.

Let us introduce notation to present an example. This notation is based on the relational algebra, ISBL, used by PRTV, although we modify it freely in order to make it better illustrate our points.

In PRTV a user manipulates relations within his workspace by expressions of the form:

```
C = A * B
C = N!A * B
```

The first command would construct a relation with a RELID of 'C' (the named entity introduced earlier with its symbolic 'value'; no tuples are accessed as yet) and a value equal to the 'join' of the values of 'A' and 'B'.

The second command would incorporate the RELID: 'A' into the relational value formed for 'C' instead of the value of A. 'N!A' should be read as 'name-A'.

Suppose we have defined 'F' by the following sequence of commands:

```
C = N!A
D = N!B
E = N!C
F = N!E * D
```

Then RDEPEND would contain the following tuples:

RDEPEND (RELID1 RELID2 DEPTYPE)

RELID1	RELID2	DEPTYPE
C	A	N
D	B	N
E	C	N
F	E	N
F	D	V

In order to obtain tuples for every dependency of F one might join RDEPEND with itself repeatedly until no further tuples appeared (detected by testing its cardinality). The type of 'join' operation required is one called an 'equi-join'. This means that the tuples from each relational operand which are to be concatenated are chosen by collating equal values within certain specified domains. It is a matter of notational design to specify an equi-join elegantly. Here we show the required components to 'overlap' by placing component names beneath each other. Thus:

```
              RDEPEND|RELID1 RELID2 DEPTYPE
            * RDEPEND|       RELID1        RELID2 DEPTYPE
```

represents a relational value with five domain occurrences. Each tuple in the set so defined is formed by taking a pair of tuples from RDEPEND for which RELID1 in one tuple equals RELID2 in the other. There is a combined tuple for all such pairs.

We may further join to this a relation, DTRANS, which contains a tuple matching each pair of values of DEPTYPE which turns up in the above relational value. Each tuple of DTRANS contains a third value from the domain DEPTYPE, representing the resulting (ie, transitive) dependency. After that, we can project out just those domains we wish to see, renaming them in the process. Note that in a relation, all duplicates of a given tuple are suppressed. A relation simply records that, say, three given objects are related in a given way. The ordered set of these three objects is what comprises the 'tuple' (3-tuple, or 'triple' in this case). Thus it makes no sense to talk about more than one 'occurrence' of this tuple. The three objects are either related, or they are not.

We may thus construct the relational assignment statement:

```
          RR = RDEPEND|RELID1 RELID2 DEPTYPE
             * RDEPEND|       RELID1        RELID2 DEPTYPE
             * DTRANS |              DEPTYPE1      DEPTYPE2 DEPTYPE3
             %        |RELID1               RELID2          DEPTYPE
```

The resulting relation RR has precisely the domains and domain-IDs of RDEPEND (the final 'project', %, has seen to that), but relates RELIDs once-removed. Thus RR contains the following tuples only:

```
          RR ( RELID1  RELID2  DEPTYPE )
               E       A       NN
               F       C       NN
               F       B       V
```

The relation DTRANS can be visualised as a function with two arguments, DEPTYPE1 and DEPTYPE2, returning the corresponding object in the domain DEPTYPE3. Indeed in PRTV it can be implemented either as a PL/I function or as an ordinary relation, with a tuple for every pair of values of DEPTYPE1 and DEPTYPE2. Thus DTRANS might contain the following tuples (among others):

```
          DTRANS ( DEPTYPE1 DEPTYPE2 DEPTYPE3 )
                   N        N        NN
                   N        NN       NNN
                   NN       N        NNN
                   NN       NN       NNNN
                   N        V        V
                   V        N        V
```

Note that the last two tuples say, in effect, that if A depends on the name 'B', and that B has the value of C, then A has only a current-value connection with C. If C is changed, A will not change, and therefore this connection will be lost. On the other hand, if B depends on the name 'C', assigning the (current) value of B to A effectively assigns the current value of C to A. This is a matter of choice of convention.

RR can be incorporated back into RDEPEND (eg, by the expression:)

```
        RDEPEND = RDEPEND + RR
```

and the process repeated until the cardinality of RDEPEND grows no more. On the other hand it may be better to derive a new relation, FULL_RDEPEND, by this process each time it is called for, so that RDEPEND may be maintained more easily by simple insertion and deletion of tuples.

When the owner of the catalogued relation, F, wishes to modify it, the command:

```
        List FULL_RDEPEND: RELID1 = 'F'
```

might be issued. This lists a selection of just those tuples in FULL_RDEPEND such that RELID1 is equal to 'F'. The relational operator ':' stands for 'SELECT'. Thus:

```
        FULL_DEPEND: RELID1 = 'F'
                  ( RELID1  RELID2  DEPTYPE )
                    F       E       N
                    F       D       V
                    F       C       NN
                    F       B       V
                    F       A       NNN
```

(2) QUALIFYING AN ORDER TO DESTROY A RELATION

This might be considered to be a special case of enforcing semantic constraints imposed by the application model upon the developers themselves, a very general topic. However it can also be viewed as a basic facility to be expected of a system which claims to inhibit members of an application development team from cutting the ground from under each others' feet. There is a temptation to build such a facility rigidly into the system itself. This ignores the possibility that what is satisfactory for one application development team may not be so for another.

The simplest such 'qualification' is of course to refuse to destroy any relation from which another relation has been derived, ie, upon which there is a name-dependency, until those dependencies have been eliminated.

(3) ENFORCING SEMANTIC CONSTRAINTS IMPOSED BY THE APPLICATION MODEL

To the theorist this is probably the most interesting use to which a relational data dictionary might be put.

One objection to the use of relational databases stems from the fact that certain properties of conventional files, such as demanding a unique value in the key field, or being hierarchical, are absent. In conventional programming, these 'structural' properties are exploited to enforce certain semantic constraints arising out of the application model, such as a particular child segment having a single parent. However the skills of a database specialist are often needed to exploit such restrictions inherent in the available structures. It is up to him to ensure that his model of the application in terms of key fields and segment deletion rules behaves like the real-world counterpart: yet it is often rather hard for a business to find a man with intimate knowledge of both realms. Thus it is attractive for our purpose that the traditional restrictions of key-fields and many-one mappings have to be modelled explicitly in PRTV, since the problem of enforcing semantic constraints can then be split off from that of providing a structure capable of holding the data in the first place.

How can one use the relational algebra here discussed to model these sorts of update constraints?

Suppose we have a standing relation, X, in the database, and a transient relation, UPD_X, holding today's new additions to X. We want to insert into X just those tuples of UPD_X whose values of the key-domain, KEY, do not already occur as values of KEY in X.

X % (KEY), is a relational value, with just one domain, of current keys occurring in X. By joining it to UPD_X we express just those tuples of UPD_X whose keys already occur in X:

```
X % (KEY)  | KEY
  * UPD_X  | KEY     <OTHER_DOMAINS>
```

By forming the 'DIFFERENCE' of this expression with the original UPD_X we express all those tuples of UPD_X whose keys do not already occur in

X. We now simply 'UNION' these with X to get NEW_X. Ignoring the special domain-overlapping notation, NEW_X is given by:

NEW_X = N!X + (N!UPD_X - (N!UPD_X * (N!X % KEY)))

Note that we have made NEW_X a <u>derived</u> relation by quoting the names of relations (N!) instead of their current values. NEW_X, upon being materialised, will contain the desired set of tuples, which may be used to replace the current value of X in the database. We must then ensure that X is only ever updated in this way. A crude way of doing this is to have the data dictionary keep a list of permissible assignments into given RELIDs, so that the application generator will not accept a command changing X except those, explicitly catalogued, which assign NEW_X into X.

Clearly a similar technique can be used to insert only those tuples into X whose KEYs occur in another relation, W. The tuples which fail to get into X can of course be recovered in the expression: UPD_X - X.

It is a critical business designing facilities for an application developer to impose constraints upon himself or his colleagues. It presupposes that both he and we know what sort of security we are supposed to be offering him. If this question is not resolved, it is so easy to end up with a security system which neither deters deliberate abuse, nor protects adequately against accidental misuse, but appears designed solely to encumber lawful operations. Our intentions with the data dictionary are primarily to reduce the incidence of subsequent mis-modifications to an application. As time goes on, or one gets further away from the designer of a particular component, the modifier of the component is unavoidably less well-informed as to the side-effects such modifications may have. On the other hand we make no attempt as yet to protect against deliberate wrecking.

Compare this with the 'facility' sometimes found in database packages which simply refuses to accept data with duplicate keys. The first non-DP user of such software is inevitably engaged in research, even if he does not know it, and is in the typical research predicament of having a file of grubby data he wishes to load up, precisely to use the sophisticated query facilities the database package may offer to report on such things as duplicate keys. He quickly has to learn a few DP skills, like how to manoeuvre around the trap for duplicate keys.

The relational data dictionary approach allows just that structure to be put up first inside the database, which suffices to store the raw data, and adequate protection to be devised later for the use of the various relations of the application.

Compared to the task of defining relations to hold and manipulate the data of the application, as exemplified by X, it is much harder to write a satisfactory UPD_X to constrain its use. The latter is as demanding as writing a foolproof macro, which is really what UPD_X is. Later work might concentrate on providing relations like UPD_X 'off the peg', so to speak, that is as a result of some non-procedural specification by the application developer, rather than require him to develop the skill to construct them himself. Such 'constraining' relations may resemble the facilities available with CODASYL/DBTG (3), or IMS. Alternatively the sort of 'semantic constraint' which would be useful in practice might be thought out completely afresh.

Our approach contrasts with the CODASYL/DBTG approach of submitting the update constraints as part of the 'data definition', to be carefully separated from the 'data manipulation' activity. In the environment described it is difficult to distinguish between the two.

SUMMARY

We have tried to indicate a relational approach to many well-known problems of so-called data definitions. The key to this approach is the use of a data dictionary, itself maintained as a relational database.

Many details of this relational data dictionary clearly remain to be finalised. However the essence of a relational data dictionary is that it can be implemented even before such questions need be resolved. Thus the basic structure of, and facilities offered by, such a data dictionary can be changed extensively without the need to reload the stored data. This allows of considerable experimentation within a particular project.

REFERENCES

(1) S J P TODD: PRTV Overview,
IBM UK Scientific Centre report No 75, 1975.

(2) E F CODD: A Database Sublanguage founded on the Relational Calculus,
Proceedings of the 1971 ACM SIGFIDET Workshop on Data Description, Access and Control.

(3) CODASYL DBTG: Data Base Task Group Report April 1971.
Available from ACM, New York.

Data Base System Evaluation

Harry L. Hill, IBM

The evaluation of data base systems embraces four very significant fields, the first being the design of resource management necessary to build into the product necessary performance attributes to make that product or system an attractive saleable item. The second part is the prediction of performance for a given configuration and workload. The third is the ability to measure the performance and confirm or deny the expectation obtained from the predictive process; and finally the ability to tune the system to accommodate changes made either in the configuration that exists or the user workload that is currently presented to the system.

To cover these four elements of data base evaluation, I have chosen to describe within this paper these topics:

1. Concepts of system performance
2. Performance and the development process
3. Predicting and measuring system performance
4. System performance tuning

I. CONCEPTS OF SYSTEMS PERFORMANCE

Let us look at some of the basic concepts behind system performance. The key question is one of systems performance sensitivity - the problem is always to find what is in the critical path. Fig. 1 describes clearly the approach that is taken, given that one can identify the bottleneck in the system; the key question is that if I remove that bottleneck, at what point and under what conditions do I hit the next one (because there is always a next one).

When we talk about the goodness of performance, i.e. how well a system performs, it is necessary to establish measures of goodness. We talk about performance in the following ways, as shown in fig. 2 - in terms of throughput, jobs per unit time, system data rate, number of accesses per second to a storage device, etc. There are perhaps more sophisticated and better ways of describing performance. For example, throughput per rental, dollars per second per access to a storage device, cost per job, cost per transaction. These latter measures of performance tend to be more revealing of the 'value to the user' as we sometimes call it, i.e. the cost performance trade-off.

It should be observed, as in fig. 3, that there are some very significant trends in performance evaluation. In the early days when we described performance in terms of component or device productivity, you will recall the measures of CPU goodness were in terms of add time, subtract time, multiply time, etc. We have emerged from that somewhat primitive measure of performance and today we talk about performance in terms of systems productivity, where the system is the sum of the hardware, the software and the workload effects. Tomorrow I am confident that we will be talking about systems performance not so much in terms of just the system but in terms of the user relationship to that system. I call that 'people productivity', where people's productivity is geared to maximise the objectives of a given enterprise or business. The computing system is then but one key element in meeting a business objective. This is particularly important for live terminal systems where the business of a company may be totally dependent on the availability and usability of the total system.

System performance is really best described in terms of the management of time spent waiting for systems resources. Fig. 4 describes a representation of systems resources because that is what performance is all about, the management of resources within a system allocated to a given profile of work. Every single system that has been constructed to date behaves in this way. The element of work is offered to the central processing unit or work engine and that work is executed by merging data with a program to a point where more data or programs are required. At that point in time the processing ceases and a request is queued in front of a storage device (i.e. a resource) in order to obtain additional data or programs to continue or complete the processing. When that work is completed, the processing engine proceeds on to another task. What we have is a serial processing engine operating on elements of work who's data and programs are queued in parallel against system resources. By placing a 'meter' in the line between the storage and the queue for processing one can get a measure in terms of transactions per second or system data rate.

Fig. 5 shows a plot of system performance against the number of tasks, that is, the depth or level of multiprocessing and the consequence on the system of these tasks executing work. Notice that as you increase the number of tasks, the system performance increases to the point where a bottleneck is reached and I have chosen in this case to show the channel at the first bottleneck. If I were to add channels to the system I would relieve that bottleneck within the system and I would hit the next one which I have, in this case shown to be storage devices. So performances progress through 'ceilings' or bottlenecks.

Work that is presented to a computing system does not represent a constant load on all resources. In fig. 6 I have shown diagramatically a time varying workload effect on the system where the height of each pedestal represents 100% utilisation of that resource - notice that I am showing only 3 resources, a channel, a CPU and a drive device. The point is that not all of the time is any one resource the bottleneck, but the bottleneck changes from rsource to resource depending upon the demand of the time varying workload placed against it. When that resource is 100% utilised, it clearly forms a black mark on top of the pedestal, so by removing that bottleneck, that is, by putting a more powerful CPU in or a larger number of channels, this serves to improve the overall system performance. Clearly we are seeking an economic design where the number of black marks on top of the pedestal is reasonably balanced, that is, resources are not wasted. Fig. 7 depicts a system transaction rate versus a time varying workload, and a similar argument applies.

All transaction-based systems tend to behave in a similar way and fig. 8 shows a three-dimensional plot of response times versus real storage versus transaction traffic rate. Notice that as the real storage available for processing is decreased, the response time increases. Similarly, as the transaction traffic rate increases, the response time increases and all systems tend to behave this way. It should be realised that in virtual operating systems the decrease of storage causes an increase in paging rate. Under these conditions the CPU utilization generally decreases and the system gradually becomes I/O bound.

2. PERFORMANCE AND THE DEVELOPMENT PROCESS

As data base systems have grown and become sophisticated, it is necessary to achieve not only good performance, but predictable performance. This has to be built into the development process of the product. I should like to take as an example the development of storage which is a key resource in any data base system. Fig. 9 shows a typical development process which, in the early days of the computer industry, started off with the research and development of what I would describe as the basic parameters of the storage device. These parameters were offered to engineering groups who designed them into products and we developed on that basis the well-known disk drive. The drives were offered to the CPUs and were integrated with software systems which in turn were offered to industries to configure and use on behalf of that industry, and those industries designed those systems together with their applications to generate useful data processing facilities. The point is that in the early days we started off with the basic technology and we did what is described as a 'bottom-up' design - that is how the technology of the industry grew up. If we look today at the basic relationship of the direct access storage device (fig. 10) you will see that only certain combinations of those basic parameters are of interest to the systems designer, such as data rate and access times - areal density is frankly not very significant to the system designer. Similarly as block size decreases data rate becomes less important than access time. The consequence of this 'bottom-up' development process has been that we have decreased in a rather dramatic way the effective cost to the user of storage.

The decrease in storage cost as seen by the user is shown in fig. 11, i.e. the relationship between dollars per megabyte per month for a variety of products versus the year of announcement. In fig. 12 you will also notice the access rate characteristics where the accesses per dollar and the accesses per second are shown for the same range of products. If we are to look now at fig. 13 we will see that the storage technology spans a range of access times, storage capacities and cost per bit. This figure is interesting - observe the gap in the continum of storage devices. This gap occupies the same time domain as task switching in several of the medium and high speed processors. The technology for storage and data base systems is rich - rich in function and rich in performance and in cost choices. There is in fact sufficient technology to reverse the process and instead of doing a 'bottom-up' design, to take the requirements of modern applications and do a 'top-down' design (again see fig. 9), that is, to define the systems and the applications that are required in a business or enterprise and to map them into the technology.

3. PREDICTING AND MEASURING SYSTEM PERFORMANCE

The timely development of performance tools forms an essential part of developing a computing system. It has two major characteristics. One, it is important to be able to predict the performance of a complex data base/data communications system prior to either the hardware or the software being in existence and two, it is important that having predicted it and built it, it is important to be able to measure it and validate the prediction. The learning process is being able to describe differences.

The essential objective in developing performance tools is to be able to establish a discipline both for developers and subsequently for users of avoiding surprises in performance, since late discoveries are hard to correct. Fig. 14 describes this objective and describes the methods that are generally used to achieve them, that is, to develop models, to validate those models, to be able to track the instruction path length within a system and, as knowledge is gained, to be able to document that experience and construct a vocabulary that communicates both the predictive and the measurement processes. Fig. 15 shows the process. There are really two types of predictive capabilities, one is analytic and the other is simulative. In the measurement area there are two types of facilities required to produce the data necessary for measurement; one is hardware and the other is software monitors.

Measurement is both time consuming and expensive, therefore there has been significant emphasis and progress placed upon the development of models in order to determine the performance of a system, while measurement techniques are increasingly used to validate these models so that performance information and guidelines can be generated spanning a range of applications, configurations and workload demands. It should be recognised, however, that multiple sub-systems operating within one operating system are often hard to handle by conventional analytic means, and one is forced to consider hybrids of analytic and simulative techniques. It is most important that the developer or user of a model has clearly in his mind the question he wants the model to answer. Rarely is a general purpose model sensitive to questions that were not known at the time the model was developed.

It is perhaps useful to examine a data base/data communication system from a performance standpoint, and for this I have chosen IMS/VS and have constructed a flow chart for the main processing blocks of that system. Fig. 16 shows the flow of such a transaction;

notice that it divides itself into three major parts. The communication part where message switching and message queues are handled; the processing of that message against program and data and the multiple calls to that data base for that particular transaction; the completion of that transaction and the generation of the output message in the message queue, and the handling of that message through a terminal access method to a terminal. That is, if you like, the life of a transaction; it is born at the terminal where it enters the system and it dies at the terminal when the transaction is completed. If we were to place 'meters' in the lines joining those function to queues and libraries, etc., we could fact measure the activity that is going on with the system. As we pass multiple messages into such a system, we see that the problem of performance resolves down to the allocation of resources, CPUs, channels, programs and data to handle the requirements of each different transaction. The job, then, is to define algorithms for using resources and for waiting for resources. These algorithms start with what priorities are associated with each transaction type and must include recovery strategies in the event that a resource, a data path or a queue discipline fails. Availability and performance are becoming increasingly dependent upon recovery schemes designed into the product.

There are really only two ways of improving the performance of a data base/data communication system. One is to shorten the transaction path length and the other is to provide either faster or parallel processing resources. It is thus often desirable to be able to calculate the number of instructions executed on behalf of an IMS transaction. Fig. 17 shows a typical appraoch to such a problem, where T is the total instructions executed for the IMS transaction, K1 through K5 are coefficients representing various IMS and VS releases; Q,U,N and C represent major parameters of most importance and significance in terms of overall systems performance.

Now if we were to take these transactions and were to apply values to those parameters, it is conceivable that one could divide the instruction processing capability of the machine by the path length of the transaction and come up with a theoretical maximum number of transactions per second that that resource could process, given that the processing unit was in fact the major bottleneck in the system. This has been done in fig. 18 and shows the difference in transactions per second processed for an 85% utilised 158 and 168. It should be clear that these are not measured values, they are predicted values, and are shown merely to demonstrate the sensitivity of system performance to changes in the key parameter values that affect it.

Fig. 18 is, then, designed to show the sensitivity of a system to changes in the major parameters that affect the system performance. Again this is not a measured environment this is a predicted environment and it is probably not possible to accurately reproduce this in a measurement environment without rigorously defining several other important system and user dependent factors. It does, however, also show on the same theoretical basis the difference in path length between an MVS system and an MVT system. Traditionally, it is thought that the systems that have higher sophistication have longer path lengths and whereas in general this is true, it is clear that in the MVS system, as the data base call structure becomes more complex, the difference in path length diminishes significantly in favour of MVS.

Independent of the investment made in developing and using models of the system, it is essential to measure the real thing as rapidly as possible. One method used in IBM is shown in fig. 19, where a simulated network is represented in both hardware and software and a data base is constructed to represent the application and system data bases. The simulated network is programmed to generate scripts at a given interval and with a given think time, or range of think times, such that the system under test appears to be loaded with transactions as though they were coming from real terminals. By the applications of suitable hardware probes and suitable software probes, we are able to measure the utilisation of resources occurring within the system under a variety of transaction rates, types and call structures. A typical measurement is shown in fig. 20, in this case an IMS/VS 1.0.1 system running under VS2 release 2. Notice the linear CPU utilisation as transaction rate goes up on this 158 CPU with 2400 Baud lines and 4800 Baud lines.

The measurement in question is designed to explore the sensitivity of line speeds to system performance. Note that in the 2400 Baud lines case, with ten lines, the line utilisation became a significant bottleneck in the system and this is evidenced by the response times starting to rise rather rapidly, whereas at 4800 Baud line speed, the response time is well contained.

System performance can be viewed in two ways and fig. 21 shows that we are either using a resource or we are waiting for it. Let us now take the flow chart (fig. 16) that we developed to show the life of an IMS transaction. Let us look at that flow chart with respect to the time we spend waiting for a resource, that is, waiting for a line, waiting for buffers, waiting for a processing region, waiting for an application program to be brought in, waiting for I/O, that is, storage accesses to bring data or programs into the system, waiting for lines to handle the output message and waiting for services to transmit that message to the terminal. Let us also look at the amount of time using the resources. Fig. 22 shows, and it is drawn to scale, where if this were 8 inches long, the response time from beginning to end would be 1 second, making 3 loops around the DL1 call. It is also clear, as we approach a 100% utilised system, the units of processing occupy a smaller and smaller portion of the total response time. This chart shows the waiting time and processing time for only one transaction within a 75% loaded system.

4. SYSTEM PERFORMANCE TUNING

The goodness of performance then, of a data base/data communication system is balancing or tuning two things. It is balancing the supply of resources with the demand on them, because we are either waiting for that supply or we are using that supply. Fig. 23 show this balancing scheme. If we have a high supply with respect to the demand, then we are wasting resources. If we have a high demand with respect to the supply of resource we are going to suffer poor response times. In general, performance is a user option since it requires the additon of resources and these generally cost money; but not alway is that the case. In some cases, it is necessary and possible that the resources be tuned to meet the demand of the workload. Performance tuning is concerned primarily with the elements shown in fig. 24, being data base profiles, transaction profiles, profiles of the IMS system, of the processing requirements of the region, of the hardware and software configuration, of the overall teleprocessing configuration, and importantly, the use of tool to measure these resources.

Fig. 25 shows the primary factors affecting the performance and the design of the system The number of transactions per second is typically in the range of 1 to 50, although within the next five years I am confident that you will see that range grow towards 200 transactions per second. In terms of EXCPs per call, we are looking today in the range 0.1 to 5 per data base call. In terms of calls per transaction, we typically find anywhere from 5 to 50 calls with several transaction types exceeding 50 and reaching close to 100 calls per transaction, so the data base designer is faced with designing a system of resources which can efficiently and economically accommodate the range of performance critical factors.

The tuning of data base systems is clearly a complex matter involving firstly an awareness of utilisation of resources, and secondly the understanding and knowledge about the sensitivity of changing the resource allocation to achieve an overall system performance level. The objective then is shown in fig. 26 - either minimise the transaction path length and/or invoke parallelism of key resources. The method recommended is firstly to quantify the profiles of the transaction and of the system; understand the behaviour of the system in response to changes in the workload; use software monitors to quantify that behaviour and resort to hardware monitors which do not interfere with the processing characteristics of the system; to define experiments to uncover and order the bottleneck; and to make changes, one at at a time, to the system and measure the effects. Only by measurements do we really get smart.

Performance tuning can be an iterative process because what one is trying to do is to optimise the utilisation of resources and match them against the workload. Frequently that workload is changing and one's job is not done until one has resolved the differences between what one expects, that is the expectation of performance, and what one has actually got. If there is significant differences between those two elements, then clearly there must be an explanation which always seems to lie in better understanding of what the system is doing. I mentioned the complexity of tuning a data base/data communication system. It is certainly not true that every one behaves differently. There are some typical causes of bottlenecks which are frequently uncovered and those really fall into three categories, as shown in fig. 27 - resources of a teleprocessing network - balancing of those resources and the selection of buffer sizes and message format buffers; the region resources, that is the amount of program loading that is done; the structure and the size of application programs; the structure and the size of the data base; the use of extended function within that data base structure; and lastly, the CPU resources, where its use is determined largely by the amount of system and user I/O and the use of bufferpool services.

Finally, I should like to discuss trends within data base/data communication system performance. Those trends really fall into three broad areas - trends in prediction, trends in measurements and trends in tuning. I think that over the next five years we are going to see generalised use of analytic tools for dedicated systems and some guidelines based on analytic tools for mixed systems. We are going to see the specific use of simulation and hybrid tools for mixed or complex systems. We are also going to see the availability of tools at an early point in the design of systems to help users choose amongst different configurations which have different price performance characteristics.

In terms of measurement trends, we are going to see integrated software performance monitors, because basically performance is a user option and it is proper that the user understands what the system is doing and what choices he has to change it. Where a software monitor impacts the basic behaviour of the system, we are going to see integrated hardware built into the product to facilitate measurement and so be able to monitor the performance with little or zero overhead. We are going to see selective performance report generation, and we are going to see dynamic performance information and monitoring of key resources, so that information can be made available to a user to permit him to manage his system in line with some overall strategic direction that has known cost performance trade-offs.

Lastly, in performance tuning, I believe that we are going to see a family of tools available for the design of major components. That is, the design of TP networks, of data bases, of multiprocessing systems to permit the designer at an early stage to become familiar with the behaviour of those elements of the system that are likely to be a system bottleneck. We are going to see system-managed performance generation reports, and tuning controls that are made available on an open loop basis. It is conceivable that in the next five to ten years many of the tuning controls can be architected into a closed loop system so that the system is able to tune itself, and at this point I refer to tuning of the system in terms of allocating resources in accordance with a predetermined set of performance strategies. Some of these can be determined by the manufacturer and some will be determined and selected by the end user.

This concludes my presentation on the Evaluation of Data Base Systems.

Concepts of System Performance Sensitivity

The Problem: Find What's in the Critical Path, i.e., What's the Bottleneck

And . . . What's the Payoff When I Remove That Bottleneck and Hit the Next One.

Because . . . There Always is a Next One

Fig. 1

Performance Measures of Goodness

How Can We Talk About Performance?

Thruput (Jobs/Unit Time)

System Data Rate

Accesses/Sec

Terminals Supported

Terminal Response Time

Or Perhaps:

Thruput/Rental

$/Sec/Access

Cost/Job

Cost/Transaction

Fig. 2

Trends in Performance Evaluation

Notice the Trend from:
Component or Device Productivity

To

System Productivity

(System = Hardware + Software + Workload)

To

People Productivity

Fig. 3 (People Productivity = Maximized Enterprise Objectives)

A Representation of System Resources

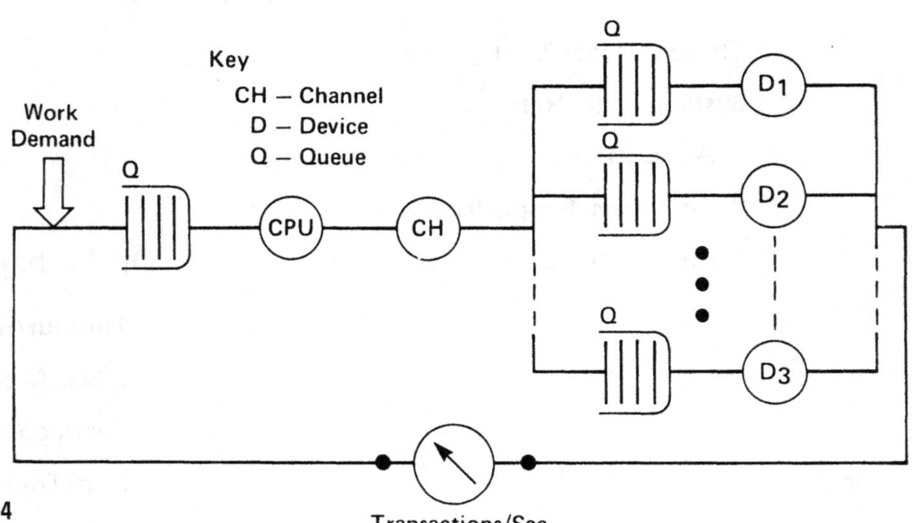

Fig. 4

A Way to Think About Bottlenecks

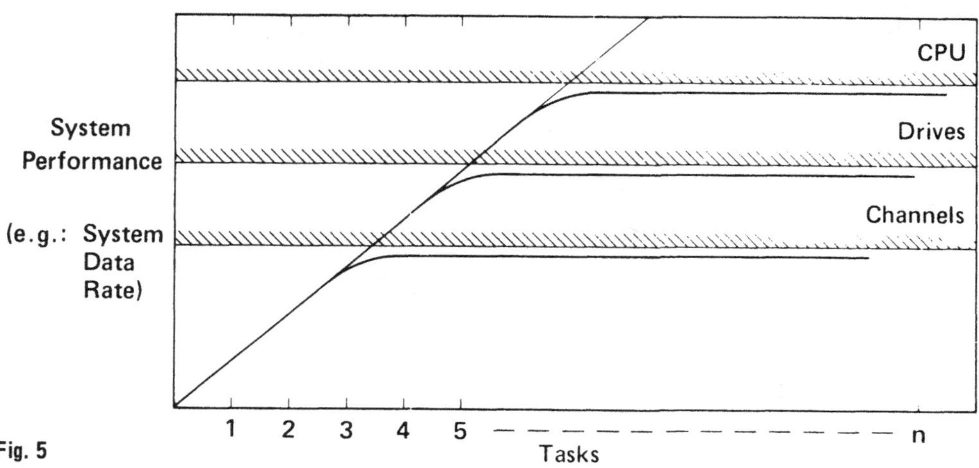

Fig. 5

SYSTEMS PERFORMANCE VS TIME
FOR A TIME VARYING WORKLOAD

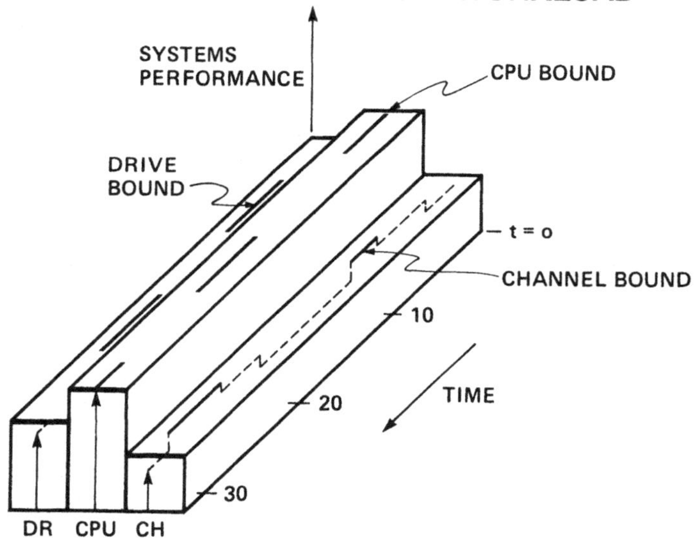

Fig. 6

TRANSACTION RATE VS TIME
FOR A TIME VARYING DBDC WORKLOAD

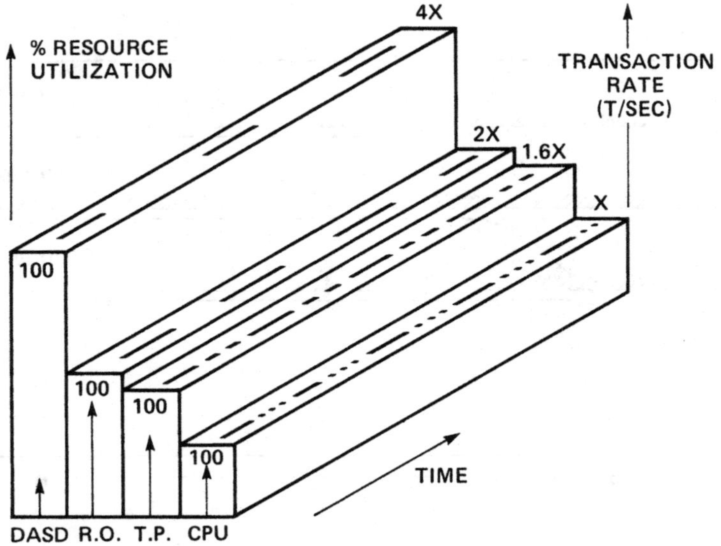

Fig. 7

DBDC PERFORMANCE RELATIONSHIPS

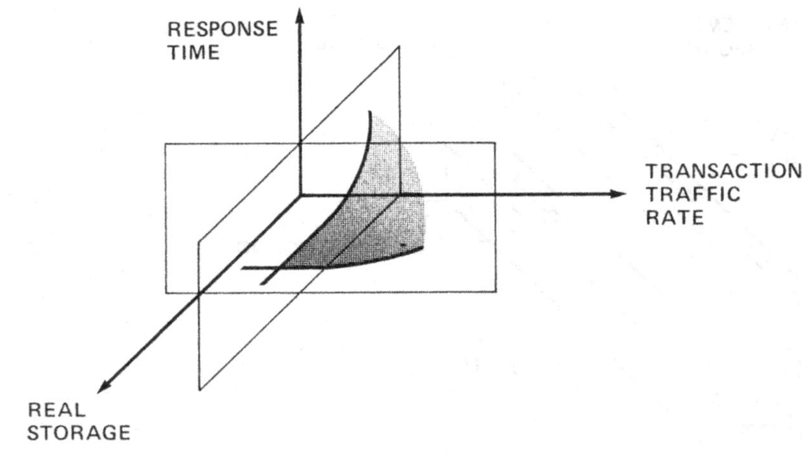

Fig. 8

The Development Process

A View of the Development Process

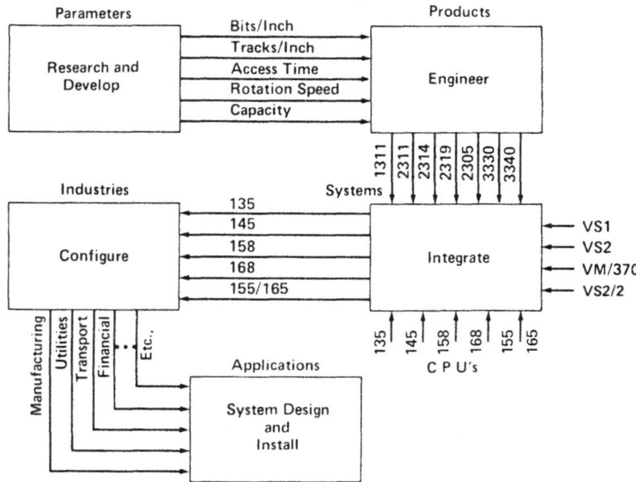

Fig. 9

DASD Parameter Relationships

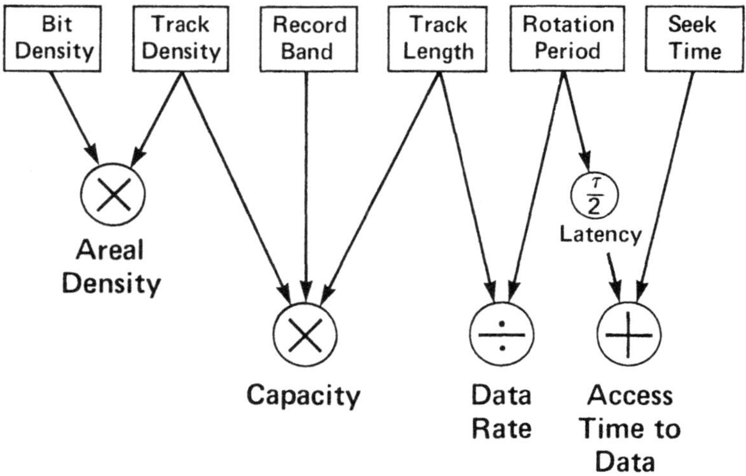

Fig. 10

The Cost of Attached Storage

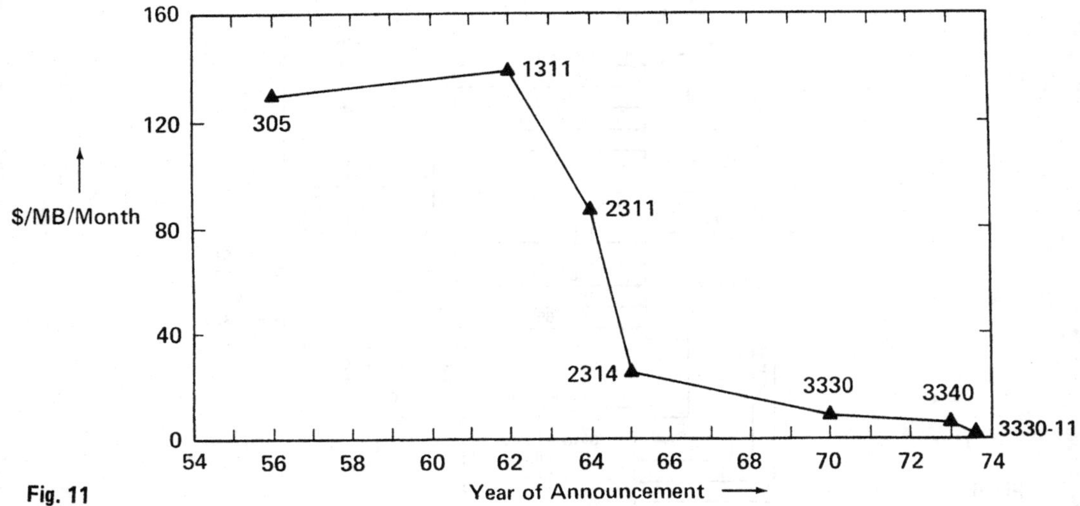

Fig. 11

Access Rate Characteristics

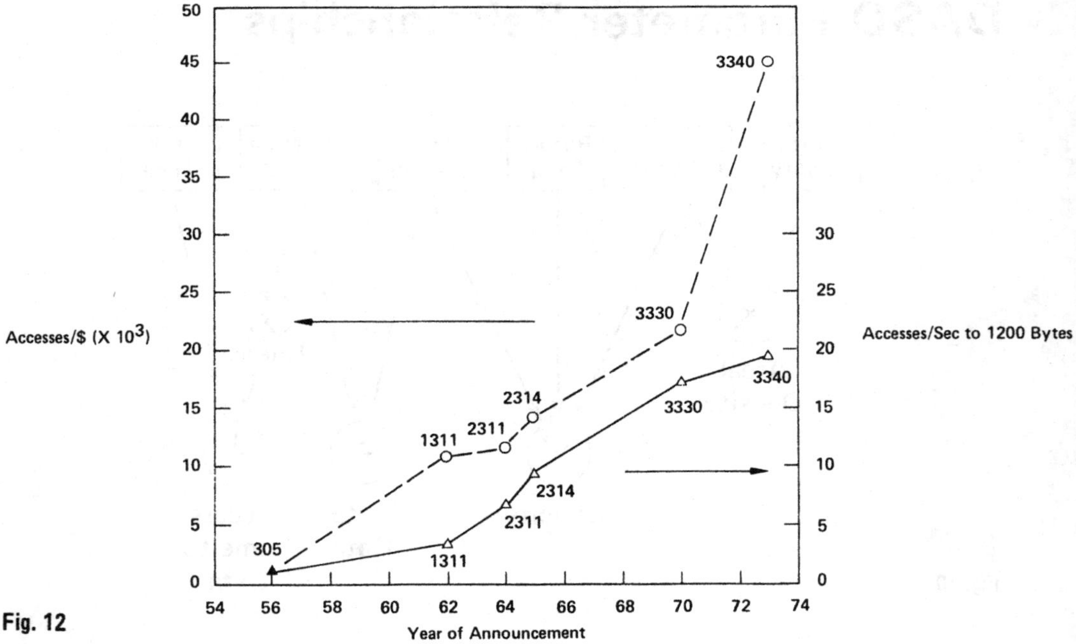

Accesses/$ (X 10³)

Accesses/Sec to 1200 Bytes

50 45 40 35 30 25 20 15 10 5 0

30 25 20 15 10 5 0

305 1311 2311 2314 3330 3340

305 1311 2311 2314 3330 3340

54 56 58 60 62 64 66 68 70 72 74

Year of Announcement

Fig. 12

Present Storage Technologies

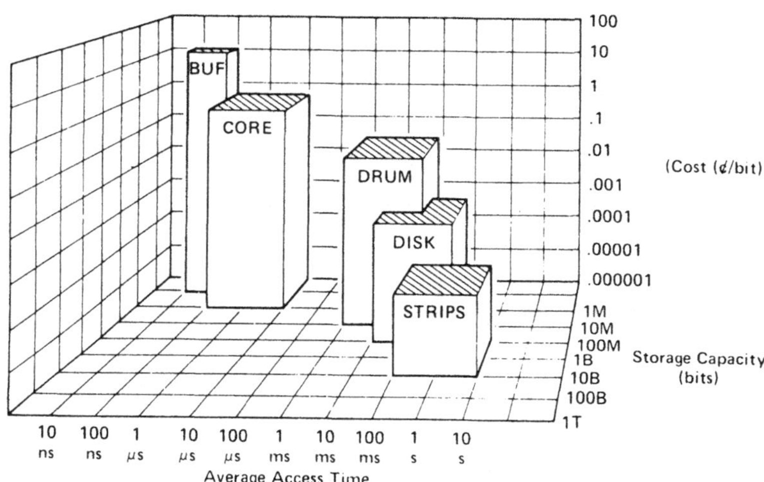

Fig. 13

OBJECTIVES AND METHODS

Objective

- DON'T CREATE SURPRISES IN PERFORMANCE – LATE DISCOVERIES ARE HARD TO CORRECT

Method

- DESIGN TOOLS (MODELS) TO ASK/ANSWER QUESTIONS IN A DISCIPLINED WAY
- DO IT EARLY TO INFLUENCE DESIGNERS
- SPECIFY AND TRACK PATH LENGTHS
- VALIDATE MODELS AND MEASURE TO GET SMART
- WHEN YOU'RE SMART – DOCUMENT IT

Fig. 14

PERFORMANCE TOOL DEVELOPMENT

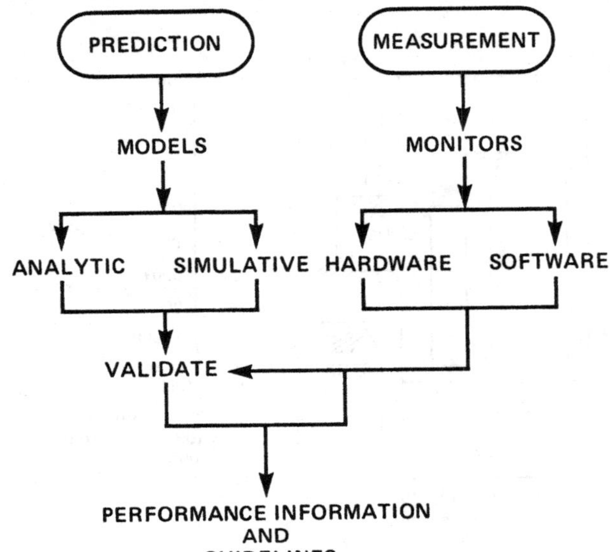

Fig. 15

MAIN PROCESSING BLOCKS OF A TRANSACTION IMS/VS

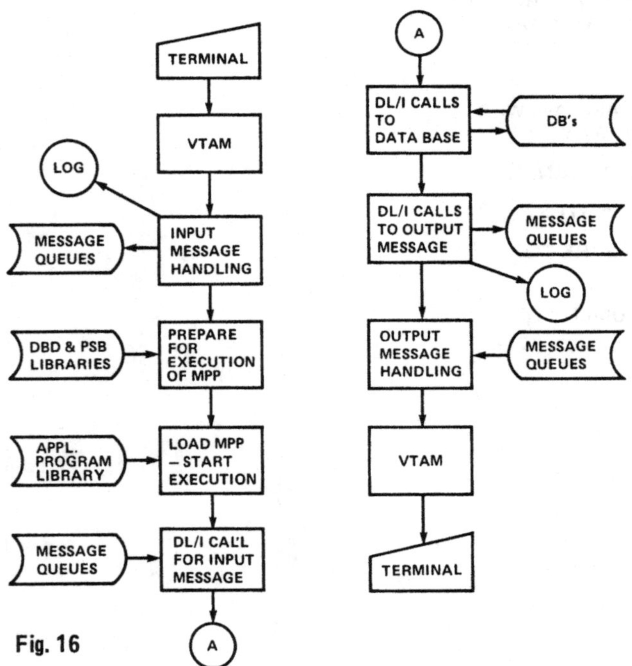

Fig. 16

IMS PATH LENGTH ANALYSIS

HOW MANY INSTRUCTIONS ARE EXECUTED
ON BEHALF OF AN IMS TRANSACTION?

$$T = (K_1 + K_1{}^1) + (K_2 \times Q) + (K_3 \times U) + N[K_4 + (C \times K_5)]$$

K_1 ---- K_5 ARE COEFFICIENTS REPRESENTING VARIOUS IMS AND VS RELEASES.

Q = FRACTION OF INQUIRY TRANSACTIONS

U = FRACTION OF UPDATE TRANSACTIONS

N = NUMBER OF DATA BASE CALLS/TRANSACTION

C = NUMBER OF DATA BASE IOS/CALL

T = TOTAL INSTRUCTIONS EXECUTED FOR ONE IMS TRANSACTION

Fig. 17

IMS PATH LENGTH ANALYSIS

IMS TRANSACTION PATH LENGTH ($INST^R \times 10^3$)								
VS	154	160	176	239	162	169	185	247
MVT	114	124	148	243	114	124	148	243

CALLS/TRANSACTION	3	5	10	30	3	5	10	30
IO'S/CALL	3.3	2.0	1.0	0.3	3.3	2.0	1.0	0.3
O/O INQUIRY	0.5	0.5	0.5	0.5	0	0	0	0
O/O UPDATE	0.5	0.5	0.5	0.5	1.0	1.0	1.0	1.0

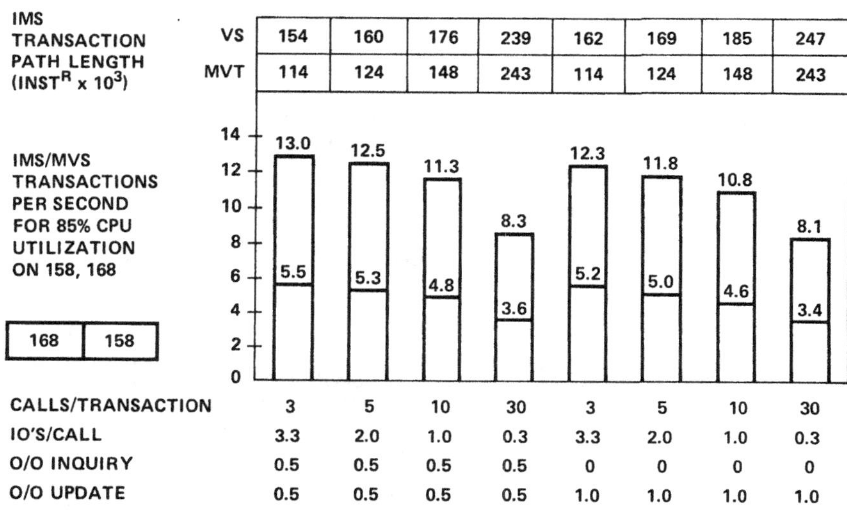

Fig. 18

PERFORMANCE MEASUREMENT ENVIRONMENT

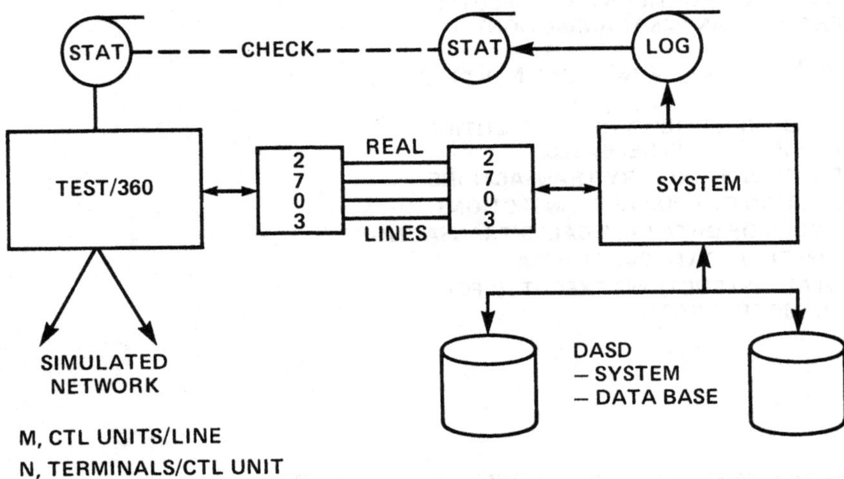

Fig. 19

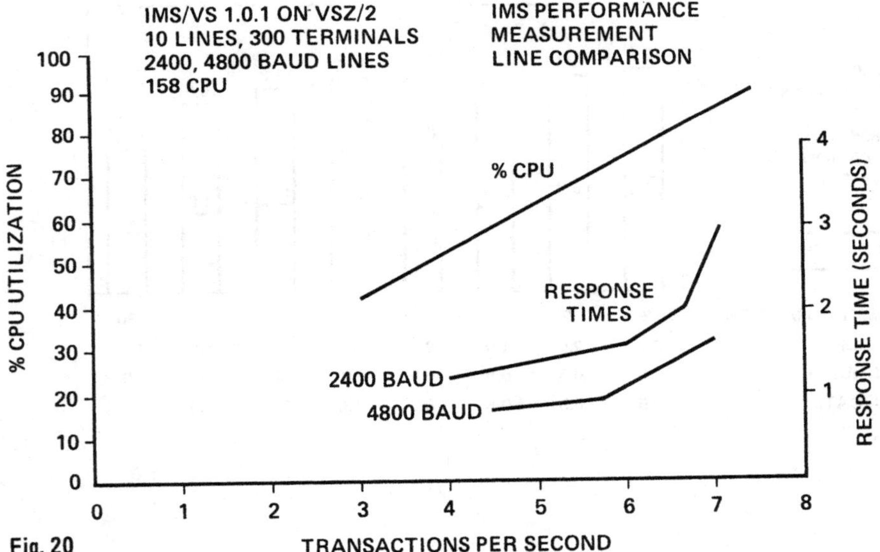

Fig. 20

WHAT IS PERFORMANCE

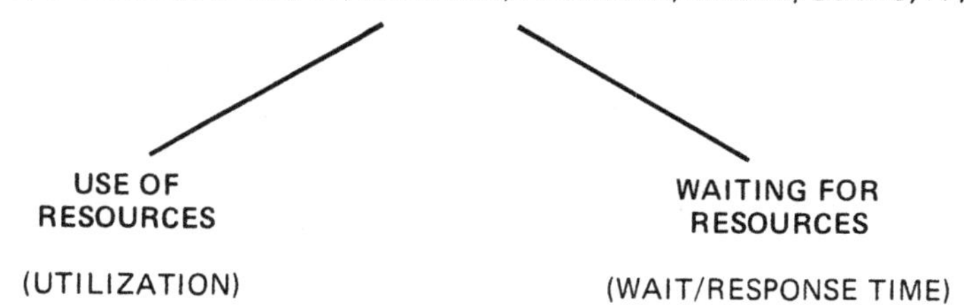

DEFINE WHAT YOU MEAN BY PERFORMANCE

Fig. 21

TIMING AN IMS TRANSACTION

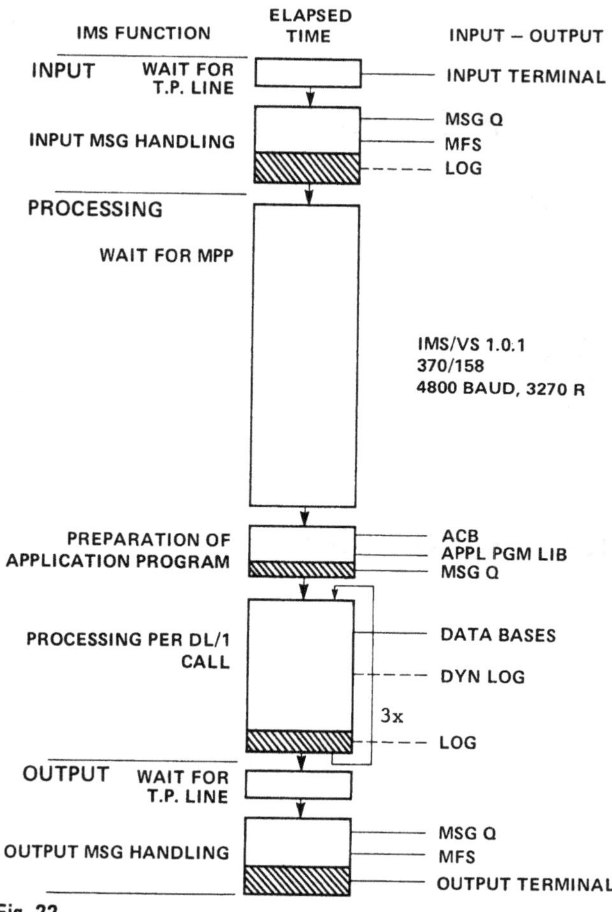

Fig. 22

DBDC PERFORMANCE TUNING

Supply ⟷ Resource ⟷ Demand

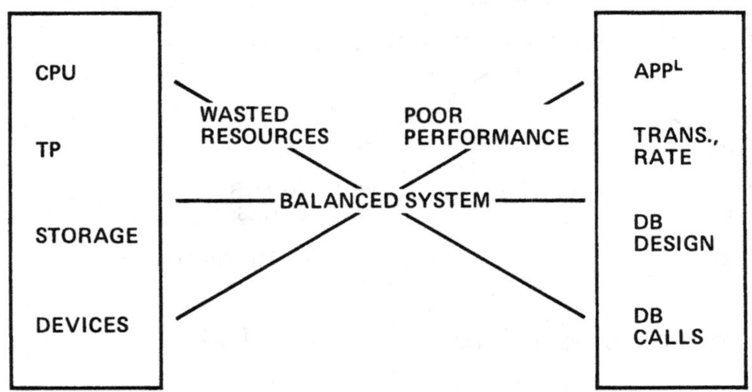

TUNING ⟶ BALANCE RESOURCE SUPPLY AND DEMAND

Fig. 23

DBDC PERFORMANCE TUNING

Primarily concerned with:

- DATABASE PROFILES
- TRANSACTIONS PROFILES
- IMS PROFILES
- MPP PROCESSING REQUIREMENTS
- HARDWARE CONFIGURATION
- OPERATING SYSTEM PROFILE
- TELEPROCESSING CONFIGURATION
- OTHER

and the use of tools to measure critical parameters

Fig. 24

PRIMARY FACTORS AFFECTING PERFORMANCE/DESIGN

PARAMETER	TYPICAL VALUES
– # TRANSACTIONS	1 – 50
– # EXCPS/CALL	0.1 – 5
– # CALLS/TRANS	5.0 – 50

Fig. 25

A DBDC TUNING APPROACH

Objective

- MINIMIZE THE TRANSACTION PATH LENGTH.
- INVOKE PARALLELISM OF KEY RESOURCES.

Method

- QUANTIFY PROFILES – TRANSACTIONS, SYSTEM CONFIGURATION AND PERFORMANCE GOODNESS.
- UNDERSTAND SYSTEM BEHAVIOR IN RESPONSE TO WORKLOAD.
- USE SOFTWARE MONITORS TO QUANTIFY BEHAVIOR (Δ TIME), MAYBE – HARDWARE MONITORS AND DETAILED TRACE.
- DEFINE EXPERIMENTS TO UNCOVER AND ORDER BOTTLENECKS.
- FORM IMPROVEMENT HYPOTHESIS, MAKE CHANGE, MEASURE EFFECT.
- DOCUMENT EXPERIMENT AND RESULTS. GET SMART.

Result

- OPTIMUM UTILIZATION OF SYSTEM RESOURCES TO MATCH WORKLOAD.
- RESOLVE DIFFERENCE BETWEEN EXPECTED AND ACTUAL PERFORMANCE.

Fig. 26

TYPICAL CAUSES OF DBDC RESOURCE BOTTLENECKS

TP RESOURCES	• BALANCING NETWORK LOADING • SIZE OF TP BUFFERS • SIZE OF MESSAGE FORMAT BUFFERS
REGION RESOURCES	• AMOUNT OF PROGRAM LOADING • STRUCTURE AND SIZE OF APPLICATION PROGRAMS • DATA BASE STRUCTURE AND # CALLS • USE OF EXTENDED IMS FUNCTIONS • AMOUNT OF I/O
CPU RESOURCES	• AMOUNT OF SYSTEM AND USER I/O • USE OF BUFFER POOL SERVICES

Fig. 27

Datensicherheit in Datenbanksystemen

Hartmut Wedekind, Technische Hochschule Darmstadt

Zusammenfassung

Die Begriffe "Datenschutz","Datensicherheit" und "Datenintegrität" werden in der Einführung gegeneinander abgegrenzt. Im ersten Hauptteil werden die Sicherheitsmaßnahmen behandelt, die sich auf technische und organisatorische Belange beziehen. Die Prozesse der Identifikation und Authentifikation, die organisatorische Bildung von Schichten, Bereichen und Berechtigungsmatrizen sowie kryptographische Methoden stehen im Mittelpunkt der Betrachtungen. Der zweite Hauptteil befaßt sich mit Sicherheitsmodellen. Unter Sicherheitsmodellen verstehen wir die sprachliche Fixierung der Sicherheitsbedingungen, um diese in ein Datenverwaltungssystem einbringen zu können. Eine Datenbank beinhaltet alle gespeicherten Daten, ein Datenverwaltungssystem alle Verfahren zu ihrer Handhabung. Wir unterscheiden deskriptive (nicht prozedurale, deklarative) Sicherheitsmodelle , die für Relationale Datenbanksysteme vorgeschlagen wurden, von prozeduralen Modellen, wie sie z.B. im DBTG der CODASYL-Gruppe für hierarchische Datenbanksysteme vorgesehen sind.

1. Einführung

Die Begriffspaare Datenschutz und Datensicherheit auf der einen Seite und Datensicherheit und Datenintegrität auf der anderen Seite liegen so nahe beieinander , daß eine gegenseitige Abgrenzung der Begriffe vor der Behandlung von Einzelheiten erforderlich ist. Unter dem Thema "Datenschutz" soll die Frage beantwortet werden "Was und wovor ist zu schützen" (15). Man bemüht sich in dieser Disziplin um die Erarbeitung von Rechtsnormen und Organisationsvorschriften die festlegen, was aus ethischen, sozialen, wirtschaftlichen oder nachrichtendienstlichen Gründen nicht jedermann zugänglich sein soll oder nicht in eine Datenbank eingebracht werden darf. Der Datenschutz ist besonders wichtig im Hinblick auf personenbezogene Daten. Aber auch für Firmendaten (z.B. Kundenstammdaten, patent- oder lizenzfähige Daten) und für Daten der öffentlichen Verwaltung (z.B. Daten über Baulandplanung) besteht ein Schutzinteresse. In Amerika ist ein Datenschutzgesetz ergangen, in Deutschland existiert ein Gesetzesentwurf der Bundesregierung.

Innerhalb der Datensicherheit interessiert man sich für die Frage "Wie ist zu schützen". Wir wollen uns in dieser Arbeit beschränken auf die Fragen der Gewährleistung einer Zugriffssicherheit, durch die unberechtigte Zugriffe abgewehrt werden. Was ein unberechtigter Zugriff ist, wird durch Datenschutzvorschriften festgelegt. Wir klammern die physische Datensicherheit aus. Hierunter werden Probleme der baulichen Maßnahmen in Rechenzentren, die Schlösser- und Schlüsselverteilung, das Anbringen von Schreibringen bei Bändern, die Berücksichtigung des Feuerschutzes und die Wiederherstellung zerstörter Dateien verstanden. Die physische Datensicherheit befaßt sich mit der Sicherung vor Datenverlust.

Die Datenintegrität betrifft die Genauigkeit der Daten. Die Daten müssen Integritätsbedingungen genügen, die sich im einfachen Fall auf Datenfelder mit einer Datentypdeklaration beziehen; in komplizierten Fällen geht eine Integritätsbedingung über viele Dateien eines Datenflußplanes hinweg. Die Teile-Nr. einer Auftragsdatei müssen z.B. eine Untermenge der Teile-Nr. sein, die in der Teilestammdatei aufgeführt werden. Abstimmkreise der kaufmännischen Praxis sind Integritätsbedingungen, die sehr komplizierter Natur sein können. Integritätsbedingungen sind Qualitätsbedingungen der Datenbank.

Datensicherheit und Datenintegrität nennt Date (9) zu recht Zwillingsprobleme. Datenintegrität ist die Forderung nach Fehlerlosigkeit der Datei; demgegenüber orientiert sich die Datensicherheit am Zugriff. Beide Probleme erfordern die Formulierung und das Einbringen von zusätzlichen Bedingungen. Während bei der Datensicherheit die Bedingungen aus den abstrakten Normen des Datenschutzes abgeleitet werden, berücksichtigen die Integritätsbedingungen das verwendete Datenmodell und die konkreten Spezifikationen der Miniwelt der Benutzer. Im Rahmen der Datenintegrität wird auch das Problem des möglichen Integritätsverlustes durch einen gleichzeitigen Änderungszugriff behandelt (shared access).

2. Sicherheitsmaßnahmen

2.1 Identifikation und Authentifikation

Wenn ein Benutzer zu einer Datenbank (DB) Zugang haben will, so muß er sich zuerst identifizieren, d.h., er muß dem System sagen, wer er ist. Diese Identifikation muß auf Richtigkeit überprüft sein, sie muß authentifiziert werden. Ein weitverbreitetes Mittel zur Identifikation aber auch zur Authentifikation ist bei DB Systemen das Kennwort (password). Jeder Benutzer bekommt ein Kennwort. Die Kennworte werden in einer Kennworttabelle vom DB-System verwaltet. Die Tabelle kann noch weitere Personenstammdaten wie Personal-Nummer, Name und Datum der Kennworterteilung enthalten. In der Tabelle kann ferner vermerkt werden, welche Terminale benutzt werden dürfen. Damit kann überprüft werden, ob der Benutzer an einem vorher identifizierten Terminal überhaupt arbeiten darf. Der Prozeß der Identifikation wird bei manchen Terminalen heute dadurch vereinfacht und auch sicherer gemacht, daß maschinenlesbare Ausweiskarten verlangt werden. Mit der Personenidentifikation geht im System die Terminalidentifikation einher. Dem System wird so bekannt, wo die Terminalsitzung stattfindet. Wenn man davon ausgehen kann, daß die Kennworte und ihre Abspeicherung geheim bleiben, so ist der Identifikationsprozeß auch gleichzeitig ein Authentifikationsprozeß. Damit die Annahme realistischer wird, können besondere Methoden für die Kennwortvergabe eingeführt werden. Sehr sicher, aber auch aufwendig, ist ein Kennwort, das nur einmal benutzt werden kann (one time password). Petersen und Turn (2o) führen aus, daß diese Art der Kennwortvergabe auch nicht vor solchen Eindringlingen schützt, die sich mit einem Terminal in den Terminalbetrieb zwischen dem berechtigten Benutzer und dem System einschalten (infiltration between the lines). Die Kennworttabelle muß auf jeden Fall geheim bleiben, wenn sie nicht in einer Geheimschrift verschlüsselt wird.
Eine weitere Möglichkeit, Identifikation und Authentifikation zusammenfallen zu lassen, wäre die Überprüfung von Finderabdrücken, die Analyse der maschinellen Stimme oder die Unterschriftskontrolle. Für auch wirtschaftlich vertretbare Verfahren sind getrennte Identifikations- und Authentifikationsprozesse notwendig. Bei einer Authentifikation sind Informationen auszunutzen, die nur der Person bekannt sind, die sich in der Identifikationsprozedur als solche ausgegeben hat. Man kann zum Beispiel ein weiteres Kennwort angeben müssen. Allein schon durch ein "Über-die-Schulter-gucken" kann auch dieses Kennwort allgemein bekannt werden. Zweckmässiger ist es deshalb, daß das System dem Benutzer, der

einen Zugang wünscht, eine Frage stellt, die nur dieser beantworten kann. Auf Vorschlag von L. Earnest empfiehlt Hoffman (16, S. 92) wie folgt vorzugehen. Beim "log-in" identifiziert der Benutzer sich; er bekommt daraufhin vom System eine Pseudozufallszahl angeboten, die wir x nennen wollen. Durch eine einfache Transformation T, die vom Benutzer im Kopf durchzuführen ist, wird eine Zahl y ermittelt. Das Ergebnis y = T(x) wird eingegeben. Das System vollzieht ebenfalls die Transformation T(x) und prüft, ob das Ergebnis tatsächlich y ist. Ein potentieller Eindringling kann höchstens x und y sehen. Die Transformation T ist für ihn kaum in Erfahrung zu bringen, wenn die Prozedur im Rechner geschützt ist. Die Prozedur ist aber geschützt, da nur der Zugriff hat, der authentifiziert worden ist. Es kann für T z.B. die folgende Transformation vorgeschlagen werden, die kaum von einem Dritten ermittelt werden kann:

$$T(x) = \Big(\sum_{i=\text{ungerade}} i\text{-te Ziffer von } x\Big)^2 + (\text{Stunde des Tages})$$

Es werden also die Ziffern auf den ungeraden Stellen summiert. Die Summe wird quadriert und zur Stunde des Tages addiert.
Die dargestellte Methode zur Authentifikation ist sehr einfach und wenig aufwendig. Sie hat darüber hinaus den Vorteil, daß die Kennworttabelle jedermann bekannt sein kann, da sie zur Identifikation benötigt wird. Geheim bleiben muß lediglich T(x).

Weitere Methoden zur Authentifikation werden von Evans u.a. (10) und Purdy (21) vorgeschlagen. Beide Verfahren ähneln sich sehr stark und bauen auf Erkenntnissen auf, die innerhalb der Kryptographie (Geheimschrift oder Chiffrekunde, kryptos=geheim) entwickelt wurden. Wegen der großen Bedeutung der Kryptographie für die Sicherheit von DB-Systemen werden wir in einem gesonderten Abschnitt auf diese Verfahren eingehen. Auf die erwähnten Verfahren von Evans und Purdy, die auf der Methode der "Ein-Weg Chiffre" (one way cipher) von Wilkes (27) aufbauen, soll hier in diesem Rahmen nicht eingegangen werden.

2.2 Schichtungen, Bereichsbildungen und Berechtigungstabellen

Es gibt drei einfache Strukturen, um ein Sicherheitssystem zu organisieren. Es handelt sich um die Schichtung (stratification), die Bereichsbildung oder Sektionierung (compartmentalization) und die Anordnung der Zugriffsberechtigung in einer Berechtigungstabelle (authorization table).

Bei der Schichtung werden die Benutzer im Hinblick auf die Zugriffsberechtigung im Sinne einer Hierarchie in Gruppen eingeteilt. Die Schichten der Daten oder die Benutzergruppen erhalten z.B. von oben nach unten die folgenden Bezeichnungen:

streng geheim	1. Schicht
geheim	2. Schicht
streng vertraulich	3. Schicht
vertraulich	4. Schicht
nicht klassifiziert	5. Schicht

Eine Person, die z.B. Zugriff zu streng geheimen Daten hat, um diese zu sehen, zu löschen oder zu ändern, hat auch Zugriff zu Daten in darunter liegenden Schichten. Kann eine Person hingegen nur zu streng vertraulichen Daten zugreifen, so bleiben die Schichten "streng geheim" und geheim" für sie unzugänglich. Allgemein gilt: Eine Person darf nur zu den Daten der Schicht, für die sie klassifiziert wurde, und zu Daten in darunter liegenden Schichten zugreifen. Die Schichtung von Personen und Daten aus Gründen der Sicherheit stammt aus dem militärischen Bereich. In zivilen Sicherheitssystemen ist diese Sicherheitsorganisation ungebräuchlich. Aber auch im militärischen Bereich kombiniert man häufig die Schichtung mit der Bereichsbildung, die im Englischen "compartmentalization" heißt. Bei der Bereichsbildung werden die Daten in disjunktive Teilmengen zerlegt. Eine Teilmenge oder ein Bereich (Sektion) wird einer Person oder auch einer Personengruppe zugeordnet. Daten dürfen nur genau einmal in einem "Bereich" vorhanden sein. Das Sicherheitssystem muß gewährleisten, daß zwischen den Bereichen Sperren liegen, die nicht durchbrochen werden können. Martin (19,S.151) sieht die Bereichsbildung als eine vertikale Aufteilung der Daten. Die Schichtung wird von ihm auch horizontale Aufteilung genannt.

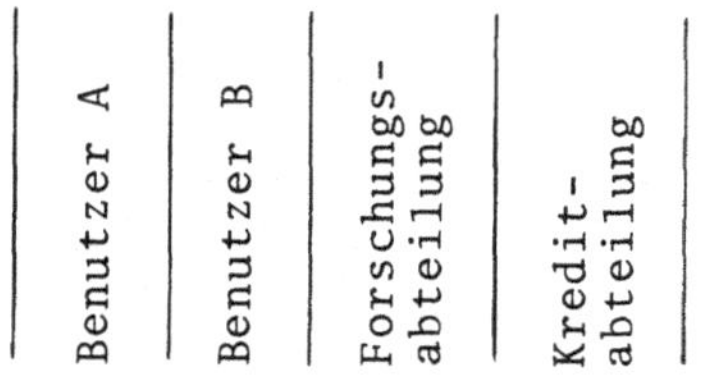

Benutzer A	Benutzer B	Forschungs-abteilung	Kredit-abteilung

In einem vertikalen Bereich sind bei Personengruppen auch horizontale Schichten denkbar. Diese Form wird häufig bei militärischen Sicherheitssystemen vorgefunden. Auch hier möchte man, daß eine

Person nur Zugang zu den Daten hat, die von ihr auch wirklich gebraucht werden. Friedman (14,S.269)nennt die Bereichsbildung eine Umsetzung des militärischen Postulats des "Need-To-Know". Jeder soll nur das wissen, was er wirklich benötigt. Eine sehr bekannte Anwendung der Bereichsbildung ist die speichergeschützte Aufteilung des Zentralspeichers für Einzelprogramme. Das Betriebssystem gewährleistet beim Multiprogrammingbetrieb, daß in einem Programm nicht der Speicherbereich eines anderen Programms adressiert werden kann. Unterstützt wird das Betriebssystem dabei häufig hardwaremäßig durch Begrenzungsregister (base limit register). Ein Register dieser Art nimmt eine Basisadresse und die Bereichslänge auf. Durch Vergleich der Programmadressen mit dem Registerinhalt kann eine Bereichsüberschreitung entdeckt werden. Die dritte Form der einfachen Strukturen für ein Sicherheitssystem ist die Berechtigungstabelle. Die Tabelle enthält das Kennwort, die Personal-Nr. und ein n-bit-langes Feld für die Berechtigung. Ist das i-te Bit eine 1, so ist ein Zugriff zum Sicherungsobjekt D_i erlaubt, bei 0 wird der Zugriff verwehrt. Die Tabelle wird auch häufig Benutzerprofil (user security profile) genannt. Der Nachteil ist, daß die binäre Regel "entweder Zugriff oder kein Zugriff" gilt. Bei Datenbanksystemen wird diese Tabelle häufig als Matrix ausgebildet, wobei die Zeilen die Benutzer und die Spalten die Sicherungsobjekte darstellen. Eine Berechtigungsmatrix soll an einem Beispiel erklärt werden, daß in einer ähnlichen Form auch bei Conway u.a. (8, S.212 zu finden ist. Wir gehen aus von der Relation PERSONAL (PNR, LSTG, GHT, LMB, VST), die außer der Personal-Nr (PNR) die sehr sensitiven Personaldaten Leistung (LSTG), Gehalt (GHT), letzter medizinischer Befund (LMB) und Vorstrafen (VST) enthält. Die bereits behandelte Kennworttabelle dient zur Zeilenidentifikation.

PNR	Kennwort	PNR	LSTG	GHT	LMB	VST	Bemerkung
A	13 C 151	R	R,W	R,W	R	R,W	Personalchef
B	74 Q 028	R,W	R	R	N	N	Organis.-Chef
C	43 F 974	R	N	N	N	N	Programmierer
D	14 Z 234	R	N	N	R,W	N	Mediziner
F	28 R 862	N	R	R	R	R	Statistiker

R = Lesen erlaubt, W = Verändern erlaubt
N = Weder Lesen noch Verändern erlaubt

Damit in einem System die Berechtigungsmatrizen für Mengen von entities nicht zu speicheraufwendig werden, wird empfohlen, Zonen und Kategorien zu bilden (19. S.6). Eine Zone ist dabei die Zusammenfassung mindestens zweier Mengen von Sicherungsgegenständen. Aus den Mengen Verkaufsteil, Einkaufsteil und Fertigungsteil wird die Zone Teil. Eine Kategorie ist die Zusammenfassung mehrerer Attribute. Aus Kunden-Name, Wohnort und Umsatz kann die Kategorie "Kundeninformation" entstehen. Eine weitere Reduktion des Speicheraufwandes ist die Bildung von Benutzergruppen. Alle Mitglieder einer Benutzergruppe haben genau gleiche Zugriffsrechte. Zwecks leichter sprachlicher Unterscheidung wird eine Benutzergruppe, die aus sicherungstechnischen Gründen gebildet wird, von Friedman (14.S.269)"Clique" genannt. Zonen, Kategorien und Cliquen sind drei sehr einprägsame Begriffe.

Gegenüber den Schichtungen und Bereichsbildungen läßt die Berechtigungsmatrix schon die Darstellung von wesentlich subtileren Sicherheitsbedingungen zu. Die Sicherheitsbedingungen dürfen jedoch nicht wertabhängig sein. Eine tabellarische Darstellung in der Form des Datenschemas "Matrix" ist dann nur noch sehr schwer möglich. Es muß zu einer sprachlichen Formulierung der Sicherheitsbedingungen übergegangen werden. Eine Bedingung ist dann wertabhängig, wenn Attributausprägungen zu ihrer Formulierung benötigt werden.
Man kann wertabhängige Sicherheitsbedingungen von beliebiger Komplexität angeben. Die Vorschriften des Datenschutzes verlangen häufig die Einhaltung nur einfacher wertabhängiger Bedingungen, wie z.B. die Personalsatzbedingung*). Wertunabhängige Bedingungen können zur Übersetzungszeit, wertabhängige Bedingungen erst zur Ausführungszeit überprüft werden. Wertabhängige Bedingungen sind sehr zeitaufwendig.

2.3 Umgehung der Sicherheitsvorkehrungen

In diesem Abschnitt werden Methoden zur Umgehung der Sicherheitsmaßnahmen beschrieben. Gleichzeitig wird die Frage behandelt, welche Sicherheitsmaßnahmen gebraucht werden, um mit Vorsatz arbeitende Eindringlinge abzuwehren. Bei den Methoden der Eindringlinge handelt es sich um "Schurkereien", die den "naiven" und "rechtschaffenen" Benutzer sehr esotorisch anmuten. Für viele Angriffe der Eindringlinge ist die Verschlüsselung der Datenbank im Sinne der Kryptographie eine wirkungsvolle Gegenmaßnahme. Die Attacken und Verteidigungsmaßnahmen auf ein DV-System sind in vorzüglicher Weise in dem viel beachteten

*) d.h. jeder darf nur seinen eigenen Personalstammsatz lesen.

Aufsatz von Peterson und Turn (20) dargestellt.

Die Ziele eines vorsätzlichen Eindringens in ein DB-System können sein:
1) Gewinnung von Information, 2) Herausfinden, welches Informationsinteresse ein Benutzer hat, 3) Ändern und Zerstören von Information, 4) Kostenlose Nutzung von Resourcen des Systems oder Nutzung von Systemresourcen auf Kosten eines anderen.

Von Peterson und Turn werden die Methoden (20) zum vorsätzlichen Eindringen in das System in zwei Kategorien eingeteilt. Es wird von passiver Infiltration gesprochen, wenn der Eindringling sich auf irgendeine Weise in das DV-System einschaltet, um zu wissen, was vor sich geht. Eine aktive Infiltration liegt dann vor, wenn der Eindringling entweder Systemressourcen nutzen will oder gezielt Informationen gewinnen, ändern oder zerstören will. Die Methoden der passiven Infiltration sind das Anzapfen von Übertragungsleitungen (wiretapping) vom System zum Terminal und das Anbringen von Sonden (electromagnetic pickups) in CPU und diversen Speichern. Die Übertragungsleitungen gelten als der Teil des Gesamtsystems, der am leichtesten verletzbar ist (20,S.291). Nach Peterson und Turn setzt man sich gegen diese beiden aufgeführten Angriffe am besten durch eine Verschlüsselung in eine Geheimschrift zur Wehr. Dem Eindringling wird dann aufgebürdet, die Chiffre zu "knacken". Wenn der Aufwand (work factor) zum Brechen der Chiffre größer ist als der Wert der gewonnenen Information, lohnen sich diese Angriffe nicht. Diese Aussage ist sehr abstrakt, da zwar der Aufwand zur Codebrechung nicht aber der Wert der Information für einen Eindringling abgeschätzt werden kann. Im Hinblick auf die aktive Infiltration können die folgenden Methoden aufgezählt werden:

1) "Masquerading". Der Eindringling hat sich z.B. über ein Anzapfen der Leitung das Kennwort eines Benutzers besorgt und "maskiert" sich nun mit diesem. Durch Verschlüsseln kann verhindert werden, daß der Eindringling durch Anzapfen das Kennwort erfährt. Das Verschlüsseln und Entschlüsseln muß selbstverständlich am Terminal stattfinden.
2) "Browsing" (Schnüffeln). Der Eindringling ist ein rechtmäßiger Benutzer, der den Identifikations- und Authentifikationsprozeß erfolgreich passiert. Er versucht jedoch Daten zu lesen oder zu verändern, zu denen er nicht zugreifen darf. Eine gut funktionierende Zugriffskontrolle ist die beste Abwehr gegen diese Art der Infiltration.

3) In die Übertragungsleitung zwischen Benutzer und System wird vom Eindringling ein eigenes Terminal eingebracht. Während der rechtmäßige Benutzer am Terminal sitzt, kann sich folgendes ereignen:
   a) Der Eindringling löscht das "sign-off" Kommando und fährt fort, im Namen des Benutzers sein Terminal zu bedienen. Dieser glaubt, daß die Terminalsitzung beendet sei.

   b) Während das Terminal des rechtmäßigen Benutzers inaktiv ist, schaltet sich der Eindringling ein, um mit der Datenbank zu arbeiten ("between the lines").

   c) Der Eindringling sucht sich die spezielle Information aus dem Verkehr zwischen dem rechtmäßigen Benutzer und dem System aus, verändert diese und läßt die modifizierte, fehlerhafte Information zum Terminal des Benutzers übertragen. ("piggyback entry").

Die Verschlüsselung ist für diese drei Fälle die beste Gegenwehr.

4) Diebstahl eines auswechselbaren Datenträgers. Neben der physischen Absicherung durch speziell verschließbare Räume ist auch hier die Verschlüsselung zu empfehlen.

5) Die Eindringlinge sind Systemprogrammierer mit Detailkenntnissen auf dem Gebiet des Speicherschutzes, des Programmierens im privilegierten Modus und des Betriebssystems. Eindringlinge dieses Typs sind naturgemäß die gefährlichsten. Sie können absichtlich undichte Stellen in Systemprogramme einbauen (trap doors) oder sich von Zeit zur Zeit den Zentralspeicher herausdrucken lassen. Die Systeme sind heute so kompliziert, daß nur ein Team von Eindringlingen erfolgreich arbeiten kann, was einen gewissen Schutz darstellt, da ein ganzes Team sich nur in seltenen Fällen auf eine "Schurkerei" dieser Art einläßt. Durch das Protokollieren gewisser Operationen, wie zum Beispiel das Herausdrucken des Zentralspeichers, können nachträglich unzulässige Eingriffe bekannt werden. Peterson und Turn nennen diese Maßnahmen "threat monitoring"; sie messen ihnen eine große Bedeutung bei. Besonders schwer zu erkennen sind Angriffe, die durch Software-Modifikationen, z.B. durch Änderungen von Übersetzern, Vorübersetzern, Texteditoren etc. zustande kommen. Da fast alle Programme durch andere Programme verarbeitet werden, stellt Bayer (1,S.78) zu recht den Grundsatz auf : Kein Programm ist sicherer als diejenigen Programme, durch die es bearbeitet wird".

Systemprogrammierer mit Detailkenntnissen können auch die Methode des "eingepflanzten Satzes" benutzen, um die Chiffre schneller zu brechen. Der Eindringling bringt Klartextfragmente in die Datei und spürt dann die Chiffre zur Codebrechung auf. Insbesondere Bayer (1) hat auf diesen Vorgang aufmerksam gemacht.

2.4. Kryptographische Methoden

Kryptographie ist die Lehre von der Erzeugung eines Geheimtextes aus einem ursprünglichen Text und von der Wiedergewinnung eines ursprünglichen Textes aus einem Geheimtext. Der erste Vorgang heißt Chiffrieren; sein Umkehrung wird Dechiffrieren genannt. Andere Bezeichnungen für "ursprünglichen Text" und "Geheimtext" sind "Klartext" und "Kryptogramm" oder "Chiffre". Eine Chiffre ist eine unverständliche Folge von Schriftzeichen. Die Sicherheit eines Chiffrierverfahrens beurteilt man nach dem Widerstand oder Aufwand (work factor) für den unberufenen Eindringling. Im einem kryptographischen Code, der keine Chiffre ist, können Teile der Schriftzeichenfolge von einem Dritten zwar verstanden, aber nicht richtig gedeutet werden. Es werden Wörter und ganze Satzteile ziemlich willkürlich ausgetauscht. Wie dieser Austausch durchzuführen ist, wird in einem Wörterbuch, das Codebuch geannt wird, festgehalten. Bei kryptographischen Codes soll in der Regel auch eine Datenkompression erzielt werden. Wegen des Speicheraufwandes, der durch das Codebuch verursacht wird, kommen kryptographische Codes für DB-Systeme nicht in Betracht. Wir benötigen algorithmische Chiffrier- und Dechiffrierverfahren und keine tabellarischen. Es können drei Arten von algorithmischen Verfahren unterschieden werden:
a) Ersetzungsverfahren (substitution methods), b) Versetzungsverfahren (transposition methods) c) Block-Chiffrierverfahren (block cipher methods)

Die Kryptographie hat eine lange Geschichte. Liebende und Diebe haben ihre Verbindungen immer so gut es eben ging verheimlicht, bemerkt Feistel (13,S.21),um in scherzhafter Weise auf die vorwissenschaftliche Kryptographie einzugehen. Erst etwa Mitte des vergangenen Jahrhunderts wurde die Kryptographie langsam zu einer Wissenschaft. Der geheime Nachrichtenaustausch bleibt jedoch bis tief in dieses Jahrhundert hinein auf Bleistift und Papier beschränkt. Durch den Computer hat die Kryptographie dann einen neuen, kaum erwarteten Aufschwung genommen. Alle historischen Anmerkungen, die wir im Verlauf der Darstellung machen werden, sind aus dem berühmten Buch von Kahn "The Codebreakers" (18).

a) Ersetzungsverfahren

Bei diesem kryptographischen Verfahren wird ein Zeichen

des Klartextes durch ein Zeichen aus dem Alphabet der Chiffre ersetzt. Im Gegensatz zum einfacheren Versetzungsverfahren bleibt die Identität eines Klartextzeichens nicht erhalten. Man kann das Ersetzen über eine Tabelle oder algorithmisch, d.h. in diesem Zusammenhang algebraisch durchführen. Innerhalb der Datenbank-Kryptographie haben die additiven Substitutionsverfahren wegen ihrer hohen Leistungsfähigkeit bei großen Datenmengen eine besondere Bedeutung bekommen. Von den additiven Verfahren wollen wir hier die Verfahren "Addition modulo q" oder die Vignère-Vernam -Chiffren hervorheben.

Im frühen 16. Jahrhundert hat der Benediktinermönch Trithemus das überhaupt erste gedruckte Buch über Kryptographie veröffentlicht. Trithemus beschreibt in diesem Buch eine quadratische Matrix mit Buchstaben als Elemente, deren Zeilen von oben nach unten jeweils um eine Position versetzt werden. Er benutzte diese Matrix als Schlüssel zum Chiffrieren in einem additiven Substitutionsverfahren. Im späten 16. Jahrhundert wurde diese Idee von Blaise de Vignère wieder aufgegriffen und verbessert. Historisch nicht ganz korrekt wird das im folgenden dargestellte Verfahren Vignère- Verfahren genannt.

<u>Klartext</u>

		0	1	2	3	.....	25
		A	B	C	D	.....	Z
0	A	A	B	C	D	.....	Z
1	B	B	C	D	E	.....	A
2	C	C	D	E	F	.....	B
	.	.	.	.	.	.....	.
	.	.	.	.	.	.....	.
	.	.	.	.	.	.....	.
25	Z	Z	A	B	C	.....	Y

Schlüsselmatrix für die Vignère-Chiffre

Die Spaltenbezeichnungen (A,B,C, etc) gelten für den Klartext.
Die Zeilenbezeichnungen werden für den Schlüssel benötigt. Das Chiffrezeichen wird im Schnittpunkt zwischen Zeile und Spalte gefunden. Wenn einem D im Klartext ein B im Schlüssel gegenübersteht, so finden wir als Chiffrezeichen E. Beim Dechiffrieren geht man umgekehrt vor.

Wir wollen "klassische" Chiffrierung mit der Vignère-Methode an einem Beispiel demonstrieren:
Gegeben sei der Klartext :"KEIN VERRÄTER" und der Schlüssel "KAISERBALL"

Klartext : K E I N V E R R A E T E R
Schlüssel: K A I S E R B A L L K A I
Chiffre: U E Q F Z V S R L P D E Z

Wenn wir den Buchstaben A bis Z die Zahlen 0 bis 25 zuordnen, wie das in der Abb. geschehen ist, so kann man den Chiffrierungsprozess als Addition modulo 26 auffassen. Für das obige Beispiel finden wir dann, ohne die Matrix benutzen zu müssen:

K + K = 10 + 10 = 20 = 20 mod 26 = U
E + A = 4 + 0 = 4 = 4 mod 26 = E
I + I = 8 + 8 = 16 = 16 mod 26 = Q
N + S = 13 + 18 = 31 = 5 mod 26 = F
. . . . .
. . . . .
. . . . .
R + I = 17 + 8 = 25 = 25 mod 26 = Z

Im vergangenen Jahrhundert nannte man die Vignère-Chiffre "le chiffre indéchiffrable". Tuckerman (23), kann zeigen, daß das Brechen dieser Chiffre mit Computermethoden kein großes Problem ist, wenn genügend Geheimtext vorhanden ist. Nicht zu brechen ist ein Geheimtext, wenn der Schlüssel nur einmal benutzt und durch einen Zufallszahlengenerator erzeugt wird, der keine periodischen Pseudozufallszahlen produziert. Je länger der Schlüssel, desto schwieriger wird es, die Chiffre zu brechen.
Der amerikanische Nachrichteningenieur Gilbert Vernam hat 1917 die Vignère-Chiffre zum ersten Mal auf einen digitalisierten Datenstrom angewendet. Vernam sah sich vor die Aufgabe gestellt, ein Alphabet zu chiffrieren, das aus $2^5 = 32$ Zeichen für Fernschreiber bestand, und in einem Digitalcode dargeboten wurde. Das Ergebnis seiner Untersuchungen war eine Addition modulo 2.

Beispiel

Chiffrieren:

Klartext: 0 1 0 0 1'1 1 1 0 0'
Schlüssel: 0 1 0 1 0'1 0 1 0 1'
Chiffre: 0 0 0 1 1'0 1 0 0 1'

Dechiffrieren:

Chiffre: 0 0 0 1 1'0 1 0 0 1'
Schlüssel:0 1 0 1 0'1 0 1 0 1'
Klartext: 0 1 0 0 1'1 1 1 0 0'

Die Addition modulo 2 und die logische Operation "Exklusives ODER" sind identisch. Mit dem "Exklusiven ODER" wird auch wieder dechiffriert. Das "Exklusive ODER" hat eine eindeutige Inverse. Die Vernam-Chiffrierung spielt in der Datenbank-Kryptographie eine besondere Rolle. Sie ist eine spezielle Chiffre nach dem "Addition modulo q" Verfahren, das von Tuckermann Vignère-Vernam-System oder abgekürzt V-V-System genannt wird.

b) Versetzungsverfahren

Bei der Anwendung von Versetzungsverfahren bleibt die Identität des Zeichens gewahrt, es ändert sich lediglich die Position. Kinder praktizieren z.B. eines der vielen Versetzungsverfahren, wenn sie ihren Namen von hinten nach vorne hinschreiben.

Eine gebräuchliche Methode für eine Versetzungstransformation ist das Aufteilen des Klartextes in Blöcke mit einer anschließenden Anordnung in einer Matrix. Auf die Matrix werden einige Operationen angewendet. Der so entstandene Text wird dann wieder nach einer bestimmten Regel in die lineare Form gebracht. Da Versetzungsverfahren alleine angewendet zu wenig Sicherheit bieten - eine Häufigkeitsanalyse der Zeichen kann schon zum Ziele führen - wollen wir sie nicht genauer beschreiben.

c) Block-Chiffrierverfahren

Ein Chiffrierverfahren, das n Informationsbits in n Chiffrebits umwandelt, wird Block-Chiffrierverfahren genannt. Die Bit-Vernam-Transformation ist in diesem Sinne ein Block-Chiffrierverfahren. Wenn man heute jedoch den Begriff "Block-Chiffrierverfahren" ohne weitere Zusätze benutzt, dann denkt man an ein Verfahren, das die folgenden Eigenschaften hat:

1. Ersetzen (substitution) und Versetzen (transposition) werden stufenweise hintereinander angewendet. Da das "Hintereinanderschalten" von Prozessen eine "multiplikative" Verknüpfung bedeutet, werden Block-Chiffrierverfahren auch Produkt-Chiffrierverfahren genannt.

2. Im Gegensatz zu den "Bit für Bit" oder "Buchstaben für Buchstaben" Ersetzungsverfahren, bei denen in der Chiffre keine Abhängigkeiten zwischen den einzelnen Bits oder Buchstaben bestehen, wird der Block aus n Bits als Ganzes behandelt. Es liegt in der Chiffre eine Symbolabhängigkeit vor. Wenn ein Symbol in der Chiffre von einem anderen abhängig ist, kann durch einen Übertragungsfehler bei einem Symbol ein ganzer Block nicht mehr dechiffrierbar sein.

3. Die Stufe "Substitution" ist eine nichtlineare Transformation. Auf diesen Eigenschaften werden wir im folgenden noch genauer eingehen.

Block-Chiffrierverfahren für die Rechneranwendung wurden insbesondere von Feistel entwickelt (13), (12) und (11). Sie zeichnen sich durch große Sicherheit aus, d.h. der Aufwand, eine Block-Chiffre zu brechen, ist beträchtlich. Block-Chiffrierverfahren wurden schon von der deutschen Armee im ersten Weltkrieg unter dem Namen ADFGVX benutzt (18). Zwischen den Weltkriegen wurden dann Chiffrier-Maschinen entwickelt, die mit einem Pseudozufallschlüssel arbeiteten. Erst die Rechneranwendungen haben Mitte der 60-iger Jahre wieder das Interesse für Block-Chiffrierverfahren belebt (13, S.99). Wir werden die Block-Chiffrierverfahren hier so darstellen, als würden die Transformationen von Geräten besorgt.

Wir beginnen mit der Beschreibung der nichtlinearen Substitution.

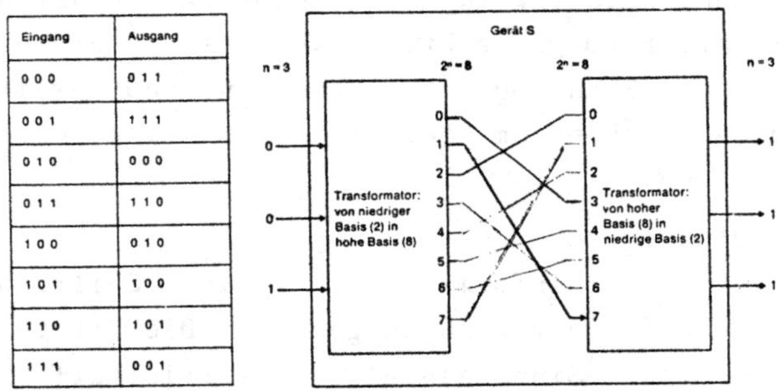

Eingang	Ausgang
0 0 0	0 1 1
0 0 1	1 1 1
0 1 0	0 0 0
0 1 1	1 1 0
1 0 0	0 1 0
1 0 1	1 0 0
1 1 0	1 0 1
1 1 1	0 0 1

Nichtlineare Substitution nach Feistel (13, S.25)

Es wird angenommen, daß der Klartext in Blöcken zu n = 3 Bits eingegeben wird. Es werden nicht wie beim Vernam-Verfahren eine Null oder eine Eins zu den Eingabeziffern addiert, sondern man substituiert einen ganzen Eingabeziffernblock durch einen beliebigen Ausgabeziffernblock. Das Substitutionsgerät (Gerät S) besteht im wesentlichen aus zwei Basistransformatoren. Der Eingabetransformator nimmt einen Block in der Darstellung zur Basis 2 auf und verwandelt ihn in eine Oktalzahl. Der Ausgabetransformator geht umgekehrt vor. Für die n Eingabebits gibt es 2^n Substitutionszeichen, die auf nichtlineare Weise durch Basistransformation gefunden werden. Die Basistransformation ist auch als ein gutes Verfahren zur Erzeugung von hash-Adressen bekannt. Bevor eine Substitution im umgekehrten Sinne stattfindet, wird eine Versetzung vorgenommen, die man sich durch eine einfache Verdrahtung realisiert vorstellen kann. Eine mögliche Verdrahtung wird in der Abbildung gezeigt. Insgesamt gibt es $2^n! = 8! = 40320$ solcher Verdrahtungen (Hardware) oder Tabellen (Software). Für n = 3 oder 4 ist ein Substitutionsgerät mit einer beliebigen Verdrahtungsmöglichkeit noch zu realisieren. Durch Eingeben gewisser "Tricknachrichten" kann der Eindringling jedoch die Chiffre brechen (13,S.26). Das ist nicht mehr der Fall, wenn z.B. n = 128 gewählt wird. Mit 128 Ein- und Ausgängen müßte der Eindringling $2^{128} > 10^{38}$ verschiedene Blöcke eingeben, um die Arbeitsweise des Gerätes zu erforschen. Das ist nicht durchführbar. Diesem Vorteil steht der entscheidende Nachteil gegenüber, daß das Verfahren für große n, z.B. für n = 128, technisch nicht realisiert werden kann. Dies ist die Ursache, die dazu führte, daß man mehrere kleinere Substitutionsgeräte, z.B. mit n = 3, in einer Stufe parallel anordnete. Da eine Substitutionsstufe mit mehreren S-Geräten noch sehr leicht überwunden werden kann, wurde ein Versetzungsgerät nachgeschaltet. Da in einem Versetzungsgerät eine Permutation von Symbolen vorgenommen wird, spricht man auch von einem Permutationsgerät (P-Gerät). Kaum zu brechen ist eine Chiffre dann, wenn mehrere P-Geräte und S-Geräter hintereinander angeordnet werden. Das "Durcheinanderwirbeln" der Bits durch eine komplizierte Transformation H ist so groß, daß eine Inversion für jemanden, der nicht eingeweiht ist, kaum noch nachvollzogen werden kann. Die Abbildung zeigt, wie aus einer einzigen 1 durch mehrmaliges nichtlineares Substituieren und Permutieren (Versetzen) eine "Lawine" von Einsen entstehen kann. Bei der Dechiffrierung werden die Stufen in umgekehrter Richtung durchlaufen. Um das Block-Chiffrierverfahren für den Gegner noch schwieriger zu machen, können für die S-Geräte jeweils andere Schlüssel vorgegeben werden, so daß wir zwischen den Geräten S_1, S_2, ...S_{20} unterscheiden können.

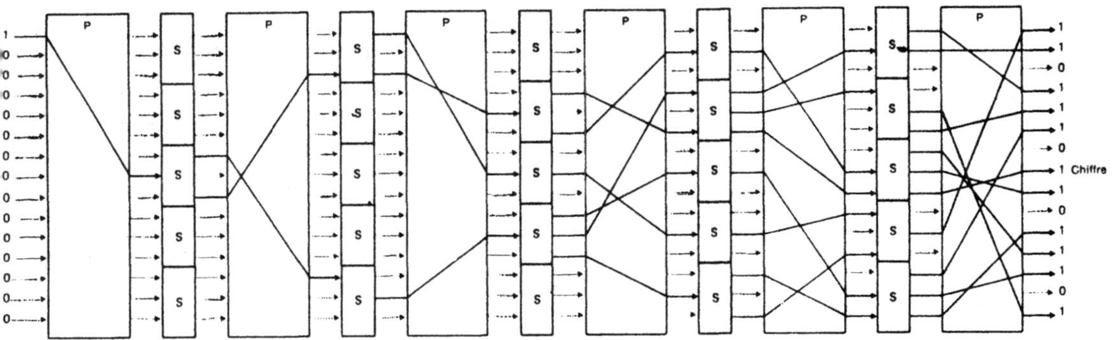

Block-Chiffrieren nach Feistel (13, S.100)

3. Sicherheitsmodelle in Datenbanksystemen

3.1 Deskriptive Modelle

Relationale DB-Systeme unterscheiden sich von anderen DB-Systemen dadurch, daß mehrere Entwurfsebenen deutlich erkennbar sind. Es können drei Ebenen erwähnt werden, die in einem relationalen DB-System mindestens vorhanden sein müssen:
1. Die logische Ebene, 2. Die Ebene der Zugriffspfade, 3. Die Ebene der physischen Abspeicherung auf den Geräten.
In DB-Systemen, die auf dem Relationenmodell der Daten basieren, wird davon ausgegangen, daß Sicherheitsbedingungen zur Miniwelt des Benutzers gerhören und daß ihre Formalisierung deskriptiv auf der logischen Ebene erfolgen muß. Sicherheitsbedingungen und auch Integritätsbedingungen werden prinzipiell genauso behandelt wie Anfragen (queries) der Benutzer. Sicherheits- und Integritätsbedingungen können sehr komplex sein. Es werden keine Sicherheitsorganisationen in Form von Schichtungen, Bereichsbildungen oder Berechtigungstabellen vorausgesetzt.

Gegeben sei eine relationale Datenbank mit n Relationen R_1, $R_2, \ldots, R_n$. Mit Hilfe einer Datenmanipulationssprache (DML) mit dem Relationenmodell als Grundlage (etwa ALPHA (7), SQUARE (3) oder SEQUEL (4)) ist es möglich, logische Bedingungen so zu formulieren, daß das Ergebnis der Qualifikation die Beantwortung einer Anfrage ist. In ALPHA wurde die Beantwortung einer Anfrage Zielliste (target list) genannt. In Anlehnung an Chamberlin (5) und Boyce (2) wollen wir das Ergebnis der Anfrage "Sicht" (view) nennen. Eine Sicht ist eine Relation, die nicht abspeichert, sondern nur durch logische Bedingungen definiert wird. "Views" sind virtuelle Relationen. Wenn die Basisrelationen (base relations) R_1, $R_2 \ldots$, R_n verändert werden, die tatsächlich zur Abspeicherung anstehen, so werden auch die abgeleiteten, virtuellen Relationen einer Änderung unterworfen. Eine "Sicht" ist im Sinne von Chamberlin (5) ein dynamisches Ergebnis einer Anfrage, in der auch built-in Funktionen wie COUNT, SUM etc. benutzt werden dürfen. Der Begriff "Sicht" stammt von Boyce (2). Er wird eingeführt, um insbesondere die Sprache SEQUEL auch als Datenbeschreibungssprache (Data Description Language, DDL) herauszustellen. Im Sinne einer DDL liegt nur dann eine vollständige Sicht vor, wenn alle Beschreibungsparameter einer Basisrelation deklariert werden. Sichten im Sinne einer DDL sollen an den Basisrelationen

LAGER_GUT (NR, BEZ, MENGE, PREIS)
LIEFERUNG (NR, LNR, DATUM)

veranschaulicht werden. Es bedeuten: NR = Nummer des Lagergutes, LNR = Lieferanten-Nummer, BEZ = Bezeichnung.
Die formale Beschreibung von LAGER-GUT lautet:

```
DEFINE LAGER_GUT TABLE AS:
  NR(SCOPE=POSINT,REPR=DEC (6))
  BEZ(SCOPE=ALPHA, DOMAIN=NAME, REPR=CHAR(*)
  MENGE(SCOPE=REAL,DOMAIN=SCHUETTGUT,UNITS=TONNE,
        REPR=FLOAT DEC (15,4)
  PREIS(SCOPE=REAL, DOMAIN=GELD, UNITS=DM PRO TONNE,
        REPR = FLOAT DEC (8,2)
  KEY=NR,
  ORDER=ASCENDING TNR
  INDEX,BEZ
DEFINE LIEFERUNG TABLE AS:
  NR LIKE LAGER_GUT.NR
  LNR LIKE NR EXCEPT(REPR=DEC (8))
  DATUM (SCOPE=POSINT, REPR=DEC (3))
  KEY NR,LNR
  ORDER=DESCENDING NR, ASCENDING LNR
```

Eine Tabelle wird zunächst durch ihren Tabellennamen, die Namen der Spalten und - wenn notwendig - durch die Ordnung der Zeilen beschrieben. Eine Spalte (Attribut) kann kenntlich gemacht werden durch einen Namen, einen Wertebereich (SCOPE) z.B. positive ganze Zahl (POSINT), eine Vergleichbarkeit (comparability DOMAIN), die aussagt, ob zwei Werte vergleichbar sind, eine Maßeinheit (UNITS) z.B. Tonne und eine Darstellung (REPR, representation). Die Begriffe SCOPE,UNITS und REPR erklären sich selbst. Zu bemerken ist nur, daß gewisse Standardausprägungen wie POSINT, REAL etc. für SCOPE und etwa FIXED BINARY, DECIMAL etc. für REPR bereitgestellt werden sollten. Was die Vergleichbarkeit anbetrifft, so sind zwei Werte nur dann vergleichbar, wenn sie aus Spalten stammen, für die der Parameter DOMAIN gleich ist. "Schüttgüter" können nur mit "Schüttgütern" und "Geld" kann nur mit "Geld" verglichen werden. Insbesondere dann, wenn mit zwei Relationen ein Verbund gebildet werden soll, spielt die Vergleichbarkeit eine große Rolle. Zur Veranschaulichung des Begriffes "Sicht" im Hinblick auf Sicherheitsbedingungen wird im folgenden ein Beispiel in der Sprache SEQUEL dargestellt:
Aus der Basisrelation "LAGER_GUT" soll die Sicht "VERKAUFS_GUT" entwickelt werden. Ein Verkaufsgut unterscheidet sich dabei von einem Lagergut dadurch, daß das Schüttgut in Säcke abgepackt und nach Stücken

gezählt wird. Die Sicht "VERKAUFS_GUT" enthält das Lagergut in einem verkaufsfähigen, abgepackten Zustand. Ein Stück, d.h. ein Sack soll 1/100 Tonnen wiegen.

```
DEFINE VERKAUFS_GUT TABLE AS:
        LIKE LAGER_GUT EXCEPT (MENGE. DOMAIN=SAECKE,
        MENGE.UNITS=STUECK, PREIS.UNITS=DM PRO STUECK)
```

Über die folgende Deklaration wird dem System die Umrechnung Tonnen in Stück mitgeteilt.

```
DEFINE CONVERT (TONNE TO STUECK):
        1/100 TONNE
```

CONVERT kann als Umrechnungsroutine aufgefaßt werden. Um die Umrechnung selber braucht sich der Benutzer der Sicht "VERKAUFS_GUT" nicht zu kümmern. Um die abgeleitete Sicht "VERKAUFS_GUT" zu einer Sicherheitsbedingung zu vervollständigen, muß geklärt werden, was dem Benutzer einer Sicht alles erlaubt ist. Wir stellen uns dabei vor, daß wir der Eigentümer der Basisrelation LAGER_GUT sind und volle Verfügungsgewalt über diese Relation haben. Der Begriff "Eigentümer" wird in diesem Sinne definiert. Chamberlin u.a. (5) schlagen nun die folgenden Verfügungsrechte vor:

1) GRANT (Gewähren): Hiermit wird verfügt, daß der Benutzer der abgeleiteten Sicht diese Sicht jedem beliebigen anderen Benutzer zeigen darf. Anders ausgedrückt: Die Weitervergabe der Leseerlaubnis wird gewährt.
2) REVOKE (Widerrufen): Die Verfügung über die Sicht wird widerrufen.
3) DESTROY (Zerstören): Hiermit wird die Erlaubnis zum Zerstören der Sicht erteilt.
4) INSERT (Einfügen): Es wird zugestanden, Tupeln in die virtuelle Relation (Sicht) einzufügen.
5) DELETE (Löschen): Es dürfen Tupeln gelöscht werden.
6) UPDATE (Modifizieren): Attribute dürfen verändert werden.

Eine Sicht und Verfügungsrechte machen eine Sicherheitsbedingung aus. Dem Benutzer mit der Nr. X sollen die folgenden Rechte zugestanden werden:

```
GRANT VERKAUFS_GUT TO BENUTZER.BNR = 'X'
        (GRANT='NO', REVOKE = 'NO', DESTROY = 'NO'
        INSERT='NO', DELETE = 'NO', PREIS.UPDATE='YES')
```

Wir wollen die folgenden Merkmale für Sichten und Sicherheitsbedingungen herausstellen:

1. Verschiedene Sichten können hierarchisch wie "Generationen von Geschlechtern" aufgebaut werden. Wir unterscheiden "Vater-Sichten" von "Sohn-Sichten". An der Wurzel des Baumes steht der "Ur-Vater", die Basisrelation, die dem Eigentümer gehört. Alle Änderungen in einer "Vater-Sicht" werden in den diversen 'Sohn-Sichten' berücksichtigt. Es wurde bereits der Grundsatz aufgestellt, Änderungen im allgemeinen nur beim "Ur-Vater" vorzunehmen.
2. Die Verfügungen oder Berechtigungen, die einer "Sohn-Sicht" zustehen, müssen immer im Umfang kleiner oder gleich sein dem Umfang, den die "Vater-Sicht" hat. Die "Sohn-Sicht" muß aus der "Vater-Sicht" produziert werden können. (Nemo plus juris transferre potest, quam ipse habet) .
3. Beim Widerrufen einer Sicht werden die zugehörigen "Sohn-Sichten" zerstört.

Aus der Sicht VERKAUFS_GUT soll in einem weiteren Beispiel für den Benutzer Y eine Sicht entwickelt werden, damit er nur die Felder NR und BEZ lesen kann.
Wir schreiben in der Sprache SEQUEL:

```
DEFINE LISTE FÜR Y1 TABLE AS:
       SELECT NR, BEZ
       FROM VERKAUFS_GUT
```

Es folgt dann:

```
GRANT LISTE FÜR Y 1 TO BENUTZER.BNR = 'Y'
      (GRANT = 'NO', REVOKE = 'NO', DESTROY = 'NO'
      INSERT = 'NO', DELETE 'NO', UPDATE = 'NO')
```

3.2 Prozedural Modelle

Bevor wir zu einer kurzen Darstellung von prozeduralen Modellen übergehen, wie sie im DBTG-Report (6) und bei Hoffman (16) ausführlicher zu finden sind, verweisen wir hier auf die Sicherheitsmerkmale des Systems IMS (siehe (26)). Alle Zugriffe zu einer IMS-Datenbank gehen über einen zugeordneten PCB (Program Communication Block), der ein Subschema beschreibt. Damit wird von der Architektur her eine besondere Sicherheitsstufe vorgesehen. Es kann von einem Programm nur zu Daten zugegriffen werden, die durch ein PCB sensitiv gemacht wurden. Das Programm darf zweitens nur solche Operationen ausführen, die im Felde PROC-OPTIONS des PCB definiert wurden. Die kleinste Sicherungseinheit ist ein Segment. Eine Berechtigungsmatrix kann mit Hilfe des IMS über PROC-OPTIONS implementiert werden. Weitere Sicherungsmöglichkeiten bietet das IMS an, wenn der Datenkommunikationsteil installiert wird. Es kann dann z.B. spezifiziert werden, daß Programme nur bei Angabe von Kennworten aufgerufen werden dürfen und daß auch ein Kennwort erforderlich ist, um an Terminalen gewisse Kommandos benutzen zu dürfen.

Für Datenbanksysteme sind das System DBTG (6) und das von Hoffman entwickelte "Formulary Model"(16) zwei wichtige Repräsentanten für Sicherheitsmodelle, in denen die Sicherheitsbedingungen von einer Zentralstelle direkt in Sicherheitsprozeduren (von Hoffman "Formularies" genannt) umgesetzt werden müssen. Dabei steht dem Programmierer eine Trägersprache, etwa PL/1 oder COBOL zur Verfügung. Wir wollen uns in unserer Darstellung auf die wichtigsten Merkmale im System DBTG beschränken.

In der Sprache des DBTG ist die kleinste, nicht weiter auflösbare Dateneinheit ein "data-item". Ein Name und eine Ausprägung machen ein "data-item" aus. Mehrere "data-items" mit einem gemeinsamen Namen sind ein "data-aggregate". Mehrere "data-items" oder "aggregates" bilden einen "data-record", der wie alle Einheiten bezeichnet sein muß. Die wesentliche hierarchische Struktur im Datenmodell des DBTG ist der "set". In einem set gibt es solche Sätze, die "owner" (Vatersatz) und solche, die "member" (Sohnsatz) heißen. Eine Ausprägung eines "set" (set occurrence) besteht aus genau einem "owner record" mit keinem, einem oder mehreren"member records". Ein "member record" kann ohne einen "owner record" nicht existieren (Integritätsbedingung). In einem "set" ist ein "record" Typ entweder "owner" oder "member" (aber nicht beides). Ein "member record" kann "member record" in mehreren "sets" sein. Damit sind dann Netzwerkstrukturen darstellbar. Ein "set" ist streng zu unterscheiden vom mathematischen Begriff "set" (Menge). Eine weitere Organisationseinheit ist eine "area". Der gesamte Speicherbereich einer DBTG-Datenbank wird in eine Anzahl von bezeichneten "areas" zerlegt. Ein "schema" enthält die gesamte formalisierte Beschreibung einer Datenbank. Ein "sub-schema" ist grob gesprochen eine vom Benutzer ausgewählte Untermenge eines "schema". Ein Programm kann nur zu solchen Daten zugreifen, die in einem "sub-schema" definiert sind. Wie im IMS, in dem das "sub-schema" durch einen PCB festgelegt wird, ist auch im DBTG durch das "sub-schema" eine gewisse Sicherheit in einer ersten Stufe gewährleistet. Die zweite Stufe wird im folgenden beschrieben. Das "sub-schema" kann als ein sehr starres und eingeengtes

Sicht -Konzept aufgefaßt werden.
Das System DBTG unterstützt Sicherheitsprozeduren im Hinblick auf alle angeführten Organisationseinheiten vom "data-item" bis zum "schema". Um nur das Wesentliche hier darzustellen, werden wir uns auf das "record-Niveau" beschränken.

Vom DBTG werden zwei Klauseln bereitgestellt: Zu einem PRIVACY LOCK im "schema" und zum anderen ein PRIVACY KEY im Programm des Benutzers. Mit Hilfe der Datenbeschreibungssprache (DDL) für das "schema" kann ein "Schloß" (PRIVACY LOCK) vor die Daten "gehängt" werden, das mit Hilfe eines "Schlüssels" (PRIVACY KEY), formuliert in der Datenmanipulationssprache (DML), geöffnet werden kann. Im einfachsten Fall ist der Schlüssel ein Kennwort, in komplizierteren Fällen wird eine Prozedur aufgerufen. Wir stellen zunächst den Fall dar, daß der Schlüssel als Kennwort aufzufassen ist. In der Sprache COBOL als Trägersprache soll im folgenden das Programm des Benutzers aufgefaßt sein. Die Sicherheitsbedingung möge lauten: Nur wer über das Kennwort 'KAISERBALL' verfügt, darf einen beliebigen Satz mit dem Namen PERSONAL löschen:

```
Schema :  RECORD NAME IS PERSONAL
                    -
          PRIVACY LOCK FOR DELETE IS 'KAISERBALL'
                    -
                    -
Programm: IDENTIFICATION DIVISION
                    -
                    -
          PRIVACY KEY FOR DELETE OF PERSONAL RECORD IS 'KAISERBALL'
                    -
                    -
          PROCEDURE DIVISION
                    -
                    -
          DELETE PERSONAL
                    -
                    -
```

Das DBTG sorgt dafür, daß die Zeichenkette 'KAISERBALL' in der Klausel PRIVACY LOCK mit der Zeichenkette 'KAISERBALL' in der Klausel PRIVACY KEY verglichen wird. Bei Gleichheit der Zeichenketten wir die Operation DELETE PERSONAL im Hinblick auf einen beliebigen Satz PERSONAL erlaubt. Bei Ungleichheit der Zeichenkette wird die Operation unterdrückt und ein Fehlerstatus-Anzeiger gesetzt.

Wir kommen nun zu dem komplizierteren Fall, der dann vorliegt, wenn die Ausführung einer Operation nicht von einem Kennwort sondern von Bedingungen abhängt. Es soll von dem folgenden Beispiel ausgegangen werden: Ein Personalleiter darf Sätze mit dem Namen PERSONAL dann löschen, wenn 1. der Inhalt des Feldes Gehalt kleiner als 10.000 ist oder wenn 2. der Inhalt des Feldes Abteilungs-Nummer gleich 15 ist.

Die erste Bedingung sei in der Prozedur mit dem Namen GAMMA und die zweite in der Prozedur mit dem Namen DELTA realisiert. In den folgenden Anweisungen wird angenommen, daß der Personalleiter nur aufgrund der 1. Bedingung einen Zugriff wünscht.

```
Schema:  RECORD NAME IS PERSONAL
           -
         PRIVACY LOCK FOR DELETE IS PROCEDURE GAMMA OR PROCEDURE DELTA
           -
Programm:IDENTIFICATION DIVISION
           -
         PRIVACY KEY FOR DELETE OF PERSONAL RECORD IS PROCEDURE  GAMMA
           -
           -
         PROCEDURE DIVISION
           -
           -
         DELETE PERSONAL
```

Mehrere PRIVACY LOCKS können durch ein OR zusammen in einer Anweisung definiert werden. In einer Prozedur wird die Zugriffsberechtigung geprüft. Die Prozedur übergibt den Parameter 'Ja' oder 'Nein' dem DBTG. Die Prozeduren selber werden im DBTG nicht weiter spezifiziert. Hoffman (16) jedoch gibt die Struktur einiger Sicherheitsprozeduren an. Man kann davon ausgehen, daß für jede Sicht mit den dazugehörigen Aktionen im Sinne des vorherigen Abschnitts eine Prozedur zur Verfügung gestellt werden muß. Bei einem komplizierten Sicherheitssystem mit vielen verwickelten Sicherheitsbedingungen wird der Installation eine beachtliche Arbeit aufgebürdet, wenn die prozedurale Lösung gewählt wird.

Literaturverzeichnis

1) Bayer, R. und Metzger, J. U.: On the Encipherment of Search Trees and Random Process Files, Institut für Informatik, TU München, März 1975.

2) Boyce, R. F. und Chamberlin, D. D.: Using a structured English query language as a data definition facility, IBM Research Report, Rj 1318, San José, Dec. 10, 1973.

3) Boyce, R. F. u. a.: Specifying Queries as a Relational Expression: SQUARE, in: Proc. ACM SIGPLANSIGIR Interface Meetings Gaitherburg, Maryland, Nov. 4-6, 1973.

4) Chamberlin, D. D. u. a.: A Structured English Query Language, in: Proc. ACM SIGFIDET Workshop on Data Description Access and Control, Ann Arbor, Mich., May 1-3, 1974.

5) Chamberlin, D. D., Gray, J. M und Traiger, I. L.: Views, Authorization and Locking in a Relational Data Base System, IBM Research Report, Rj 1486, Sam José, Dec. 19, 1974.

6) CODASYL DATA BASE TASK GROUP (DBTG) REPORT, April 1971, erhältlich bei IFIP Administrative Data Processing Group, 40 Paulus Potterstraat, Amsterdam.

7) Codd, E. F.: A data base sublanguage founded on the relational calculas, in: 1971 ACM SIGFIDET Workshop on Data Description, Access and Control, San Diego, Nov. 11, 1971, S. 35-68.

8) Conway, R. W., Maxwell, W. L. and Morgan, H. L.: On the Implementation of Security Measures in Information Systems, in: Com. ACM, Vol. 15 (1972), No. 4, S. 211-220.

9) Date, C. J.: An Introduction to Data Base System, Addison Wesley, Reading (Mass.), 1975.

10) Evans, A. und Kantrowitz, W.: A User Authentication Scheme not requiring Secrecy in the Computer, in: Com. ACM, Vol. 17 (1974), No. 8, S. 437-442.

11) Feistel, H., Notz, W. A. und Smith, J. L.: Cryptographic techniques for machine to machine data communication, IBM Research Report, RC 3663, Yorktown Heights, Dec. 27, 1971.

12) Feistel, H.: Cryptographic coding for data-bank privacy, IBM Research Report, RC 2827, Yorktown Heights, 1970.

13) Feistel, H.: Chiffriermethoden und Datenschutz, in: IBM Nachrichten, Teil 1, 24. Jg. (1974), Heft 219, S. 21-26. Teil 2, 24. Jg. (1974), Heft 220, S. 99-102. Übersetzung aus dem Englischen: Feistel, H., Cryptography and computer privacy, in: Scientific American, Vol. 228 (1973), No. 5, S. 15-23.

14) Friedmann, T. D.: The authorization problem in shared files, in: IBM Systems Journal, Vol. 9 (1970), No. 4, S. 258-280.

15) Hentschel, B., Gliss, H., Bayer, R. und Dierstein, B.: Datenschutz-fibel, Verlag J. P. Bachem, Köln 1974.

16) Hoffman, L. J.: Computer and Privacy, A Survey, in: Computing Surveys, Vol. 1 (1969), No. 2, S. 85-103.

17) IBM-Broschüre: The Consideration of Physical Security in a Computer Environment, Oktober 1972, Fr. Nr. 6520-2700-0.

18) Kahn, D.: The Codebrakers, McMillan, New York, 1967.

19) Martin, J.: Security, Accuracy and Privacy, Prentice Hall, Englewood Cliffs, 1973.

20) Petersen, H. E. und Turn, R.: System Implication of Information Privacy, in: AFIPS Conf. Proc., Vol. 30 (1967), SJCC, Thompson Book, New York, S. 291-300.

21) Purdy, G. B.: A High Security Log-in Procedure, in: Com. ACM, Vol. 17 (1974), No. 8, S. 442-445.

22) Stonebraker, M. und Wong, E.: Access Control in a Relational Data Base Management System by Query Modification. University of California (Berkeley) Research Report ERL-M438, 14 May, 1974.

23) Tuckerman, B.: A Study of the Vigenère-Vernam Single and Multiple Loop Enciphering Systems, IBM Research Report, RC 2879, Yorktown Heights, May 14, 1970.

24) Turn, R.: Privacy Transformation for Databank Systems, Rand Corporation, Forschungsbericht für die National Science Foundation, AD-761563, March 1973, veröffentlicht auch in: AFIPS Conf. Proc. Vol 42 (1973), S. 589-601.

25) Turn, R.: Privacy and Security in Personal Information Databank Systems, (Prepared for the National Science Foundation), Rand Corporation, R-1044-NSF, March 1974.

26) Wedekind, H. und Härder, Th.: Datenbanksysteme II, Bibliographisches Institut, Mannheim, 1975. (noch unveröffentlicht)

27) Wilkes, M. V.: Time-Sharing Betriebe bei digitalen Rechenanlagen (Übersetzung aus dem Englischen), Carl-Hanser Verlag, München, 1970.

28) Scherf, J.A.: Computer and Data Security, A Comprehensive Annotated Bibliography, MIT Project MAC, January 1974

On the Integrity of Data Bases and Resource Locking

Rudolf Bayer, Technische Universität München

Abstract

The problem of providing operational integrity of data bases as opposed to operating systems is discussed. Techniques of resource locking, mainly individual object locking and predicate locking, are surveyed, improved, and unified. An efficient on-line transitive closure algorithm for deadlock discovery is presented and analyzed. Several strategies for preventing indefinite delay of transactions are proposed. Phantoms and the need for predicate locking are surveyed and reconsidered. Several strategies for handling phantoms are proposed: one without predicate locking and two in which predicate locking is needed for writing transactions only, and in which individual object locking sufficies for pure readers.

I. INTRODUCTION

Providing data base integrity means to guarantee the correctness of the data (more precisely their accuracy, consistency, and timeliness) through

1) the proper operation of the hardware,
2) the proper operation of the software, as well as
3) the proper use of the system.

This paper only covers part of the software aspect of integrity. The problem of guarding data bases against hardware failures has been covered extensively by M.V. Wilkes [Wil 72]. Proper use of the system is mainly concerned with quality control in data acquisition and with prevention of accidental or mieschievous misuse, i.e. with the security of computer systems.

As opposed to many other computing environments, data bases give rise to especially high integrity requirements for at least the following reasons:

1) Longevity: Even rare errors will in the long run lead to a certain contamination and degradation of the quality of a data base. Completely purging erroneous data and all their consequences from a data base is difficult.
2) Limited repeatability: Even if data or processing errors are discovered, it may be impossible or useless to rectify the situation due to time constraints, unavailability of the correct source data, unavailability of a correct system state preceding the fault.
3) The need for immediate and permanent availability: This prevents a practice often used elsewhere, namely running a program and then checking by careful inspection and analysis whether the result is or at least "looks" right, correcting and rerunning the program otherwise.
4) Multiaccess: Data bases are manipulated by many users with probably quite different quality standards. It is infeasible to completely entrust the quality control to these users and difficult to track the source and the proliferation of errors.

II. SEMANTIC AND OPERATIONAL INTEGRITY

We wish to distinguish between semantic and operational integrity of data bases:

By _semantic integrity_ we mean the compliance of the data base contents with constraints derived from our knowledge about the meaning of the data. Semantic integrity might be enforced by allowing on certain data only a limited set of precisely specified meaningful operations, by adopting a set of programming and interaction conventions, by dynamically checking the results of updates, or by proving for each program manipulating the data base, that the semantic integrity constraints are satisfied.

Little is known about how to describe, to enforce, and to implement such semantic integrity constraints. Still we believe, that semantic integrity is of a much more basic nature than operational integrity, and that a better understanding of semantic integrity would greatly help the solution of other integrity problems as well. An approach has been described in [Bay 74] to obtain semantic integrity via the definition of "aggregates" which limit the processing of data to the use of a set of carefully designed operations directly associated with the data.

Operational Integrity: For the purpose of this discussion let a "transaction" [EGLT 74] be the unit of processing for scheduling purposes and for external data base manipulation. A transaction is a sequence of more primitive "actions". Most work to date concerned with integrity has been limited to those integrity problems arising from the activity of the operating system:

1) the effort to schedule transactions to be processed in parallel as far as possible [EGLT 74], [Eve 74], [KiC 73], [CBT 74],
2) the need to acquire resources, in particular sets of data objects or individual data objects (also called "records" in [CBT 74] and "entities" in [EGLT 74], for exclusive or shared use by a transaction and to lock those resources accordingly,
3) the induced problems of deadlock among locking transactions, of deadlock discovery, of deadlock prevention, and of preemption of resources from transactions to resolve deadlocks.

III. OPERATING SYSTEMS AND OPERATIONAL INTEGRITY

As opposed to semantic integrity there is at least a brute force, straightforward solution for operational integrity, namely to avoid parallelism between transactions completely and to sequence in time the execution of transactions. This is unsatisfactory for many reasons, and better solutions have been developed for use in operating systems. We will survey these solutions briefly and indicate, why they are not satisfactory for data base applications. As usual in this field we use "process" as the analogon for "transaction". The list of techniques is adopted from G.C. Everest [Eve 74]:

Presequence Processes: Processes potentially competing for resources must be presequenced and must execute one after the other. For data base transactions it is often not known a priori, which data resources will be needed. This means that any two transactions will be potentially competing and must be sequenced. As a consequence, no parallelism is possible and we have the unsatisfactory brute force method mentioned before. Still presequencing transactions, e.g. through time-stamping, may be useful for other purposes, like preventing indefinite delay of transactions by introducing an aging mechanism to increase the priorities of transactions.

Preempt Processes: This technique relies on discovering deadlocks after they have occurred. It then terminates (or backs up to an earlier state) one of the processes involved in the deadlock, the resources locked by that process are freed. As we shall see, this technique plays an important role in data base locking, too, but there its application is much more difficult due to the large number of transactions and resources involved. This makes deadlock discovery and preemption quite complicated and expensive.

Preorder all System Resources: The processes are then required to claim their resources according to such a total order. It has been shown, that more general than linear orders, e.g. hierarchical orders, are sufficient to support a deadlock-free locking strategy [Ram 74]. In data bases the resources are data objects, which often do not have such an natural order. Furthermore a process might not be able to claim resources according to such an order, since his needed resources might be data dependent [EGLT 74], [CBT 74].

Preclaim needed Resources: Before starting to execute, a process has to claim all the resources it will ever need. Typically they are specified on the control cards preceding a job or job-step, and the process is not started until the operating system has granted to it all the requested resources. This is probably the most common technique for assigning non-sharable resources.

In a data base environment this technique requires considerable modifications to become feasible. Claiming resources may itself be a complicated and lengthy task requiring searching through large areas of a data base. These searches should run concurrently if possible.

Deadlock Prevention Algorithms: They often rely on too special properties of resources - like Habermann's banker's algorithm [Hab 69] - or on too special models of computation - like Schroff's algorithm [Sch 74]- to be generally applicable here.

IV. THE CHAMBERLIN, BOYCE, TRAIGER METHOD

In [CBT 74] a technique is proposed to provide operational integrity for data bases. The technique can be considered as a modification and combination of several methods described in section III. Integrity of the data base must be guaranteed at the beginning and again at the end of a transaction, it may be - and generally must be - violated by the single actions. Due to the potential interference of two or more transactions executing in parallel, transactions must lock certain parts of the data base for exclusive or shared use. The scheme proposed in [CBT 74] therefore requires each transaction to lock all its resources (parts of a data base, e.g. individual records or fields of records) during a so-called "seize phase" before starting the "execution phase". During the seize phase the data base must not be modified by the seizing transaction and therefore

1) preemption of locked resources from a transaction still in its seize phase is feasible, and
2) backing a transaction in its seize phase up to wait for the preempted resource is rather easy.

Once a transaction has started its execution phase, it is not allowed to claim more resources, thus no backup will be necessary. At the end of an execution phase a transaction must free all its resources before starting a new seize phase.

The seize phase may be a rather complicated task, thus seize phases of transactions should be run in parallel. This raises the deadlock problem again as usual: Let t_1, t_2 be two transactions. t_2 trying to seize resource r_1 already locked by t_1 must wait until r_1 is freed by t_1. But since resources are not locked in any particular order, t_1 may wish to lock first r_1, then r_2. If t_1 successfully seizes r_1 and t_2 successfully seizes r_2, then a deadlock has occurred. Such deadlocks must be discovered and a resource must be preempted from a transaction involved in the deadlock, say r_2 from t_2, causing t_2 to wait for t_1 on r_2.

In [CBT 74] an aging mechanism is attached to transactions to avoid deadlock due to indefinite delay of transactions. It is then shown in [CBT 74] that the scheme described is deadlock-free in the sense, that each transaction will eventually be processed. This requires, of course, the proper algorithms for discovery of deadlocks between transactions in their seize phases, for preemption or resources, and for backing up transactions to certain points within their seize phases.

It is now clear, that the scheme proposed in [CBT 74] is a shrewd modification and combination of the following:

1) Try to preclaim needed resources.
2) If 1) would lead to deadlock, preempt resources.
3) Superimpose a presequencing scheme for transactions - e.g. through timestamping - to enforce an aging mechanism and to avoid deadlock due to indefinite delay of transactions.

V. SOME MODIFICATIONS AND AN ON-LINE TRANSITIVE CLOSURE ALGORITHM

The deadlock discovery algorithm mentioned as useful in [CBT 74] is not really applicable, since it requires that a transaction t_1 may wait for at most one other transaction to release resources. In the CBT-scheme, however, t_1 may be waiting for resources to be released by arbitrarily many transactions t_{w_1}, t_{w_2}, ... t_{w_k} as the result of arbitrarily many preemptions of resources from t_1:

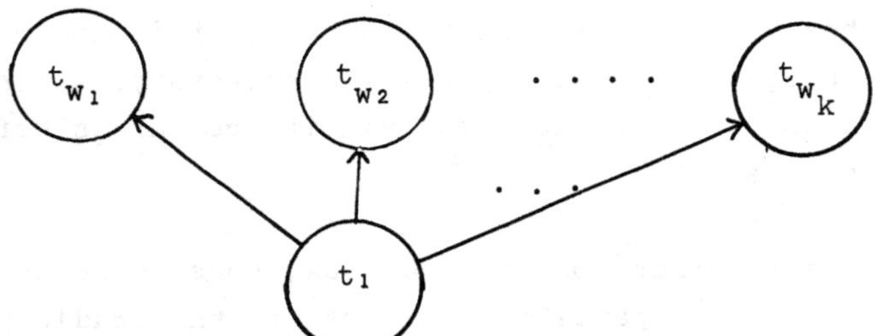

Fig. 1: Transaction t_1 waiting for other transactions.

The resource state of a transaction t_i is determined by the set

$$A_i = \{r_{i_1}, \ldots, r_{i_{q_i}}\}$$

of resources which it has so far acquired, and the set of request pairs

$$B_i = \{(r_{i_1}', t_{i_1}), \ldots, (r_{i_{p_i}}', t_{i_{p_i}})\}$$

where (r_{i_j}', t_{i_j}) indicates that resource r_{i_j}' is desired from transaction t_{i_j}. Any transaction t_i for which B_i is non-empty is in a wait state.

We may then define the wait relation $w \subseteq T \times T$ where T is the set of transactions, such that

$$(t_i, t_j) \in w \text{ iff } \exists\, r : (r, t_j) \in B_i .$$

We say that t_i is <u>waiting for</u> t_j (to release r). t_i may be waiting for several transactions as noted above, and for several resources from the same transaction.

The wait graph G_w is the directed graph

$$G_w = (T, w).$$

Deadlock discovery amounts to finding cycles in G_w or, equivalently, to finding pairs (t, t) in the transitive (but not reflexive) closure w^+ of w. Thus deadlock exists iff $\exists t \in T : (t,t) \in w^+$.

Maintaining w is trivial, since something like the B_i's will have to be maintained in any case. Calculating w^+ from w is, on the other hand, quite expensive, the best known algorithms requiring $O(n^3)$ [War 62] or $O(n \cdot m)$ [Bay 74] steps, where n is the number of nodes in G_w and m the number of arcs.

It would be sufficient, however, to have a good "on-line" transitive closure algorithm since w^+ need only be partly modified as arcs are added to and deleted from w.

More precisely, "on-line" transitive closure algorithm means an algorithm solving the following problem:

$$\begin{array}{lll} & \text{Given } w,\ w^+, & \text{calculate} \\ & \quad w',\ w'^+, & \text{where} \\ w' & = w \cup \{(t_i, t_j)\} & \text{or} \\ w' & = w \setminus \{(t_i, t_j)\}. & \end{array}$$

Although it is quite simple to add an arbitrary arc and calculate w'^+ from w^+, it seems in the general case notoriously difficult to delete an arbitrary arc and calculate w'^+ from w^+. No better alternative seems to be known than calculating w'^+ from scratch, i.e. starting with w' and ignoring the fact that we already have w^+.

For our purpose, we need a highly simplified version of the on-line algorithm for the transitive closure only. By closer inspection one observes, that we need to delete sinks of G_w and the arcs leading into sinks of G_w only. This is the decisive property which makes the difficult general problem tractable in our special case. To get w'^+ from w^+ now simply amounts to deleting or zeroeing out a column from the Boolean matrix describing w^+.

We will now develop such an on-line transitive closure algorithm in more detail. We assume that transactions will wait in queue q(r) for an already locked resource r. The first transaction on a queue has successfully locked (or seized) the resource, it may be in its seize or execution phase. All other transactions on the queue are waiting (or blocked). We indicate this as in Fig. 2.

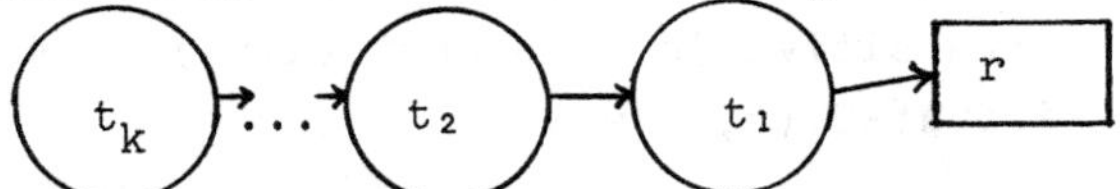

Fig. 2: Transactions waiting for resource r.

t_1 has locked r,

t_{i+1} is waiting for t_i to release (or free) r; i=1,2,...,k-1,

when t_i eventually releases r (and no preemptions have occurred in the meantime), then t_{i+1} will seize r.

Let us first consider the state transition diagram of a transaction (Fig. 3) and the operations relevant to that diagram, which a transaction may perform:

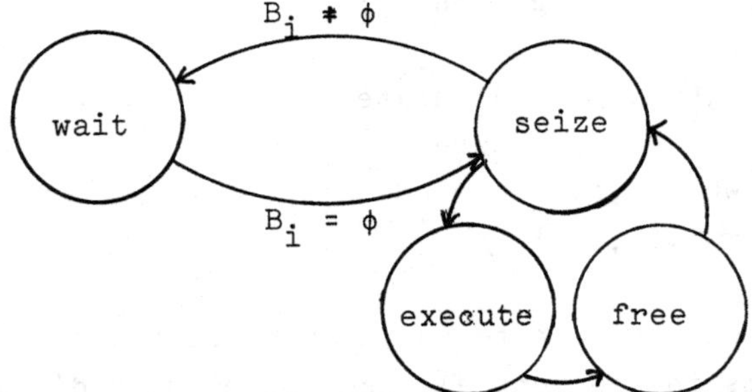

Fig. 3: The state transition diagram of a transaction.

A transaction t_i can perform the following operations involving resource r and another transaction t_k:

<u>Seize r:</u> $A_i := A_i \cup \{r\}$; update $q(r)$;

<u>$\forall r \in A_i$: Free r:</u> $A_i := \phi$;

$\forall r \in A_i$ <u>do</u> <u>if</u> t_k is next in queue for r
<u>then</u> <u>begin</u> (r,t_i) must be in B_k;
$B_k := B_k \setminus \{(r,t_i)\}$;
$A_k := A_k \cup \{r\}$;
update $q(r)$;
<u>if</u> $B_k = \phi$ <u>then</u> make t_k
continue to seize
<u>end</u>;
update w and w^+;

<u>Seize unsuccessfully:</u> t_i is still in the seize state, let t_k be last in queue for r:

<u>Case 1:</u> no deadlock arises, if t_i is queued behind t_k in $q(r)$:
$B_i := \{(r,t_k)\}$;
put t_i into wait state;
update w and w^+;

<u>Case 2:</u> A deadlock would arise, if t_i were queued as in Case 1. This deadlock is discovered by tentatively, but not definitely queueing t_i as in Case 1, updating w^+ and checking, whether w^+ contains cycles. In this case t_i might have to preempt r from t_k. t_k must be in wait state, since we have a cycle:
In this situation t_i should move forward in $q(r)$ until it can be inserted and no deadlock arises; update $q(r)$ accordingly.
Let t_ℓ be the first transaction in $q(r)$ (starting from t_k) such that inserting t_i between t_ℓ and $t_{\ell-1}$ causes no deadlock, then we have Case 2a. If there is no such t_ℓ then we have Case 2b.

<u>Note:</u> In [CBT 74] t_i is always inserted as close to the head of the queue as possible. This strategy favors the younger transactions and must rely heavily on an aging mechanism to prevent indefinite delay. The processing costs of this aging mechanism are not analyzed.

<u>Case 2a:</u> $B_\ell := \left(B_\ell \setminus \{(r,t_{\ell-1})\}\right) \cup \{(r,t_i)\}$;
$B_i := \{(r,t_{\ell-1})\}$;
update q(r);
t_i goes into wait state;
update w and w^+;

<u>Case 2b:</u> t_1 cannot be executing, otherwise t_i would queue behind t_1 according to Case 2a. Therefore t_1 is seizing or waiting. We make t_i preempt r from t_1, i.e. we queue t_i in front of t_1;
<u>if</u> $B_1 = \phi$, <u>then</u> make t_1 wait;
$B_1 := B_1 \cup \{(r,t_i)\}$;
$A_1 := A_1 \setminus \{r\}$;
$A_i := A_i \cup \{r\}$;
update w and w^+;

<u>Necessary Changes to w and w^+ and Analysis of their Complexity</u>

For the following analysis we assume that w^+ is represented in an n×n Boolean matrix K with the meaning

$$K[i,j] \equiv (t_i,t_j) \in w^+.$$

Operation	Description of Operation	Complexity of the Change to w^+
<u>Seize r:</u>	No change to w or w^+	0
<u>$\forall r \in A_i$: Free r:</u>	Since t_i frees all its resources at the end of its execution phase, we can remove all arcs (t_k,t_i) from w, and delete or zero out column i of K.	O(n)
	For the analysis of the following operations we need two auxiliary procedures first. Let t_i be in its seize state. To insert an arc (t_i,t_k) into w and to update w^+ accordingly we need the procedure INSERT1.	

Operation	Description of Operation	Complexity of the Change to w^+
	To insert (t_ℓ, t_i) we need the procedure INSERT2.	
<u>INSERT1 (t_i, t_k):</u>	<u>Comment</u> t_i is in seize state;	
	$w := w \cup \{(t_i, t_k)\}$;	constant
	$\forall t_j \atop (t_j,t_i)\in w^+$: $\forall t_\ell \atop (t_k,t_\ell)\in w^+$ $: w^+ := w^+ \cup \{(t_j, t_\ell)\}$;	$O(n^2)$ at worst, $O(m)$ average, see lager analysis
	$\forall t_\ell \atop (t_k,t_\ell)\in w^+$ $: w^+ := w^+ \cup \{(t_i, t_\ell)\}$;	$O(n)$
	$\forall t_j \atop (t_j,t_i)\in w^+$ $: w^+ := w^+ \cup \{(t_j, t_k)\}$;	$O(n)$
	$w^+ := w^+ \cup \{(t_i, t_k)\}$;	constant
<u>INSERT2 (t_ℓ, t_i):</u>	<u>Comment</u> t_i is in seize state;	
	$w := w \cup \{(t_\ell, t_i)\}$;	constant
	$\forall t_j \atop (t_j,t_\ell)\in w^+$ $: w^+ := w^+ \cup \{(t_j, t_i)\}$;	$O(n)$
	$w^+ := w^+ \cup \{(t_\ell, t_i)\}$;	constant
	<u>Note:</u> Since t_i is in the seize state, there is no t such that $(t_i, t)\in w^+$. Consequently no cycle in w^+, and therefore no deadlock can arise due to the operation INSERT2 (t_ℓ, t_i).	

<u>Seize r unsuccessfully:</u>	As before, let t_k be last in queue for r:
	for j := k step -1 until 1 do
	  begin tentatively INSERT1 (t_i, t_j);
	   if no deadlock then
	    begin ℓ := j+1;
	     exit to perform Case 2a
	    end end;
	perform Case 2b;
		for each deadlock $O(n^2)$ or $O(n+m)$ resp.

Operation	Description of Operation	Complexity of the Change to w^+
	Case 2a: make last INSERT1 operation definite;	at worst $O(n^2)$ or $O(n+m)$
	if $\ell \neq k+1$ then begin INSERT2 (t_ℓ, t_i);	$O(n)$
	if $\exists r' \neq r: (r', t_{\ell-1}) \in B_\ell$ then	search of B_ℓ
	else $w := w \setminus \{(t_\ell, t_{\ell-1})\}$ end;	
	Case 2b: INSERT2 (t_1, t_i);	$O(n)$

Analysis of INSERT1:
Adding a single arc to w, according to INSERT1, say (t_i, t_k), requires oring row k of the Boolean matrix K to all rows j with $(t_j, t_i) \in w^+$. At worst this part of INSERT1 requires $O(n^2)$ operations. If, however, there are m arcs in w^+, then each node on the average will have m/n arcs into it and m/n arcs out of it. Accordingly the average number of operations will be

$$O\Big(n \cdot (m/n)\Big) = O(m).$$

VI. FOUR STRATEGIES FOR PREVENTING INDEFINITE DELAY

With the locking and preemption schemes proposed it is still conceivable, that a transaction is delayed indefinitely from its executiton phase. To deal with this problem, we propose four increasingly effective, but also increasingly costly strategies. It seems quite reasonable to employ several strategies within one system successively in order to force transactions which have passed a certain age threshold into their execution phase and out of the system.

Strategy 1: Let t_e be the eldest transaction. Schedule all transactions t, such that $t_e w^+ t$, with highest priority. This clearly has a tendency to speed up the processing of t_e. It is easy to find those t from the t_e-row of the Boolean matrix describing w^+.

Strategy 2: Stop all transactions in seize phases from further seizing except those t for which $t_e w^+ t$.

Strategy 3: For all r such that t_e is waiting in q(r) let t_r be the transaction that has locked r. If t_r is seizing or waiting, preempt r from t_r and give r to t_e. If t_r is executing, insert t_e in q(r) directly behind t_r. No new deadlocks can arise if we assume that all these preemptions are performed together in one step. Then recalculate the new w'^+.

Strategy 4: Stop all transactions, which are not executing from seizing further. Then apply strategy 3 for t_e until t_e has reached its execution phase. Then let the other transactions proceed.

Some Oberservations on Strategies 1, 2, 3, 4: It is clear that all strategies will tend to bring t_e closer to its execution phase.

Strategy 1 can be generalized to establish a partition of the transactions into a linearly ordered set of priority classes, which can serve as the basis for a general scheduling strategy. Strategies 1 and 3 might still allow indefinite delay. It is easy to construct a plausibility argument, that strategies 2 and 4 will prevent indefinite delay of transactions.

VII. AN ALTERNATIVE APPROACH: PREEMPTION AND PARTIAL BACKUP

Although it seems feasible to maintain the basic locking and preempting mechanism proposed in [CBT 74] using the special algorithms described in the preceding sections, there is another argument supporting a more radical preemption than that proposed in the CBT-scheme:

Let us assume that r_1 is preempted from t_1 by t_2, which probably updates r_1. Depending on the value of r_1, t_1 might have locked other resources r_1', r_1'',... already. But since the value of r_1 changes, the decision of t_1 to lock r_1', r_1'', ... should be reconsidered. In other words, t_1 should be backed up within its seize phase to precisely the state it was in just before seizing r_1, it should then be waiting for t_2 on r_1, and the resources r_1', r_1'', ... locked by t_1 should be freed again.

In such a preemption scheme a transaction t_1 will generally be waiting for at most one other transaction t_2 on precisely one resource r_1. The wait relation $t_1 w t_2$ shall now mean that t_1 waits for the holder t_2 of r_1 and not for the predecessor in $q(r_1)$, since we do not need to maintain such queues. The resulting G_w is obviously a forest of oriented trees, the arcs pointing towards the roots. Only roots are processing in the execution or seize phases. All other transactions are waiting.

Since a transaction t_1 is waiting for t_2 on precisely one resource r_1, we may label that arc with r_1.

The following simple algorithms then describe the necessary operations.

Seize unsuccessfully:

Case 1, no deadlock arises: t_1 trying to lock r already locked by t_2 means that the tree with root t_1, i.e. $T(t_1)$, is appended as a subtree to t_2, the new arc being labelled with r.

Case 2, deadlock arises: Deadlock discovery is quite simple: Each seizing or executing transaction is the root node of one tree. Deadlock arises precisely when t_1 is also the root node of the tree in which t_2 is. To find this out, just follow the arcs from t_2 to the root. In this case a cycle would be generated by inserting an arc (t_1,t_2). The deadlock is resolved by preempting the resource r from t_2.

Preemption works as follows: t_2 must free r and all resources it locked after r. In the process - see the Free operation - corresponding subtrees of t_2 will be detached - allowing their roots to continue seizing - and the arc (t_2,t_3) from t_2 to its father t_3 in $T(t_1)$ will be deleted. The tree $T'(t_2)$ remaining after pruning $T(t_2)$ will be attached as a subtree of t_1 by introducing the new arc (t_2,t_1) with label r.

Free r': If t_2 frees a resource r' either due to being backed up in its seize phase or due to finishing an execution phase and there is an arc (t_4,t_2) labelled r', then this arc can be deleted, thereby t_4 becomes a root and can proceed in its seize phase. To free such arcs one must represent these trees by data structures in which it is possible to follow arcs in both directions.

VIII. PREVENTING INDEFINITE DELAY

It is possible that for individual transactions t a situation similar to a deadlock might again arise due to t being preempted and backed up in its seize phase again and again. Strategies 1 and 2 of section VI are easily adapted to work for the preemption and backup technique of section VII.

The analogon to strategy 3 of section VI is much easier to implement now: Let t_e be the eldest transaction in the system again. Assume that t_e is waiting for t on r and t is not executing. (If t is executing, nothing can be done except scheduling t with highest priority until t has finished executing.) Then t_e will preempt r from t and t will be backed up in its seize phase to a state just before seizing r. t_e becomes a root and continues seizing. A new arc (t,t_e) labelled r is introduced. The preemption process works precisely as described in section VII. The main difficulty of strategy 3 of section VI has disappeared, since we do not explicitly store w^+. Instead, cycles are discovered by just following the path from an arbitrary node of a tree to its root, a simple and fast operation. To prevent pathological cases of data bases changing faster than t_e being able to catch up in its own seize phase, we can apply an analogon to strategy 4 of section VI again. Instead, however, it suffices to prevent that transactions will enter from their seize phases into their execution phases. Let this be strategy 5. Since only finitely many transactions are in the system at any one time, and since each executing transaction will run only a finite time, t_e will eventually be able to finish both its seize and execution phase, and indefinite delay of t_e cannot occur.

IX. PHANTOMS AND PREDICATE LOCKS

In [EGLT 74] a technique is described to use so called predicate locks ("predicate locking") for locking logical, i.e. existing as well as potential subsets of a data base instead of locking individual data objects ("individual object locking"). This technique also solves the "phantom problem". To explain briefly, what phantoms are, let us assume that there is a universe $\mathcal{D}$ of data objects (called "entities" in [EGLT 74] and "records" in [CBT 74]) which are the potential data objects in the data base B. Thus $B \subseteq \mathcal{D}$. Two transactions t_1, t_2 may have successfully locked all their needed resources, and they may be executing. t_1 may add a new object $r_1 \in \mathcal{D}$ to B and t_2 may add a new object $r_2 \in \mathcal{D}$ to B, such that t_1 would have locked r_2 and t_2 would have locked r_1, if t_1 or t_2 would have seen r_2 or r_1 resp. during their seize phases. r_1 and r_2 are called "phantoms", since they might, but not necessarily will appear in B (materialize) while t_1 or t_2 are in their execution phases.

The appearance of just a single phantom, say r_1, does not cause any difficulty, since this has the same effect as running the transactions t_1, t_2

serially, namely in the order t_2 followed by t_1. In this case also t_2 would not see the object r_1 created by t_1 and therefore t_2 could not be able to lock r_1. It is the goal of predicate locking to schedule transactions in parallel as far as possible under the restriction, that the parallel schedule is equivalent to - i.e. has exactly the same total effect on the data base as - a serial schedule. One also says that such a schedule is a "consistent schedule", or that each transaction sees a "consistent view" of the data base.

To enforce consistent schedules each transaction t is required to lock (for read or write access) all data objects $E(t) \subseteq \mathcal{D}$ - irrespective of whether they are in B or are just phantoms - which might in any way influence or be influenced by the effect of t on B. E(t) shall be locked by specifying a predicate P defined on $\mathcal{D}$ (or on a part of $\mathcal{D}$, e.g. on a relation [Cod 70]) such that $E(t) \subseteq S(P)$ where S(P) is the subset of elements of $\mathcal{D}$ satisfying P.

Two transactions t_1, t_2 are then said to be in conflict, if for their predicates P_1, P_2 it is true that $\exists r \in S(P_1) \cap S(P_2)$ and t_1 or t_2 performs a write action on r. Thus conflict can arise even if r is a phantom. In this case t_1, t_2 cannot run in parallel, but must be run serially. The order in which they are run is irrelevant for consistency. This order might be important for other reasons which are not of interest here.

The main difficulties in using such a locking and scheduling method seem to be the following:

1) Find a suitable predicate P_t for t. Ideally $E(t) = S(P_t)$ should hold, but then P_t might be too complicated. If P_t is chosen in a very simple way, then $S(P_t)$ might be intolerably large, increasing the danger of phantoms, which are really artificial phantoms.

2) The problem "$S(P_1) \cap S(P_2) \neq \phi$" may be very hard. In general this problem is even undecidable. Thus for practical applications and a given it is necessary to find a suitable class of locking predicates, for which the problem "$S(P_1) \cap S(P_2) \neq \phi$" is not only decidable, but for which a very efficient decision procedure is known. For more details and a candidate class for suitable locking predicates see [EGLT 74].

3) Phantoms might turn out to be a very serious but mostly artificial obstacle to parallel processing in the following sense: phantoms in

$S(P_1) \cap S(P_2)$ prohibit t_1 and t_2 from being run in parallel. But if these phantoms do not materialize, and if furthermore $S(P_1) \cap S(P_2) \cap B = \phi$, then, of course, t_1 and t_2 could have been run in parallel. How much of an artificial obstacle phantoms are to parallel processing seems to be unknown and can probably be answered only for concrete instances of data bases.

X. A UNIFICATION OF INDIVIDUAL OBJECT LOCKING AND PREDICATE LOCKING

Let us start with the crucial observation for this section:

"Transactions,which are pure readers, do not need to lock phantoms".

A transaction is a "pure reader", if it is composed of read actions only. Obviously for many data base applications the pure readers are a very important class of transactions.

To understand our observation, consider two pure readers t_1, t_2 first. Since there are no write actions at all, there is no possibility for phantoms to materialize, thus they need not be locked. Phantom locking is only necessary to control the interaction with a transaction, say t_3, which also performs write operations. We call t_3 a "writer". Consider the interaction between t_1 and t_3. Let us assume that there is a phantom $r \in S(P_1) \cap S(P_3)$ such that t_3 might perform a write on r. Then t_1 and t_3 could not run concurrently, if t_1 would use predicate locking. If however, t_1 uses individual object locking and successfully terminates its seize phase, then t_1 can run in parallel with t_3 provided that

$$\widehat{S(P_1)} \cap S(P_3) = \phi$$

where $\widehat{S(P_1)} = S(P_1) \cap B$, i.e. the set of real data objects (without phantoms) in B which t_1 needs to lock in order to see a consistent view of B. But now $\widehat{S(P_1)}$ can be locked by t_1 using conventional "individual object locking" as e.g. described in [CBT 74] instead of predicate locking. If t_3 should materialize phantoms, then running t_1 and t_3 in parallel still is consistent and has the same effect as the serial schedule t_1 followed by t_3.

The following observation should also be clear now: To control the interaction between the writer t_3 and the pure reader t_1 if suffices, that t_3 use individual object locking according to [CBT 74]. t_3 need not lock its phantoms, since t_1 is not interested in phantoms anyway. We can conclude that the problem of phantoms - and therefore predicate locking - arises only between writers.

The preceding observations suggest several alternative approaches for handling the phantom problem:

Strategy 1 - Serialize Writers:

Since, as we just observed, phantoms cause difficulties only between writers, the simplest solution is, not to schedule any writers to run concurrently. Concurrency is possible between arbitrarily many pure readers and at most one writer. Consistency is guaranteed by individual object locking and by handling deadlocks and preemptions as described in the earlier part of this paper. The problem of phantoms does not arise.

As mentioned before, in many applications most transactions are pure readers. Serializing writers in those cases should notcause a significant loss of concurrency and has the advantage that predicate locking with its associated difficulties is not needed.

Strategy 2 - Predicate Locks between Writers:

Use predicate locks as described in [EGLT 74] only to determine whether two writers t_3, t_4 can run in parallel. After a writer is allowed to proceed on account of his predicate locks, he then starts individual object locking to compete for further processing with other transactions, which are pure readers, exactly as in strategy 1. For more details on the individual object locking phase, in particular the types of locks, see strategy 3.

Using predicate locking and individual object locking at this point allows a more general notion of conflict than that used in [EGLT 74]. Let U_1 or R_1 be the set of objects including phantoms which are updated or only read respectively by a transaction t_1. Define U_2 and R_2 for t_2 analogously. Obviously $U_1 \cap R_1 = \phi$ and $U_2 \cap R_2 = \phi$.

Then define

$$\begin{aligned} B_1 &:= U_1 \cap U_2 \\ B_2 &:= U_1 \cap R_2 \\ B_3 &:= R_1 \cap U_2 \\ B_4 &:= R_1 \cap R_2 \end{aligned} \qquad (X.1)$$

Diagrammatically this can be shown as in Fig. 4.

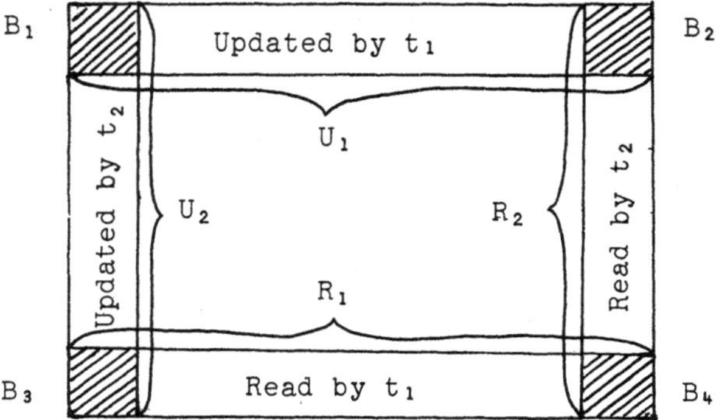

Fig. 4: Possible intersections of update and read-only sets.

For t_1 and t_2 to proceed in parallel with individual object locking the following conditions must hold:

$$\begin{aligned} B_1 &= \phi \\ B_2 &= \phi \vee B_3 = \phi \end{aligned} \qquad (X.2)$$

Without individual object locking the stronger condition $B_2=\phi \wedge B_3=\phi$ is required in [EGLT 74]. To see that our weakend condition suffices let us assume without loss of generality that $B_2=\phi$ and $B_3 \neq \phi$.

B_3 is read only by t_1, but is updated by t_2. Also B_3 may contain phantoms which are materialized by t_2. Let us assume that both t_1 and t_2 are successful in their seize phases, i.e. while locking individual objects excluding phantoms, and then continue to run in parallel. We claim that this is equivalent to the serial schedule t_1 followed by t_2.

Since B_1 and B_2 are both empty, the effect of t_1 on B cannot in any way influence t_2, thus t_2 has the same effect on B if it is run after t_1 or parallel to t_1.

B_3 is not empty, but t_1 successfully locked all the resources it needed to see a consistent view of the data base. t_1 may have missed phantoms materialized by t_2 , thus the effect of t_1 will be the same as in the serial schedule t_1 t_2. Consequently running t_1 and t_2 in parallel is equivalent to the serial schedule $t_1 t_2$, and is therefore consistent.

The conditions (X.2) for t_1 and t_2 to proceed in parallel can be generalized for $t_1, t_2, \ldots, t_n$ to proceed concurrently. This is left to the reader.

Strategy 3: This strategy sacrifices some concurrency, but is much simpler to implement than strategy 2. There a writer t_i was required to perform individual object locking both in the sets U_i and R_i. It turns out that with the conflict condition of [EGLT 74] between writers, writers need perform object locking only within U_i, but they need not set any read locks.

Assume that a writer t_i first locks the sets U_i and R_i by specifying the predicates P_U^i and P_R^i. The condition for two writers t_i and t_j to run concurrently then is:

$$
\begin{aligned}
S(P_U^i) \cap S(P_U^j) &= \phi \\
S(P_U^i) \cap S(P_R^j) &= \phi \qquad \qquad (X.3) \\
S(P_R^i) \cap S(P_U^j) &= \phi
\end{aligned}
$$

After successfully locking U_i and R_i the writer then proceeds to perform individual object locking within U_i by setting "u-locks" for exclusive use of data objects to be updated. These u-locks are necessary for preventing pure readers from reading those objects while they are being updated. Since the sets $S(P_U^i)$ are pairwise disjoint, there is never any possibility for conflict between u-locks of different writers.

We observe that writers need not set any individual read-locks, called "r-locks", since $S(P_R^i) \cap S(P_U^j) = \phi$, and conflict of u-locks of one writer and r-locks of another would not be possible anyway. Furthermore, several r-locks of readers and writers on the same data object would be allowed, since data objects are shareable as long as they are only read.

The only potential conflict still remaining is between read-access of pure readers and update-access of a writer to the same data object s, which is not a phantom. To control this we require pure readers to set r-locks on individual data objects s to be read. This must happen during a seize phase. Several r-locks can be on s, but not both r-locks of pure readers and a u-lock of a writer. Thus if a reader (writer) sets an r-lock (u-lock) first then a writer (reader) trying to set a u-lock (r-lock) on the same data object must wait for the reader (writer) to release s. This leads to the usual wait situations with the possibility for deadlock and the need for preemption and backup as described in the first part of this paper.

If a deadlock is discovered then a reader or a writer is backed up within its seize phase for setting r-locks or u-locks resp. as described before. For simplicity we can assume that locking with the predicates P_U and P_R is one indivisible operation, thus deadlock between writers is not possible during this phase of predicate locking.

To summarize, a writer t_i proceeds as follows:

1) Lock predicates P_U^i and P_R^i. If conditions (X.3) are satisfied for all other writers t_j which have successfully locked their predicates P_U^j and P_R^j then proceed with step 2), otherwise wait, until P_U^i and P_R^i can be successfully locked, then proceed with step 2).

2) Start a seize phase setting u-locks on individual data objects to be updated within $S(P_U^i)$. In case of conflict with r-locks wait or be backed up within this seize phase.

3) A pure reader performs a seize phase setting r-locks on data objects to be read. In case of conflict with u-locks the reader must wait or be backed up within this seize phase.

Summarizing the main advantages of strategy 3 we observe:

- o Only writers use predicate locking to handle phantoms.
- o Concurrency between writers is possible.
- o Writers need an individual object locking phase for setting u-locks in their update areas only. In this phase phantoms are ignored.
- o Pure readers do not use predicate locking, they set r-locks during an individual object locking phase only and ignore phantoms completely.

Note: Since predicate locking is now needed for writers only, it might be quite feasible to replace arbitrary predicates by a fixed partitioning of the data base or by a fixed family of subsets of $\mathcal{D}$, whose intersection properties are known once and for all and recorded in a Boolean matrix (intersection between two subsets is empty or not). Instead of locking predicates the above subsets are then locked by writers.

Acknowledgement: I wish to thank Mr. John Metzger, with whom I had many useful discussions during the writing of this paper.

Bibliography

[Bay 74] Bayer, R., "AGGREGATES: A Software Design Method and its Application to a Family of Transitive Closure Algorithms". TUM-Math. Report No. 7432, Technische Universität München, Sept. 1974

[Bjo 73] Bjork, L.A., "Recovery Semantics for a DB/DC System". Proceedings ACM Nat'l. Conference 1973, 142-146

[CBT 74] Chamberlin, D.D., Boyce, R.F., Traiger, I.L., "A Deadlock-free Scheme for Resource Locking in a Data Base Environment". Information Processing 1974, 340-343

[Cod 70] Codd, E.F., "A Relational Model for Large Shared Data Banks". Comm. ACM 13, 6 (June 1970), 377-387

[CES 71] Coffman, E.G. Jr., Elphick, M.J., Shoshani, A., "System Deadlocks". Computing Surveys 3, 2 (June 1971), 67-78

[Dav 73] Davies, C.T., "Recovery Semantics for a DB/DC System". Proceedings ACM Nat'l. Conference 1973, 136-141

[EGLT74] Eswaran, K.P., Gray, J.N., Lorie, R.A., Traiger I.L., "On the Notions of Consistency and Predicate Locks in a Data Base System". IBM Research Report RJ 1487, Dec. 30, 1974

[Eve 74] Everest, G.C., "Concurrent Update Control and Data Base Integrity". In: Data Base Management (ed. Klimbie, J.W., and Koffeman, K.L.), North Holland 1974, 241-270

[Fos 74] Fossum, B.M., "Data Base Integrity as Provided for by a Particular Data Base Management System". In: Data Base Management (ed. Klimbie, J.W., and Koffeman, K.L.), North Holland 1974, 271-288

[Hab 69] Habermann, A.N., "Prevention of System Deadlocks". Comm. ACM 12, 7 (July 1969), 373-377, 385

[KiC 73] King, P.F., Collmeyer, A.J., "Database Sharing - an Efficient Mechanism for Supporting Concurrent Processes". AFIPS Nat'l. Comp. Conf. Proceedings 1973, 271-275

[Oll 74] Olle, T.W., "Current and Future Trends in Data Base Management Systems". Information Processing 1974, 998-1006

[Ram 74] Ramsperger, N., "Verringerung von Prozeßbehinderungen in Rechensystemen". Dissertation, Technische Universität München, 1974

[Sch 74] Schroff, R., "Vermeidung von totalen Verklemmungen in bewerteten Petrinetzen". Dissertation, Technische Universität München, 1974

[War 62] Warshall, S., "A Theorem on Boolean Matrices". Journal ACM 9, 1 (January 1962), 11-12

[Wil 72] Wilkes, M.V., "On Preserving the Integrity of Data Bases". The Computer Journal, 15, 3 (August 1972), 191-194

DATA BASE STANDARDIZATION

A STATUS REPORT

Thomas B. Steel, Jr.

Equitable Life Assurance Society

New York, N.Y., USA

This paper is a report on the current (1975 September) status of the Study Group on Data Base Management Systems in the United States, together with some remarks on the ISO activity in the area. While the official purpose of this Study Group is an investigation of standardization potential in the area of data base management systems, an important by-product of the work of the Group has been the development of a set of requirements for effective data base management systems. As no existing or proposed implementation of a data base management system satisfies these requirements, it is appropriate to expose these ideas as widely as possible for evaluation.

Among the responsibilities of the Standards Planning and Requirements Committee (SPARC) of the American National Standards Committee on Computers and Information Processing (ANSI/X3) is the generation of recommendations for action by the parent Committee on appropriate areas for the initiation of standards development. For some time it has been evident that data base management systems are in the process of becoming central elements of information processing systems, and that there is less than full agreement on appropriate design. In addition to the existence of a number of implementations of such systems (CODASYL 1969), there are several documents generated out of the collective wisdom of some segment of the information processing community which are either proposals for specific systems (CODASYL 1971) or statements of requirements (GUIDE-SHARE 1970), (CMSAG 1971). As is well known there is a debate in the community on whether existing and proposed implementations meet the indicated requirements or whether the requirements as drawn are all really necessary. Further, there are serious questions about the economics of meeting all the stated requirements.

In addition to the above considerations there is argument on the appropriate data model to use: relational, hierarchical, network. This particular debate has been referred to as the "theological" discussion of the data base management system theorists. There has been criticism of the use of this word; I can only respond to that criticism by quoting Hilaire Belloc: "All political questions are ultimately theological". Indeed, such it seems to be, from which it follows that the correct answer to the question of what data model to use is necessarily "all of the above". One of the outcomes of the work reported in this paper is a mechanism that permits this answer in a meaningful sense.

In the autumn of 1972, responding to the clearly perceived need to rationalize the growing confusion, SPARC, then under the Chairmanship of the author, took formal action to initiate investigation of the subject of data base management systems in the context of potential standardization. Consistent with its normal practice when confronted with a complex subject, SPARC established an _ad hoc_ Study Group on Data Base Management Systems, initially under the Chairmanship of D. M. Smith of the EXXON Corporation and now under the Chairmanship of the author. This Study Group was convened with a charge to investigate the subject of data base management systems with the objective of determining which, if any, aspects of such systems are at present suitable candidates for the development of American National Standards. The "if any" qualification is important because a negative response is just as meaningful as a positive response in a standards context. The "at present" qualification is equally significant, indicating the continuing need for review as the requirements, technologies and economics change over time.

The eventual result of the deliberations of this Study Group will be a series of reports in a specified format (SPARC 1974), identifying potentially standardizable elements of data base management systems and recommending whether or not there is a need, technological feasibility and economic justifications for the initiation of a standards development project in the area. The first interface to be examined is 7 with respect to COBOL. The present target date for completion of this work is the beginning of 1976. As an Interim Report the Study Group has prepared a document (SPARC 1975) which has had wide circulation and is soon to be generally published.

It is appropriate at this juncture to provide a list of the members of the Study Group and their affiliations to indicate the breadth of representation. It is worth noting the extent to which the user community is participating in this effort, a rare event in data processing standardization on any continent.

Bachman, C.W.	Honeywell Information Systems
Cohn, L.	IBM Corporation
Florance, W.E.	Eastman Kodak Company
Kirshenbaum, F.	Equitable Life

Kunecke, H.	Boeing Computer Services
Lavin, M.	Sperry Univac
Mairet, C.E.	Deere and Company
Sibley, E.H.	University of Maryland
Steel, T.B., Jr.	Equitable Life
Turner, J.A.	Columbia University
Yormark, B.	The RAND Corporation

The initial tasks of the Study Group were the difficult ones of understanding and coming to respect the varying views of the different individuals--all theologies were (and still are) represented--and developing a vocabulary that was consistent and mutually comprehensible. It is not clear whether this last task has yet been fully accomplished, although considerable closure has been attained.

In the course of the early discussions it emerged that what any standardization should treat is interfaces. There is no merit and potential disaster in developing standards that specify how components are to work. What is potentially proper for standards specification is how the components are meshed together; in other words, the interfaces. With this notion in mind a generalized model of a data base management system has been developed that highlights the interfaces and the kind of information and data passing across them. Figure 1 is a simplified diagrammatic view of this model.

It should be noted that, except for the man-system interfaces, the technological nature of the interface is not determined; it could be hardware, software, firmware or some mixture. Indeed, some of the interfaces could be man-man, although pursuit of that notion is not germane to what follows. The important point is that the implementation of the system is not prescribed, only the requirements that must be satisfied. As was noted above, this is a simplified diagram, but in order to maintain consistency with the detailed picture, the numerical identifications of the exhibited interfaces have not been changed so there are some numbers missing.

The hexagonal boxes depict people in specific roles. The rectangular boxes represent processing functions, the arrow terminated lines represent flow of data, control information, programs and descriptions, and the dashed boxes represent program preparation and execution subsystems (including compilation and interpretation functions). Finally, the solid bars represent essential interfaces, the ultimate subject matter of the Study Group's deliberations. These interfaces are numbered rather than conventionally named for simplicity of discussion and to avoid confusion.

Among the processes and interfaces omitted on this cut down version of the diagram are the various ways that system programmers and machine operators can invade the system to make _ad hoc_ repairs, certain bypasses of the system mechanism that are asserted to promote efficiency but of debatable desirability in view of their impact on data independence, integrity and security, and the entire structure of physical mapping of data onto specific storage devices. All of the latter structure is to be found to the left of interface 21, much of it will be dictated by the laws of physics and, as such, is of little concern to the current investigation. The principal elements of the Study Group's view of a data base management system are displayed and, in particular, the _three_ schema approach, reflecting the new element introduced by this work, is illustrated.

The lower right hand side of the diagram, the hexagon labelled "application programmer", the dashed rectangle labelled "application program subsystem" and the two interfaces labelled "7" and "12" comprise the entire non-data base activity of preparing and executing an application program. This structure may be viewed as replicated into a variety of subsystems, all interfacing with the data base management system through interface 12, differing in the nature of the language used by the programmer to communicate across the man-machine interface. This language may be a conventional procedure language such as COBOL, ALGOL or PL/I, recognizable special languages like report generators, inquiry languages or update specifiers, or some potentially new type of procedure or problem language. The critical thing to note here is that all data description passes into the application program subsystem across interface 12 from the data base system itself. This, of course, is nothing new.

The lower left hand side of the diagram, the hexagon labelled "system programmer", the dashed rectangle labelled "system program subsystem" and the two interfaces labelled "16" and "18" comprise the entire <u>normal</u> interface available to the system programmer when it is necessary to bypass the ordinary mode of access to the system. Routine system maintenance and modification will occur through this subsystem. There are some exceptions, as noted above, but they do not concern the thrust of this paper. It should also be noted that there is clearly available the installation option of permitting application programmers to operate across this interface, potentially dangerous as that may be. Again, there is nothing new in this construction.

It is the upper portion of the diagram that is of concern in this paper. Current data base systems envision a two level structure; the data as seen by the machine and the data as seen by the programmer. A plethora of confusing terminology has been employed to distinguish between these views. The Study Group has chosen to employ the terms "internal" and "external" to make this distinction. In addition, the Study Group has taken note of the reality of a third level, which we chose to call the "conceptual", that has always been present but never before called out explicitly. It represents the enterprise's view of the structure it is attempting to model in the data base. This view is that which is informally invoked when there is a dispute between the user and the programmer over exactly what was meant by program specifications. The Study Group contends that in the data base world it _must_ be made explicit and, in fact, made known to the data base management system. The proposed mechanism for doing this is the _conceptual_ _schema_. The other two views of data, internal and external, must necessarily be consistent with the view expressed by the conceptual schema.

This required consistency can be maintained and verified in a reasonably fail safe manner only if the conceptual schema is machine processable. The bulk of the remainder of this paper will discuss the nature of the conceptual schema and how it may be made explicit to the system. However, it is worth examining what its presence means to the dynamics of the data base management system operation in terms of the diagrammatic representation of Figure 1.

Ignoring the system programmers, who are extraneous to normal operation, there are four human roles identified: the enterprise administrator, the data base administrator, the application administrator(s), and the application programmer(s). Notice that these are roles as opposed to individuals. The same individual may function in different roles and one role may involve several individuals simultaneously. It is critical, however, that there is only one enterprise administrator and one data base administrator (viewed as roles) while there may be several application administrators and several application programmers. This leads to the notion that there can be several external schemas, each representing a different view of the data, provided each is consistent with and derivable from the single conceptual schema. By extension there can be several application programmers, not necessarily working on the same program, that use the same external schema.

Each "administrator" is responsible for providing to the system a particular view of the necessary data and the relevant relationships among that data. The central view, as noted above, is that of the enterprise administrator who provides the conceptual schema. It must be emphasized, and apparently with repetition as this point seems to be the most frequently missed by those not on the Study Group who have examined its work, that the conceptual schema is a real, tangible item, made most explicit in machine readable form, couched in some well defined and potentially standardizable syntax. Much of the remainder of this paper is concerned with conceptual schemas and the author's view of the possibilities for the semantics of such schemas. In order to provide a context, however, a preliminary examination of the dynamics of the process envisioned is appropriate.

The enterprise administrator defines the conceptual schema and, to the extent possible and practicable, validates it. Some, but in general not all, of this schema can be checked for consistency by mechanical means. As the conceptual schema is a formal model of the interesting (for the data base management system) aspects of the enterprise, if the situation is at all complex then the problem of logical incompletability will be encountered (Godel 1931). The conceptual schema will contain, among other things, definitions of all the entities to be comprehended--up to the isomorphism determined by identity of those properties defined in the schema as relevant. Relatonships amongst these entities will also be explicated, as will the constraints on allowable values of "data". By defining those persons with some access to the data base management system as entities of interest, it is possible to directly model the rules of access and, thus, provide security control at the level of the conceptual schema. This is a key point. It is well known that there are substantial problems with security control and the importance if a centralized point having a view of the entire system must not be overlooked.

The data base administrator (a definition of this role somewhat at variance with the conventional conception of the task) is responsible for defining the internal schema. This schema contains an abstract description of the storage strategy currently employed by the data base management system. Whether the data is actually stored flat, hierarchical, networked, inverted or otherwise, including any meaningful combination, is contained in the internal schema. The "internal syntax" of the data values will also be found in the internal schema; such items as the radix for numeric values, coding schemes used, units of measure, and the like. Access paths and the relational connectivity between data representations will be defined. All of this must be consistent with and derivable from the conceptual schema, which, therefore, must be available for display to the data base administrator,. The internal schema processor (see

Figure 1) provides a mechanical check on this consistency. Within the limits imposed by this requirement of consistency with the conceptual schema, the data base administrator is free to alter the internal schema in any way appropriate to optimization of the data base management system operation. Indeed, by use of suitable interpreters it will be possible to reorganize the internal structure of the data base dynamically while normal operations continue. In view of the massive size of some data bases currently comtemplated, this is an essential requirement, and it would seem that only the guarantee of separation of the users' view and the system's view of data provided by interposition of the conceptual schema permits this.

The third "administrator" role, the application administrators, provide the external schemas (analogues of the DBTG "sub-schemas") which define the application programmers' views of the data. These external schemas are a multiplicity in concept and will, in general, only encompass the portion of the data base relevant to a particular application. It is envisioned that each general application area will have its own application administrator who provides the appropriate schemas for that area. These are the only data descriptions (schemas) seen by an application program and provide the only avenue of data name resolution. It would carry this essay too far afield to discuss the complexities of name resolution and symbol binding; suffice it to say that all external name resolution, whether performed at compile time, program invocation time, or module execution time are done across interfaces 7, 12 and 31 through the intermediation of the appropriate external schema across interface 5.

Exactly the same remarks about the consistency of the various external schemas with respect to the conceptual schema as was noted about the internal schema are to be understood, with the qualification that one external schema may be a true subset of another and, under the hypothesis that consistency in this sense is transitive, the external schema processor may only validate one external schema against a more comprehensive one known to be consistent with the conceptual schema.

After the appropriate schemas are defined, the system dynamics becomes quite straightforward and little different from current systems. The application programmer (report specifier, inquiry specifier, etc.) does his job in the usual way, using the provided external schema, both explicitly and implicitly, as his set of data declarations, providing procedural input across interface 7 and invoking compilation, generation or other relevant processes through the application program subsystem. Upon entry to execution mode, requests for data are passed across interface 12 to the conceptual/external transformer which computes the mapping between the external data description and the conceptual data description. This description passes across interface 31 to the conceptual/internal transformer which in its turn computes the mapping between the conceptual data description and the internal data description. In general, the internal and conceptual schemas will be static, so, depending upon the mapping complexity and the nature of the implementation, it may well be possible to collapse the two transformers (<u>into</u> and <u>out of</u> the conceptual data description) by computing the composite mapping function. This should not obscure the face that in order to maintain true data independence it must always remain possible to force this process to occur in two steps.

Finally, the data request as transformed is passed across interface 30 to the internal/storage transformer. The internal schema will recognize storage as something like a linear, multioriginated address space, and it will be necessary to remap this abstract model of storage onto hardware constructs such as tracks, cylinders and the like. This "dirty" description then is passed across interface 21 into the bowels of the machine (and may go through other transformations therein) until actual data is obtained and the process reversed. This brief description has been couched in terms of obtaining data but, of course, storage of data proceeds in the same way, mutatis mutandis.

Question of locks, avoidance of "deadly embrace", security, integrity and other data base management system problems all have their place in this scheme of things, but it is beyond the scope of this paper to consider them. By and large they present no distinct aspects in this three level view from those found in conventional approaches, except that in some instances--security, for example--the solutions may be both easier and more assured.

Before turning to a discussion of the conceptual schema it is appropriate to insert a brief excursus on the status of data base management system standardization in ISO. At the Eight Plenary Meeting of ISO/TC97, held 1974 May 14-17 in Geneva, Resolution 11, passed with 14 affirmative and two negative (Canada, France) votes, assigned responsibility for data base management to Subcomittee 5 (Programming Languages) and instructed SC5 to establish a study group on the subject (ISO 1974).

Such a Study Group was established by SC5 and several countries submitted position papers. The USA position paper was the SPARC Interim Report. An 1975 June 24-26, the Study Group met in

Washington, DC with delegations from France, Germany, Sweden and the USA. Written input was also available from Switzerland and the United Kingdom. The following six points are the conclusions of that meeting:

1. The Study Group concludes in response to the Netherlands Proposal on Data Base Management (ISO/TC 97/598), that any standardization action in the area of data base management systems based on existing proposals is premature in the absence of criteria against which to measure such proposals.

2. The Interim Report of the ANSI/X3/SPARC Study Group on Data Base Management Systems (ISO/TC 97/SC 5 (USA-75) N359) is accepted by the ISO/TC 97/SC 5 Study Group on Data Base Management Systems as an initial basis for discussion on a gross architecture of data base management systems.

3. The Study Group acknowledges the need to identify all types of data base management systems users and to specify their requirements.

4. The Study Group proposes to review and augment the terminology used in N359 and the concepts therein. As the initial effort, the Study Group will establish priorities in terms of the interfaces identified in N359 for further investigation. These priorities will be chosen to optimize the benefits derived from standardization.

5. As a parallel activity to those identified above, the current CODASYL data base specifications will be evaluated. The Study Group notes at this time that preliminary studies by various national and internationl bodies have indicated that the CODASYL specifications are not suitable for standardization as they

stand.

6. The Study Group will recommend development work for those interfaces appropriate for standardization for which no adequate candidate exists.

The next meeting of this Study Group will be in Paris, 1976 January 12-15.

The underlying notion behind the conceptual schema as envisioned by the Study Group is the "entity-property-value" trinity made explicit in GUIDE-SHARE requirements study (GUIDE-SHARE 1970). There is general agreement among the members of the Study Group on the overall nature and objectives of the conceptual schema, but in my judgment there is less real agreement on its exact place in the scheme of things than might seem the case from the Study Group reports. To a considerable extent this lack of agreement does not hamper progress, and may well not matter in the long run provided the distinct views are carefully articulated. What follows is the author's view of the conceptual schema notion and some indications on how it can be formalized.

Figure 2 is a schematic illustration of how one can proceed from "reality" to the data models actually used by application programs. It is derived from a metaphysics that may not be wholly congenial to everyone but should at the very least be familiar to those acquainted with the principles of scientific explanation (Braithwaite 1953). It is assumed that a "real world" exists in some meaningful sense. Subordinate to this "true" reality can be found the "perceived" reality obtained through our sensory inputs as transformed by our brains. This immediate, primitive image of reality is, or at least can be, transformed into a rational mental model of reality by a process known as scientific abstraction.

This process can be roughly described as: (1) observation (noting one's perceptions); (2) experimentation (stimulation of the perceived reality to generate new perceptions); (3) generalization (intuiting that similar stimulation will generate similar perceptions); (4) theorizing (identifying fundamental generalizations); (5) deducing (inferring that new and different stimulations will produce new, albeit expected, perceptions); and, finally, (6) verification (initiating these new stimuli and observing the results). Repeated iteration of this sequence leads to a gradually more refined mental model of the real world.

In order to communicate this model to someone--or something--else, it is necessary to use a language. As is well known, natural languages are unsatisfactory media for precise communication of the content of scientific models. At present the best available vehicle for such precise communication is that of formal languages (Tarski 1930). While there are complications in the reduction of scientific descriptions of reality to existing formalisms, most of these problems are to be found on the outer limits of the models. Generally one does not really wish to describe a total model of all reality--the "best" model whose boundary is fuzzy and moves with the growth and modification of scientific knowledge. What is desired is to describe some limited model of a portion of reality, extracted from the "best" model by a process we can call "engineering abstraction". While it may be the case that the universe is "best" described by the interactions of 3.10^{80} quarks, the typical engineer is more apt to build his bridge by combining girders, cross braces and rivets. The molecular biologist may view the human being as a complex structure of water, protein molecules, DNA and other, assorted chemicals, but to the insurance agent a human being is not much more than an age, sex and checkbook. For any application one abstracts those aspects of "reality" considered relevant and ignores the rest. Thus, formal descriptions need only deal with the appropriate level of abstraction.

This resultant formalism--the "symbolic" model--is derived from the limited, "engineering" model of the interesting subset of reality as embodied in the mind of the perceiver by a process we will call "symbolic abstraction", and is the linguistic expression in some conventional, predetermined syntax of a set of forms to which suitable semantic content is given by the adoption of rules of designation and rules of truth (Carnap 1942). It expresses the totality of what is known and interesting about the enterprise being modeled. It *is* the conceptual schemma. The processes of mapping from this formal model to the data models we call "internal schema" and "external schemas" may be complex and difficult in practice, but they are straightforward in principle, providing only that the conceptual schema has sufficient detail to permit all necessary expression.

In the author's view the proper choice of formalism--indeed, the only acceptable choice--is that of modern symbolic logic; the first order predicate calculus with identity (Hilbert & Ackermann 1938), together with a suitable axiomatic set theory (Bernays & Fraenkel 1958), augmented by appropriate modal logics (von Wright 1951), and, finally, supplemented by "individuals" (Quine 1961) and the associated non-logical predicates and the axioms for their behavior. The reasoning behind this position is quite simple. Use of the conventional formalisms of symbolic logic and set theory permit the invocation of all the analysis that has been devoted to this topic by three generations of logicians. Both the pitfalls and possibilities are well understood and the limitations clearly defined. Further, it is in some sense the most general scheme available. If one accepts Church's Thesis (Kleene 1952), as do most contemporary logicians, it *is* the most general scheme that can be contemplated for use with digital machinery. From this it is possible to deduce that anything expressible to a machine with precision at all is necessarily expressible in this fashion.

As an aside let me emphasize a point which should be obvious but is, perhaps, worth making explicit for clarity. Whenever in this paper I use the word "set" I intend it in the strictly logical sense as a synonym for "collection" or the German "Menge" or the French "ensemble", *not* in any way as that linguistic atrocity perpetrated by the DBTG Report wherein the nineteenth, fifth and twentieth letters of the Roman alphabet are used in that order as the name of a peculiar object. This may seem harsh, but the point at issue represents a prize example of the manner in which the information processing sciences generate confusion for themselves and others by casual misuse of words. Indeed, it reminds me of Orwell's Newspeak.

In a paper of this character it is not possible to probe the possibilities of the sketch above in any depth. However, certain examples may clarify the power of the approach. It is unequivocally precise in any modern version of set theory as to what is meant by a "relation". A relation is a set of ordered pairs (the ordered pair $<x,y>$ being definable as $\{\{x\},\{x,y\}\}$) and one can say that x bears the relationship R to y provided that $<x,y> \in R$ ("$\in$" being the predicate of set membership). Thus, the confusion between a "relation" and a "relationship", which is another example of terminological idiocy, is made quite precise.

Relations of interest can be given names and defined either by enumeration of their members or by any property that must be possessed by a pair to enjoy membership, in exactly the same fashion that any other set is completely defined by its members.

The equally troublesome concept of "order" can be explicitly defined. A partial ordering is any relation having the properties of reflexivity, anti-symmetry and transitivity. A linear ordering is a partial ordering where any two elements in its field are comparable and a well-ordering is a nowhere dense linear ordering.

Structures of arbitrary complexity can be constructed. The concept of a general array (Steel 1964) developed out of some early data structure studies, and it can be shown that any nondense complex is expressible as a general array so defined. As digital computers cannot deal with dense structures except in finite approximation, this would seem to be sufficient.

The modal predicate of deontic logic, "O" (for "obliged to"), and its derived predicates "O-" ("obliged to not" ≡ "forbidden to"), and "-O-" ("not forbidden to" ≡ "permitted to") provide the required paradigm for expressing either legal constraints in the model or defining the rules of access.

These examples could be multiplied a considerable length, but should be sufficient to illustrate the point. From a theoretical point of view there is no more suitable vehicle for expressing a conceptual schema. This is, of course, not the whole story.

First, theoretical possibility and practical possibility are not identical. There is the danger that the necessary expressions get too large and cumbersome for effective use. In an age where we deal with million instruction operating systems, this is not a fully persuasive argument in any event. It is, however, moot. The number and character of the necessary expressions do not get excessive; unlike, say, the contrast between conventional procedure languages and Turing machines. On the contrary, nearly a century of search for compact notation has resulted in definitional sequences that provide more compact expression than one typically finds in programming language data descriptions (or sub-schemas) which perform less of the task. Some of this is due, of course, to the use of large character sets, but in any case economy of notation is not a problem.

A second potential difficulty is the actual use of the tools to construct the desired models, which is a task that is necessarily an art rather than a science. Clearly, if the process of constructing a model could be itself formalized one would already _have_ the model in the input. To this point I can only say that I have personally been partially successful in constructing models of relatively complex insurance procedures, and in a matter of a few days, inventing notation as I went along. This effort was only partially successful in the sense that, while I was able to generate static models with no difficulty, the problem with time and the dynamic behavior of the model caused difficulties of two types. First, thre was the philosophical problem of the potential as opposed to the actual. How does one treat the property "age at death" prior to the actual death of the individual? Formally, of course, this is trivial, but obtaining some assurance that the formalism does not hide an ambiguity or paradox is far from trivial.

The second problem with time has to do with the inelegance of making the variable denoting time distinguished and, therefore, a special case. While there is nothing inherently wrong with mathematical inelegance per se, several thousand years of logical and mathematical history suggest intuitively that something is wrong. Some recent work (Thomasen 1974) on the reduction of tense logic to modal logic hints at a solution to this problem.

I have gone far enough with this work to become convinced that the approach is sound and no fundamental invention is required; only some hard work to refine the ideas. There remains, however, one further potential criticism of this approach with which it is necessary to deal. It is a criticism to which I would prefer to comment "a pox on those who raise it" and then ignore the matter. As a practical consideration, however, it will not go away. It is much the same argument that has been raised in the past against every programming language except COBOL; i.e., the language is too much like algebra, only the mathematicians can use it. The argument is irrefutable for if people believe they cannot understand something, they won't! However, there is one difference between this situation and the programming language situation. The only one who must construct models is the enterprise administrator and only the data base administrator and the applications administrators need to read such models. These individuals are presumably senior and well compensated. They can be required to have a little education. Furthermore, while I have no proof, it is my belief that once the barrier of belief in its esoteric character is overcome, it is no harder to teach reasonably intelligent people the relevant logic than it is to teach them COBOL and the DDL.

To summarize this personal view of the nature of a conceptual schema, any alternative is either equivalent and therefore equally complex while being less understood for lack of familiarity, or it is not equivalent and therefore can only model a subset of that reality otherwise amenable to modelling. The only real issue is whether some less powerful but more acceptable formalism exists that is adequate for modelling anticipated enterprises for a reasonable future. In my view neither data structure diagrams (Bachman 1969) nor normalized relations (Codd 1970) nor the CODASYL DDL (CODASYL 1971) being discussed at this Working Conference are candidates for such an alternative. As overlaid structures for internal and external schemas they may be quite suitable; the criteria for acceptability being different.

In conclusion, let me reiterate that the latter portion of this paper is my personal view of the appropriate structure for a conceptual schema and does not necessarily represent the view of other members of the ANSI/SPARC Study Group on Data Base Management Systems. On the other hand, the general principle of the three level approach and the essential requirement for the conceptual schema _is_ fundamental to the deliberations of the Study Group. It is reasonable to claim that this position will be maintained in the Final Report of the Study Group and will continue to characterize the official position taken by ANSI on behalf of the USA in any deliberations on data base management systems in the ISO.

REFERENCES

Bachman, C. W.: "Data Structure Diagrams", Data Base, 1:2 (1969).

Bernays, P. and Fraenkel, A. A.: "Axiomatic Set Theory", North-Holland (Amsterdam 1958).

Braithwaite, R. B.: "Scientific Explanation", Cambridge University Press (London 1953).

Carnap, R.: "Introduction to Semantics", Harvard University Press (Cambridge, MA 1942).

CMSAG Joint Utilities Project: "Date Management Systems Requirements", CMSAG (Orlando, FL 1971).

CODASYL: "A Survey of Generalized Data Base Management Systems", available from NTIS (Washington, DC 1969).

CODASYL": "Data Base Task Group Report", ACM (New York 1971).

Codd, E. F.: "A Relational Model of Data for Large Shared Data Banks", CACM, 13:6 (1970), pp. 377-387.

Gödel, K.: "Uber formal unentscheidbare Sätze der Principia Mathematica und verwandter Systems I", Monatshefte, 38 (1931), pp. 173-198.

GUIDE/SHARE: "Data Base Management System Requirements", SHARE Inc. (New York, N. Y. 1970).

Hilbert, D. and Ackermann, W.: "Grundzuge der Theoretischen Logik", Julius Springer (Berlin, 1938).

ISO: ISO/TC97 (Geneva-3) 669.

Kleene, S. C.: "Introduction to Metamathematics", van Nostrand (Princeton, N. J. 1952).

Quine, W. V. O.: "Mathematical Logic", rev.ed., Harvard University Press (Cambridge, MA 1961).

SPARC: "Outline for Preparation of Proposals for Standardization", document SPARC/90, CBEMA (Washington, DC 1974).

SPARC: "Interim Report: Study Committee on Data Base Management Systems:, SIGMOD NEWSLETTER (forthcoming).

Steel, T. B., Jr.: "Beginnings of a Theory of Information Handling", <u>CACM</u>, 7:2 (1964), pp. 97-103.

Tarski, A.: "Fundmentale Begriffe der Methodogie der deduktiven Wissenschaften I", <u>Monatshefte für Mathematik und</u> Physik, 37 (1930), pp. 361-404.

Thomason, S. K.: "Reduction of tense logic to modal logic, I", J. Symbolic Logic, 39:3 (1974), pp. 549-551.

Von Wright, G. H.: "An Essay in Modal Logic", North-Holland (Amsterdam 1951).

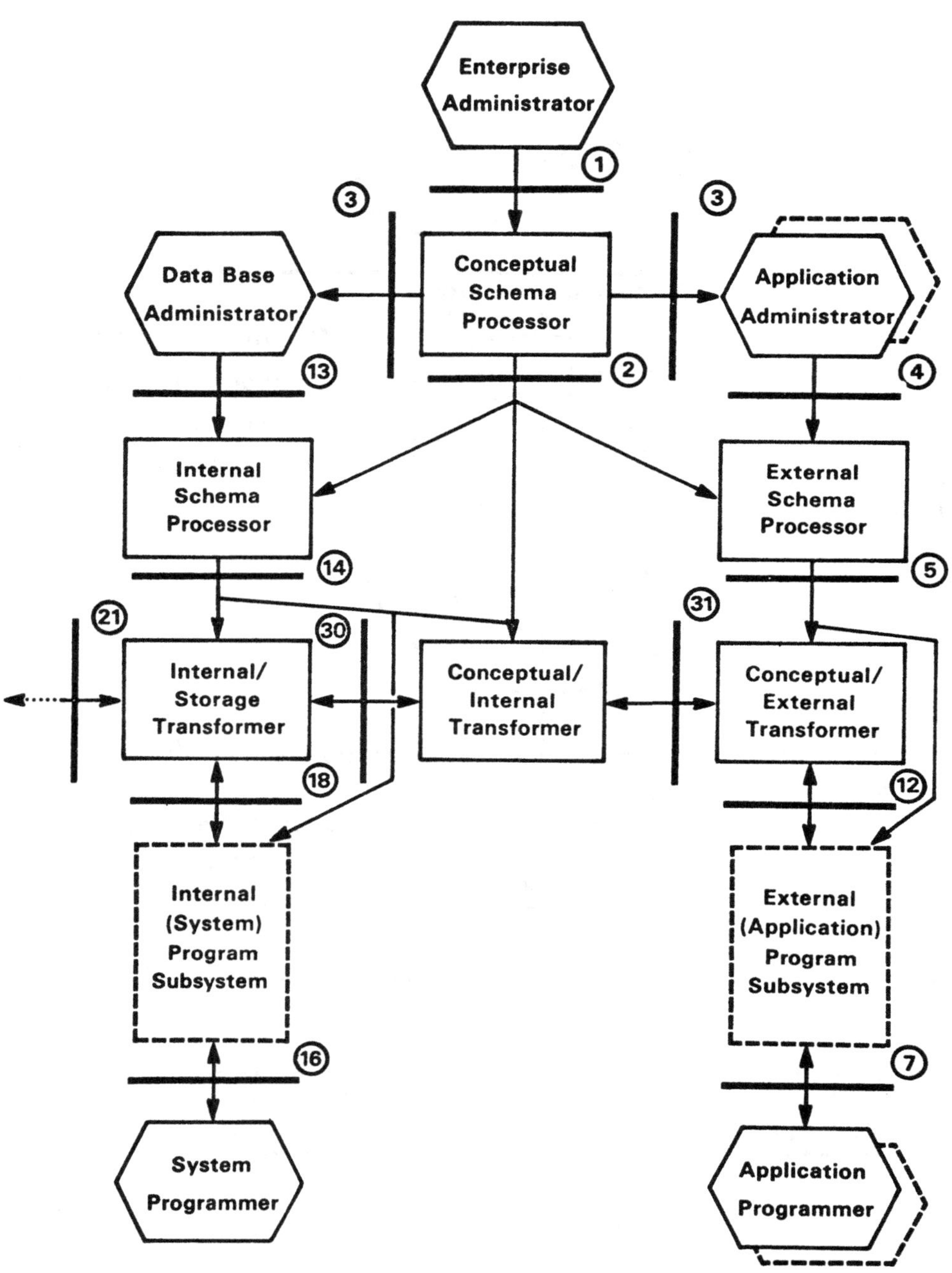
Enterprise Administrator
1
3
3
Data Base Administrator
Conceptual Schema Processor
Application Administrator
13
2
4
Internal Schema Processor
External Schema Processor
14
5
21
30
31
Internal/ Storage Transformer
Conceptual/ Internal Transformer
Conceptual/ External Transformer
18
12
Internal (System) Program Subsystem
External (Application) Program Subsystem
16
7
System Programmer
Application Programmer

Figure
1

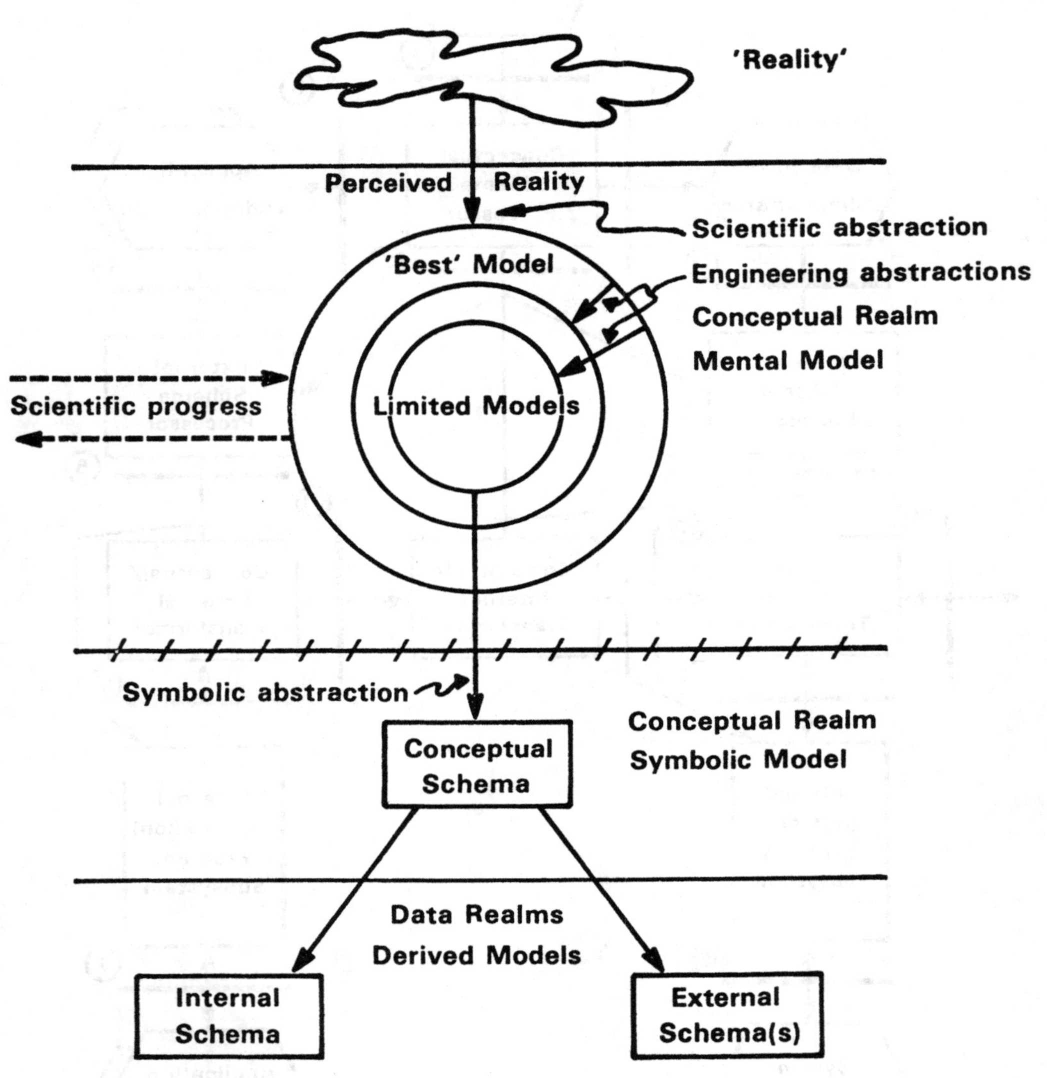
'Reality'
Perceived Reality
Scientific abstraction
'Best' Model
Engineering abstractions
Conceptual Realm
Mental Model
Scientific progress
Limited Models
Symbolic abstraction
Conceptual Schema
Conceptual Realm
Symbolic Model
Data Realms
Derived Models
Internal Schema
External Schema(s)

Figure
2

A New Series

Texts and Monographs in Computer Science

Editors:
F. L. Bauer, Munich,
and D. Gries, Ithaca, N. Y.

This series will consist of high quality, definitive texts, both at the undergraduate level and graduate level, and monographs of interest to researchers in computer science. The undergraduate texts will serve as guides to further study in all the basic areas of computer science; the graduate texts and monographs will thoroughly investigate advanced topics and lead the reader to the frontiers of computer science research.

H. W. Gschwind, E. J. McCluskey

Design of Digital Computers
An Introduction

2nd edition 1975
375 figures. IX, 548 pages.
ISBN 3-540-06915-1

Contents: Number System and Number Representations. Boolean Algebras.
Integrated Circuit Gates. Storage Elements. Computer Circuits. The Basic Organization of Digital Computers. The Functional Units of Digital Computers. Unorthodox Concepts. Miscellaneous Engineering and Design Considerations.

The Origins of Digital Computers Selected Papers
Edited by **B. Randell**

2nd edition 1975
120 figures. XVI, 464 pages
ISBN 3-540-07114-8

Contents: Analytical Engines. Tabulating Machines.
Zuse and Schreyer. Aiken and IBM. Bell Telephone Laboratories. The Advent of Electronic Computers. Stored Program Electronic Computers.